Milton Caniff
Conversations

Conversations with Comic Artists
M. Thomas Inge, General Editor

Milton Caniff
CONVERSATIONS

Edited by
Robert C. Harvey

University Press of Mississippi
Jackson

For Julia and Kit and Linda, too—
a poor but deeply felt proxy for hours lost

www.upress.state.ms.us

Manufactured in the United States of America

10 09 08 07 06 05 04 03 02 4 3 2 1
∞

Library of Congress Cataloging-in-Publication Data
Caniff, Milton Arthur, 1907–
Milton Caniff : conversations / edited by Robert C. Harvey.
p. cm.—(Conversations with comic artists)
Includes index.
ISBN 1-57806-437-6 (cloth : alk. paper)—ISBN 1-57806-438-4 (pbk. : alk. paper)
1. Caniff, Milton Arthur, 1907—Interviews. 2. Cartoonists—United States—Interviews. I. Harvey, Robert C. II. Title. III. Series.

PN6727.C3 A5 2002
741.5'092—dc21

2001046666

British Library Cataloging-in-Publication Data available

Contents

Introduction

The interviews collected in this volume provide details and insights into the life and career of one of the world's most acclaimed comic strip artists. Milton Caniff is one of the few authentic giants in the history of cartooning: his achievements in the comic strip form shaped the genre and set standards by which all storytelling strips were subsequently judged.

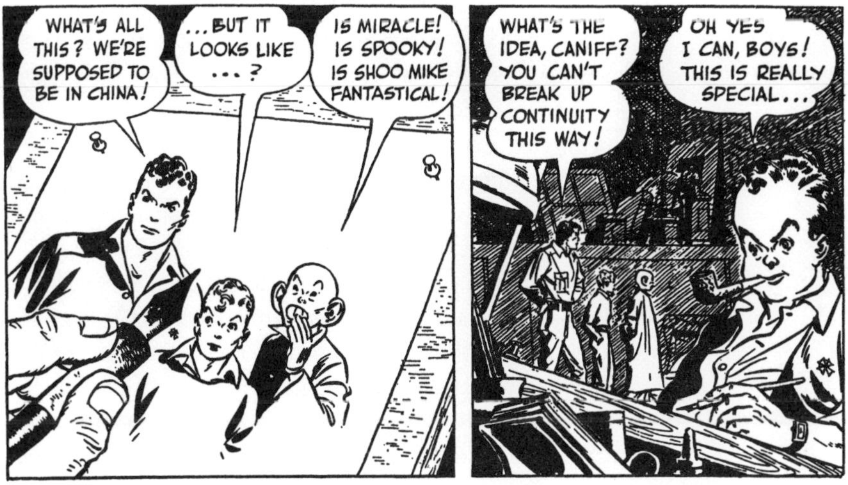

Pat Ryan, Terry, Connie, and—Caniff.

Born in 1907 and reared in Hillsboro and Dayton, Ohio, Caniff apprenticed in the art department of the *Dayton Journal* while attending Stivers Manual High School, where he excelled in both art and drama courses. He continued to indulge his thespian aptitude at Ohio State University, but he earned his way as an artist at the *Columbus Dispatch* already fully aware of the practical wisdom in the advice given him by the *Dispatch*'s noted cartoonist, Billy Ireland: "Stick to your inkpots, kid; actors don't eat regularly." At Ohio State, Caniff pledged Sigma Chi fraternity, entering one of many associations he would later be able to exploit as avenues of publicity by which he promoted the circulation of his comic strip creations. After graduating in 1930 with a degree in fine arts, he married his high school sweetheart, Esther "Bunny" Parsons, and began to earn his living (precariously in those Depression times) as a commercial artist.

In March 1932, Caniff was offered a staff artist job with the Associated Press in New York. By September, he was doing a panel gag cartoon, *Mister Gilfeather,* that he inherited when another young staff cartoonist, Al Capp, abandoned it to return, briefly, to his native Boston—but not before he and Caniff had bonded for life. In March 1933, Caniff took over an illustrated jingle feature, *Puffy the Pig;* in May, he converted the panel about the pompous Gilfeather into the topical *Gay Thirties;* and on July 31, the AP launched his first nationally syndicated strip, *Dickie Dare,* which dramatized a young boy's dreams of adventure. Dickie, falling asleep over books about Robin Hood, Robinson Crusoe, and Aladdin, dreams of joining his literary heroes on their exploits. Within a year, however, Caniff realized that Dickie's adventures lacked a certain element of suspense: readers invariably knew how some of the adventures would turn out. To remedy the situation, he arranged for his young protagonist to give up dreaming of deeds of derring-do and to begin performing them. In May 1934, Dickie meets a freelance writer and adventurer named "Dynamite Dan" Flynn, an old friend of the family, who takes Dickie on a trip around the world. They have actual adventures en route, but they never get all the way around the world. After only a couple of escapades, Caniff left the strip for greener pastures, and *Dickie Dare* was inherited by Coulton Waugh.

In October 1934, Caniff was summoned by Joseph Patterson of the *New York Daily News* to create another strip about "real" adventures. Beginning on October 22, *Terry and the Pirates* embodied Patterson's prescription as John Bainbridge detailed it in a 1944 *New Yorker* profile: a kid hero with a rugged and handsome adult mentor, wandering through China ("Anything can still happen out there," Patterson said) and encountering exotic dangers and beautiful femmes fatales at every pagoda. Adventure and sex appeal were the ingredients in Patterson's recipe for success with an adventure comic strip. Although Caniff always credited Patterson with creating the basic *Terry* formula, this new strip was virtually a carbon-copy of *Dickie Dare.* Dickie's dark hair faded to blond and he became Terry; Dan Flynn's blond hair turned dark, and he became Pat Ryan. Even the Pat Ryan–Normandie Drake unrequited love affair, which Caniff claimed Patterson alerted him to by referring him to *Wuthering Heights,* was blooming in *Dickie* with Dan Flynn and Kim Sheridan. But what wasn't in the earlier strip was the Dragon Lady, undoubtedly Caniff's most inspired creation.

As Caniff complained to Jay Maeder in 1972, the strip's title was a plot direction: "[I]t threw you into a mold, in the sense that you couldn't escape from it . . . in terms of trying to do anything other than pirate stories." All the prewar adventures in *Terry* involved one kind of pirate or another. Fortunately for the realistic aura he was seeking to conjure in the strip, the unsettled almost medieval milieu of China after the 1911 collapse of the Manchu Dynasty provided the cartoonist with ample material of the buccaneering sort. Ryan, another of those free-lance globetrotting writers, and his charge, Terry Lee, arrive in China on a treasure hunt and acquire a native guide-cook-factotum named George Webster Confucius, "Connie" for short. But Terry and Pat are diverted from their expedition as they fall into the hands of one after another of the marauding bands of provincial warlords and other kinds of brigands that infested the Oriental landscape—Captain Blaze (an old reprobate who becomes more friend than foe), Papa Pyzon, Captain Judas, General Klang. And the Dragon Lady.

The Dragon Lady is the first villain Caniff created in the strip, and, as Caniff explains to Maeder, she is "the strongest of all because she had the double weapon of beauty and absolute ruthlessness, which everybody, man and woman, dreads and anticipates with shuddering pleasure." A pirate queen, she so fascinated Caniff that he returned to her again and again during the first several years of the strip, each time exploring some new facet of her personality. To the stock femme fatale of melodrama, Caniff had added two final and masterfully delicate touches: a note of doubt about her ruthlessness and the poignant suggestion that perhaps the Dragon Lady would rather be loved of men than lead them.

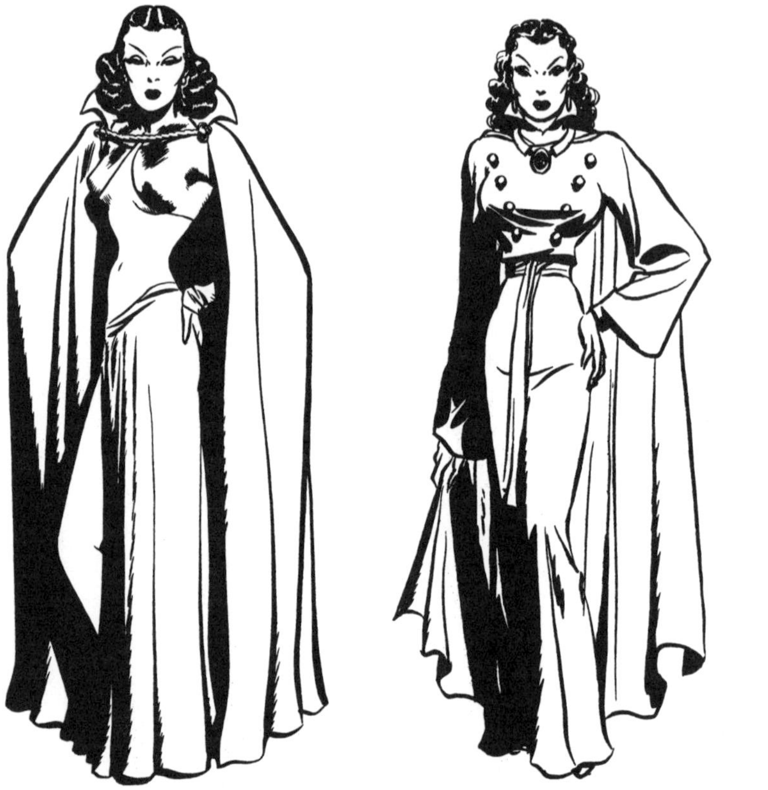

The Dragon Lady's appearance changed slightly over the years with each successive return to the strip.

Another recurring character was Burma, Caniff's Sadie Thompson character, a bad girl with a heart of gold. Burma has no last name but she has a past—something vaguely illegal—and despite the gold-digging motive that animates much of her activity, she falls for penniless Pat Ryan. Meanwhile, Pat Ryan meets and falls in love with his Catherine, Normandie Drake. And, later, Terry meets his paramour in April Kane, a southern belle patterned somewhat on Scarlett O'Hara in *Gone with the Wind.* But Normandie marries the craven Anthony Sandhurst, leaving Pat forever frustrated in love; and April is simply too much a belle to reveal any genuine feeling for Terry (or anyone else).

In pursuing stories that involved these characters, Caniff went well

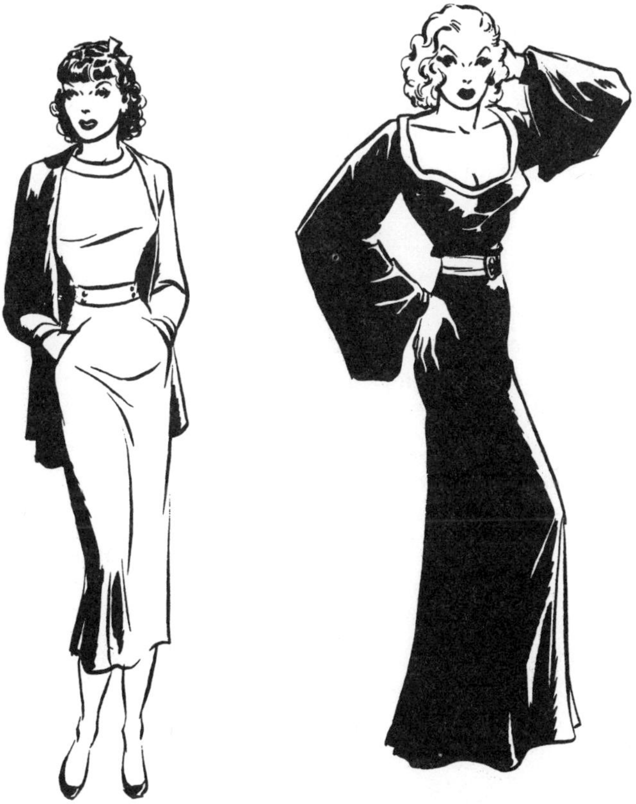

Normandie Drake, Pat Ryan's true love, and Burma, the strip's blonde bombshell (inspired by Hollywood's Jean Harlow).

beyond Patterson's prescription and effectively redefined the adventure continuity strip by raising new standards of excellence for most of the genre's basic ingredients. Inspired by the work of his studio-mate Noel Sickles, Caniff developed an impressionistic style of drawing that suggested reality economically with shadow rather than with painstakingly rendered details. Describing this method to Shel Dorf in 1978, Caniff acknowledges that Sickles, "[who] was much more concerned with method and technique than with setting up a cartoon character, . . . contributed more to the success of the *Terry* drawings than any single person."

To the realism of the graphic technique he appropriated and developed, Caniff added realism of detail, striving for absolute authenticity in depicting every aspect of the setting for *Terry* whether Oriental or, later, military. He explains this evolution in a 1982 interview for *Airman:* "I had been putting Terry through his paces in the Yellow Sea when I began getting letters saying my characters were floating east on rivers that coursed west. And I was told they were holding up Chinese pants with buttons that were sold exclusively by an Ohio dime-store chain. . . . I didn't sell comic strip realism to my readers. They sold it to me." He polished the prose of his dialogues, and as speech balloons grew larger, he resorted to cinematic technique to rejuvenate visual excitement in the strip—shifting his "camera" rapidly from panel to panel to portray scenes from dramatically different distances and angles.

But Caniff's signal accomplishment was a storyteller: with his actor's sense of the dramatic potential of the medium, he enhanced the simple adventure story by making character development integral to action-packed plots. To weave into the tapestry of Terry's history two such intriguing characters as the Dragon Lady and Burma (to mention only these two) was to add to the strip's exotic locale a powerful attraction: their characterizations complemented the mysteriousness of the Orient with the mysteries of their personalities. Still, each woman's personality seemed so true-to-life that it lent the authority of its authenticity to the strip's stories, making the most improbable adventures real. This complex evocation of realism and exoticism in character, setting, and incident raised the appeal of Caniff's work to the level of mystique. And with the opening of hostilities worldwide in 1941, the cartoonist would incorporate new elements of reality into his fiction.

Caniff reached the pinnacle of his fame during World War II. In the strip, Terry joined the Army Air Corps (Air Force), and one of Caniff's stellar creations of the period was the pilot who teaches Terry to fly. Caniff had earlier introduced a knockabout flyer named Dude Hennick, who was deliberately patterned after an Ohio State chum named Frank Higgs. Higgs had joined the Chinese war effort in the late 1930s, serving with Claire Chennault. But when Caniff turned to Terry's training as a pilot, he chanced upon another Ohio State alum in the Air Corps, Phil Cochran, who would become Flip Corkin in the strip. In a 1970 interview with Jim Taylor, Caniff reveals the moment of inspiration: "I went up there and watched [Phil] fly a routine day's training mission. . . . And suddenly it dawned on me that I was sitting there on top of one of the most colorful characters that I or anybody else had ever seen. . . . I had a perfect wild-type fighter pilot." Pat Ryan faded away during the war years, and Flip

Corkin took his place, becoming one of the most popular comic strip characters of the era. Thereafter, Caniff often resorted to using real personages as models for his "paper dolls" (as he called his cast).

Caniff's realistic and sympathetic treatment of military life championed the achievements of ordinary men and women in uniform. Moreover, since his stories were set in the China-Burma-India theater of the war, they raised the visibility of that otherwise much-neglected region of the allied undertaking. The cartoonist became an American Kipling. *Terry*'s trenchant, pragmatic patriotism warmed hearts and steeled nerves on the homefront as well as at the battlefront. The Sunday page for October 17, 1943, so incisively captured the wartime spirit of the day that it was read into the *Congressional Record* to become a part of the national archive.

Another of Caniff's famous creations came about through one of his numerous contributions to the war effort: Miss Lace, a curvaceous bundle of camaraderie, was the central figure (so to speak) of *Male Call,* a mildly risqué weekly strip he drew without remuneration for distribution as a morale-booster to camp and unit newspapers. Caniff provides his own description of Miss Lace for an article in *Editor & Publisher* commemorating her retirement from active duty in 1946: "Her chief characteristic, very carefully planned, was her direct appeal. . . . She had to hold the guys' interest—not so much in that they tried to make her, but in that she was a good sport." Immensely popular, the strip was published regularly in more than three thousand papers, the greatest circulation in number of individual publications ever attained by any comic strip.

After the war, Caniff caused a new sensation: he abandoned *Terry,* which was owned by the Chicago Tribune-New York Daily News Syndicate, to create for Field Enterprises a new strip. As Caniff explained to Dorf in 1978, he asked for and received "full ownership of the property and full editorial control," neither of which he had with *Terry.* The new strip was a long time in coming, and its conception and birth were attended by peculiar restraints and great anticipation.

Launched while Caniff was at the height of his fame and popularity with *Terry and the Pirates, Steve Canyon* hove into public view on the crest of a wave of unequaled ballyhoo, the culmination of a promotional campaign unique in both its length and content. The news that Caniff would start a new adventure comic strip broke in early 1945, when he still had two years to go on his *Terry* contract. Since he was leaving the Tribune-News Syndicate chiefly to gain ownership as well as control of his new strip, Caniff would do nothing during that two-year period to endanger his future proprietary rights: he didn't draw a line on the new strip until his old contract expired on October 14, 1946. Then he had less than a month to create a new cast of characters and to get strips into production for the debut date early in January 1947. But Caniff knew exactly what he wanted for his adventure strip, and once he was no longer under contract with the Tribune-News, he promptly sought out *Editor & Publisher*'s Helen Staunton, to whom he described his new creation in November 1946. His hero would not be a continuation of Terry, he told her. "I had to back away from all that. Steve Canyon's been around. I couldn't have Terry smoke, or even fall in love really without showing everything that led up to it. But this guy might have been in love a dozen times."

While waiting for his Tribune-News contract to run out, Caniff concentrated on *Terry,* purposefully aiming to do in his last two years his very best work—"so they'll miss me when I'm gone," he told me. His last *Terry* daily strip appeared on Saturday, December 28; the Sunday, one of his most celebrated pages, the next day. On Monday, Terry's fate was taken over by George Wunder, another AP alum, who had won a competition for the job. Meanwhile, Caniff's new syndicate, having nothing of the new strip to display to prospective subscribing newspapers, sold it solely on the basis of its creator's reputation. And that was apparently enough for an unprecedented number of editors. On January 13, 1947, *Steve Canyon* began in 234 newspapers, 162 of which had bought the feature before seeing even the earliest promotional drawings of the characters that appeared only seven weeks previously in Staunton's November *E&P* preview.

Even with the strip's debut, Caniff continued to deny his audience a glimpse of the character they'd been waiting two years to see: perhaps indulging an impish sense of humor, the cartoonist built suspense during the strip's first week through the chancy device of keeping his hero offstage. What they finally saw was a tall, lean, square-jawed, hawk-nosed, worldly-wise soldier of fortune. In personality, he was a more mature Terry, but Caniff had taken pains to make him look markedly different, giving him a theatrical dark streak in his blond hair—a feature of his appearance that excited great comment in the promotional materials. Deliberately contrived to appeal to postwar readers many of whom would be ex-G.I.s, Canyon had been an Army Transport Command pilot, and, like thousands of other veterans after the war, he had set himself up in business, operating his own cargo airline. It was a vocation that gave Canyon the plausible excuse he needed to go anywhere to do anything, and it had a name that rang with the romantic resonance of adventure—Horizons Unlimited. Although Caniff consciously guarded against repeating himself in the new strip, he attempted to recreate the *Terry* mystique at the onset by confronting Canyon with a femme fatale as powerful and unscrupulous in financial circles as the Dragon Lady had been in the China Sea. Even Copper Calhoon's nickname on Wall Street, "the Copperhead," evoked the serpentine character of her predecessor.

Steve Canyon was conceived as a modern sophisticated incarnation of the plainsman of the American West ("airplanes man," the publicity punned), and Caniff gave him a grizzled old-timer sidekick reminiscent of the stock character Gabby Hayes had virtually invented in Western movies. With the old would-be Seventh Cavalry trooper Happy Easter at his side, Canyon spent the next four years barnstorming around the globe in a loping saga of footloose adventure. And Caniff waylaid his hero with an array of fascinating friends and foes: the pneumatic Madame Lynx and the mysterious Maid of Nine were aspects of the Dragon Lady; Delta and Fancy, of Burma; but the pairing of antihero Doagie Hogan with the innocent idealist Princess Snowflower was an original conception. And in Summer Smith, Steve met the woman he would court for eighteen years before marrying (a case of unrequited love that equaled Daisy Mae's more celebrated wait for Li'l Abner).

Still, as Caniff reveals in an interview with Jules Feiffer, the cartoonist felt that he was "foundering:" "I couldn't quite get the act together." So in 1950, he added the youth Reed Kimberly to his cast, intending to have Canyon play mentor to the boy as Pat Ryan had to Terry. But when the Korean War broke out, Caniff abandoned that plan. Instead, Canyon reenlisted in the Air Force, and from that time on, *Steve Canyon* was a military strip. Canyon's adventures took place in military settings and with such an authentic representation of the military point of view that he became an unofficial spokesman for the Air Force and was often written about in military publications by Air Force reporters like Major Jim Taylor and Master Sergeant Alan Prochoroff (both writing for *Airman* magazine).

While military custom inhibited Canyon's free-wheeling style somewhat (and a regulation haircut muted the melodrama of the dark streak in his hair), he could still rescue such damsels in distress as the provoca-

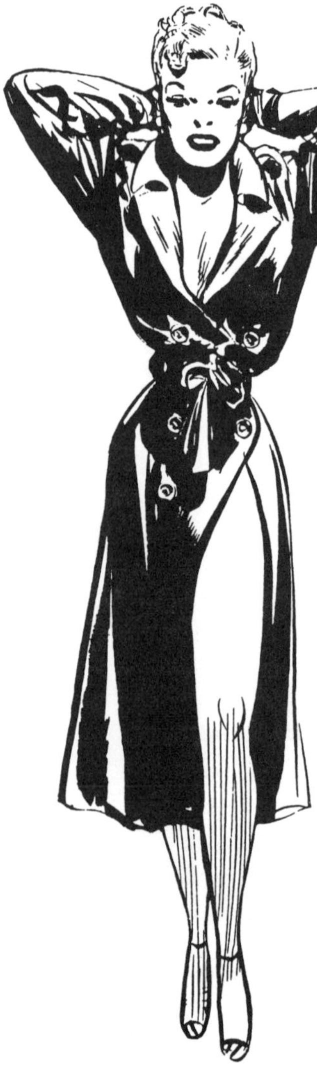

At the left, the most frequently employed promotional picture of Mizzou; but she never flaunted her charms like this in the published strip. And the even more brazen drawing below was never completed.

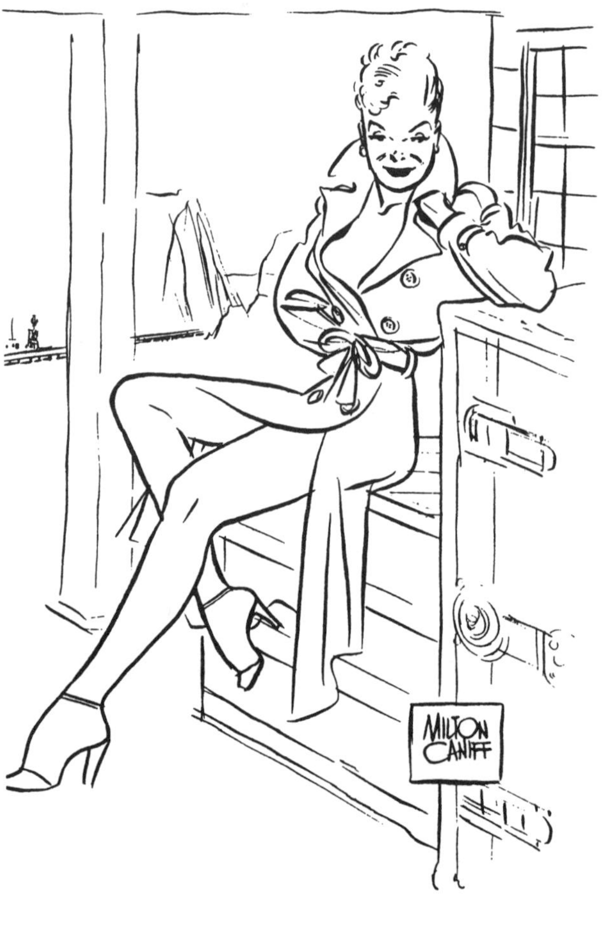

tive Miss Mizzou, who showed up in the North Woods wearing nothing under her trenchcoat. Caniff continued to practice the tricks and tropes of storytelling that he had perfected in *Terry.* And in 1956, he once again sought to appeal to a youthful audience, this time introducing a young woman, Poteet Canyon, Steve's "kissin' cousin" and his ward, who would dog her guardian's steps for the rest of the strip's run, her adolescent infatuation for him never fading. Throughout these years, Caniff played variations on the theme most prevalent in his work—loyalty, in both its personal and patriotic forms. Maintaining the high standards of craftsmanship that he had raised in *Terry,* Caniff scarcely rested on the laurels of his technical achievements there. In *Canyon*'s later years, he continued to explore the medium's potential. He introduced the repertory theater concept, rotating stories among several leading players, and then the element of fantasy, with adventures in which his characters dreamed themselves into other times and places (a distant echo of his first strip). Featuring Poteet as a college student and then as a journalist, he deftly shifted the focus of the strip to hold reader interest with topical stories.

But during the Vietnam War, Caniff underestimated momentarily the extent of anti-war sentiment in the country. Caniff's fatal misstep in this regard is perhaps scarcely surprising. He has always acknowledged, as he did in 1982 in *Airman* magazine, that he was "an out-and-out unabashed patriot." But the cartoonist's rhetorical posture during the Vietnam period has about it an irony of classical proportions. His career and life enacted the American dream—establishing its efficacy in his mind and creating thereby his hubris. He proved that hard work and talent can yield success, and during World War II, the trenchant patriotism he infused into Terry inspired both soldiers at the front and their families at home and brought Caniff unprecedented fame. But when he sought to invoke the same spirit during the Vietnam War in *Steve Canyon,* he inspired only virulent protest, and newspapers canceled the strip by the score. Caniff eventually realized his mistake. In a 1972 interview with Jay Maeder, Caniff would reflect on the changing perceptions of the American public: "The whole Vietnam thing has brought out the attitudes of the younger people. An abhorrence of the whole thing which everybody feels, and the misery of supporting a conflict in an area which they not only don't understand but can't pronounce—the World War II point of view was quite different. . . . There's no Hitler today, there's no Hirohito, there's none of that. Just a big fat nothing to get killed for."

When readers objected to what they perceived as Caniff's hawkish stand in the strip, Caniff tried to recover by taking Canyon out of uniform to serve the Air Force as a special agent in mufti. As Caniff explains to Feiffer, "I kept thinking of James Bond; when he was sent out on an assignment he was a lieutenant in the British Navy. . . . If [Canyon] went wherever under questionable circumstances, I could fall back on the fact that he was sent there. There's more freedom to operate, because he had no freedom." Caniff also frequently avoided the military milieu altogether by addressing other topical concerns of the era, such as drug abuse in a story line with Summer's son Oley. And after Canyon's marriage in 1970 to Summer, Caniff tried to refocus the strip, featuring the couple as a team in light comedy-mysteries like Mr. and Mrs. North of the old radio program. But the strip's circulation was irreparably damaged: it never regained the distribution it had enjoyed at the peak of its popularity in the late fifties when, with a Steve Canyon television series boosting the strip's popularity, it was running in over 600 newspapers.

Steve Canyon ended in June 1988. Written and drawn by long-time assistant Richard Rockwell during Caniff's final two-month illness, the strip could not survive his passing. He died on Easter Sunday 1988. For his many fans, it was not a happy Easter. By the time of his hospitalization, something Caniff had drawn had been in print every weekday continually for nearly fifty-five years, every Sunday for fifty-three years—a publication record without equal.

Caniff was undoubtedly the most honored cartoonist in the profession. He received honorary degrees from several institutions and awards from dozens of organizations to which he contributed time and talent. His support of the U.S. Air Force earned him many accolades, including the USAF Exceptional Service Award (the highest for a civilian). For his work with the Boy Scouts, he received both the Silver Beaver and Silver Buffalo. He was twice (1947 and 1972) named "outstanding cartoonist of the year" by his peers in the National Cartoonists Society, an organization he helped found, serving as its second president (1948–49) and as honorary chairman for seventeen years. Despite his many accomplishments, Caniff persisted all his life in thinking of himself as a newspaperman whose job was to sell tomorrow's paper.

The interviews on the following pages were selected from the file of material assembled during the five years I was working on a "definitive biography" of this cartooning legend. I have silently corrected typographical errors and other occasional errors of facts. Because Caniff was frequently asked the same questions, some repetition is inevitable. A few recurring recitations of details have been edited out, but for the most part, the interviews are reprinted as they first appeared.

R.C.H.

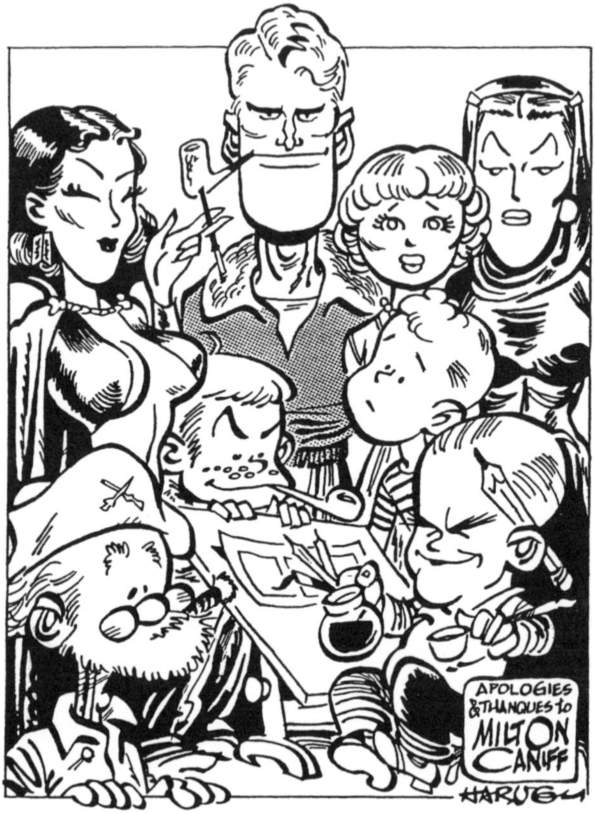

Milton Caniff (lower right) and some of the cast from Terry *and* Steve Canyon, *caricatured by editor Harvey. Clockwise from Caniff: Happy Easter, the Dragon Lady, Steve Canyon, Summer Smith Olson Canyon, Copper Calhoon, Terry, and, smack in the middle with a pipe, Hotshot Charlie.*

Chronology

1907 February 28: Milton Arthur Paul Caniff is born at home, 149 East North Street, in Hillsboro, Ohio, the only child of John William Caniff, a printer, and Elizabeth Burton Caniff.

1912 John Caniff, acting upon his doctor's orders, quits the printer's trade in order to cure himself of a persistent cough and becomes a chauffeur for Colonel Livy Blair Boyd, vice president of the Bell Foundry in Hillsboro; that fall, the Caniffs go with the Boyds to their winter home in Redlands, California, the first of many annual treks across country.

1913 Spring: The Boyds and the Caniffs return to Hillsboro for the summer; and in the fall, back to Redlands, a cycle that would be repeated each spring and fall for the next five years.

1919 Summer: Milton joins the Boy Scouts.

Fall: John Caniff quits his job with the Boyds, and the Caniffs move to Dayton, Ohio, first to 221 Clinton Street then to 648 Richard Street; Milton attends Ruskin Elementary School.

1920 Milton starts giving chalk talks at churches and other locales around town.

1921 Winter: Milton enrolls in a cartooning correspondence course offered by Charles N. Landon in Cleveland, Ohio.

Summer: Milton goes to work part-time in the art department of the *Dayton Journal,* where he serves an apprenticeship with Ferd Appel, the art director. Through high school, Milton reports for work after school and Saturdays during the school year, and every day during summers.

Fall: He enters Stivers Manual High School and falls under the considerable influence of the art teacher, Martha K. Schauer.

1922 Milton meets Esther "Bunny" Parsons and begins dating her. He also becomes involved in high school drama under the tutelage of Florence Lange and undertakes a whirl of extra-curricular activities, which lasts throughout his high school career. He draws a comic strip, *Chic and Noodles,* for the school newspaper.

1923 Milton meets an enterprising freshman, James Reston.

1925 Milton graduates from high school and takes a summer job at the *Miami News* in Florida. While there, he visits the Everglades and gets bitten by a mosquito, a seemingly inconsequential occurrence that eventually results in phlebitis—and a 4-F draft classification.

Fall: Caniff enrolls in Ohio State University (majoring in fine arts), pledges Sigma Chi fraternity, and gets a part-time job in the art department of the *Columbus Dispatch* through the good offices of Billy Ireland, the newspaper's celebrated cartoonist. Through his college years, Caniff also appears in campus as well as community theater productions and does art work for the yearbook and the campus humor magazine. During his years at Ohio State, Caniff meets Bil Dwyer, Tom Cochran (whose brother Phillip, Caniff will make famous), Frank Higgs, Curtis LeMay, Noel Sickles, Charles Raab, and numerous others whom he will encounter later in life. Caniff also makes regular weekend trips to Dayton to see Bunny.

1928 Spring: Caniff drops out of school for a quarter, incapacitated by an infection that will later develop into phlebitis.

Summer: With earnings from his job as art director for the college year book, he goes on a tour of Europe.

Fall: Caniff freelances artwork for the yearbook of another Ohio college, Ohio Wesleyan, at the behest of the editor, Frank Stanton (who will later become president of CBS).

1930 June: Caniff graduates from Ohio State and goes on full-time at the *Dispatch.* August 23: He and Bunny marry in Cleveland.

1931 November: Caniff joins Sickles part-time in a commercial art enterprise.

1932 January: The *Dispatch,* feeling the pinch of the Depression, begins laying off staff, and Caniff is among those laid off. He tours nearby Ohio cities with a traveling theatrical group, first as advance publicity agent, then as an actor. The enterprise fails within months, and Caniff throws in with Sickles full-time.

March: Caniff gets a telegram from Wilson Hicks, assistant editor at the Feature Service of the Associated Press in New York, offering him a position in the art department. He arrives in New York on April 1 and begins moonlighting at once, ghosting the female characters in a comic strip Bil Dwyer just inherited, *Dumb Dora.* The next day, Caniff reports for work at the AP and during his first day there, he meets Alfred Caplin, who will become Al Capp and a life-long friend.

September 12: Caniff inherits *Mister Gilfeather,* a single panel cartoon that carries forward from day-to-day a slender thread of storyline about a blow-hard young man.

1933 March 6: Caniff's first *Puffy the Pig* appears, an illustration over a jingle written by Hicks; later, Caniff produces the jingle as well as the drawing.

Spring: Sickles gets a job at AP based upon Caniff's recommendation.

May 4: Caniff's revitalized *Gilfeather,* now without Gilfeather and re-named *The Gay Thirties,* begins.

July 31: Caniff's first nationally distributed comic strip, a daily (no Sunday) called *Dickie Dare,* debuts.

December: When John Terry, creator of the aviation comic strip *Scorchy Smith* for AP, falls ill, Hicks assigns Sickles to fill-in for Terry.

1934 Winter: James Reston comes to New York, sleeps on the Caniffs' couch for a few nights, and gets a job with the AP after Caniff introduces him to Hicks.

April: When John Terry dies, Sickles inherits *Scorchy Smith* and begins to improve the quality of the artwork on the strip. Shortly thereafter, Sickles and Caniff set up a studio together.

Fall (early October): Caniff is summoned to meet Captain Joseph Patterson, who offers him the chance to do a comic strip for the Chicago Tribune–New York Daily News Syndicate. Caniff agrees, and *Terry and the Pirates* debuts on Monday, October 22. The Sunday page begins on December 9, and the Dragon Lady appears the next week.

1935 January–February: *The Magazine of Sigma Chi* issue of this date carries a lengthy story about Caniff's success in getting syndicated.

Fall: Alfred Andriola joins the Sickles-Caniff studio as secretary to the cartoonists; Andriola would later create the comic strips *Charlie Chan* and *Kerry Drake.*

1936 Summer: The Caniffs and Sickles move out to "the country" for the summer, renting a renovated barn as a studio-apartment in Rockland County outside Haverstraw near New City.

1937 February–March: Caniff is laid up with phlebitis.

June: The Caniffs move permanently to Rockland County, renting a white stucco building called "Contempora House." Andriola moves with them, taking a room in the house. Sigma Chi dubs the cartoonist a Significant Sig at its annual convention.

November 1: *Terry and the Pirates* radio program debuts on NBC's Red Network.

1939 February: The Dayton Art Institute mounts an exhibition of Caniff's artwork—selected *Terry* strips as well as other sketches and paintings of Oriental subjects.

June: The Caniffs move again, this time to a place designed for a studio on Camp Hill Road (still in Rockland County). Caniff hires Adelaide Gilchrest as a secretary, replacing Andriola who left the previous fall to produce *Charlie Chan;* Caniff also hires a maid, a young black woman named Wilhelmina Robinson. ("Willie" will marry Otis Tuck and remain in the Caniff household, serving most of the time as a kind of office manager, until the death of Bunny Caniff almost fifty years later.)

1940 April: Columbia's abysmal movie serial version of *Terry and the Pirates* debuts; Caniff watches part of the first chapter but runs out of the theater, "screaming," as he put it.

December: An exhibit of Caniff art from *Terry* and elsewhere opens at the fashionable Julien Levy Art Gallery in the East Fifties in Manhattan.

1941 January: *Harper's Bazaar* for this month carries an article illustrated by Caniff with drawings of his strip heroines wearing garments he designed.

July: The Caniffs move again, renting a home designed by Henry Varnum Poor on South Mountain Road in Rockland County. Their neighbors include the playwrights Maxwell Anderson, John Houseman, and Kurt Weill. The Caniffs will remain here for the next twenty-three years. They maintain a small apartment in the City so that their frequent forays to the theater won't entail long trips back home at the end of the evening.

October 16: Raven Sherman, a character in *Terry,* dies in the strip, inspiring a great outcry among Caniff's readers.

December 7: Japanese bomb Pearl Harbor, and Caniff is caught with his cast in Hong Kong when the Japanese attack there, too.

1942 August 1: Flip Corkin arrives in *Terry.*

October 11: The "Burma strips" debut with a special GI version of *Terry and the Pirates* that Caniff produces for the Camp Newspaper Service, the military "syndicate."

1943 January 10: The last "Burma strip" appears.

January 24: Miss Lace bows on stage in *Male Call,* the strip Caniff concocts to replace the Burma version of *Terry and the Pirates.*

March: Caniff is drafted but fails the physical because of his phlebitis and is classified 4-F. He will be recalled in a few months but again be rejected for active service.

October 18: Representative Carl Hinshaw of California reads into the *Congressional Record* the previous day's installment (a Sunday page) of *Terry* that records Flip Corkin's speech to Terry when Terry finally wins his wings as a flyer.

1944 December: Caniff signs a contract with Marshall Field to produce a new comic strip for Field Enterprises Syndicate; Caniff's *Terry* contract has two years to run.

December 25: Caniff's first Christmas Day special strip, "White Christmas."

1945 January 1: Walter Winchell reveals that Caniff has signed with Marshall Field and will leave the Tribune-News Syndicate after his contract expires in October 1946.

May 8: V-E (Victory in Europe) Day.

August 14: V-J Day.

1946 March 1: The National Cartoonists Society is formed.

March 3: The last *Male Call* is published.

May 26: Joseph Patterson dies; Caniff's *Terry* is still running in the *New York Daily News* (albeit no longer on the prestigious back page; Patterson had moved it inside the funnies section when Caniff's defection became known).

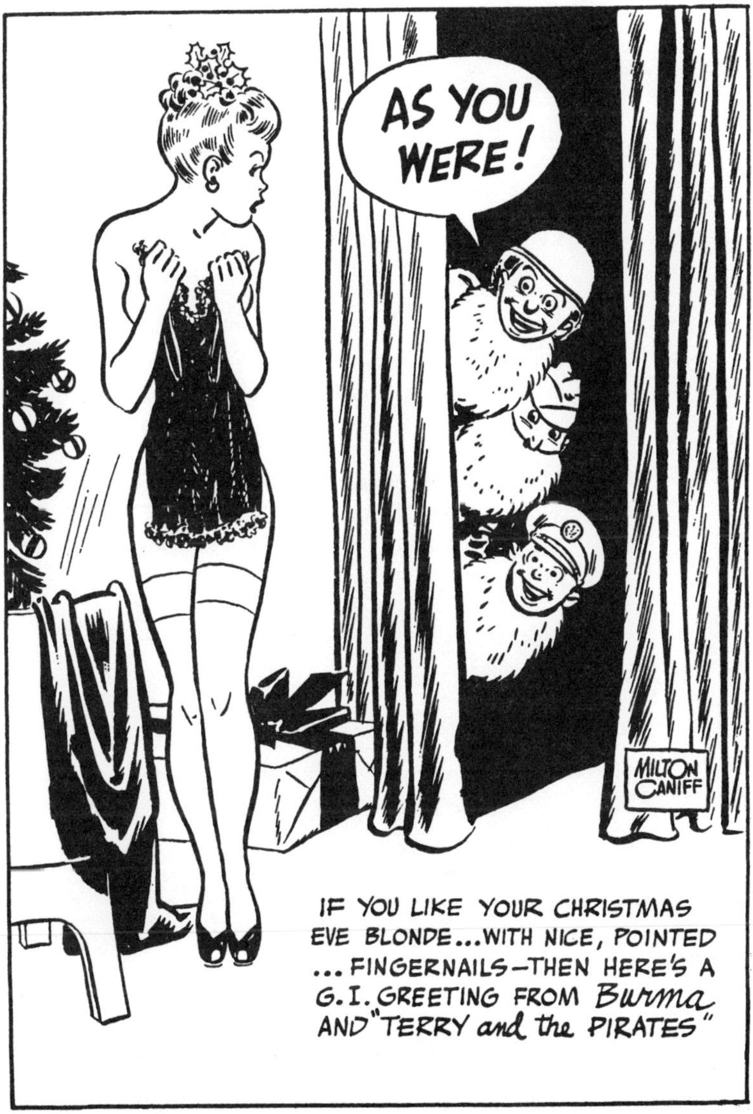

The Camp Newspaper Service, the armed forces syndicate for which Caniff produced his war-time morale-building strips, offered its numerous features by means of the "Clip Sheet," a printed page from which base newspaper editors could clip such illustrations as this for their papers. Burma starred briefly in Terry *strips created for CNS, but Caniff also did special drawings and pin-ups like this one for unusual occasions and holidays; here, we have Burma for Christmas 1942.*

October 15: Caniff's contract with the Tribune-News Syndicate expires; he begins work on his new strip, which will be named *Steve Canyon.*

December 28: The last daily *Terry* by Caniff.

December 29: The last Sunday *Terry* by Caniff.

Caniff joins the Air Force Association soon after it is formed this year.

1947 January 13: *Steve Canyon* begins, but the hero doesn't appear until the following Sunday, January 19. This week's *Time* magazine carries a cover story on Caniff and his new strip.

May 11: Caniff receives NCS's first "cartoonist of the year" award, known officially as the Billy DeBeck Memorial Award. (Later, "cartoonists of the year" will be awarded the Reuben.)

June 15: Happy Easter debuts in the strip.

1949 Caniff is awarded Sigma Delta Chi's (journalism fraternity) Distinguished Service Award.

Bill Mauldin, the celebrated wartime cartoonist, moves into the Rockland County neighborhood, buying the house of another soldier whose wartime creation had made him famous—Marion Hargrove, who wrote *See Here, Mr. Hargrove.*

1950 April 24: Caniff is the subject of a cover story in *Newsweek* of this date.

June: North Korea invades South Korea.

October: Steve Canyon is back on active duty in the Air Force.

1951 November: Caniff produces a comic book, *Steve Canyon's Air Power,* designed to foster interest in the Air Force. For the comic book, he creates a new character, a young man named Dart Davis.

1952 Caniff is awarded the Air Force Association's medal of merit for distinguished service to air power.

February 17: Steve proposes to Summer Smith Olson. She accepts but it will be eighteen years before they finally marry.

August: Miss Mizzou arrives in *Steve Canyon,* wearing only a trenchcoat.

On the Dumont tv network, *Terry and the Pirates* runs in thirty-minute weekly shows.

1953 Caniff receives citation from the Treasury Department for patriotic service in aiding the savings bond program and the Americanism Award from the Philadelphia lodge of B'nai Brith.

February: Caniff hires Richard Rockwell as his drawing assistant.

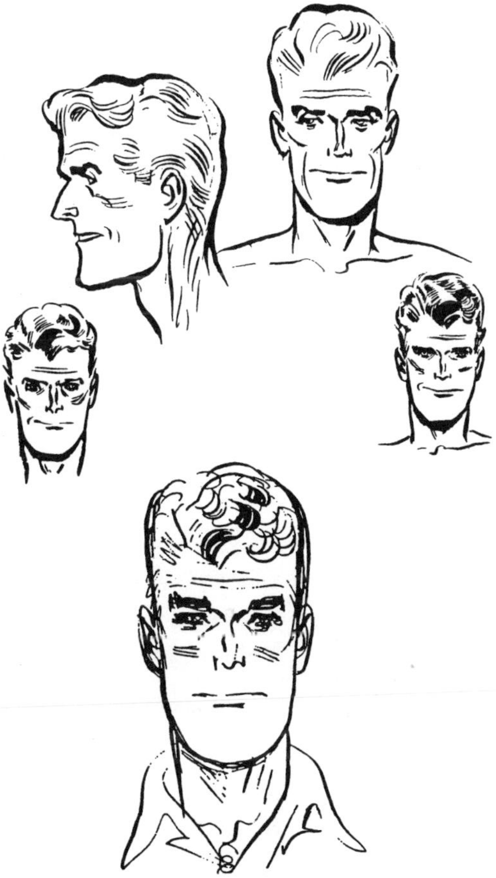

To illustrate the sort of doodling he did in determining Steve Canyon's appearance, Caniff produced the four drawings at the top years after the fact. The larger drawing immediately above was done for a fan during a 1947 promotional trip to Chicago the week before the new strip debuted.

1954 Ohio awards Caniff its Career Medal as a "distinguished son of Ohio."

April 21: Caniff and other members of NCS testify before the U.S. Senate Judiciary Committee's Subcommittee to Investigate Juvenile Delinquency (specifically in this case, the possible influence of comic books upon young readers, an allegation made conspicuously public by Fredric Wertham in a crusading diatribe entitled *Seduction of the Innocent,* published early in 1954).

Caniff becomes a founding member of the Newspaper Comics Advisory Council late in the year.

1956 Rollins College of Winter Park, Florida, confers upon Caniff an honorary Doctor of Fine Arts degree.

Bill Mauldin runs for Congress, campaigning throughout the district in his own Piper Cub (which he pilots himself) and a jeep. Caniff designs posters for the effort, and Bunny serves as Mauldin's financial manager.

August: Poteet Canyon enters the strip as a teenage ward of Steve's; she promptly and irrevocably falls in love with her guardian.

1957 The U.S. Air Force awards Caniff its highest civilian honor, the Exceptional Service Award; and NCS presents him with the Silver T-Square award.

1958 August 29: Steve and Poteet are in Colorado Springs, Colorado, for the official opening of the Air Force Academy.

September 13: *Steve Canyon* television show, starring Dean Fredericks, premieres; runs for two years.

1959 May: The Caniffs are in Berlin when Nikita Krushchev threatens to close the West's access to the city. Although Krushchev subsequently does nothing, Caniff covers the events surrounding the threat for the *Chicago Sun-Times,* sending reportorial drawings to the paper.

December 7: *Life* magazine celebrates the "silver jubilee" of the syndicated careers of Al Capp and Milton Caniff. The two were to appear on the cover but at the last minute, a photograph of the glamorous new fiancee of the Shah of Iran appeared. "An editor decided that old men don't sell magazines—pretty girls do," Caniff said, "I had to agree with him."

John Caniff dies this year.

1960 May: The Caniffs make a month-long tour to Japan. It is the longest he ever spends away from the drawing board since joining AP in 1932.

November 12: Caniff does a chalk talk at Carnegie Hall for the Golden Jubilee Recognition Ceremony of the Greater New York Council of the Boy Scouts of America at which Eagle rank is awarded to Scouts from the five burroughs. The cartoonist was recruited for the job by Scout Executive George Cahill, who persuaded him to produce drawings and verses to be given to all new Eagles and their mothers. It was a ploy to boost flagging attendance, and it worked: Caniff's celebrity status attracts a capacity-straining crowd that overflows into the street.

November 17: The Banshees Club of New York gives Caniff its Silver Lady award as the Cartoonist of the Year.

1961 Caniff is awarded the Silver Beaver by the Allegheny Trails Council of the Boy Scouts of America.

He becomes a founding member of New York City's Air Force Association chapter, the Irongate Squadron ("irongate" referring to the gate guarding the entrance to "21," the restaurant and watering hole of one of the other founders, Maxwell A. Kriendler). The chapter becomes noted for its extremely successful annual fund-raisers for Air Force charities. The secret to the success, Caniff told me, was in devoting the chapter's annual ball to honoring some worthy dignitary. At the second of these events in February 1965, Curts Le May is the honoree, and Caniff, who had co-chaired the first with Kriendler, is again a key player: he is now commander of the Irongate Squadron. Before long, the Irongate Squadron's annual Air Force Ball becomes known as the Air Force Salute, which eventually eclipses all similar Air Force Association efforts and becomes the National Air Force Salute.

1962 Dayton's city fathers establish the National Aviation Hall of Fame, chartered by Congress in July, and Caniff (one of the official incorporators and a member of the Board of Nominations for the rest of his life) supplies portraits of the honorees, who are selected at the rate of four a year.

1964 The Caniffs move back into the City, leaving the Poor House forever and taking two apartments at 360 East 72nd Street—one on the 19th floor for a studio; the other, on the 12th floor, as a residence. They give up a penthouse suite they've maintained at Woodstock Tower in Tudor City (an apartment complex on East 42nd Street).

February: Caniff becomes the third commander of the Irongate Squadron.

September 15: During ceremonies marking "Steve Canyon Day" at the New York World's Fair, Caniff receives the Aerospace Citation from the U.S. Air Force, the Golden Scroll of the National Cartoonists Society, and the World's Fair Silver Medallion of Honor.

1966 Caniff shortens the strip's storytelling time from 12–14 weeks to 9–10 weeks, responding to a frequent criticism from newspaper editors that readers won't follow long continuities on the funnies pages when they can get a whole story—beginning, middle, and end—in an hour in front of the television set in their living rooms.

October–November: Caniff gets a one-man show in Paris at the Gallery of the French Society of Photography.

1967 April–May: Caniff's work is in the Louvre as part of an NCS exhibition tracing the history of the comic strip.

1968 June 14 (Flag Day): A giant 10×11-foot Caniff-designed mural about Scouting and patriotism is installed at Flag Plaza, the Scout Center in Pittsburgh, where George Cahill is now the Scout Executive for the Allegheny Trails Council.

At Cahill's behest, Caniff also produced a poem, "You Are the Flag," which, with the mural, is part of a daily flag raising ceremony that rehearses the history of the country by hoisting, in a thirty-one day rotation, each one of the flags that have flown over the nation throughout its history. The Caniffs attend the dedication ceremonies on July 4.

1970 April 24: Steve Canyon and Summer Smith Olson are, at last, married.

August: The Caniffs move to Palm Springs, California. Bunny's relatives live in California, and she and Milton had been spending a few months of every year there for some time. Adelaide Gilchrest commits suicide on the day the Caniffs leave. Willie Tuck moves to California to become Caniff's studio manager.

Caniff designs the Centennial Medallion commemorating Ohio State University's anniversary.

Nostalgia Press publishes *Terry and the Pirates,* a hardcover volume reprinting the first three stories in the daily strips. Later, Nostalgia will issue reprint volumes for the first Burma sequence and for the Dragon Lady's first appearance in the daily strips.

1971 NCS presents Caniff with the first Elzie Segar award in recognition of "unique and outstanding contributions to the profession of cartooning."

1972 April: Caniff receives his second "cartoonist of the year" award, now called the Reuben, from NCS.

1973 February 23: the last *Terry and the Pirates* (bylined George Wunder) is published. Caniff's mother dies this year.

1974 March: Caniff abandons a kidnaping story in the strip because of the Patricia Hearst kidnaping. The eleventh issue of a new magazine, *People,* carries the story. Originally, Caniff was slated for the cover, but, as before with the 1959 *Life* article, a pretty girl, Cybill Shepherd (and the man she was living with, Peter Bogdanovich), elbow him out of the way.

June: Caniff receives an honorary doctorate from Ohio State University and addresses the graduating class.

1976 May 21: Caniff receives the Silver Buffalo from the Boy Scouts of America.

Summer: The nation's 200th birthday anniversary is celebrated in *Steve Canyon* with the first dream sequence: Steve dreams he is in colonial America on the eve of the signing of the Declaration of Independence; the sequence concludes, fittingly, on July 4.

1977 October 27: Sigma Chi ushers Caniff into the Order of Constantine.

Comic Art Publishing begins reprinting all of *Steve Canyon,* starting with the first releases from 1947. Reproduction is poor, but the project lasts only four volumes, ending with the strip for June 18, 1948.

1979 Spring: Caniff receives the NCS category plaque for Best Story Strip of the year.

May 19: The Milton Caniff Research Room is dedicated at Ohio State, where the cartoonist's papers and memorabilia will be archived.

1981 NCS gives Caniff its Gold Key Award, signaling his entrance into the Society's Hall of Fame. He has now won every award NCS confers.

1982 Caniff is named to the Hall of Fame of the Museum of Cartoon Art in Rye, New York. (The institution, founded by *Beetle Bailey* cartoonist Mort Walker, later moved to Boca Raton, Florida, and assumed a new name, the International Museum of Cartoon Art.)

March 28: Caniff is the honoree at the annual National Air Force Salute staged by the Irongate Squadron in New York. After dinner, he is presented with the Maxwell A. Kriendler Memorial Award (which Caniff had designed) in recognition of his "devoting his brilliant creative talents for more than four decades to champion the cause of men and women in uniform thus enhancing the image of the United States Air Force and our nation."

1983 January: Kitchen Sink Press publishes the first issue of *Steve Canyon Magazine,* which undertakes to reprint all of the strip. Issues are sporadic after the first year or so, culminating in four paperback volumes that take the reprinted strips to April 7, 1958, as of 1992, when the project ended.

Summer: Steve dreams he's in the China-Burma-India theater of World War II for the glider invasion of Burma with Phil Cochran.

The Caniffs move back to New York, selling their home and studio in Palm Springs. They had always spent the theater season in New York, so they were living six months on the West Coast and six months in the East—"the worst six months for weather in each place," Caniff once quipped. As before, they rented in the same building (on East 45th Street) two apartments—one as a residence, the other as a studio.

1984 November: The Museum of Cartoon Art mounts a special exhibit of Caniff's work to commemorate the fiftieth anniversary of the debut of *Terry and the Pirates.* Nantier-Beall-Minoustchine (NBM) Publishing begins a twelve-volume three-year project that will reprint all of Caniff's *Terry and the Pirates* at the rate of one volume each quarter, Sundays (albeit in black-and-white) as well as dailies.

1986 May: Caniff has heart surgery, but before the operation, he gets a month ahead in the strip by getting permission to re-run a 1947 story on the pretext that Steve Canyon has been asked to write his autobiography, which he does by dictating into a tape recorder his recollections of his first encounter with Copper Calhoon.

Fantagraphics Books reprints all of Caniff's AP strip in *The Complete Dickie Dare.*

1987 *Milton Caniff's America: Reflections of a Drawingboard Patriot,* a collection of the special strips Caniff did for

Christmas Day, Armed Services Day and Air Force Day, is published by Eclipse Books.

Ohio State University names Caniff Alumnus of the Year, and the Alumni Association gives him the Alumni Medalist Award, its highest honor.

December: King Features renews Caniff's contract for another two years of *Steve Canyon.*

1988 January: Caniff has cataracts removed. To create a work-free recovery period, he re-runs a 1948 sequence about the Persian Gulf.

February: Caniff is diagnosed with lung cancer. Hospitalized for treatment, he plans to continue to draw the strip while in bed (as he had done during other hospital stays with bouts of phlebitis) but finds his energy not up to the task. Dick Rockwell and Shel Dorf undertake to produce the strip during Caniff's recuperation.

March 28: Given a choice—home or a hospice—Caniff returns home.

April 3: Caniff dies at 2:20 p.m. It's Easter Sunday.

May 11: Bunny, in the middle stages of Alzheimer's disease, dies at 2:35 a.m. in the hospital to which she'd been taken after suffering a heart attack a week after her husband's funeral on April 6.

June 3: The Rockwell continuity in *Steve Canyon* ends so that Rockwell can take the next day's strip, a Saturday release, to pay tribute to his boss of thirty-five years.

June 5: The final strip, a Sunday, is designed and executed by Bill Mauldin. Unique in the annals of syndicated cartooning, the strip depicts one of Mauldin's celebrated World War II characters, Willie, marking a battlefield grave, but instead of embedding a rifle to mark the spot, he's using a drawing pen. Another serviceman, this one in flying togs with the word "Canyon" on his helmet, is placing a helmet on the pen; the helmet carries the name "Caniff." This picture is signed by seventy-eight cartoonists. There are no other words except "In Memory, Milton Caniff—1907–1988."

1990 NBM Publishing begins reprinting all the Caniff *Terry and the Pirates* Sundays in color in twelve slim volumes.

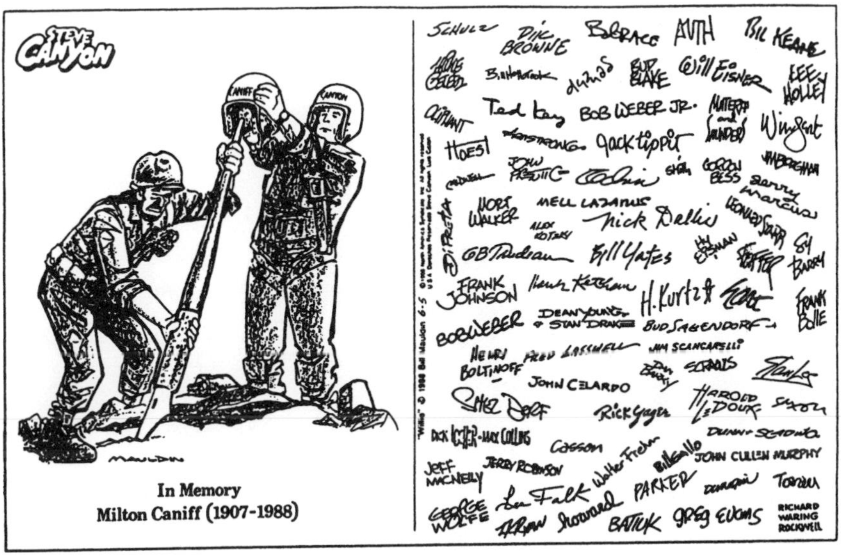

Milton Caniff
Conversations

Notes and Interview

CHESTER CLEVELAND / 1937–1945

Excerpted from *The Magazine of Sigma Chi*, February–March 1945, n.p. Reprinted by permission.

Like any good fraternity brother, Caniff relied upon his brethren. From the very first, he made his fraternity part of his promotional network, knowing that among the ranks of Sigma Chis were a certain number of newspaper editors who would be interested in buying the work of a fraternity brother. When Terry and the Pirates *was launched in October 1934, Caniff conspired immediately with Chester Cleveland, editor of* The Magazine of Sigma Chi, *to do a lengthy article about the cartoonist's success. And Caniff continued to appear in the magazine: he contributed drawings regularly, and Cleveland retailed anecdotes and news about Caniff. With the tenth anniversary of* Terry and the Pirates, *Cleveland produced a "Special Tribute Issue for Milton Caniff," and in it, he collected many of the articles and notes he'd run in the past about the cartoonist. A couple of these appear below. The Don Wilson to whom Cleveland refers is another Sigma Chi, the genial announcer on the "Jack Benny" radio program. Cartoonist Fontaine Fox is another fraternity brother.*

In correspondence, my usual salutation for Caniff is "Dear Budge" or "Dear Budget." He generally signs his letters in the same fashion. The darned thing has been going on since November 29, 1937, the day that we drove to Manhasset, Long Island, with Russ Easton and Ed Nell to meet Fontaine Fox for the first time. We had a 2 p.m. appointment with the famed Σ X creator of "The Toonerville Trolley" at his studio in a downtown business block. For once in our lives we arrived a half hour ahead of schedule. We were hellbent upon rushing up the stairs to exchange the grip with Brother Fox when Milt threw a wet blanket on our plans in an oration which went something like this: "All syndicate cartoonists like Fox work at least 18 hours a day, to the point of exhaustion, in front of a drawing board. . . . Every minute counts. . . . Every moment of the all too short day must be carefully budgeted. . . . Y'know, just one damned deadline after another. . . . It wouldn't be fair to bust in on Brother Fox a half-hour early and rob him of precious time when he has been good enough to grant us an interview. . . . As I said

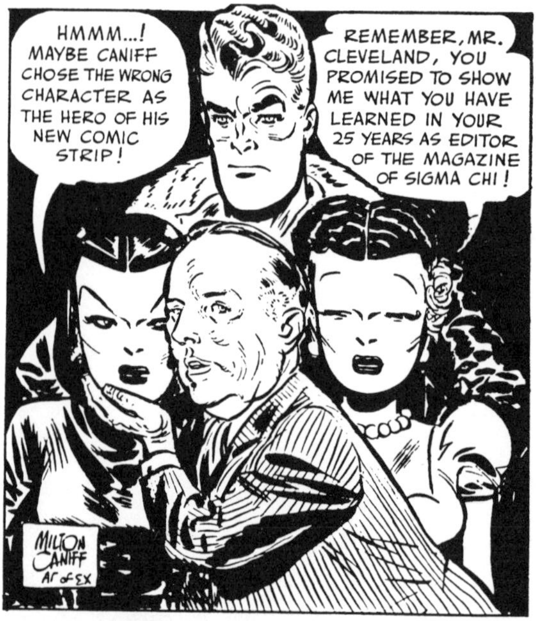

When Caniff launched Steve Canyon *in 1947, Cleveland again gave the cartoonist and his new strip extensive coverage in* The Magazine of Sigma Chi. *And Caniff reciprocated with such special drawings as this, in which Cleveland himself appears with Caniff's new cast (Copper Calhoon, Steve, and Feeta-Feeta) in the March 1947 issue.*

before, fellers, a great and noted cartoonist like Mr. Fox has no choice other than to budget, budget, budget his time all day long." So the four of us repaired to a nearby tavern where the next half-hour seemed like five minutes. Promptly at 2 o'clock we knocked on the studio door, were warmly greeted by Mr. Fox's assistant, and of all things, found our Louisville-born brother in a perfectly relaxed mood. If he had done any work that day there was little evidence of it. He was certainly glad to welcome us and got just as much of a kick out of meeting Milt as the Ohio Stater got in meeting him. After the formalities were over we enjoyed Brother Fox's Southern hospitality in the form of a couple of bottles of rare sparkling Burgundy. No one mentioned the word "budget" the rest of the afternoon, let alone Milt. But Milt has heard it plenty since that memorable red-letter day. A couple of years later Fontaine Fox moved his studio to 1 W. Elm St., Greenwich, Conn., where he undoubtedly keeps on budgeting, budgeting, budgeting the live-long day.

Cleveland: When I inquired, Budge, as to your preferred brand of cigarettes I had no idea whatever of sending you several cartons. I did have a carton of Luckies but Don Wilson, of all people, wangled them out of me when he dropped in on February 10. That was simply the first of many questions that I am not asking. You know how folks relish this intimate stuff, so give, brother, give!
Caniff: Bitter as I am, Simon (Legree), about the fact that you are not going to send me 17 cartons of Old Golds, I hasten to send the information you requested.

Attached you will find bank statements and birth certificate. Photostat of my draft registration will follow in time for the Third World War (for date—see editorial page of the *Chicago Tribune*—any edition).

Cleveland: What are your favorite books and authors, and how in the world do you ever find time to read at all?
Caniff: My extra-curricular reading is done through the courtesy of Mrs. Caniff who is kind enough to read aloud to me while I am toying with my paper dolls. After the dialogue is done it is fairly easy to listen while doing the actual drawing on *Terry.* This is a great boon, since I would otherwise be limited to the tragic papers which I read, not so much for entertainment as to find out what the other pariahs are doing and how the color of the blood comes out in the Sunday editions. The

current opus is Volume II of Carl Sandburg's *The War Years.* I must say you Illinois boys do all right.

I would be hard put to name an absolute favorite author since my tastes are so definitely sub-divided by type categories. Also, I am the victim of immediate-itis. I so often like the book I just finished. For instance, just now my favorite biographer is by all odds, Carl Sandburg. However, I was completely enamored of Lloyd Lewis after finishing *Sherman, The Fighting Prophet.* Likewise do I beat the drum for Howard Fast and his fictionized biographical writing *Citizen Tom Payne, Conceived in Liberty.* I am fickle, but I have fun.

Cleveland: Now that you are in the money and no longer have to eat at Wimpy's and the Automat, what places attract you most from the culinary standpoint? Also, where do you stand in matters of cuisine? As a matter of fact, I have never seen you back away from any dish.
Caniff: I am a ham and eggs boy at heart, but I am a red point* epicure at present. Neither Ganzi's (The Palm), Toot Shor's, Sardi's, The Stork Club or "21", or places I used to think of as being my favorite beaneries in New York, can touch the concoctions we now have at home made from the meat that used to go to the dogs. Of course, this is tough on the dogs, but in spite of my Great Dane's 200 lbs. I still outweigh him by 10 and he can catch rabbits and I can't (I have seen too many Walt Disney movies). He doesn't go to the movies. That is, without an escort. He hasn't been the same since Rin-Tin-Tin died; neither has Rin-Tin-Tin.

Cleveland: What are your hobbies? In responding to this question, please remember that we are running a family magazine.
Caniff: Are you kidding about this hobby business? Every once in a while I go to the window, carefully take aim with the binoculars and watch the people on the golf course across the valley. It wears me out so I usually have to take a nap after that.

Seriously, the theater is probably my hobby, if simply sitting on the folding chair side of the footlights could be called a hobby. However, since hobbies are supposed to be diversions and/or avocations, such divertissement produces the desired end while I sit on mine and do nothing more than let the mummery drip on me.

**A reference to the war-time rationing system whereby civilian purchases of food and gasoline and other materials were controlled by an allotment of points contained in booklets of coupons.*

Cleveland: "Prof" Scheuch agrees with me that *Harvey* is the most entertaining play that has hit Broadway in many seasons. Both of us freely admit that we actually saw Elwood P. Dowd's 6'1½" rabbit companion. Have you shared this memorable experience?

Caniff: Rabbit, hell . . . I haven't even seen Barbara Stanwyck, let alone Frank Fay from whom she was divorced some years ago. After sleeping in the library of the Players Club a couple of times this year, my current theater-going has been somewhat curtailed. You see, my trouble is that I can't let an evening at the theater end there and I too often find myself (by the merest chance, of course) lifting a lager at the bar of said emporium of the Arts in the small hours of the morning. Ergo: no beds to be had anywhere in town, not even a board . . . so I chase Hamlet's ghost out of the library of the Player's Club and lay me down among the playbills. By Rube Goldbergian reasoning: the damn sofa is too short at the Players. Therefore, I have not seen many plays this season.

A play or movie often lingers pleasurably in my mind for cockeyed little reasons. For instance I was practically driven to tobacco by the delicious odor of cigar smoke when George Arliss was playing the Hartman Theater in Columbus in *Old English.* Arliss' enjoyment of his last meal and a cigar in the final act of that tidbit left its mark.

I shall never forget the scene in *My Maryland* when practically every flat-broke at Sigma Chi then at Ohio State turned up on the stage of the Hartman Theatre in Confederate uniforms marching bravely across the boards, then hurrying noisily behind the backdrop to re-appear until the army seemed of magnificent proportions. That *My Maryland* company does not know to this date that the terrific burst of applause came from the solvent members of the Chapter who were on hand to see that the hard-earned pay of the super-numeraries thus engaged traveled back to the pockets of those who had been making loans against the security of this week's engagement.

Cleveland: Recalling that unforgettable suspense we suffered while Candy's mongrel dog was being shot off-stage in John Steinbeck's terrific play, *Of Mice and Men,* I want you to name a few other plays which in your opinion have made theatrical history.

Caniff: Among the plays that left the greatest impress over the years were *What Price Glory, Of Mice and Men* (remember that night?), *Mary of Scotland, Design for Living, Abe Lincoln in Illinois, Green Pastures.*

As to movies, one of my earliest recollections and still a top favorite—*Birth of a Nation, Wings, Hell's Angels, The Big Parade, Gone with the Wind.*

Cleveland: The record shows that Kay Francis and Fredric March once supported you in a Dayton summer stock company. On second thought, I guess it was the other way around. Well, anyway, this places you in an enviable position to enumerate your Thespian greats, legitimate, illegitimate, and motion picture.
Caniff: Chester, you know goddamn well this is a bunch of assorted defecation, for want of a better word. How the hell do I know what movies I like best. I always like the one I just saw. As a matter of fact, Pearl White and Helen Holmes are really my all-time loves. The best that Bette Davis can do will hardly equal the consummate agony on the face of poor Helen when she was strapped to the drive-wheel of a Southern Pacific locomotive. That's the kind of stuff I like. Real Ee-motion.

Cleveland: Seriously, Milt, you are one of the prize assets of the Sigma Chi Fraternity. Personally I think that you are the logical successor to our beloved George Ade in the hearts of Sigma Chi. That's a pretty big order but you are rapidly on your way to that distinction. Now that it can be told, just what other fraternities rushed you at Ohio State and why did you pick the Norman Shield?
Caniff: I was desultorily rushed by Beta Theta Pi, Phi Kappa Psi, and Delta Upsilon. I think the Betas threw a meal at me because I had been previously rushed at Miami by Beta and Sigma Chi. The good Beta brothers at Ohio State probably got a penny post card from the Miami Chapter calling me in for a duty job.

I fell asleep at the Phi Psi House which must not have raised my stock particularly. Since I was illegally carrying a Sigma Chi pledge button in my pocket, I rather imagine the Phi Psis had word of my affiliation and didn't waste much time. I recall that they did wake me up in time to go home before my roommate thought I had transferred to Wisconsin or some place. I don't know why the DUs invited me down for a meal and I am sure they don't either.

The fact of the matter is that I was completely sold on Sigma Chi before I ever arrived at the University. There was too much Sigma Chi background dating as far as childhood in Hillsboro, followed by my close friends from the previous year's graduating class at Stivers who had taken Sigma Chi pledge buttons, for me to consider anything else very seriously. I had gone to Columbus the previous year for a football game and they could have pledged me then if they had cared to. I guess I have a one-track mind.

Lee Beardshear was the boy who really put the pressure on, however. Lee had been president of the senior class preceding the one of which I was president and he had also been president of our high school fraternity the year before I was, so that I listened closely when he told me of the wonders of the Lodge. Then, of course, there was John McCutcheon, Fontaine Fox, et al, so the sales talk was hardly necessary.

The Consul when I was initiated (early fall of 1926, sophomore year at Ohio State) was Richard McCann, now dead. The Rushing Chairman the year before had been Ray Davisson.

Cleveland: Where in the world did your Mom dig up the handle, Milton Arthur?

Caniff: The Milton Arthur resulted from the situation shown in the attached clipping from a recent issue of the *Hillsboro* (Ohio) *News-Herald* (operated, incidentally, by Granville Barrere, a Sig from Miami). My father was 1st Sergeant of the National Guard Company in Hillsboro when I was born. The Captain's name was Arthur Underwood and the 1st Lieutenant's name was Milton Wedding. Voila!

There is a third name (Paul) which was added at baptism because of the lack of a saint's name prescribed by Catholic ritual.

Significant Sig and the Funnies: Milton Caniff

JOHN BAINBRIDGE / 1944

Excerpted from *The New Yorker* profile, January 8, 1944, pp. 25–30.

The genesis of *Terry and the Pirates* goes back to one afternoon late in the summer of 1934, when Captain Joseph Patterson, publisher of the *News,* was sitting in his office looking through an early edition of the *Sun.* After reading the comic-strip page, which is the section of any paper he always turns to first, he turned to a syndicated cartoon feature titled *The Gay Thirties,* which showed a young woman, just back home from a Mae West movie, saying something to her husband about his coming up to see her some time. Patterson laughed out loud. This was an event, for, although Patterson's affection for comics approaches idolatry, his risibility is not easily touched. Three days later, Caniff, the man who drew the cartoon that made the Captain laugh out loud, was summoned to Patterson's office and offered a job doing a new comic strip for the Chicago *Tribune*-New York *News* syndicate. "The offer from

Patterson," Caniff has since remarked, "was the end of the line. I knew then that I had arrived." He had.

When Caniff kept his appointment with Patterson at the *News,* he found that the publisher had been a constant reader of both *Dickie Dare* and *The Gay Thirties.*

In the interview, Caniff behaved with proper humility. He was aware that he was in the presence of the man who, having assisted in the birth of *The Gumps, Smitty, Harold Teen, Winnie Winkle,* and *Dick Tracy,* had midwifed more comic strips than any other person in the country. Caniff listened respectfully to Patterson's specifications. He told Caniff he wanted an adventure strip with a universal appeal. That meant, he said, a youngster to get a juvenile following, a handsome hero to provide the love interest, and, for comedy, a daffy character who could logically become involved with the two principals. Make the locale the Orient, since that's the last outpost of adventure, Patterson added, put the heart throbs in the daily strips, and draw the Sunday color page primarily for youngsters. Finally, Patterson said that somewhere in the action he'd like to see a character called Old Pop and that he wanted plenty of blood and thunder. "Get Old Pop hanged," Patterson said. "Show him hanging."

Caniff met with Patterson on a Thursday and Patterson wanted to see sample strips the following Monday. In his spare time during the next three days and nights, Caniff, who had never been nearer the Orient than the corner of Mott and Pell, read some books by Pearl Buck to pick up background material, invented and named a cast of characters, worked out the beginning of a plot, and drew a two weeks' supply of strips. He named his youngster, a tow-headed American boy of twelve, Tommy Tucker, and his hero, a wavy-haired, pipe-smoking brunet, Pat Ryan. The first episode began with Tommy and Pat landing in China to search for a secret gold mine, the map of which had been willed to Tommy by his grandfather. Pat and Tommy immediately hired an English-speaking Chinaman, comically named George Webster Confucius, as their combination interpreter, guide, and valet. To get up the river to the gold mine, Tommy, Pat, and Confucius engaged a boat owned by an ancient American mariner called Old Pop, who had a daughter named Dale.

One thing Patterson hadn't mentioned was a villain, but Caniff provided one. Instead of the orthodox oily male, he invented a beautiful half-caste woman who led a gang of river pirates. Caniff named her the Dragon Lady.

. . . .

Caniff named his strip *Tommy Tucker.* Patterson liked everything about it except the title. That night Caniff jotted down a list of fifty other names on a sheet of foolscap and sent it over. Toward the end of the list, he put in the name "Terry." When the sheet came back to him, Caniff saw that Patterson had circled "Terry" and written "and the Pirates" in the margin. *Terry and the Pirates* was launched in the *News* in October, 1934.

. . . .

[At the time] the trend toward realism in the comic strips was on. It has reached its extreme in *Terry and the Pirates,* which has changed in the past nine years from a comic strip to what Patterson describes as a "romantic and dramatic continued serial." Caniff now tries to make his strip as real as life. He has exchanged comedy for accuracy and is proceeding on the premise that facts are more entertaining than fantasy. He not only has his characters grow up, he even arranges matters to indicate that they have a well-rounded sex life.

. . . .

It is inevitable that a few of the kiddies who read *Terry* may miss some of the Krafft-Ebing undertones, but this doesn't worry Caniff. "I'm interested in pleasing their daddies," he says simply.

Most *Terry* characters are more or less imaginary, but several bear considerable resemblance to real persons, both living and dead. The many similarities between one of Caniff's leading women and the late Jean Harlow cannot be called coincidental, since he planned her that way. Caniff's devotion to accuracy approaches delirium in the delineation of a half-dozen characters whom he models after living people. Colonel Philip G. Cochran, the Air Forces hero, has been a friend of Caniff's since they were at Ohio State and is, as most everyone probably knows by now, the original of Caniff's character called Flip Corkin. Caniff not only has Corkin look, talk, think, dress, and act like Cochran, but he also faithfully promotes him soon after Cochran is promoted in the Army Air Forces. About the only important difference between the original and the facsimile is that Cochran has no steady girl, while Corkin is in love with a nurse named Taffy Tucker. When Cochran returned a few months ago from North Africa, where he won six medals and five citations, he found, to his momentary annoyance, that most of the people he met here were not especially interested in the details of the Tunisian campaign. What they were really interested in was how he was getting along with the Tucker girl.

Caniff's method of creating a character is rather different from that of an old-school cartoonist. . . . Caniff estimates that he put in about three months, off and on, in creating Taffy . . . [and] spent several days just worrying about a name for Taffy. Since he visualized her as a pert, snub-nosed girl from Georgia, he wanted a name with a typically Old South sound. He finally settled on Guinevere Marianne Tucker, nicknamed Taffy because of her candy-colored hair. She had to be short, because she was scheduled to fall in love with Flip Corkin, who is short, and she had to be blond for contrast with Flip, who is dark. Caniff decided to make Taffy a Red Cross nurse, so he got in touch with the Red Cross, which sent a representative to his studio to tell him how Red Cross nurses are selected and trained and to supply him with a set of nurse's uniforms as models. Caniff went through much the same routine with the War Department, since he planned that Taffy would eventually transfer from the Red Cross to the Army Nurse Corps. He was put in touch with an exceedingly articulate Army nurse, who furnished him with details about Army nurses—their slang, their special problems, how they feel about dates with soldiers, and other minutiae. People often ask Caniff whether he believes that his readers appreciate all this painstaking work. He replies by producing from his files a stack of letters from Red Cross and Army nurses. With considerable ecstasy, all these correspondents say that Taffy Tucker is simply wonderful and as real as life. "They're the critics," Caniff says. "If you get rave notices from them, you can figure the rest of the customers aren't going to walk out on you."

If Caniff has unconsciously patterned any of his characters after himself, it is Pat Ryan. Caniff, like Ryan, has changed in the past decade from an ambitious collegian to a poised, easy-going man in his middle thirties. Caniff, who is tall, dark, and handsome, has been described for the ages by a reporter on *Mademoiselle* as "sweet and kinda plump, with nice big blue eyes." Being old Boy Scouts, Caniff and Ryan have not forgotten the sound teachings of Uncle Dan Beard, and, being members of Sigma Chi, both are paragons of fraternal friendliness. Caniff's fraternity means a good deal to him. He keeps in touch with many of the chapter brothers and frequently contributes drawings to the *Magazine of Sigma Chi* with rousing captions like "Hold the Cross high, Gang!" In 1937, at the annual Grand Chapter convention, the gang awarded Caniff a Significant Sig Medal. He is the youngest member ever to be so honored. Ryan is not so significant, but Sigma Chi has meant a good deal to him, too. He was once saved from a horrible death because he was wearing his fraternity pin. Unlike Ryan, who is on very active war duty in the Pacific, Caniff was turned down by the services because of a childhood leg injury. Since we got into the war, however, he has been spending much of his time doing jobs for the armed services, such as illustrating the Army's "Pocket Guide to China," published for soldiers. His biggest task for the Army is producing a weekly strip titled *Male Call,* which is furnished free to over a thousand Army camp newspapers and to a couple of dozen Navy and Marine publications. *Male Call,* an extremely racy series which some service papers label a "comic-strip-tease," features an alluring little number named Lace and her spicy adventures among enlisted men. The strip has been denounced as immoral by the Brooklyn *Tablet* and praised by at least one chaplain for its "frank, clever, and tasteful" way of treating sex.

Caniff and his wife, a reserved, statuesque blonde who reads Proust but not *Terry* or any other comic strip, live in a large, modernistic house outside Haverstraw. The house, which he rents from Henry Varnum Poor, the painter, is on the top of a small mountain near High Tor, Maxwell Anderson's mountain. Anderson and his wife are Caniff's near neighbors and close friends. Caniff owns two cars and a station wagon, has a Great Dane called Captain Blaze (after a *Terry* character) and a wire-haired terrier called Flip Corkin, and keeps two servants to take care of the house and a full-time gardener to take care of the property, which covers several acres. Caniff, however, is too busy to have much chance to enjoy his possessions. He puts in around fifteen hours a day at his work, but, even though, like most comic-strip artists, he has assistants, he is always behind schedule. According to his contract with the *News,* he must deliver his daily strips to the syndicate office four weeks in advance of publication and keep nine weeks ahead on the Sunday color page. Caniff has managed to meet this deadline twice in the nine years the contract has run.

. . . .

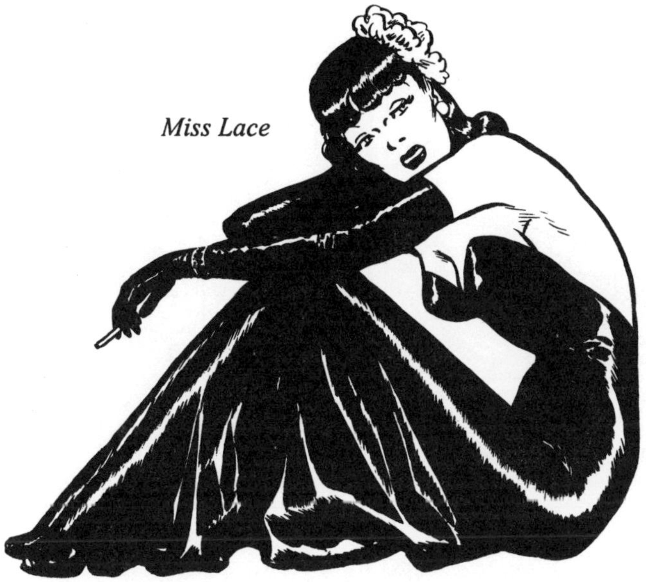

Miss Lace

As a man who would rather be right than punctual, Caniff is willing to spare practically no expenditure of time or effort to avoid making a mistake. He has accumulated a reference library of a couple of hundred volumes, ranging from the Bible and a Sears Roebuck catalogue to Marshall's *Common Legal Principles* and Henry Savage Landor's *China and Her Allies.* In addition, he subscribes to twenty-one popular and technical periodicals, eight newspapers, and a Washington newsletter. Pictures and articles clipped from them go into a row of steel filing cabinets that takes up one of the studio walls. Caniff's files, which are indexed and cross-indexed, contain folders of material on approximately thirty-four hundred subjects, arranged alphabetically from "Abyssinia (Scenes)" and "Abyssinia (Types)" to "Water (Waves, Brooks, Rivers, Waterfalls)" and "Weddings (See Divorce)."

In preparing a recent sequence in which Pat Ryan was involved in a large-scale amphibious operation, Caniff felt obliged to read or at least consult thirty-eight books. He found in his library many of the references he wanted, such as Jane's *Fighting Ships* and Lovett's *Naval Customs, Tradition, and Usage,* but he had to buy seventeen other books. A couple of the strips in the sequence dealt with the construction of a submarine base, so Caniff bought *Submarines,* by Herbert Zim. Since a panel in

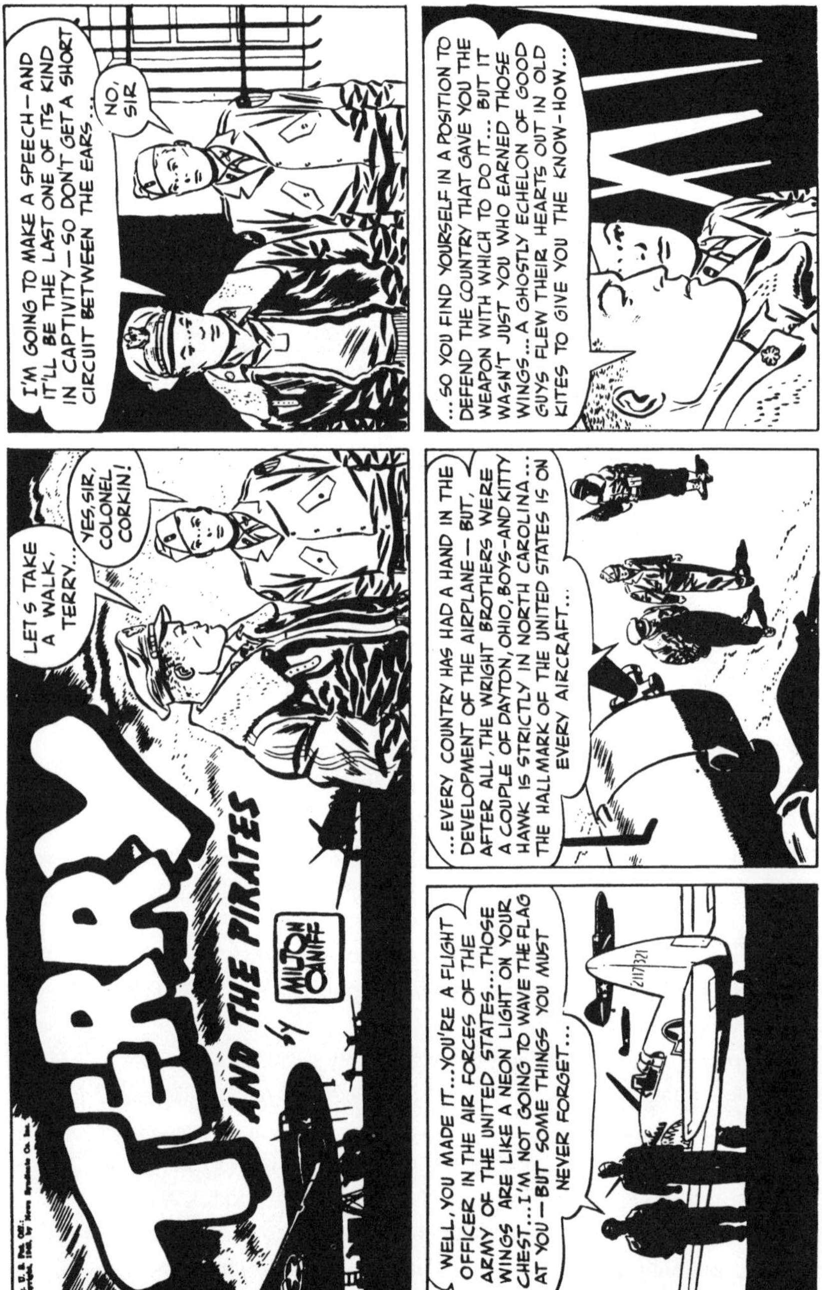
TERRY AND THE PIRATES
by MILTON CANIFF
LET'S TAKE A WALK, TERRY...
YES, SIR, COLONEL CORKIN!
I'M GOING TO MAKE A SPEECH—AND IT'LL BE THE LAST ONE OF ITS KIND IN CAPTIVITY—SO DON'T GET A SHORT CIRCUIT BETWEEN THE EARS...
NO, SIR
WELL, YOU MADE IT...YOU'RE A FLIGHT OFFICER IN THE AIR FORCES OF THE ARMY OF THE UNITED STATES...THOSE WINGS ARE LIKE A NEON LIGHT ON YOUR CHEST...I'M NOT GOING TO WAVE THE FLAG AT YOU—BUT SOME THINGS YOU MUST NEVER FORGET...
...EVERY COUNTRY HAS HAD A HAND IN THE DEVELOPMENT OF THE AIRPLANE—BUT, AFTER ALL, THE WRIGHT BROTHERS WERE A COUPLE OF DAYTON, OHIO, BOYS—AND KITTY HAWK IS STRICTLY IN NORTH CAROLINA... THE HALLMARK OF THE UNITED STATES IS ON EVERY AIRCRAFT...
...SO YOU FIND YOURSELF IN A POSITION TO DEFEND THE COUNTRY THAT GAVE YOU THE WEAPON WITH WHICH TO DO IT... BUT IT WASN'T JUST YOU WHO EARNED THOSE WINGS... A GHOSTLY ECHELON OF GOOD GUYS FLEW THEIR HEARTS OUT IN OLD KITES TO GIVE YOU THE KNOW-HOW...

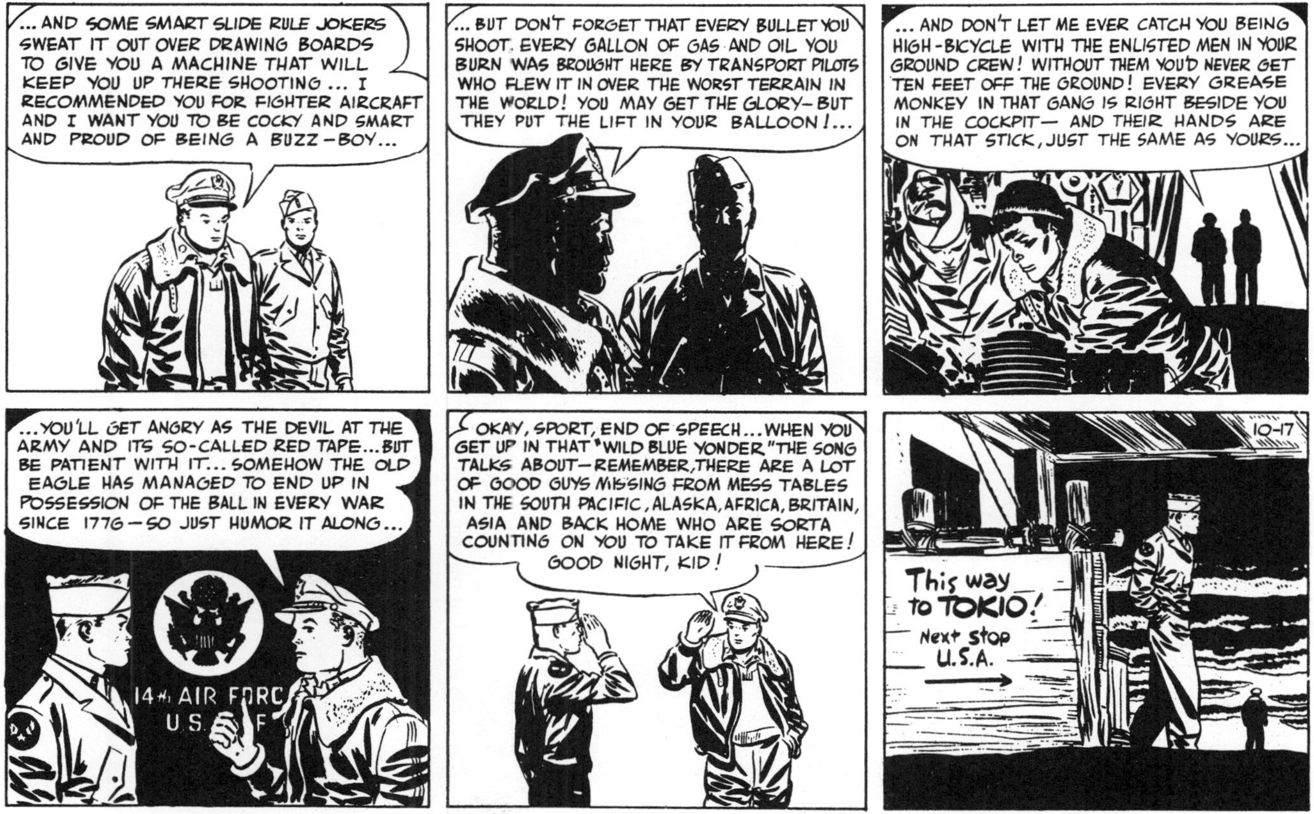

When Terry receives his wings, ending his pilot training, Flip Corkin gives a short sermon on Sunday, October 17, 1943. The most famous of Caniff's strips, it was read into the Congressional Record *and reprinted all around the world in military publications.*

a later strip was to show a field hospital, he bought the *Military Medical Manual*, which shows how a field hospital is laid out. The climax of this series began when Japanese medium bombers took off from an aircraft carrier to bomb an American installation. This presented a serious problem. Do medium bombers, after leaving a carrier, turn to the right or to the left? Caniff thought they would turn to the left, as they do when they take off from the ground, but he wasn't sure, and there was no answer to the question in military or aircraft manuals because the only medium bombers that ever took off from a carrier were the Doolittle raiders that bombed Tokio. Caniff learned that Army Signal Corps photographers aboard the carrier had filmed the take-off and that prints of the picture had been put out as home movies by Castle Films. He dispatched an assistant to the city to buy the reel, and when he ran it off in his studio, he saw that the bombers turned to the left, as he had thought all along. When he came, a few panels later, to drawing a Navy chaplain, he found that none of his books could tell him whether the crosses on the chaplain's shoulder boards sloped inward or outward. Since his maid was already waiting to take the strips to the city, he gambled and drew the crosses sloping outward. Within a few weeks, he received letters from three Navy chaplains—one in the South Pacific, one outward bound from Seattle, and one in North Carolina—all of whom kidded him about his mistake. Caniff was not amused. "That hurt," he says. "When I fumble even some little thing like that, readers begin to distrust the strip. They lose faith. I can't have that."

One Sunday last October, Caniff devoted his entire page to a monologue delivered by Flip Corkin to Terry on the occasion of Terry's receiving his wings in the Air Forces. It was a kind of illustrated commencement address, full of patriotic sentiment and authentic flier slang. When Congress convened the next day, Representative Carl Hinshaw of California opened the day's proceedings with a speech about *Terry and the Pirates*. The congressman expressed his admiration for the "finest and most noble sentiments" he found in Flip Corkin's lecture and suggested that it should be read into the *Congressional Record*. "It is deserving of immortality," he said, "and in order that it shall not be lost completely, I present it, wishing only that the splendid cartoons in color might also be printed here." After finishing with the funnies, the congressman and his colleagues went on to consider other legislative business.

The Story of an Amazing Comic Strip

MARCIA WINN / 1945

Excerpts from an article originally published in the *Chicago Tribune* and *Detroit Free Press* and subsequently reprinted in *The Magazine of Sigma Chi*, "Special Tribute to Milton Caniff," February–March 1945, n.p. Reprinted by permission.

High in the Catskills, on a peak overlooking the slopes down which Benedict Arnold once crawled to betray his country, the lights burn all night every night in a glassed-in studio where labors a man who writes with his right hand and draws, paints, and prints with his left.

The studio has a true north light, but this is of little use to its current owner, for he rarely sees the day. He works with three drawing boards, a Rube Goldberg arrangement of fluorescent lights, a 24-hour around-the-world clock, and a tremendous library on the Orient. Copies of the *National Geographic Magazine* and *Asia* are piled man-high behind him, and on the mantel rest a Chinese hat, a Chinese tongue scraper, a Chinese compass, and a wicked curved blade used for cutting brush in the South Pacific.

On one wall is a black plaque edged in Chinese red. On it in gold are the Chinese characters that mean "Terry and the Pirates, by Milton Caniff."

Milton Caniff (pronounced *cn-iff'*) is a blue-eyed, black-haired Irishman from Ohio, and someday he is going to drop in his tracks. Artistically he is a flagellant. He loves work, flogs himself on into more, and now, white-faced and hollow-eyed, is turning out the work of three men. One man's work is for pay. This is his justly celebrated comic strip, *Terry and the Pirates.* The others are Caniff's contribution to the war. Just as Terry has gone to war, so have the pen and paint brush of his creator.

Caniff is 38, and Terry is somewhere around 20 or 21. Actually he is 10, for he was born, a wide-eyed, adventurous American boy in short trousers, on October 22, 1934. He was just an average little boy, but in less than a year his antics had girdled the globe and he was speaking in 11 languages.

. . . .

Since the early days his adventures have been breath-taking realistic, for the strip progressed into a counterpart of the Flying Tigers, but always liberally splattered with voluptuous women, beautiful and just a little wicked. Many amateur sociologists and students of human nature have studied the strip to no avail to decide which is the greater drawing card, Terry's adventures or them gawgeous ladies in it.

The most gawgeous of all is the Dragon Lady, that phenomenal Eurasian with white skin and slant eyes and a figure beside which that of Helen of Troy was just a canoe sinker.

The Dragon Lady, incidentally, was modeled from a real person, as are all Caniff's characters. In fact, Caniff had a succession of models for her, all of whom married one by one and moved away from his vision. The first one, Phyllis Johnson, a professional model, now is Mrs. William Bippus and lives in Nashville, Tenn.

"She is brunette," Caniff describes the Dragon Lady, using the present tense so tenderly that the hearer suspects that the Dragon Lady will be back any day now. "I actually modeled her hair-do from this model right off the bat, but the model had no slant-eyed business at all.

"What I wanted was an Oriental villain who was not a Fu Manchu. Putting this into a woman made it ten times more interesting, an irresistible combination, mean and beautiful. I never mentioned her age, but she had an adult personality. That was why goings-on between Pat and the Dragon Lady were watched so carefully. It was no 17-year-old love-making. The readers really hung on every word—or so they said in their letters."

Pat played around with all the girls—the Dragon Lady, Burma, that slangy number who tossed wisecracks with her hips as well as her lips and drew her grab-bag name from Kipling's line, "There's a Burma girl a—sitting"; Normandy (his only true love, who married an oaf and can't get rid of him now), and Rouge, the Dragon's successor in artifice—and Terry watched. Heretofore Terry has been the hero only vicariously, for no one can have a wide-eyed child in knee pants kissing *femmes fatales,* blowing up Jap locomotives, and bringing villains to their just end. Terry has watched and learned and waited, and now, a fledgling aviator, he is coming into his own at last. In a sense the strip is starting all over again.

Any one who would like to get a Distinguished Service Cross in this war should meet Caniff and pose as a prototype for one of his characters. It is a sure-fire formula for becoming a flesh and blood hero.

Consider Phil Cochran. Cochran and Caniff went to Ohio State together, but their paths actually crossed little, for Cochran was in the school of commerce and Caniff in fine arts. But back before Pearl Harbor, Cochran, by that time an officer in the air corps, was training the 6th pursuit, or Fighting Cock, squadron at Groton, Conn., a few miles away from Caniff's eyrie. Caniff drew an insigne for the squadron, a red rooster in a green circle with a shamrock around its neck, just as Cochran wore a green shamrock on his helmet and let his good boys wear one as a merit badge.

On July 4, 1942, Cochran and Taffy Tucker, an Army nurse from the "island" (Manila), appeared in the strip. Cochran was there to wipe out the Japs. He appeared as Flip Corkin (he has always been called "Corkin" by his men), and his career in the strip has been meteoric. It has been equally meteoric since then in actual warfare, for he now is Colonel Cochran, wearer of the Silver Star, the D. F. C. with two Oak Leaf Clusters, the Air Medal with three Clusters, and the French Croix de Guerre with Star and Palms.

. . . .

Frank L. Higgs, another Ohio State classmate, was the prototype of Dude Hennick, that handsome daredevil. He now is Captain Higgs of the C.N.A.C., or China National Aviation Corporation, a part of Pan

American Airways under Chinese governmental control for the duration. Higgs once served as a fighter pilot under Chennault in Hawaii, then resigned his commission with Chennault, then a Colonel, to teach Chinese flying cadets. When the Chinese cadet program was reorganized he became a transport pilot for the C.N.A.C.

Then there was Peggy Vincent, the San Antonio girl who wrote Caniff that her husband, Col. Clinton D. (Casey) Vincent, was Chennault's chief of staff. (Chennault,* thinly disguised, is in the strip.) At Caniff's request she forwarded some pictures of the handsome 28-year-old Colonel. Soon he was in the strip as Vince Casey. As Vincent he prevailed upon Chennault to release him as Commander of an advance fighter squadron (just what he was doing in the strip). In one week he got six Japs and the D.F.C. in his plane, the *Peggy II.*

"Each one," Caniff says almost wistfully, "has done something more spectacular by far than anything I ever did in fiction in the strip."

Many persons ask how he happened to get Terry into the war. His answer was that he didn't; the war came to Terry. Terry was in China. China was too torn by war for them to avoid it, so as long ago as 1937, when the rest of the world was labeling Japanese aggression in Manchukuo an "incident," Caniff began showing Japanese troops complete with insignia and labeled "the invaders." At that time the Terry gang was opposed to the Jap feeding of opium to the Chinese through making addicts of young children.

"There was no talk of war," he says, "but any one who could read newspapers could put it together.

"The war just served as a beacon for future sequences. I foresaw a terrific struggle for the Allies, all with vested interests. About that time the military began to creep in. Girls don't like the military—they didn't then—but little basic truisms simply had to be included. Pat, a neutral, got a pass from the Jap army to go out through Japan to get something he needed. His two body servants were not neutrals, but they were admitted with him, and at night they would go out and wreck locomotives and create general havoc.

"The strip began to mold itself in that period. It couldn't be other-

---

**Claire Chennault (1890–1958) was a pioneering military aviator and advocate of aviation pursuit tactics. In 1937 he resigned from the U.S. Army and became aviation adviser to the Chinese government, then at war with Japan. For the Chinese he organized volunteer American pilots into a corps known as the "Flying Tigers." The corps became famous for defending the Burma Road, the Chinese supply route from India.*

wise with that background. I showed the Jap-Nazi-Italian collaboration as long ago as 1940, but without names."

Caniff had predicted the Japanese attack on the United States, but when it came he was caught off guard. Ordinarily he avoids specific geographic locales, but this time he had his characters in Hong Kong, all set for months of guerrilla warfare. April Kane, Terry's love, was off Hong Kong in a small boat. And—bing!—Hong Kong fell. He was seven weeks ahead of publication date in his work, and he had to work day and night to get the crew into a less doomed area. In doing it he had to abandon April Kane, who still is drifting about in the mists of time, an innocent victim.

"I think the public just understood," he said rather mournfully. "They know you get caught like everybody else got caught."

When, however, it came time for Terry to enter the war his course was inevitable. It was made so by a letter from a junior high school class:

"Our class voted that Terry will go into aviation."

He did.

Naturally Terry couldn't come all the way back to the United States in time of war to become an aviation cadet. Instead he began to train with Chinese cadets in China, a reciprocal arrangement on the part of the two Allies, for Chinese cadets were training with American boys in the United States.

Check back over Terry's training day by day, week by week, and you will find it synchronizes exactly, as far as the time element goes, with that of an aviation cadet in this country. Even in training Terry was not a remarkable character. He was an ordinary bright, run-of-the-mill American whose background differed principally in that he could pronounce strange names and had learned mathematics from the back of a truck in China.

You might be interested in Terry's graduation—the day he received his commission as a Flight Officer in the Army of the United States. You might be interested in how Caniff wrote that particular strip, the color page of Sunday, October 17, 1943, for he had just completed it the day this writer went to see him early that September.

"I wanted to have Corkin talking to Terry," he said. "He had to talk to him man to man, friend to friend, yet as a superior officer to a fledgling. I didn't have any idea what he would say. And all at once the thing just wrote itself. Maybe you know how it is. You get an idea and don't do anything with it, just let it lie around in the back of your head, and then all at once there it is, moving on its own momentum."

It turned out to be a masterpiece, in the minds of Army men, newspaper men, and readers. It has been reprinted by the thousands for morale purposes.

Was Caniff pleased? Naturally. He is modest, but he is human. Moreover, he is a consummate artist, and he had achieved a complete art, both of prose and of line, which moved.

Caniff frankly says he owes much to his readers. Scores of persons send him pictures, books on the Orient, clippings, corrections. He now has scouts, volunteers all, scattered over the world, but especially in China and the South Pacific. As a result of this, and of Caniff's extraordinary appetite for accurate detail, *Terry and the Pirates* is carefully documented.

Taffy Tucker produced a splendid example of this. After her introduction in the strip, Caniff had a letter from Lieut. Florence Hunter, an Army nurse stationed at Fort Benning, Ga., thanking him for using a nurse (Taffy was a Red Cross nurse, joining the Army Nurse Corps) and asking for his autograph. In reply he asked if she could send him any background material on Red Cross nurses. That was a year and a half ago. She hasn't stopped writing since. She reports any changes in nurses' uniforms, what nurses say, how they talk, what they do off duty, and wrote one entire series on what men say to the nurses and vice versa. "I've never seen her," Caniff says in wonder. "She's just a name and an Army serial number, but her aid is invaluable."

. . . .

"I have one problem that only I can solve," he says. "I write my own stuff. Then I have to go back and draw it, and I write myself into some of the damnedest difficulties."

So far he has managed to get every one out but April Kane.

Caniff Returns "Lace" to Her Ink Bottle

HELEN M. STAUNTON / 1946

From *Editor & Publisher,* March 23, 1946, p. 70.

When this appeared, Caniff's impending departure from Terry and the Pirates *was already widely known in the newspaper industry, some members of which had speculated that Caniff's new strip would feature a character like Miss Lace.*

When Milt Caniff couldn't go to war himself, he sent Miss Lace in *Male Call* to help the GI's morale—and almost any GI will applaud the substitution.

Miss Burma might have done that morale job, but Caniff's special weekly version of the *Terry and the Pirates* strip which he draws for the *Chicago Tribune–New York News* Syndicate, ran into an exclusive territory contract, and so Miss Lace, with her personal topography well outlined, walked into camp and saluted all the men without stripes, "Hi, Generals!"

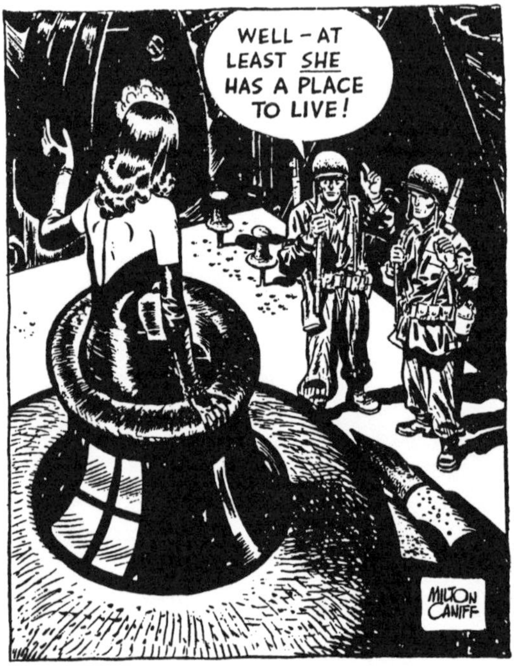

Miss Lace does a disappearing act in this drawing made for E&P. The solider's reference is to the postwar housing shortage that emerged with the arrival of thousands of returning G.I.s.

She arrived at the end of 1942, intended to fill that interim period before the Army found its own cartoonists, but so well did she fill a need that she stayed in service newspapers everywhere, mimeographed and printed, for 180 weeks and returned to her ink bottle only this month.

"My mission has been accomplished," she wrote in the last strip. "I've gone back where I came from—I'll be there if you ever need me again. So long! Love, Lace."

When Caniff starts working on his new strip for the *Chicago Sun* Syndicate after midnight Oct. 14, Miss Lace will not be a character as rumored, the cartoonist told *E & P.* Lace was created, he said, "for the drafted men, the involuntary soldier who needed a morale builder. That, by the way, is why I stopped doing *Male Call* because the audience disappeared. I couldn't do a *Male Call* strip for a bunch of high school boys, and I wasn't interested in doing it for volunteers. They don't need it."

Lace was a great many things to a great many men, *E & P* learned in talking with Caniff. To censors she was a problem, to some chaplains a menace, to officers an able assistant, to GIs and other servicemen, as hundreds of letters testified, a substitute for the femininity they were missing, and to Caniff the strip he most enjoyed doing.

He volunteered to provide a stop-gap feature for draftees in a letter to the War Department written well before the need was clear, he revealed in an interview at his studio among the hills of the Hudson.

"They said they had filed the letter and would write back, and I thought 'Oh, nuts! Like hell they will.' "

Col. Egbert White who organized *Yank,* headed *Stars and Stripes,* and now is back at Batten, Barton, Durstine and Osborn, fooled him, however, by asking for the strip and from October to December, 1942, he drew the special *Terry* free for service publication until one day it cropped up mysteriously in a civilian newspaper.*

To Caniff Miss Lace was more than just one of his voluntary contributions to the war effort and a boost to GI morale (he also chalk-talked for bond drives and visited innumerable hospitals and camps). One could tell despite his almost unsmiling, matter-of-fact, "I still have all the originals that weren't swiped. I like to look them over. Each one was done in the heat of something that was going on in the world at that time."

Asked for his own description of Lace, the stocky cartoonist cocked his leg on a low table and took time to think.

"Her chief characteristic, very carefully planned, was her direct appeal. I always dressed her very carefully. That's what caused the chaplains to howl. But it was perfectly clear to everyone that she was in good taste. She was never overdressed, never wore furs in summer. She was never a floozy." To demonstrate Caniff brought over some pinups that were definitely not overdressed.

"I picked the name Lace because it was a short, easily remembered word that suggested femininity. The only rule I had was that she shouldn't wear slacks. She had to hold the guys' interest—not so much in that they tried to make her, but in that she was a good sport. It isn't that they expect to meet anybody like Lace—some of them do—but that they'd like to meet somebody like Lace.

"I knew exactly what I wanted to do with Lace. That's what kept the strip from being off-color. She was a good sport. Not that I think of her as a sister, but they can make cracks and she snaps right back.

"She's a very hep babe when it's necessary, but completely childish in her naivete when she wants to egg a guy on to talk. She's seductive, but she never seduced anybody. Actually she's the kind of gal who would be at home anywhere.

*Dubbed the "Burma strips," these *Terry* strips featured Burma and mildly risque comedy. When some of them were pirated by a weekly suburban civilian newspaper (which also published the base newspaper for a nearby installation), the metropolitan daily complained to the syndicate on the grounds that it had an exclusive contract to publish *Terry* in that area. Caniff was directed to stop producing the Burma strips: he could do a strip exclusively for circulation to military papers, but he could not use the *Terry* title or any of his Terry characters.

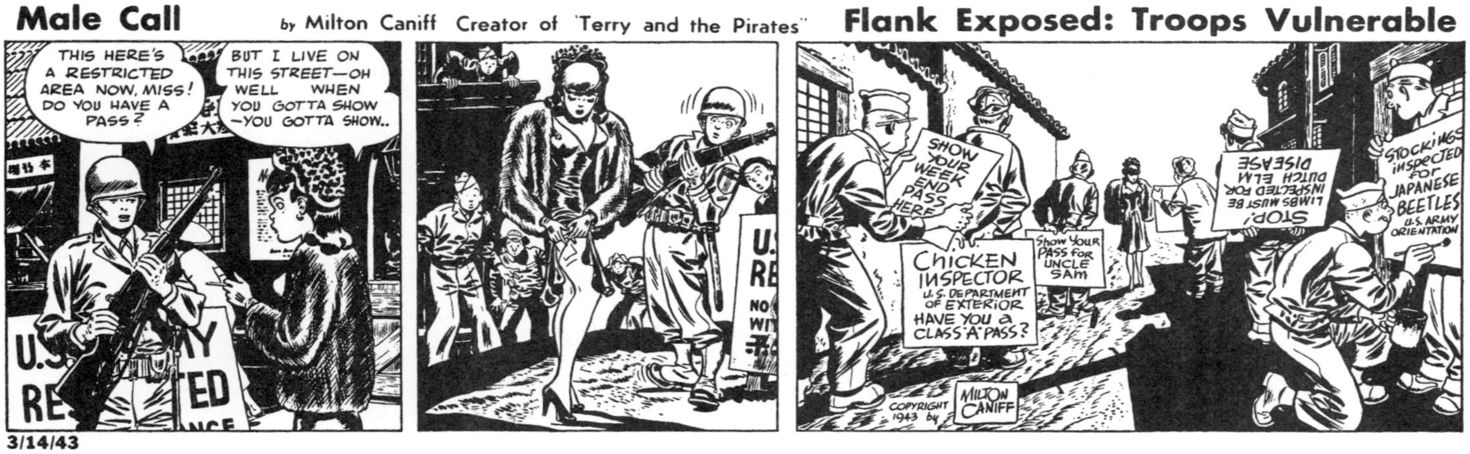
Male Call
by Milton Caniff Creator of "Terry and the Pirates"
Flank Exposed: Troops Vulnerable
THIS HERE'S A RESTRICTED AREA NOW, MISS! DO YOU HAVE A PASS?
BUT I LIVE ON THIS STREET—OH WELL WHEN YOU GOTTA SHOW—YOU GOTTA SHOW..
SHOW YOUR WEEK END PASS HERE
CHICKEN INSPECTOR U.S. DEPARTMENT OF EXTERIOR HAVE YOU A CLASS "A" PASS?
SHOW YOUR PASS FOR UNCLE SAM
STOP! LIMBS MUST BE INSPECTED FOR DUTCH ELM DISEASE
STOCKINGS INSPECTED FOR JAPANESE BEETLES U.S. ARMY ORIENTATION
COPYRIGHT 1943 by MILTON CANIFF
3/14/43

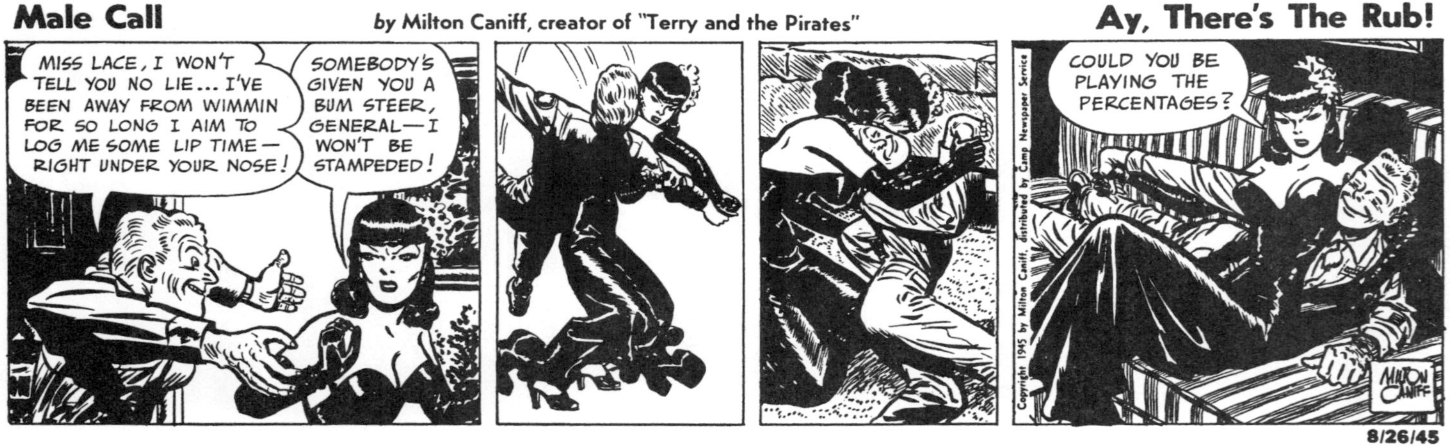
Male Call
by Milton Caniff, creator of "Terry and the Pirates"
Ay, There's The Rub!
MISS LACE, I WON'T TELL YOU NO LIE... I'VE BEEN AWAY FROM WIMMIN FOR SO LONG I AIM TO LOG ME SOME LIP TIME—RIGHT UNDER YOUR NOSE!
SOMEBODY'S GIVEN YOU A BUM STEER, GENERAL—I WON'T BE STAMPEDED!
COULD YOU BE PLAYING THE PERCENTAGES?
Copyright 1945 by Milton Caniff, distributed by Camp Newspaper Service
MILTON CANIFF
8/26/45

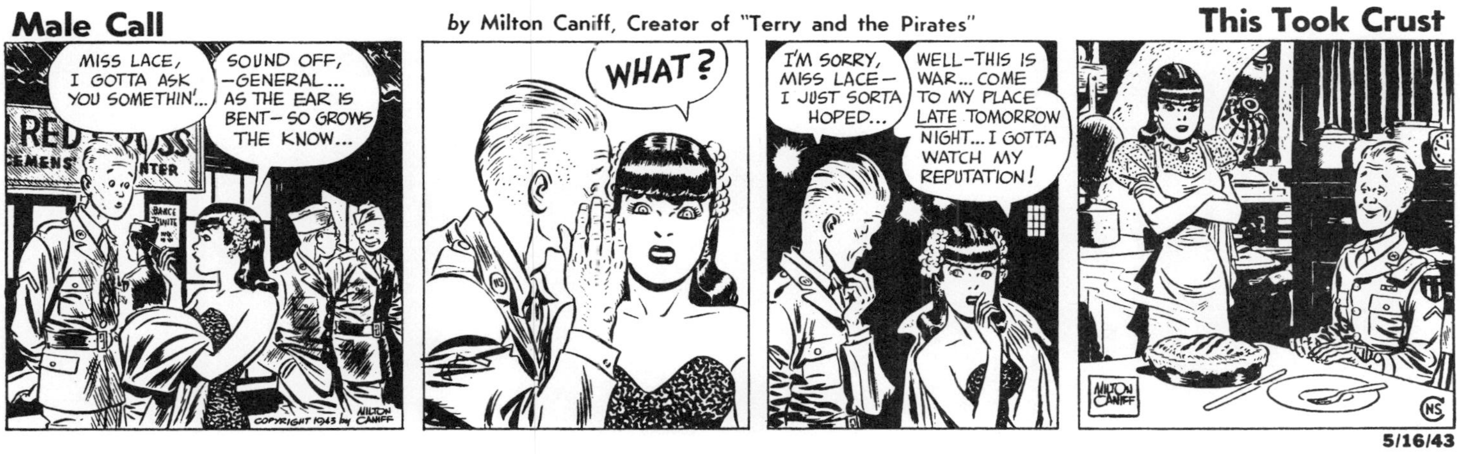

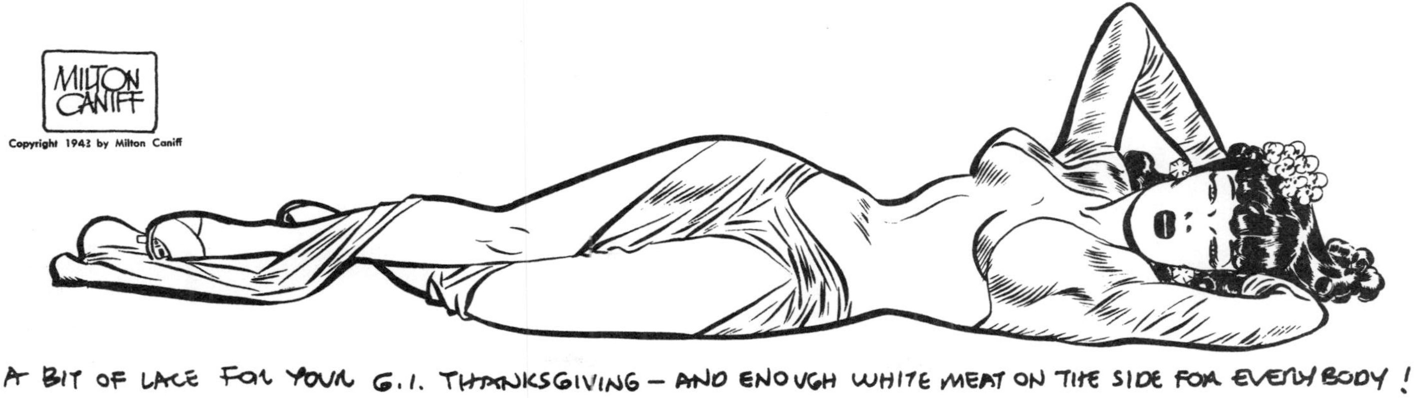

Innuendo galore, but the recumbent Lace (above) was too much; censored, she appeared everywhere as a promotional image.

"At the beginning I used to dress her according to the mode of the moment, but at the end I dressed her in a tight fitting evening dress that became practically a uniform."

The future *Chicago Sun* strip, he said, probably won't use China as a locale, but the details of the feature will remain vague, he declared, until he can start sketching, except that: the central figure will probably be a hero rather than a heroine, "because a hero uses so much elbow room while a heroine will get married and have a baby"; the strip will combine outdoors, flying, adventure and detective elements, and "it's going to be a novel about people in which the people are more important than anything else."

"I don't know what the characters will be like because it comes easier when you begin to draw. You think you've got them visually, but actually you don't till you put them on paper and change this and change that."

Meanwhile life may be less hectic for the fast-working cartoonist, now that he has only *Terry* to work on, but not everyone agrees that he has written "30" to Miss Lace.

The editor of the *Trooper* at Fort Benning, Ga., declares he's going to bring Miss Lace back from the mat files.

Milton Caniff Unveils His New Strip with Hero "Who Has Been Around"

HELEN M. STAUNTON / 1946

From *Editor & Publisher*,
November 23, 1946, n.p.

For nearly two years one of the most interesting topics among news-paper features has been, "What will Milton Caniff's new strip for the Chicago Sun Syndicate be like?"

Ever since the announcement in January, 1945, that he would leave the Chicago Tribune–New York News Syndicate and *Terry and the Pirates* when his contract ended and that he would create his own strip for CSS syndication and King Features' sale, that question has been exciting readers of *Terry*—and of his *Male Call* strip for servicemen.

That interest has created an unprecedented response from newspapers. Though the strip is not scheduled to start until Jan. 13 and though Caniff has been free to plan the new strip for only one month, 162 daily newspapers and 96 Sunday papers have already ordered *Steve Canyon.*

Another recumbent pose, this time for the bad girl in Steve Canyon, Copper Calhoon; seldom seen, this drawing was not as widely circulated as the more dignified (not to say glacial) standing figure (below).

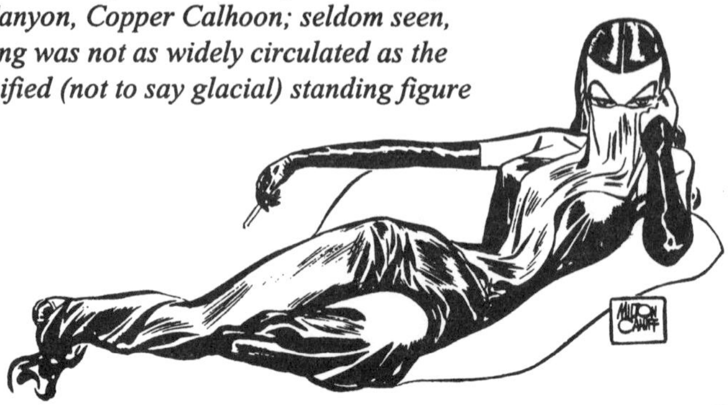

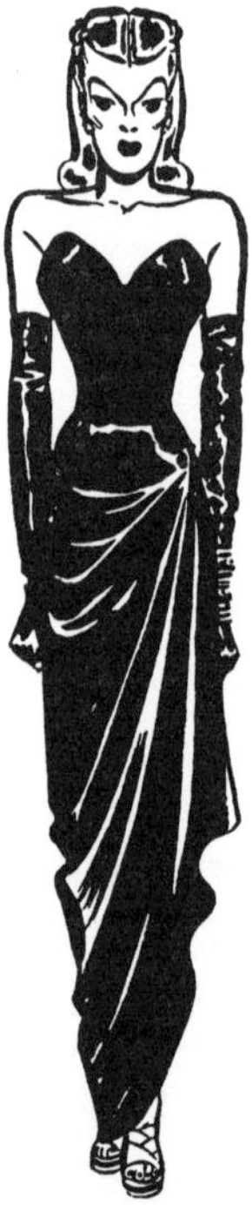

COPPER CALHOON

For these newspapers Caniff was ready at last to describe his new strip and Sunday page this week through *E & P.*

The strip will not be another *Terry,* nor a "kid strip"—Caniff's new hero, Steve Canyon, has been around a lot more than Terry. Nor will it be another *Male Call,* as it has continuity and a man as its hero.

"I had to back away from all that," explained Caniff. "Steve Canyon's been around. I couldn't have Terry smoke, or even fall in love really without showing everything that led up to it. But this guy might have been in love a dozen times."

Although Canyon's business will be an air taxi service that serves the world, the strip "actually isn't an airplane strip at all," said Caniff. "That's merely a means of getting them somewhere. I'll leave that to the boys who know planes. With me it's synthetic. I'm not a pilot. I have to go look it up. We will not scream in the promotion, 'The latest in flying . . .' "

"Essentially this is a novel . . . a picaresque novel."

"I don't want a formula, so it'll be wide open at both ends, a fast-moving he-and-she strip. It can be straight adventure or have a different kind of action, the kind you get when there's contact between two people. It doesn't have to be physical, but when there's love or hate, there are sparks!"

Face alert with enthusiasm, Caniff settled back in his chair with a glass of milk and brought his characters verbally on stage for *E&P*, with quick, vivid phrases.

He began with Copper Calhoon—"not exactly a good girl, yet within the legal limits. She's the daughter of a Wall Street wolf and just as tough as her old man, maybe a little bit tougher, being a woman. They call her Copperhead. She's hard to handle, got a lot of dough.

"Her secretary's a man—simply because no woman would stand it around her long without shooting her. He makes the contact for her with Canyon for the flying job. First four weeks will be the buildup to that job—I haven't yet decided what the job is to be, to tell the truth.

"I've made her a speculator so that I can use her as a running character in the story."

Copper will be the kind of gorgeous, highpowered, unscrupulous girl he enjoys drawing—perhaps because she keeps him guessing what she'll do next.

"It's much easier to make a gal a baddie than a goody," he grinned—"and more interesting."

Steve Canyon, explained Caniff, would be in business for himself after having been a couple of years in college and during the war in service as a captain in the Air Transport Command. His business would be Horizons Unlimited, with the Slogan "You furnish the reason—We'll furnish the ride" and the insignia a double two-headed eagle derived from American Indian symbols.

Canyon would operate the super air taxi service from a large city in the United States and be helped by other former GIs who stood ready to desert their own businesses or jobs at the ring of the telephone from Horizons Unlimited.

"He's a sort of modern Davy Crockett," Caniff added. "He knows the tower operator at every field or the chap who'll get you there. It's strictly high echelon stuff. Canyon never makes much—that would sort of defeat the purpose. He was in the Transport Command so he could have been everywhere, and he has been.

"He's a guy that will come in from a trip and forget to change his money, yens or rupees. . . . There'll be a little lunch place that will always take his money. The guy'll grumble, but he'll really save the money—I'm just mentioning some things I have in my mind. I may not use them. . . .

"He'll have lots of gals—one at every port. With a big C-54 airplane they can move around very fast. Naturally one of the problems will be to keep him single.

"He'll be always broke . . . have to sleep in the office . . . keeps his files in his pants pockets . . . keeps blankets in the filing case. . . . His secretary is always after him for the rent.

"I want to make him one of those guys that's sloppy as hell in his flying clothes, then can get dressed up in the evening and look like $700,000,000. . . . One of those long guys that'll never put on weight. . . .

"I'll never mention his age, because kids associate that age with themselves—whether they're that age or not. I want him to be liked by every group."

Through Canyon's blonde hair will run a streak of black—"You have to have a trademark."

Canyon's business will take him all over the world from his headquarters city. "What I'm trying to do," Caniff pointed out, "is to keep from being tied down to one locale. . . . If I have to name it, I'll name it New York rather than Chicago. Because they'd scream if I got the street signs wrong."

"I've been getting away with murder for years in China," Milt chuckled. "I've made my own signs."

Canyon's secretary will be another girl in his life—Feeta-Feeta he calls here. She's the one that knows all the answers. She's Samoan but has never been out of Manhattan in her life. She'll be a slick chick.

Feeta-Feeta, explained Caniff, means "guard" or "stand off."

When Caniff works on his characters, he figures out some of the characteristics he wants and what he wants to do with them, then he puts them "on stage" in his strip and develops them as he works out their appearance and action. Canyon's second-in-command is gradually shaping up: "He'll be a fixer, a brilliant guy. I haven't decided on his name yet. . . . A guy who says he ought to have been a lawyer, but who can't resist the ringing of the telephone—you know, horizons unlimited!"

Then another girl is taking shape—a girl whose career keeps them apart, "probably an actress because no career so absorbs a girl."

"It isn't a kid strip," declared the cartoonist who once made Terry's

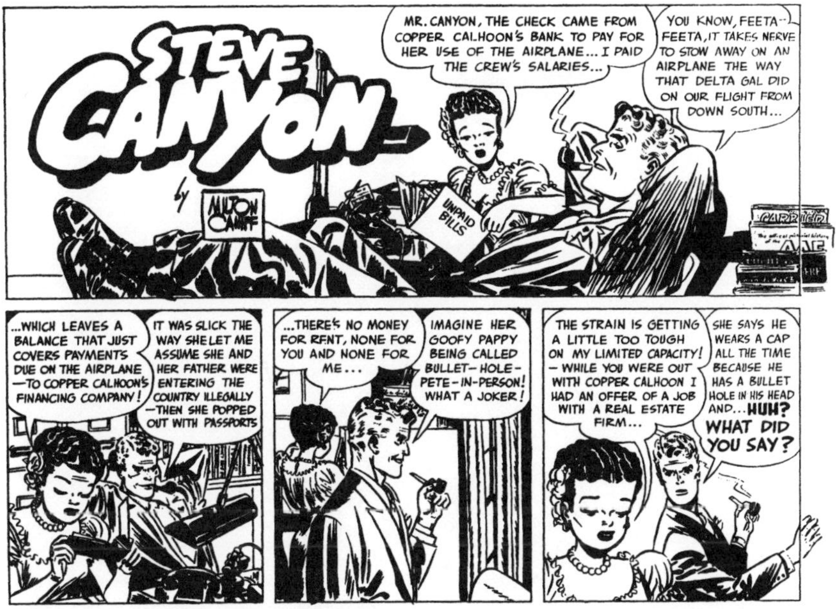

A rare depiction of Steve in his office, where he slept and lived when "home." After the first year, his office was in his pants pocket with the rest of his files.

group grow up quite fast so that the CT-NYNS strip would suit him better. "I couldn't do a kid strip—yes, I could, too! What am I saying? I used to do *Puffy the Pig* for AP. And portraits of presidential candidates with the other hand."

"My plots are complicated," he went on, "And that was Captain Patterson's idea, too. You've got to read it every day so that you'll know what happens—make it so they can't stand it. Make 'em buy the paper every day. After all that's what we're trying to do, isn't it—sell papers."

Escape Artist

1947

In the big white house on Tor Ridge, west of the Hudson, a light burned all through the winter night. Inside, in a cavernous studio, it glared down on a drawing board where a heavy-set, black-haired man put careful strokes on a paneled page. He ignored the accusing clock at his back, but sometimes paused for sips of coffee. Once he dozed off, and his pen scratched a crazy zigzag down the sheet. It was daylight when Milton Caniff took off his glasses, pushed his work away and stumbled off to bed.

Behind him, on the desk, he left his night's work: the last Sunday comic page of *Terry and the Pirates* he would ever draw. Its frames held deftly drawn figures, caught in the restrained gestures of a farewell. The fadeout was appropriately up-to-the-minute: a transport plane lifting into a sky that was streaked like the wan sunrise outside his studio.

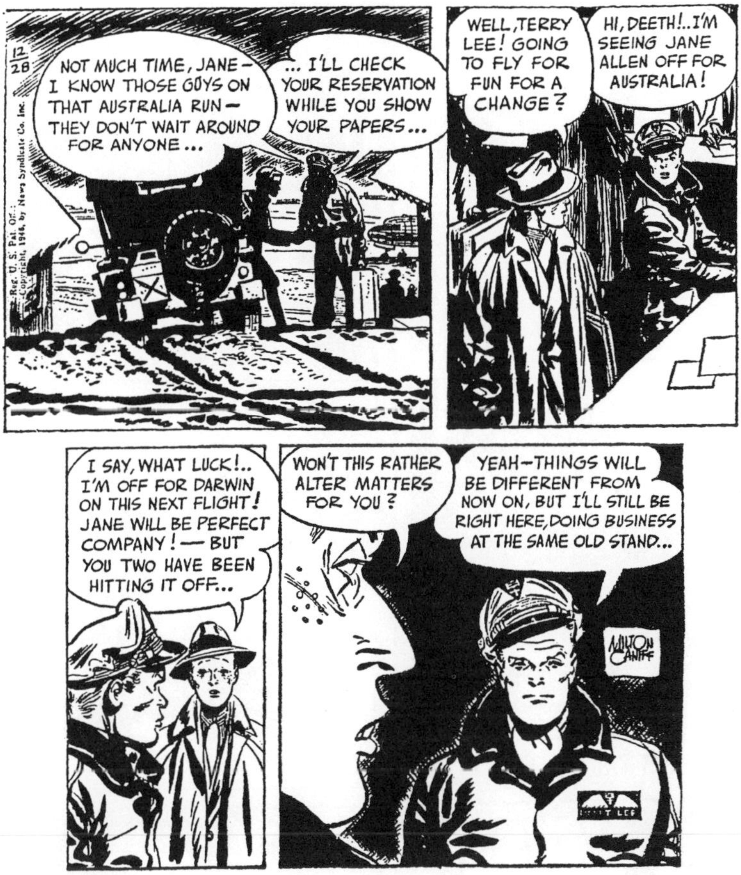

The last Terry *strip that Caniff drew (above) appeared on Saturday, December 28, 1946. The final Sunday strip, which appeared the next day (see pages 38-39), is one of the most highly regarded of Caniff's oeuvre, but, because the preparation of color plates took longer, it was drawn several weeks before the Saturday strip. Both of these pen-and-ink finales contain ironic references to Caniff's pending departure from the feature and the advent of a new cartoonist—references only the cognizanti would appreciate. But there were millions of those. Oddly, Terry in the last panel looks decidedly Canyonesque.*

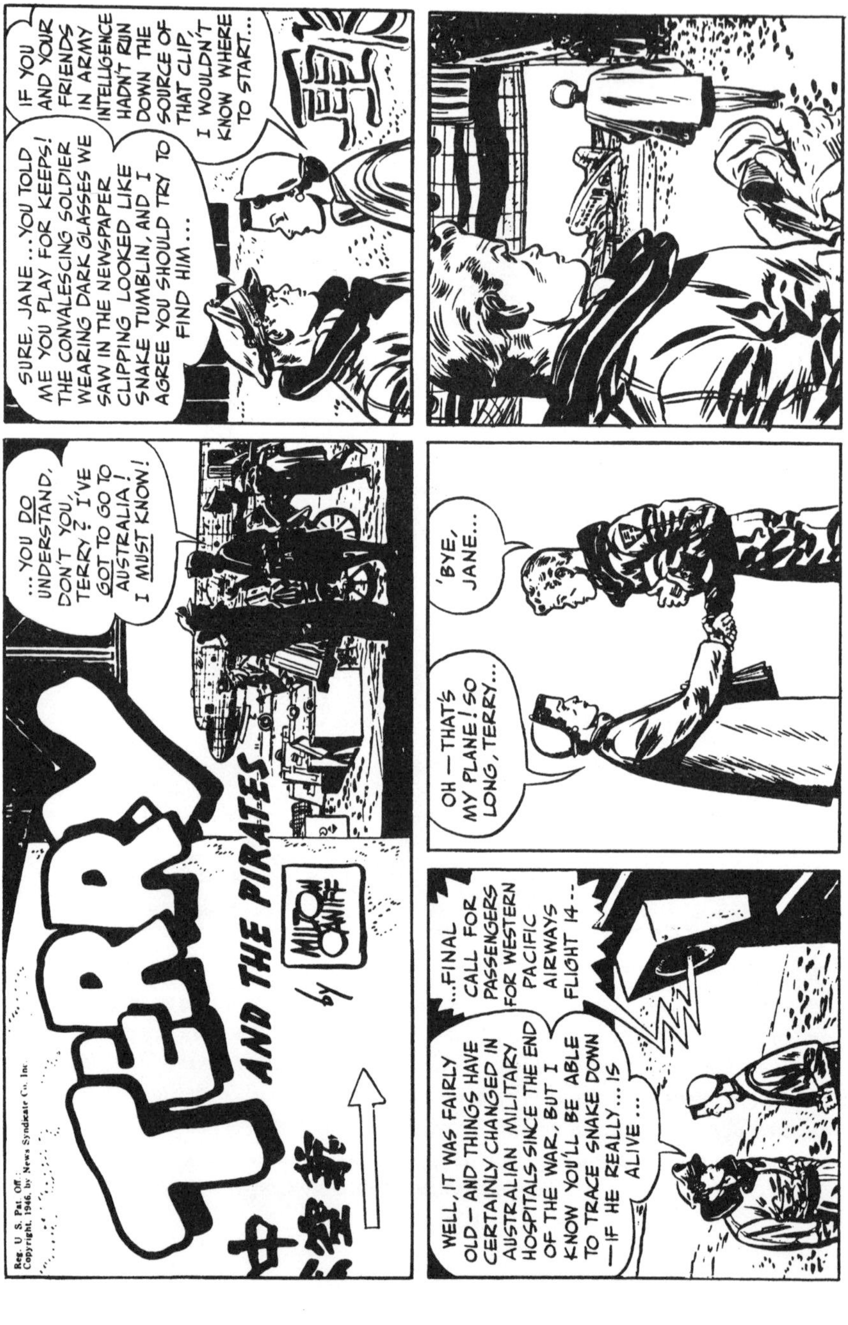
Reg. U. S. Pat. Off.
Copyright, 1946, by News Syndicate Co. Inc.
TERRY AND THE PIRATES
by MILTON CANIFF
...YOU DO UNDERSTAND, DON'T YOU, TERRY? I'VE GOT TO GO TO AUSTRALIA! I MUST KNOW!
SURE, JANE...YOU TOLD ME YOU PLAY FOR KEEPS! THE CONVALESCING SOLDIER WEARING DARK GLASSES WE SAW IN THE NEWSPAPER CLIPPING LOOKED LIKE SNAKE TUMBLIN, AND I AGREE YOU SHOULD TRY TO FIND HIM...
IF YOU AND YOUR FRIENDS IN ARMY INTELLIGENCE HADN'T RUN DOWN THE SOURCE OF THAT CLIP, I WOULDN'T KNOW WHERE TO START...
WELL, IT WAS FAIRLY OLD—AND THINGS HAVE CERTAINLY CHANGED IN AUSTRALIAN MILITARY HOSPITALS SINCE THE END OF THE WAR, BUT I KNOW YOU'LL BE ABLE TO TRACE SNAKE DOWN —IF HE REALLY...IS ALIVE...
...FINAL CALL FOR PASSENGERS FOR WESTERN PACIFIC AIRWAYS FLIGHT 14...
OH—THAT'S MY PLANE! SO LONG, TERRY...
'BYE, JANE...

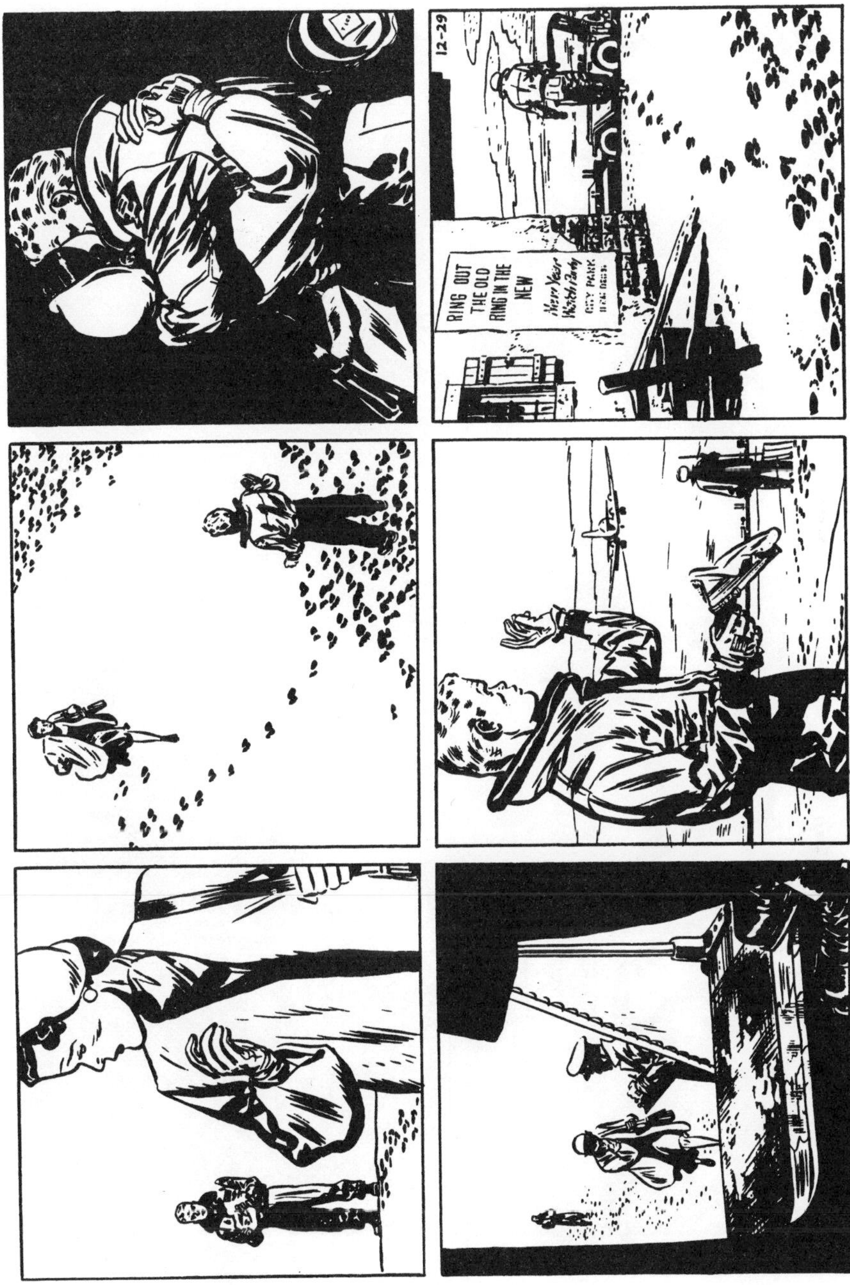

The last Sunday Terry *strip—one of the best pages he ever did, Caniff said.*

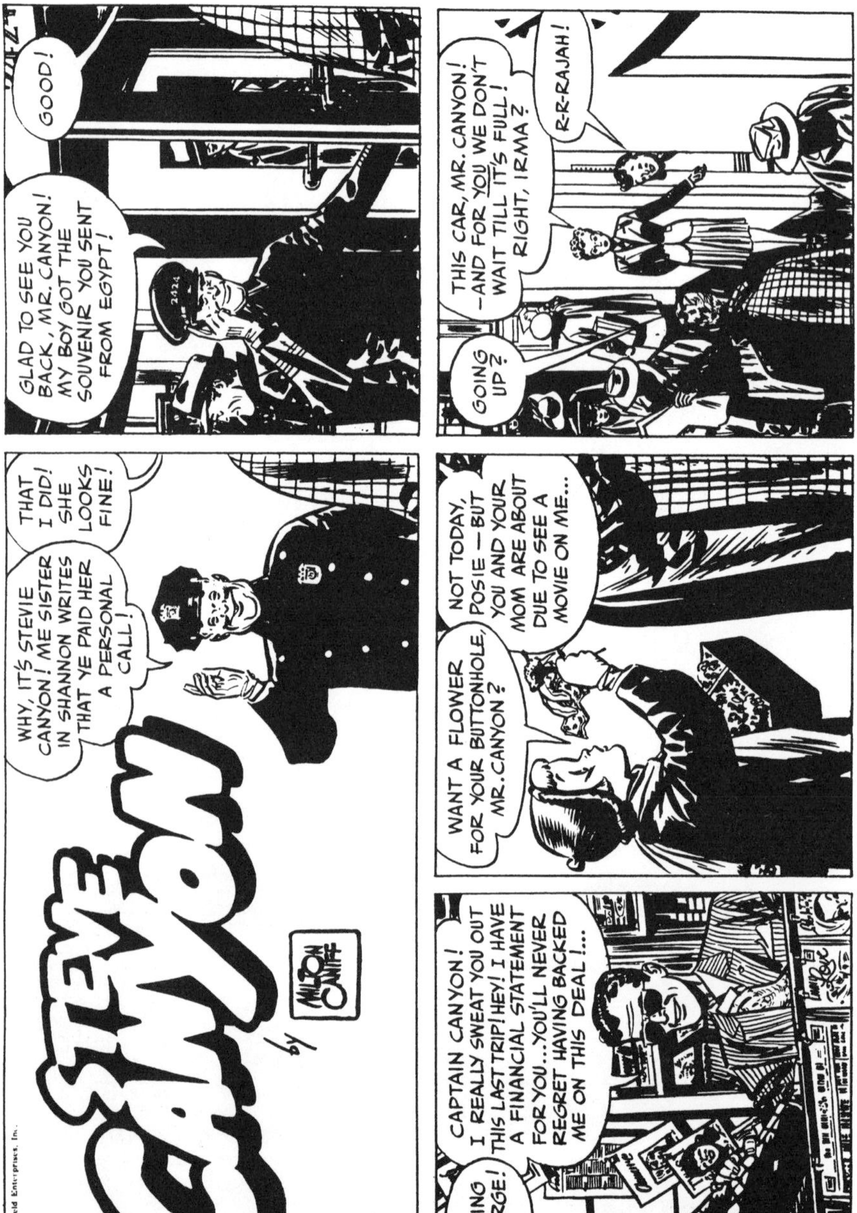
Copyright 1946 by Field Enterprises, Inc.
STEVE CANYON
by MILTON CANIFF
WHY, IT'S STEVIE CANYON! ME SISTER IN SHANNON WRITES THAT YE PAID HER A PERSONAL CALL!
THAT I DID! SHE LOOKS FINE!
GLAD TO SEE YOU BACK, MR. CANYON! MY BOY GOT THE SOUVENIR YOU SENT FROM EGYPT!
GOOD!
CHECKING IN, SARGE!
CAPTAIN CANYON! I REALLY SWEAT YOU OUT THIS LAST TRIP! HEY! I HAVE A FINANCIAL STATEMENT FOR YOU...YOU'LL NEVER REGRET HAVING BACKED ME ON THIS DEAL!...
WANT A FLOWER FOR YOUR BUTTONHOLE, MR. CANYON?
NOT TODAY, POSIE—BUT YOU AND YOUR MOM ARE ABOUT DUE TO SEE A MOVIE ON ME...
GOING UP?
THIS CAR, MR. CANYON! —AND FOR YOU WE DON'T WAIT TILL IT'S FULL! RIGHT, IRMA?
R-R-RAJAH!

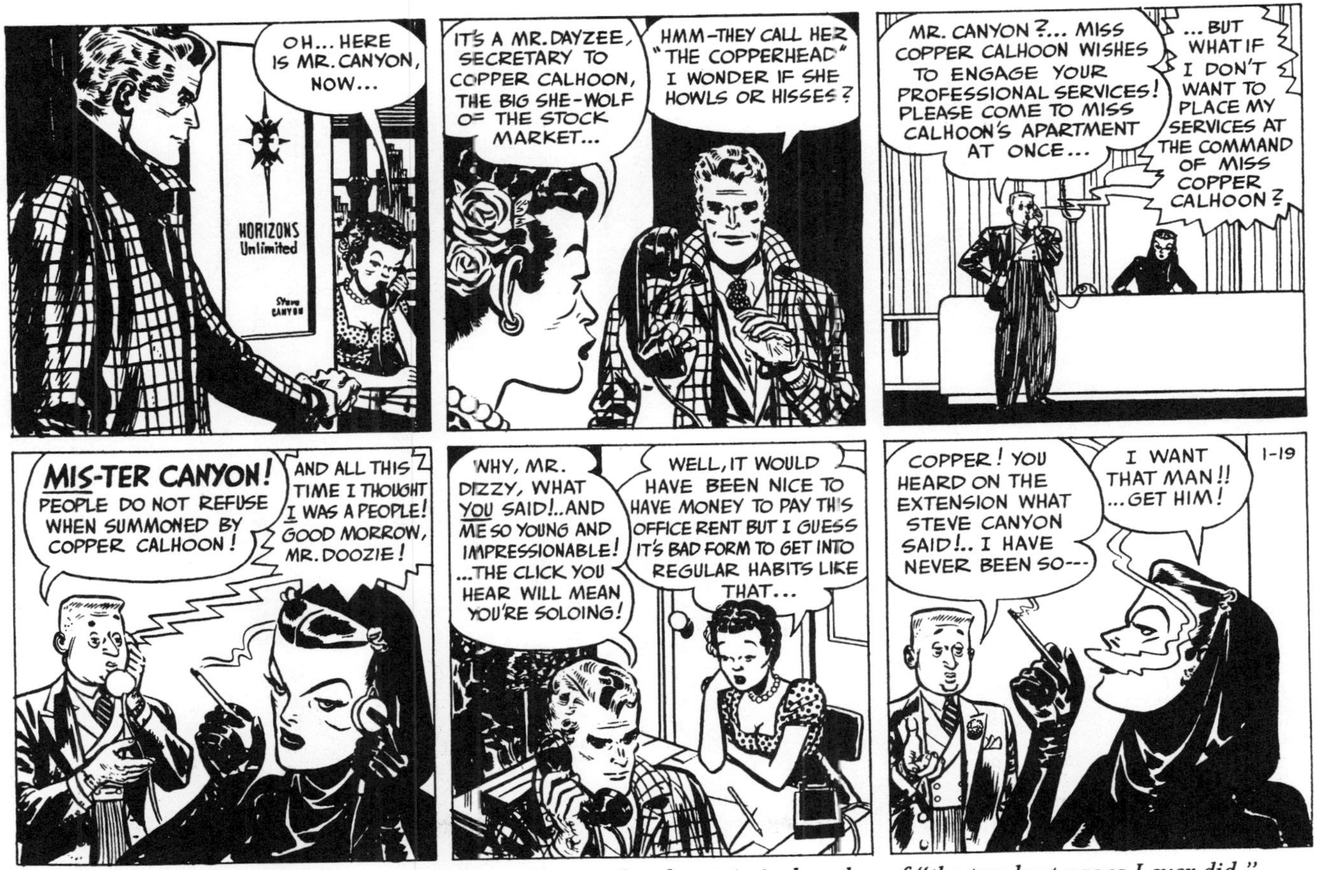

Brimming with teasing suspense, the first Steve Canyon *Sunday strip is the other of "the two best pages I ever did."*

Whether Terry Lee and Jane Allen would ever meet again, their creator did not know. He had surrendered his godlike right over them and their actions, which he had guided for eleven years past. Next week, in 220 newspapers including papers as far away as the *Times* of Seoul, Korea, Milton Caniff's byline will appear on a new comic strip, to be known as *Steve Canyon.*

In the never-never world of the funnies, this was the news of the year—comparable to Henry Ford quitting his motor company and setting up shop in competition across the street. It was a move involving three of the biggest U.S. press lords: the Chicago *Tribune's* Colonel Robert Rutherford McCormick (who lost Caniff), and Marshall Field and William Randolph Hearst, who gained him. For Caniff himself, it meant a guarantee of $520,000 for his next five years' work, and a stiff challenge—to outdo the best of his past.

There may be professors of journalism who have never heard of Milton Caniff's *Terry and the Pirates,* but every U.S. newspaper publisher has. Many a publisher spends more effort shaping up his comic page than he does in seeing that Palestine or North China is properly covered. Highbrows had once dismissed the comics as the poor man's literature; now to read at least one of them (usually *Terry*) was proof of being a regular fellow. (After all, hadn't Dickens begun *Pickwick Papers* as a text for a cartoon series?) Only the New York *Times,* among major U.S. dailies, refuses to run comics.

Innocents & a Broad. Cartoonist Caniff's contribution to the industry was to throw in some curves and give it glamor. Long before he came along the "comics" had generally ceased to be funny. They had learned a thing or two about narrative from Sidney Smith's chinless *Gumps* and Frank King's morality play about the Wallets of *Gasoline Alley.* But mostly their idea of action was to have a character jump out of his shoes. Into *Terry* and the wartime *Male Call* (for the G.I. press) Caniff poured fast-breaking dialogue, credible adventure—and one touch of Venus. He knocked himself out to make his brain children (he has no others) seem real. His Dragon Lady, Burma and Miss Lace were fashioned after lush, living models. (*Steve Canyon's* mean and sexy villainess, Copper Calhoon, was drawn from a model, Carol Ohmart, "Miss Utah of 1946.")

Undergrads, Upper Classes. In the readership polls Caniff seldom beats out Ham Fisher's hammy *Joe Palooka* or Chic Young's just-folksy *Blondie.* But his comparatively small (31 million) audience is, comparatively speaking, a class audience. It includes collegians (from Harvard to Siwash) and their professors, the Duke of Windsor, Margaret Truman, John Steinbeck—and, significantly, hundreds of newspaper executives. Two years ago, when a score of syndicate salesmen began to spread the word of a new, as yet unnamed and undrawn comic by Caniff, they had nothing to sell but Caniff's name. For U.S. publishers, that was enough.

Dig, Dig, Dig. In the last months of his '30s, Milton Arthur Caniff is a handsomely hefty (195 lbs.), blue-eyed, relaxed man with an indoor look and a sociable nature. He is almost never seen in the Stork Club or at El Morocco, although many a G.I. or plain reader might naturally assume that *Terry's* generally sophisticated dialogue was clutched from some such glamor-scented air.

Actually, it comes out of Caniff's head. Among cartoonists—fellow members of what he calls "the pariah profession"—he is well liked, but seldom seen. He lives and works (12 to 18 hours a day) on the outer suburban ring of New York City, in a town with the confusing name of New City, N.Y. (pop. 992). Neighbors in the New City intellectual colony include Playwright Maxwell Anderson, Artist Henry Varnum Poor and Author J. P. McEvoy.

A year ago, clearing his decks for the big change from *Terry* to *Steve Canyon,* Caniff swore off smoking and drinking. Though he hates to exercise, he even went for walks on brooding Tor Ridge (the locale of Anderson's 1936 play *High Tor*), to keep his weight down. Says he: "All I could think of was 'God, I wish I were inside!' " So he reminded himself that the ridge was full of copperhead snakes anyway, and gave it up.

No Idle Hands. A man who hates to know the time of day (it is always later than he thinks), Caniff gets to his studio late in the forenoon, spends his daylight hours writing with his right hand, drawing and drinking coffee with his left. "It's hell being your own master," he says. "You work a 40-hour day instead of a 40-hour week." His pretty blonde wife, Esther—he calls her Bunny—brings the coffee, gets the meals and keeps guests from gumming up the production line. Slim, slack-clad Bunny Caniff doesn't have much to say when her talkative husband has visitors. Says she: "I'm afraid people will miss something Milt is saying."

The production line cannot stop, but Caniff, a dreadful procrastinator, does his best to slow it to a calm, unhurried pace. He seizes on any excuse—like the postman's arrival with fan mail—to break off work. To his [lettering] assistant, Frank Engli, he is a casual boss who slings the slang along with the strips they hand back & forth for inking, lettering and checking.

To keep his story as fresh as the news on Page One, Caniff shamelessly picks the brains of his pals, and even copies their faces. Colonel Phil Cochran, an old college chum, gave him a correspondence course in flying—and won more fame as Colonel Flip Corkin than for leading the glider invasion of Burma under his own name. Caniff had been to Britain, Europe and Africa, but never to the Orient, where all the action in *Terry* took place.

Keep 'Em Guessing. Caniff's house on Tor Ridge, a spectacular modern affair designed and owned by Neighbor Henry Varnum Poor, was a port of call for scores of flyers during the war. The tabletalk kept Caniff abreast of servicemen's slang; the grateful flyers paid their bread-&-butter calls by buzzing the house. As a favor, the Army flew him across the U.S. in a jolting B-24, to give him the feel of it. He can "still hear the nyaaa-aaaa-aaaa of those motors—and feel the cold, going on hour after hour. Jeez, it was cold!"

To keep his audience on the edge of their chairs, Caniff, a frustrated actor, has borrowed many a trick of stagecraft. He is a staunch Alfred Hitchcock fan, fond of the director's way of opening a suspenseful sequence with a silent sound track. He has aped the best Hollywood techniques (and some of the worst) by switches from closeups to long shots to trick camera angles—and fadeouts with profiles turned to a corn-tinted sunset.

By building up to a lovemaking crisis and not letting it come off—as Hitchcock did in *Notorious*—Caniff has become the best tantalizer in the profession. It is the same heartless treatment that keeps housewives suffering daily with radio's *Young Widder Brown,* and it has the same crass commercial purpose. "It forces 'em to buy the paper," says Caniff, "to find out what the hell is going on."

At night, alone in his studio or his bedroom, he wrestles with dialogue, penciling it into the blank strips he will sketch next day, and erasing it over & over until it rings true. Somehow he finds time to contrive bright new baubles of incident to hang on his thin thread of plot.

Ink & Grease Paint. Like millions of boys who wanted to be cartoonists when they grew up, Milt Caniff never missed a day of *Mutt & Jeff* or *Polly and Her Pals.* But the Chicago *Tribune's* prize old political cross-hatcher, John T. McCutcheon, was his ideal. Milt's father took him west in 1916 and nine-year-old Milton worked for a short time as a child extra in two-reel movies. At twelve he created (for family circulation) his first cartoon, something known as *Si Plug.*

At Ohio State he saw Harold Lloyd in *The Freshman,* bought a yellow slicker and an open Ford, and was pledged by Sigma Chi, which never got over it. The fraternity has since elected him—like Cartoonist McCutcheon before him—to its select group of "Significant Sigs" (others: Booth Tarkington, Roy Chapman Andrews and George Ade).

While still an insignificant Sig, Caniff imitated John Held Jr., tried editorial cartoons for the Columbus *Dispatch.* He was jobless in 1932 when the Associated Press Feature Service beckoned him on to New York.

. . . .

A Lady Pirate. One day in 1934 brown-haired Mollie Slott, mother-hen of the Chicago Tribune-New York Daily News Syndicate, marched in to the late Captain Joseph M. Patterson, the P. T. Barnum of the U.S. comic strip. "There's a young chap in my office," she told him, "with a letter from John McCutcheon." Patterson groaned: "What, another fraternity brother?" Said Mollie: "But this is the one who does *Dickie Dare.*" Her sons had sold her on *Dickie,* and she had given the boss a batch of the strips to look at.

Patterson stalked out to her office, stared coldly at Caniff and asked: "Ever do anything on the Orient?" Caniff hadn't. "You know," Joe Patterson mused, "adventure can still happen out there. There could be a beautiful lady pirate, the kind men fall for. . . ." In a few days Caniff was back with samples and 50 proposed titles; Patterson circled "Terry" and scribbled beside it "and the Pirates."

Better than any other press lord, the moody genius of the *Daily News* knew how to make the modern mass-circulation daily an attractive grab-bag, with prizes to please either sex and every taste.

. . . .

Most of the strips that helped his lusty tabloid grow were named by him *(Dick Tracy, Orphan Annie, Moon Mullins, etc.),* often after a thoughtful thumbing of the telephone book. All the artists felt his sensitive, shrewd touch. From Caniff he wanted adventure, suspense, and pretty women.

Keep It Crisp. "I didn't know how to draw women at first," Caniff, admittedly no anatomist, recalls. "Women are always harder to draw than men. And there's the nudity problem . . . you just have to know how much is in good taste. Once in a while, if I hadn't had a good-looking babe in the strip for a while, Patterson would send me a note saying how about bringing in the Dragon Lady or some other chick. And he used to hate it when the balloons were too long. . . . I didn't agree with many of the things he did in his last years. He seemed to feel that in wartime there's a place for a newspaper that is the voice of the disgruntled—and he became that voice. But he was a great guy."

One of the few times Caniff ever preached to his readers was when he had Terry Lee win his wings in China. Terry and the readers got a long, stern graduation speech from his commander Flip Corkin on courage, skill and honor among air-men. That Sunday page was read into the *Congressional Record.* An aide showed it to Patterson, who growled: "Who does Caniff think he is, Robert Emmet Sherwood?" ("He had to go and name a playwright I admire," says Caniff.) Once Caniff, excited by the morale value of his strip, suggested that the *Daily News* be sent free to remote post exchanges. He got a curt no from Captain Patterson.

Caniff seldom heard more than querulous peeps out of Colonel Bertie McCormick's Chicago end of the *Tribune-Daily News* axis. Sample: early in 1941 he was informed that Colonel McCormick "objects to Defense Bond stamps being used in the comics, so will you please refrain from using them." And once McCormick and Patterson, reading *Terry* together, came to a sequence where the lissome Burma was carrying on with a German named Kiel. "Why," said the Colonel, turning to his cousin in alarm: "Burma is *living* with that man!"

"I'm sure," says Caniff, "that Patterson had known it for a long time."

Chained Seal. At 37, Milton Caniff was a widely imitated, $70,000-a-year success. His *Terry* strip was on the radio; a Douglas Fairbanks Jr. movie was in the works. Why give it all up? For a reason of his own, Caniff wanted more. In Florida, when he was 18, he was bitten by a mosquito and got phlebitis, an inflammation of the veins that made the Army—and insurance doctors—turn him down. Because of his quick-clotting blood, says Caniff, "even a bad bump on the leg could bump me off."

It made him more aware than most men of the nearness of death. He owned not a hair on *Terry's* head, and if he died his wife would get not a cent of *Terry's* future income. Like nearly every trained seal in his line, he was held prisoner by the "shop rights" system. Its major premise: comic strips are owned, not by their creators, but by the syndicates that sell them.

In the fall of 1944 Millionaire Marshall Field, whose young Chicago *Sun* had not succeeded in rising above the commercial horizon, decided to grab the best talent his money could buy—preferably by taking it away from his rival, Colonel McCormick. Field invited Caniff to his apartment at 740 Park Avenue, blandly asked him: "What do you want?" Caniff hardly needed to answer: ownership of copyright. "I'm out to emancipate you," smiled Field. Then he added comfortably: "I imagine you're a well-paid slave."

Caniff was the first cartoonist who ever left Joe Patterson, though not the first to abandon his brain children. Patterson and Caniff never spoke or met, after Caniff joined Field. (In Patterson's *Daily News,* and in most of the other 310 papers that print *Terry,* the strip was being drawn last week by George Wunder. Wunder, like Caniff—whom he has never met—is a left-handed graduate of the A.P. Judging by his first week, his drawing was a reasonable facsimile of Caniff's, but his dialogue was a long way below it.)

Caniff's new five-year contract with Marshall Field calls for a $2,000-a-week minimum. The Field organization was not equipped to sell the new strip nationally, so left-winger Field, who shudders at William Randolph Hearst on his editorial page, made a deal with the old lord of San Simeon. For selling *Steve Canyon,* Hearst's King Features Syndicate got first rights to run the new strip in all Hearst papers outside Chicago (including the tabloid *Mirror* in New York, instead of Field's small *PM*).

Retooling for Steve. In the airy, booklined studio at New City, Milton Caniff cleared away the oriental props that had served *Terry.* The morgue was crammed with Americana, for a change of scene: state guides, the *Rivers* series, hundreds of photographs of city streets and airports. Marshall Field, no comics expert, had no advice to give, but Caniff knew what the publishers and readers wanted: a strip with all the thrills of *Terry* and nearly all the sexiness of Lace rolled into one.

His new hero, Steve Canyon, would be a lean and squinty, older version of Terry; a fellow with an easy, insolent, Gary Cooperish grace that marked a breed of plainsmen, and airplanesmen. Canyon knew the world and its airlanes—and its women—as his granddaddy would have known the way stations on the Overland Trail. So he went into business

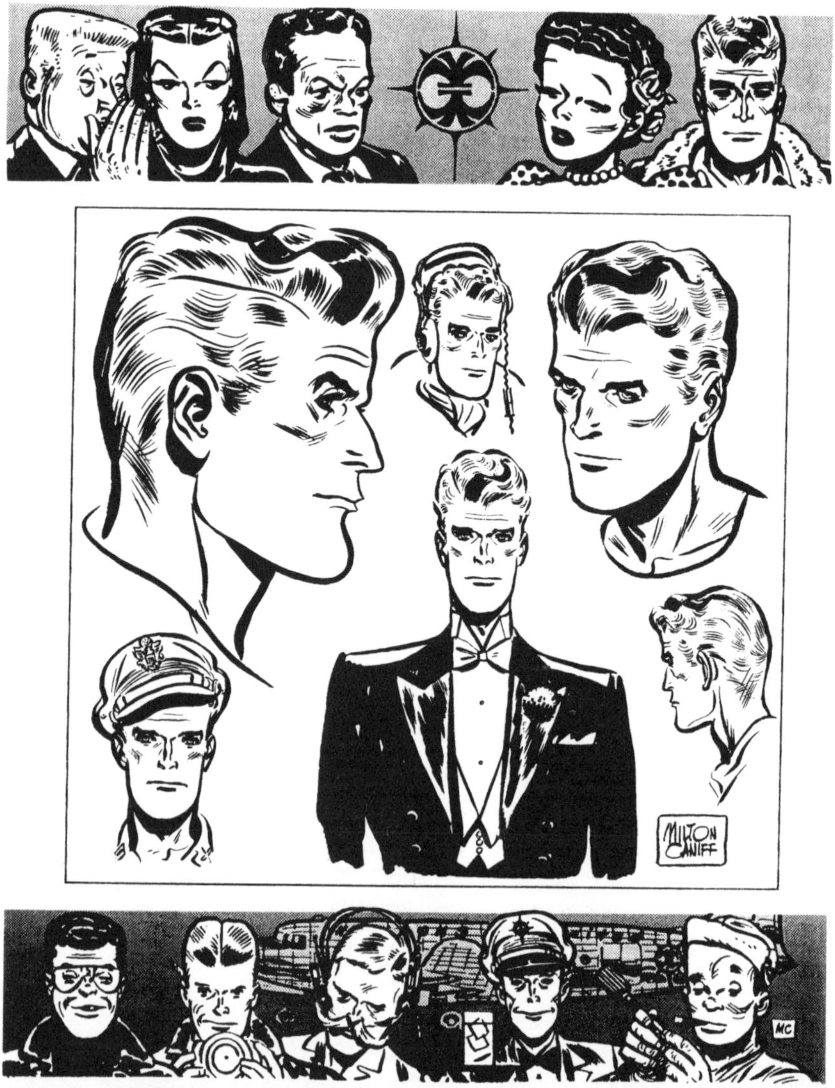

An early model sheet for Steve Canyon, these mug shots display the distinctive (and trade-markable) dark streak in his hair. The top frieze depicts Mr. Dayzee, Copper Calhoon, and Kroon (her body guard) from the first sequence in the strip, then the Navajo double-eagle logo for Horizons Unlimited, Feeta-Feeta, and Steve; at the bottom are Steve's flight crew members, each of whom, according to Caniff's initial thinking, would spin-off into separate stories in repertory theater fashion, a plan abandoned once Steve gave up the airline for freelance trouble-shooting.

on a shoestring as Horizons, Unlimited, and took for his trademark an old Navajo double-eagle design. His first customer would be a tough one: a wolverine of Wall Street, slinky Copper Calhoon.

Caniff plotted his new characters as carefully as any fiction writer. "The guy, now, had to have a name that would stick," Caniff explained. "It had to be three syllables, Dead-eye-Dick, or John-Paul-Jones. . . . *Steve-Can-yon.* Not a real name, or one you could turn into a dirty word. But a guy who'd have a girl in every port, and could do all the things that a youngster like Terry couldn't. Why, Terry couldn't even smoke. And with people in the Orient we couldn't use those casual, normal insults that pass between Americans."

Beginning his new strip, Caniff was confident and cool: "It's almost a mathematical equation," he said. "If I don't know my trade by now, I'd better quit."

Close-up of the Artist: Milton Caniff

MARY ANNE GUITAR / 1960

Excerpts from *Famous Artists Magazine*, 8:3, 1960, n.p.

Editor's Note: Famous around the world as the creator of Terry and the Pirates *and today's front-running* Steve Canyon, *Milton Caniff is disarmingly modest. "I have always told myself to write for the man on the bus or the woman having her second cup of coffee," he says. Even though his work has hung in the Metropolitan Museum and he is a favorite of such celebrities as Clare Boothe Luce and John Steinbeck, Milton Caniff remains unaffected. He has never lost contact with his audience and this is why he has been so successful. We visited him recently in his studio overlooking the Hudson River some thirty miles from New York to ask him questions about his craft and his philosophy as an artist. With his customary generosity Milton Caniff told us everything he thought you should know.*

Q: How early in life did you begin cartooning?
A: I was in kindergarten when I began to be aware of what I was doing. But nobody but my mother could have told they were cartoons.

Q: I'm curious to know if you ever took a course in cartooning or if you were completely self-taught?
A: When I was in the eighth grade I took a correspondence course in cartooning. It was the best one of its kind in its day. Many of the up-and-coming men in the field took that course. It was the Landon Cartoon Course, which no longer exists.

Q: How do you think this kind of training helped you?
A: First of all, it taught me that you are supposed to draw so you can be reproduced. To be specific, I learned to work with black ink instead of blue. The "blue inker," as we call him, may be great, but he hasn't heard about the professional way of working and so he is handicapped.

Q: The thing that interests me is that you started your career so early. You were working as an office boy at the local paper all the time you were in high school, as well as drawing for publication. How did you manage it all?
A: It was wonderful for me and I loved it. As an office boy in the art department of the Dayton *Journal* I learned the mechanics of my trade. By the time I was out of high school I knew my business. It was a combination of being a working stiff and the cartoon course that did it.

Q: Should the student of cartooning work at a job while he is studying?
A: Yes. It is important. If he can make a connection within the field, on a newspaper or in an engraving plant, this is ideal. But a cartooning job anywhere has its advantages.

Q: How else can a cartoonist "break into print?"
A: He can offer to do signs and posters for worthy causes. He can give his pictures away. I think every beginner should do this. The work isn't worth much at first anyway, so you may have to give it away. Later on, when you are known, you can begin to charge. The important thing is to reach the public eye.

Q: Did you have any art training in school?
A: I had a wonderful high school art teacher. I still go to her with my hat in my hand. She had a sense of the fitness of things. I knew from

the beginning that I was a commercial kind of guy. I didn't want to be an easel artist. She told me to go to college because, she said, there are so many outlets for the cartoonist in college. You can work on the yearbook, the humor magazine and design programs for football games and dances. I did all of these things. In high school the same thing can be achieved. And the experience is invaluable. I did a strip in high school for our student paper. It was called *Chic and Noodles.* I named it after the cafeteria fare and built it around high school life. Students often ask me where they can get ideas for a strip. If they would just look around them they would find hundreds of ideas.

Q: Did you get paid for any of this work?
A: The college activities paid very well. In fact I made enough one year to go to Europe that summer. That was in 1928. Then came the Depression.

Q: Did you take any college courses which were directly useful to you as a cartoonist?
A: I majored in fine arts and everything I learned turned out to be valuable. But the hard-nose practical stuff I was getting every day after class. I had a job on the Columbus *Dispatch* and there I learned more about mechanical reproduction and the tools of the trade. You have to know the practical side of the business. This is true in any field of art.

Q: You were always bent upon being a cartoonist? Didn't you ever consider any other form of art?
A: Oh, people would say to me, why don't you become a painter. I just didn't want to. I was never naturally skilled. I had to learn how to be a cartoonist. For example, I couldn't draw girls. I simply had to sit down and learn to draw them because I knew I would never get anywhere until I did. It is extremely important to find out what your market is and learn how to do what you must do in order to reach it. Every day when I was downtown working I heard the pros talking about what they really wanted to do and how some of them had missed the boat. I wanted to learn to do what would sell and I've never been unhappy that I chose cartooning.

Q: Do you work from photographs and models?
A: Oh yes. I have to, because I want it to be accurate. But I can't afford to have models around all the time, so I shoot them for an hour on location and then work from photographs.

. . . .

Q: There is so much suspense in a strip, so much cliff-hanger business, that I was wondering if you read mystery stories?
A: Yes indeed. The technique is just like cartooning. But we never make a mystery about who-dun-it. We tell you, *Dick Tracy* always shows you the villain along with the hero. You know how it's going to come out. But the way it's going to be done is what holds your interest.

Q: I suppose your early interest in the theater also contributed to the sense of drama which is so apparent in *Steve Canyon* . You have to build to a second act curtain in every episode. Isn't that hard to do when you know how the story is going to come out?
A: You take a single, tiny segment and you dangle baubles of suspense before the reader. Not that you give him false leads, but you introduce secondary characters and all sorts of side situations. The movies have done this for years. There will be a bearded prospector who is supposed to carry some great secret with him. He never tells the secret or even has one, but he serves to divert the audience and capture their interest. Sometimes the secondary characters take over. *Popeye* is a good example. He was only a minor character in the beginning, but he got to be far more interesting than anybody else, so he finally inherited the strip.

Q: Where do you get ideas for your stories?
A: For me the idea well is the front page of the newspaper. It's always a boy-meets-girl story against a gigantic news story. I try to be very realistic. In the old days we used to avoid this kind of thing.

Q: Why? Because you might tread on toes, political or otherwise, and become too controversial?
A: I suppose so. But I think you have much more fun if you are dealing with real people. I always felt that *Lost Horizon* was enormously political and that didn't bother anybody. And *The Thirty-nine Steps.* There the author didn't come right out and tell you who the villain was. But you felt the big, burly presence of the Nazis in the background. I avoided calling the Japanese by name until after Pearl Harbor. They were simply called the "invaders," but they wore Japanese uniforms and insignia. I don't always use the Communists as villains today.

Q: How do you keep up to date, or even far ahead of the news, when you have to have your strip finished nine weeks in advance?
A: I have to guess what's going to happen. The great danger is that you may guess wrong. I guessed wrong on Pearl Harbor but so did a lot

of others. I was never chided for this. The closest I ever got to the news was when the Air Force Academy opened. I knew the date and I wrote asking for the Orders of the Day. I had everybody wearing the right uniform and marching the right way as a result. One thing I didn't know was the weather. Turned out I was right.

Q: What kind of a day was it?
A: A lovely September day. The Denver *Post* gave me a big story because I had hit it right.

Q: Typical Caniff luck and, I would say, attention to detail. I know how thoroughly you research the details of your strip. Looking around the studio, I would guess that you have a small library here on military operations. Is research as important to a cartoonist as it is to an illustrator?
A: It is to me. Not to [Al] Capp or *Blondie*. I've got to be authentic. I had Canyon landing in London recently and I had the British flag upside down. An Englishman wrote right away to tell me about it. When it flies that way it means London is in distress. There's no compromise with reality. You either do it right or you become the laughing-stock of those who know. I always do my own research because that's the only way I can get the feel of it. I went through the course at the Space Medicine Center recently and took some of the tests myself. I've got it now. It's all in my head.

Q: What about these files of research clips? Do you really use them?
A: They are invaluable and any young cartoonist should start building his own file. Students will say to me, what's the point of clipping pictures of the new cars from the paper. Well, you have to start somewhere. I keep photographs, but not drawings, because the artist who made the drawing might have made a mistake and I will just repeat it.

Q: You have been accused of having "inside information" on military feats because you have anticipated the news so many times. Do you?
A: No. I've just been lucky and guessed right. Once I had something in the strip about an earth-hardening device. You dropped it from the air and it turned a swamp into a landing strip. When that came out I got a call from MIT and one from Ohio State asking me what I knew about such a device. It turned out that they were all working on it. They asked me to speak at MIT and tell them what I knew.

Q: And did you?
A: I did not. I said I didn't know anything. It was just a wild idea.

Q: Do you model your characters after real people?
A: That I do. I have a curious problem now. I'm bringing back a character patterned after President Kennedy. He was named Pipper the Piper and was a Navy lieutenant when I first drew him. I don't know how to handle him yet.

Q: How important is drawing to the success of a cartoon strip?
A: Obviously it is very important, but writing is the key more than drawing. There are syndicates which insist the artist be backed up by a writer.

Q: You mean they want writer-artist teams?
A: Yes. But I think this waters it out. If the strip doesn't work, the artist blames the writer and vice versa. One man should stand up and take it, whether it's success or failure. Of course there are teams which work very well. But I don't like to work this way. In the end you cut a deeper furrow if you can both write and draw. All the old-time successes did both.

Q: The writing seems so simple. Isn't it really just a story line, not fancy writing full of literary devices?
A: On the face of it, it looks simple. But it is the absolute distillation of what you want to say. And that is not easy. Only a writer like Al Capp could have created the wonderful world of Dogpatch.

Q: What qualities make a good main character in a cartoon adventure strip?
A: I have to speak for myself, of course, but you want your heroine to be virtuous and your hero to be heroic. The handsome hero never changes. In the beginning, when you are a boy, your hero image is your father. He is the strong, square-jawed figure. If you are a girl, the hero is the boy you were out with. In your mind, of course, this is a private sort of business. I am happy to have my reader alone for the few minutes each day when we rendezvous.

Q: Do you ever worry that the cliché of the handsome hero will change?
A: I try to keep up with public taste. But I am a romantic by nature and the essence of the hero never changes for me.

Q: What is that essence? I suppose the hero must be strong and good and on the side of the right?
A: Yes. But he must also know all the villain's tricks so he can outwit him. When I thought up Steve Canyon I wanted a hero who could smoke and drink. Terry couldn't do this. I can't have Steve fight when he is in uniform but I fix it so he is out of uniform once in a while. Then he can engage in physical combat. Sometimes I decide he hasn't been hurt in a long time so I have something happen to him.

Q: How do you know when it's time to make these changes?
A: You tune yourself to these things. You have to. I want people thinking of Steve Canyon ten years from now.

Q: Your hero, then, is someone people can admire, but he has human frailties as well?
A: Yes. I don't believe in making him a perfect person, a champion. Robin Hood wasn't very good at anything except the long bow. Canyon can fly an airplane, but he's not the world's champion.

Q: Do you think that people resent absolute perfection?
A: A little. My guy is never in the center of the vortex. He's always around the edges. If he were the champion of the world I'd have written the end of the story.

Q: How do you guard against limiting story possibilities in your choice of locale or the occupation of your main character?
A: The airplane just about solves this problem for me. He lands the airplane anywhere in the world, and a jeep drives up and a beautiful girl steps out.

Q: How far ahead do you plan your story line?
A: I have two or three stories that are sort of fluttering around on the outside edges of my head. Canyon will visit a college this fall and that will give me a whole new set of circumstances to work with.

Q: You think in terms of the seasons, then, when you are plotting?
A: Yes. And locale to some degree. I have made up a college which doesn't really exist, much the way Sinclair Lewis made up his city of Zenith. You stay away from libel this way.

Q: Which comes first, the story line or the characters?
A: You start always with your main characters and think of things for them to do which would be natural to them. Of course you also invent secondary characters to advance the plot.

Q: When you choose an assistant, what do you expect of him and what kind of samples do you want to see?
A: Obviously he has to be able to draw in the same general style that I use. I couldn't have a guy who would be just right for Al Capp or *Dick Tracy.* I have to have an illustrator who can draw my stuff right off the bat. He must show me samples which indicate that he is capable of taking my job away from me or creating a strip of his own. Of course he's not going to take my job away from me because I'm not going to let him. But he has to be a guy with ambition. My assistant, Richard Rockwell, was a flyer and then he worked on comic books. He wanted to find something to do so he could live out here in the country. He has a house down the road from me and that makes it convenient and also allows him to run his own operation. He wants his own strip but he hasn't hit upon anything yet that he cares to work up. I start the strip and finish it and he does the middle. Almost everybody who is anybody once worked for somebody else. I used to work for *Dumb Dora.* It's the best way to learn your craft.

Q: You do see it as a unit, then, before you start working? You don't let the plot develop spontaneously out of the material?
A: The middle part can be developed as you go along, but you have to know the beginning and the end. The danger is really quite great if you get them up this endless trail and can't get them out. You don't always have to satisfy the reader with the ending. There are certain advantages to not satisfying him. Particularly when it comes to killing off the villain. A good villain is hard to find. It's much better to let him escape and live to fight another day.

Q: Are you ever going to let Steve Canyon get married?
A: I don't know the answer to that. Offhand, I would say not. The danger is that if he is married he can never blink at another girl.

Q: Do you need a pretty girl in an adventure strip?
A: I get a cast of pretty girls around the edges but I don't use a girl as a primary character. The idea is to have one hero and a lot of cuties.

Q: Did you read romantic adventure stories as a boy?
A: No more than any other boy. But I went back and reread my books when I was doing *Terry.* Among them was *Wuthering Heights.* Captain Patterson of the *Daily News* told me to read it. I discovered that all I wanted to say in *Terry* could be found in that book. Tragedy is the real essence of what I do here all the time—a great hope getting fouled up

either by fate or the people themselves. It's no different from *Romeo and Juliet.*

Q: Isn't that a downbeat idea to base the "funnies" on?
A: If I can have a nugget of tragedy I can go breezing along. I can do anything, propagandize even. Al Capp says I am a propagandist. I propagandize for love. But the tragedy is the base of it all. You throw the shaft into the reader and he is mad as hops at you, but he has been with you all the time. I murdered one of my characters once and I'm still getting mail.

Q: You have mentioned the word danger again and again. Do you think you are in a dangerous business?
A: Oh yes. I can be chopped off any time. If a paper cancels you there is no recourse.

Q: You are sort of living a Caniff cliff-hanger then. But there must be great satisfactions or you wouldn't do it?
A: The satisfaction lies in not being bored. You've got something you want to say—not that you try to influence people consciously, but it is a most satisfying thing to have a platform. I'm not just trying to make a living. I'm trying to have some fun at it. Trying to say something. The best part is that you are allowed to in my business.

The World of Milton Caniff

MAJOR JIM TAYLOR / 1970

From *Airman*, February 1970,
pp. 55–62.

Colonel Steve Canyon is alive, well, and lives in an attractive apartment on New York's East 72d Street.

So does Milton Caniff.

To Air Force people around the world, the two are synonymous. And probably no two have ever done so much for Air Force morale, nor given the Air Force a nicer tinge of glamour throughout the civilian world.

The younger of the two, who celebrated his 23d "birthday" last month, has been in the Air Force for most of his existence. The senior has never been, at least in the usual sense of the term.

Stevenson Burton Canyon first appeared in 234 newspapers on January 13, 1947. Today, he appears in 650 papers around the world.

Canyon was a bit thinner then, in the Gary Cooper tradition. And although his hair was a shade darker, it had that same streak of black in it that it has now. His parent gave him that to identify Canyon as his own creation— for copyright purposes. The handsome, firm-jawed Canyon's first encounter was with the one and only, beautiful but bitchy, Copper Calhoon. He was then a Reserve Air Force major, serial number A0041044. Today, he is an active duty full colonel, complete with social security number (Caniff's own). He is also listed on the official rolls of Caniff's college fraternity, Sigma Chi, and on those of the Athletic Association of the Air Force Academy.

But what of the creator of this highly popular comic strip hero? What kind of person is he? How can he portray so accurately the US Air Force?

To find out, *Airman* visited Milton Caniff in his New York apartment. There, amidst the memorabilia of this renowned artist's outstanding career, mementos and honors for his contributions to the Air Force and to others, and the drawings of the people who today march through his strips, we discovered Milton Caniff.

He is a friendly, articulate person; easy to meet, easy to talk with. He is quick to laugh and quick to recount anecdotes. There, propped up in bed recovering from a leg operation, he was assiduously working away on *Steve Canyon.*

The son of a printer, Caniff was born February 28, 1907 in Hillsboro, Ohio. He was a Boy Scout, eventually becoming an Eagle Scout.

"At summer camp with the scouts, we put out a daily newspaper called the *Hodag,* for which I drew illustrations, a comic strip, and a full page comic for the Sunday edition," he recalled.

"At this time, the Dayton *Journal* carried a Scout page in its Sunday edition. It was through making some illustrations for this page that I got my first newspaper job—as office boy in the art department of the *Journal.*" He was then 13 years old.

Caniff was also quite interested in acting in those days.

"All through high school and college days," he said, "I had more irons in the fire than the village blacksmith.

"I would leave high school around 2 p.m., work at the Dayton *Journal* office until theater time, run to the theater, do whatever was called for, later returning to the *Journal* office to finish up the work I had to do.

"I continued this odd triple life even in college . . . and strangely enough, I became quite adept at it."

Caniff's high school art teacher had a lasting influence on him. And in large measure, because of her, he went to college, choosing Ohio State.

"She taught me *pu-lenty,*" he says. "I still go to her with my hat in my hand. The strip is not exactly her world, but she says she likes the drawings. I remember she once thought I was goofing off and she said, 'If I were able to, I would lick you!' She was right, I was goofing off.*

"She hadn't gone to college. But she always maintained that anybody who was going to be an editorial cartoonist, which I had started out to be, should have a college education. She was absolutely right. She had that teacher's sense of what was right."

But it may have been the art department of the newspaper that became his most important school. Under a discerning art director, he handled virtually every type of art job, from retouching, to cartooning, and sketching courtroom scenes. It wasn't always easy, especially in the beginning.

"I worked the nightside after class. Everything had to be ready at 7 a.m. when the engravers came in. If I finished early, I went home early. But the dayside guys took great delight in keeping me late. Everything they could get rid of, they dumped on me."

There were people then at Ohio State who were later to become important, and who he would encounter again in a variety of ways. He first met a future Air Force Chief of Staff there, ROTC Cadet Curtis E. LeMay.

Here too, he first met Philip G. Cochran, later to appear more than once in his strips.

"I didn't see much of him in school, although we both belonged to the Dramatic Club. He once showed up late with a pair of black and white shoes on for ROTC Governor's Review . . . A pair of black and white shoes in a long line of cadets passing in review, you could see for a mile!"

In 1930, Caniff left Ohio State, possessor of a bachelor's degree in fine arts. He immediately went to work full time with the Columbus *Dispatch.* Within two months he married Esther "Bunny" Parsons, his high school sweetheart, and within one year he was fired from his job.

It was the depression. Being among the newest members of the staff, Milton was among the first to be laid off. It may have been a fortuitous firing. Within three months he landed a job with the Associated Press Feature Service in New York. He made the trip on borrowed money.

**Caniff's high school art teacher was Martha Schauer, who lived into her nineties and who, according to Canif, was still telling him "how to do it."*

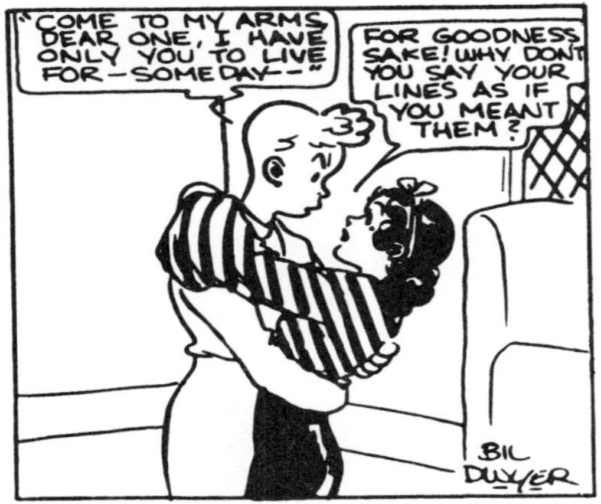

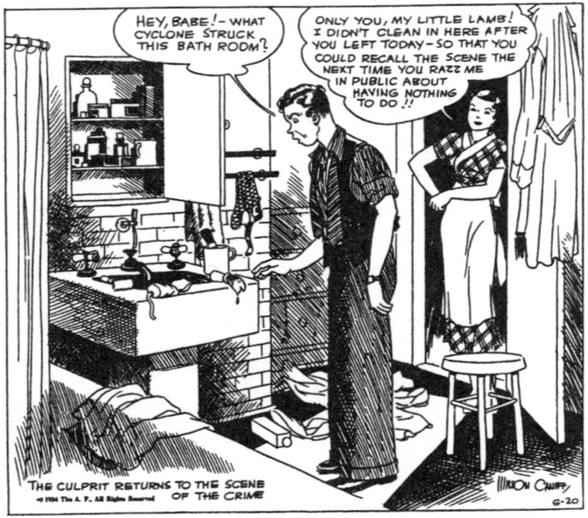

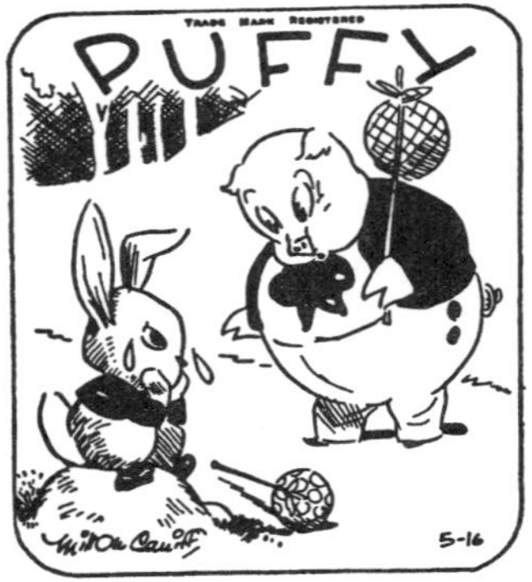

(FOR PMS, MAY 16)

As Puff skips along down the road through the park,
He sees a young rabbit alone in the dark.
"Halloo!" says the Puff, to the long-eared young chap,
"What causes that sorrowful look on your map?"

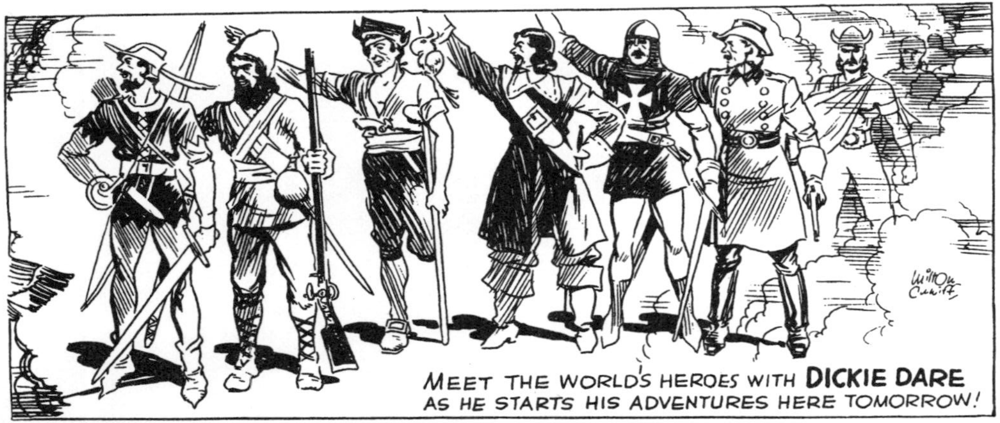

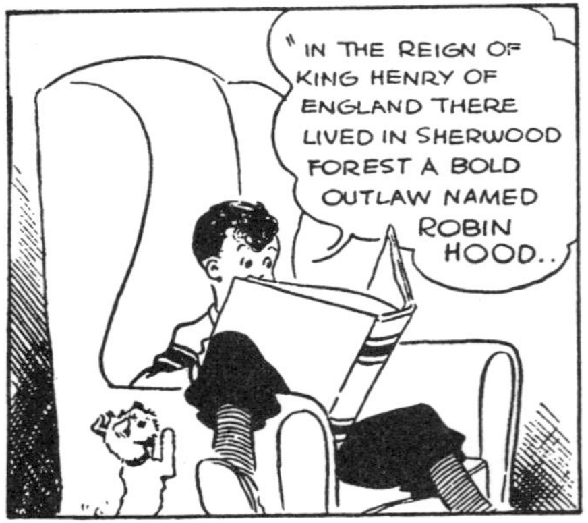

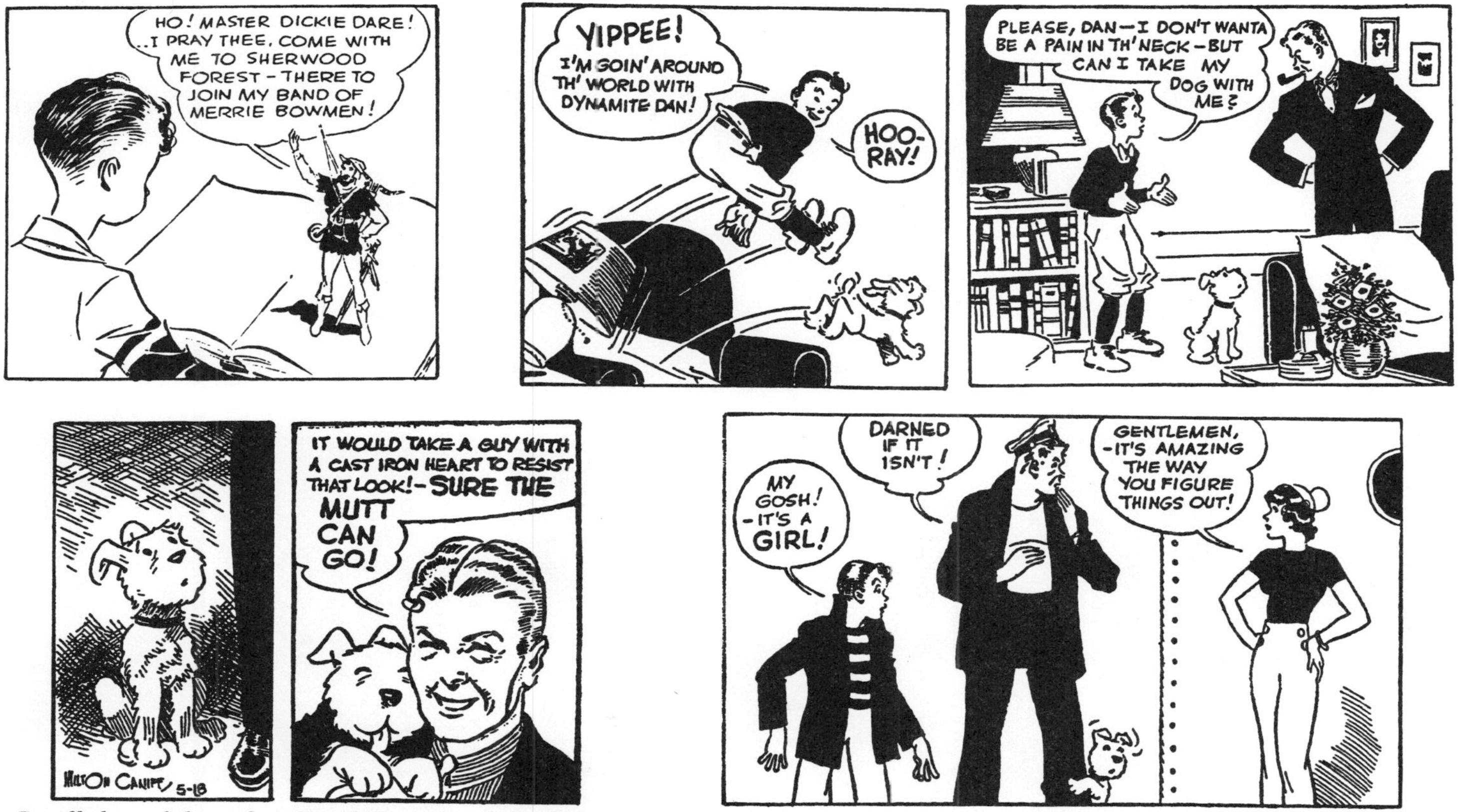

Caniff ghosted the girls in Dumb Dora *(top left) while doing* Gay Thirties, Puffy the Pig, *and* Dickie Dare *at AP. In the next assortment of panels, we see Dickie give up daydreams with literary figures in favor of real adventures with Dynamite Dan Flynn, who, before long, finds himself in love with the unattainable Kim Sheridan (last panel), a prelude to Pat Ryan and Normandie.*

Soon a spot opened up for Caniff to do a three-column human interest panel, *The Gay Thirties.* Then, in short order, he started his adventure strip, *Dickie Dare,* which appeared in the old New York *Sun.* It was the kind of adventure strip that had kid appeal on the one hand, but there was a strong arm guy standing behind him. The publisher of the New York *Daily News* (Joseph M. Patterson) saw it and wanted this kind of strip.

"Patterson had a great deal of skill in knowing what the public wanted and would buy. 'Like to do a strip for the *News*?' he asked on the phone. Of course I was just busting to illustrate for the *Daily News.*

"Patterson thought the strip should have adventure and girls, and that it should be as funny as it could be without stretching it too much. And he said, 'I think the locale should be China because it's still the place where anything can happen—off the China coast. I have two books I'd like you to read.'

"One book was about Chinese pirates, and it was kind of an obscure work, as I learned. And the other was *Wuthering Heights,* with its unrequited love theme. There's a sad but tender quality in it as well as a frustrating quality. As you can see, I've continued to use it."

Thus, on October 22, 1934 with the birth of *Terry and the Pirates,* Milton Caniff became America's youngest major cartoonist.

"I had set out to compete with Dick Tracy and Orphan Annie and the other stuff. I wanted to do something loud and dramatic, and that's why I started to draw the things as if each of the panels was an illustration for the *Saturday Evening Post.* I wanted to make each one as carefully as possible, working out the light and shade and the composition and have it believable."

That new sophisticated strip has been credited by students of the subject with having produced more imitators than any comic strip in history. No strip had ever tried complete realism in an exotic setting and, in a sense, *Terry* became a war novel. Caniff was also the first to introduce current history, as reported in the newspapers, into the comic strips.

Terry grew up in the strip, as the strip itself rapidly matured. And long before Pearl Harbor, Terry and Pat Ryan, his muscular and adventuresome protector, and their friends were backing the Chinese against the "invaders." Caniff's newspaper syndicate was careful not to offend these otherwise well identified invaders as the Japanese. He had even shown the Japanese-Nazi-Italian coalition as early as 1940, but without names.

When the war came, Caniff had already been drawing war action in Asia for four years. Now, as Pat Ryan began fading from the strip in 1942, his place was taken by "Flip Corkin"—none other than Col. Philip G. Cochran of the Army Air Corps, his former schoolmate.

Shortly before the war, Caniff had again run into Cochran through a mutual friend. When the war came, Cochran was stationed at Groton, Conn., flying fighters.

"I went up there and watched him fly a routine day's training mission. He was a first lieutenant at the time. And suddenly it dawned on me that I was sitting there on top of one of the most colorful characters that I or anybody else had ever seen.

"The guys themselves called him 'Corkin.' Just by taking the name Philip and making it 'Flip,' I had a perfect wild-type fighter pilot.

"I'd already decided to have Terry learn to fly, but I wanted to have him do it on an exchange basis, like the Chinese were coming over here and learning. . . . The Pentagon said they knew of no precedent, but on the other hand, they knew of no reason why he couldn't.

"So I asked Phil just to write out the procedure of how you would teach a kid to fly. I hadn't told *him* yet that I was going to use him as the basis for a character. By the time I had gotten around to showing him, he was already in Africa. The first knowledge he had of any of this was when people started sending him these things from the states.

"Then he got called back to the States—by Hap Arnold! By then, he was a lieutenant colonel. He thought, 'Holy Smokes, I'm ruined.'

"When he walked into Arnold's office, Arnold said, 'Hi, 'ya, Flip!' And Phil knew he was home free."

General Arnold, wartime chief of the Air Force, promoted him to full colonel and then assigned him as commander of the 1st Air Commandos. As Arnold said, in his memoirs, *Global Mission,* "Its equipment included everything from helicopters to puddle-jumpers, to light and medium bombers, to fighters, gliders, and transports and all the latest gadgets and means then known for snatching gliders off the ground. This Commando organization played a most important part in making (Maj. Gen. Orde) Wingate's mission a success and in making interior Burma too hot for the Japanese."

But when Cochran was still preparing to form the 1st Air Commandos, he would not visit Caniff for fear he'd inadvertently say something he shouldn't.

"He used to run like a thief when he saw me coming," says Caniff.

"But I had used the general background of what they were doing, because by then we had found out they were out there. You just put two and two together and sit back and play general. So I guessed pretty closely. There was a big noise about it in the British papers. They thought I was a spy."

The airborne invasion of Burma appeared in Caniff's strip *two days before it actually started.*

. . . .

But there was another strip that Milton Caniff did in World War II that was readily the most popular thing carried in military newspapers during the war.

Nobody, but nobody, from those days could ever forget the lovely, languorous, luscious lady known as Miss Lace. The strip, *Male Call,* appeared weekly in some 3,000 military newspapers, then known as Camp Service Newspapers.

. . . .

After the first year, Caniff had intended to stop *Male Call,* but he received such overwhelming complaints from editors that he continued it right until the end of the war.

"There was a funny kind of ambivalence with *Male Call.* I was doing one strip a week. But sometimes it would take me as long to do that one as it did all six of *Terry.* It had to have a point, a gag, or a sentimental outpouring. I tried to mix it up, so that it wasn't always the same old stuff. Apparently, it worked out all right. I still get a lot of mail from guys about it."

A survey in 1944 showed that *Male Call* was the most popular single item distributed to military newspapers, more popular even than news from home.

. . . .

During the war the strips were donated to the War Department. All royalties from *Male Call* reprints were assigned to the Army Relief Fund. After the war, when they had again been reprinted in book form, receipts were reassigned to the Air Force Aid Society. Even today, royalties continue to come in to Air Force Aid.

By the end of the war more than 75 Air Force planes had flown into combat proudly displaying his comic strip personalities [painted on the sides of the aircraft]. Many tributes, many honors, came to Milton Caniff for his numerous selfless contributions to the military services during the war years.

With *Terry,* Caniff had been working purely on a salary plus royalty basis. All rights to the character were owned by his syndicate. His contract was to end on October 14, 1946. Two years prior to that he gave his syndicate notice that he was going to give up *Terry* and create a strip of his own.

Such was the pulling power of the Caniff style that within three months of the announcement of the new strip, more than 125 newspapers had signed up for it. Even though he had not yet decided what he was going to draw!

"In the beginning I had to make a different type of character than Terry. I thought first of a grown man, rather than just a boy who had grown up. I wanted a guy who had all that behind him.

"I wanted a guy who had already been through the war. So the Air Force personnel boys dreamed up a whole file on him, including a serial number—when he got his wings, when he checked out in B-25s, when he got his Purple Heart and everything else that had happened to that date."

How did he come to choose a name for his protagonist?

"'Canyon' suggested open spaces, adventure and escape from the humdrum. . . . Steve, or Stevenson, has always been a virile-sounding appellation. In order to avoid the 'NMI' on his military records, I used my mother's maiden name, Burton, as the middle name for our hero."

Squadron Order 451, dated 23 January 1948, of the 55th Troop Carrier Squadron, Northeast Airport, Philadelphia, Pa., required Canyon to participate in the normal Reserve training minimums of that unit.

Then a major in the Reserves and a member of that unit, David F. McCallister made the arrangements. Caniff attended a special luncheon there and was master of ceremonies in welcoming Canyon into the squadron.

McCallister had been Caniff's inspiration for 2d Lt. Charles C. Charles, better known as "Hot Shot Charlie," in the *Terry* strip. He was later to appear again as "Soup" Davey, jet fighter pilot, in *Steve Canyon.*

"Canyon is really a composite. He's the one person I'm not using out of real life," says Caniff. "In a sense he's a molding of Pat Ryan and Terry into one character, which simplifies the plot situation. Instead of two characters you have one."

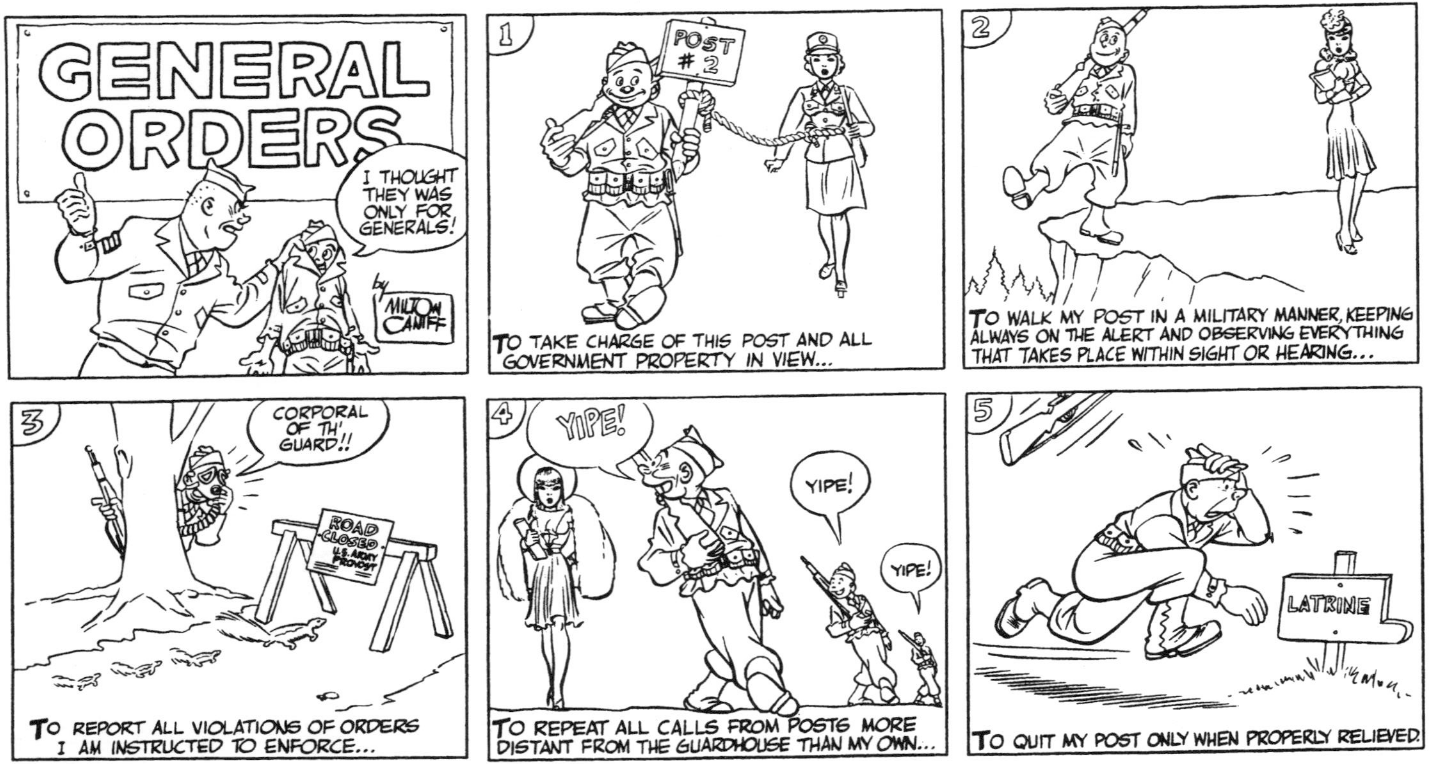
GENERAL ORDERS
I THOUGHT THEY WAS ONLY FOR GENERALS!
by MILTON CANIFF
1
POST # 2
TO TAKE CHARGE OF THIS POST AND ALL GOVERNMENT PROPERTY IN VIEW...
2
TO WALK MY POST IN A MILITARY MANNER, KEEPING ALWAYS ON THE ALERT AND OBSERVING EVERYTHING THAT TAKES PLACE WITHIN SIGHT OR HEARING...
3
CORPORAL OF TH' GUARD!!
ROAD CLOSED
U.S. ARMY PROVOST
TO REPORT ALL VIOLATIONS OF ORDERS I AM INSTRUCTED TO ENFORCE...
4
YIPE!
YIPE!
YIPE!
TO REPEAT ALL CALLS FROM POSTS MORE DISTANT FROM THE GUARDHOUSE THAN MY OWN...
5
LATRINE
TO QUIT MY POST ONLY WHEN PROPERLY RELIEVED.

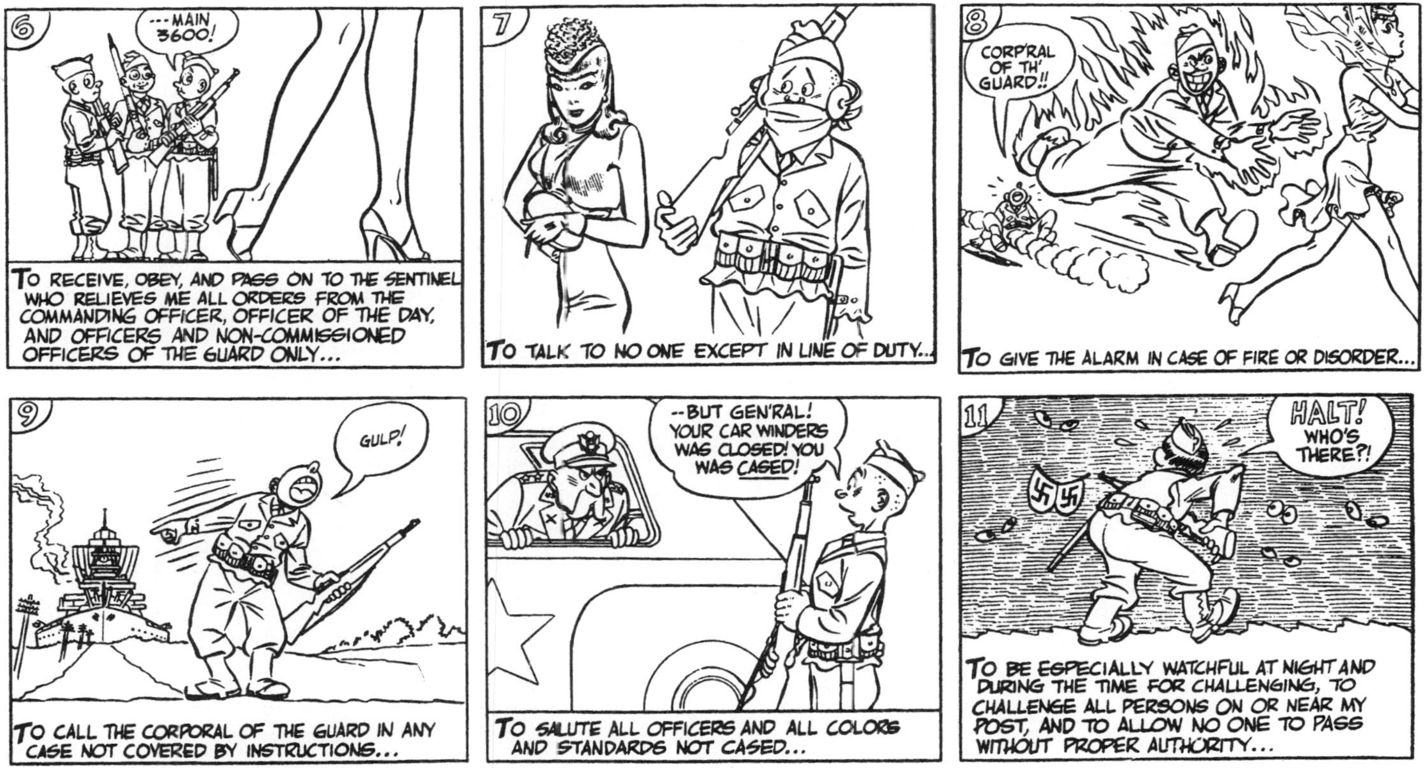

Caniff's wartime work for the Camp Newspaper Service was not confined to Male Call *and Miss Lace. He also did an assortment of other cartooning, like this strip that illustrates the meaning of "General Orders." All of Caniff's CNS art was first done in outline form like this to permit A.B. Dick to make mimeograph masters; after which, Caniff would brush in shadowy solid blacks.*

When the Korean War came along, Canyon, along with thousands of others, was called up. This was his first full time appearance in uniform since his mythical beginning.

His adventures since then have been legend. Certainly he is the Air Force's most widely known colonel. His exploits are read daily by more than 30,000,000 people around the world.

"He is a flyer, a gentleman, a brawler, a bit of a linguist, and a man unashamed of his intelligence," Caniff once wrote in a magazine article. "His habitat is the globe, and there is only one condition laid upon his natural environment: it must contain beautiful women."

In 1950, Steve Canyon first met the beautiful Summer Olson at a secret air base in the Far East. He was attracted to her, but it turned out that she was married. Caniff has since brought them together on a number of occasions, the most recent being when her teenage son was involved in taking drugs. Canyon continues to love her, but her husband is still alive, albeit a "vegetable" in a hospital.

"Canyon and Summer couldn't be married, because her husband is alive. And he doesn't dare be around her, because she's the kind of girl who could obviously change her mind. She could divorce this guy because almost every state has laws covering such circumstances.

"If I ever did really want to have Canyon married, I'd just have the old boy die off. I'll save this in the wings if I need it. And as time goes on, it becomes more and more of a potential weapon."

The personalities who act on Milton Caniff's stage come largely from real life. "Bitsy" of Power Puff Derby and other fame, is posed by a professional model, Lynda Morrow. In this instance, Caniff began with sketching the type of girl he wanted and then found a model to fit his sketches. He photographs her in color in a variety of poses. The hat she always wears is one of the things set up to protect his trademark. But Caniff insists on staying contemporary.

"When Lynda changes her hairdo, I change. She calls me up and may say, 'I've just shaved my head,' or something like that, and I'll say, 'Come on over.' And she'll come over and sit down in the same chair and we'll take more pictures, even though she may not be appearing in the strip at the time."

(Mrs. Morrow has recently had a baby who she has nicknamed "Itsy Bitsy.")

Another personality was Brig. Gen. "Casey" Vincent, who had appeared earlier in *Terry* as "Ȯl' Vincent Casey" and returned to appear in *Steve Canyon* as "General Shanty Town." Both were based on one of the youngest officers to make general officer, probably since Custer made it.

. . . .

One of the most moving stories in *Steve Canyon* was when General Shanty Town died from overwork in helping work out the defenses of the United States. General Casey's death, at age 40, was indeed attributed to overwork.

Among a great variety of other personalities have been the then Senator John F. Kennedy as "Pipper the Piper," Cartoonist Bill Mauldin as "Upton Bucket," Nancy O'Neal of Houston as "Poteet Canyon," Air Force Major Bill Lookadoo as "Major Luke Adew," Alice McDermott, wife of the then Dean of Students of the Air Force Academy, as "Allee McDean," and the daughter of Caniff's secretary appears as "Holly Hall."

Philip Cochran returned to the *Steve Canyon* panoply of characters as "General Philerie." Phil hails from Erie, Pa.

And many prominent personalities have appeared as themselves.

On an average day, Milton Caniff gets up about 9 o'clock, having gone to bed about 1 or 2 o'clock in the morning. He takes the elevator from his 12th floor apartment to the 17th floor—as far as it goes—and walks up the remaining two flights to his 19th floor studio. There he goes through the morning papers with his secretary, Adelaide Gilchrest, and they clip as they go along. (He laughingly calls her "sergeant." She fondly calls him "general." Both she and Wilhelmina "Willie" Tuck, his charming cook and all-around assistant, have been with him for more than 30 years.)

Normally, he begins work around 10 o'clock.

"I work on an assembly line basis, in that I first write all six daily strips at one time. Then I start over and pencil in all six. I rough it out in almost shorthand drawing, and my assistant carefully inks in the lettering. I have two assistants, really. The man who inks in the lettering does nothing but lettering [Frank Engli]. Then my other assistant [Richard Rockwell] goes over it and does the 'tight' drawing, in this case these horses. He's also a pilot. He was a pilot in the Troops Carrier Command and he flew a Gooney during the war and never got a scratch. He knows far more about flying than I do and I've sometimes put an airplane in a situation doing things that a plane just couldn't do. Then he catches me before I get into some kind of pickle."

Dick Rockwell [is] Norman Rockwell's nephew.

"While my drawing assistant is working on the middle phase, I'm doing something else. Then it comes back to me. I start it and I finish it.

"All the daily strips take three days, roughly two strips a day. For the Sunday papers, since there's a lot of illustration, I allow two days. On the sixth day, I answer mail and catch up on all the loose ends. I manage to get one full day away from the drawing board. But seldom can I avoid doing some work at night. I can't get it all done in an ordinary 40-hour week. I don't dread the drawing, but I like to have enough time to do it right.

"The story line is the hardest because so much counts on that. Doing a story that captures a reader and holds onto him is something else again. First of all, you're doing a contemporary picture, and it's meant to be contemporary and continually so.

"You try to please yourself, because you can't possibly know what all the readers are thinking at any given time. . . . It's a job to anticipate things. Like this dope [drugs] thing that I ran with Summer Olson."

Caniff's story ideas come from a variety of sources, but largely they come from the daily newspapers. Yet there are exceptions, such as the sequence that is just ending now.

"When I was in the hospital I had one of those hospital germs (of an idea) that is always drama—high drama. And I was thinking of a story line that would include the hospital and I thought I'd do it while it was still fresh in my mind, and the relationships between people were still fresh. So I began to think of what a good place to hide the hospital is . . . I started asking questions around the hospital. . . ."

We won't repeat the storyline, but it has just ended as we come off the press. If you're an *aficionado* of *Steve Canyon,* you'll know how it all happened. If you aren't—well, there's always a new sequence coming up.

Lead times are a problem in any publishing business.

"I'm always roughly two or three stories ahead. My finished lead time for actual art is eight weeks. But, in my mind at least, I'm writing 16 weeks in advance, and literally writing 12 weeks.

"I've cut the length of a story down to about eight weeks. I used to go about 12. In some cases I've actually cut it down to three weeks or so if I wanted to make some point rather quickly. Only twice a year do I do an editorial type thing, once on Christmas and once on Armed Forces Day."

Since the early days of *Terry,* Caniff has been widely acclaimed as giving the greatest attention to detail, as being the most authentic of cartoonists. Research for this is demanding.

"I do all my own research when I can. My assistant can do research for me, but I still need the personal contact. It's always better to go out and smell it. We've worked out a system that is so simple I don't know why in the world I didn't think about it during the war.

"Now, when I'm on a base, the Information officer loans me a photographer. And we'll walk around and I'll ask for a picture of this and that. In the event there's a picture of something sensitive they'll just send me back the prints I can have."

But no one who must be appealing to the public everyday, who must be finely attuned to its moods, its sensitivities, can live in a vacuum if he is to be successful. Caniff had once written that "letters are like applause to an actor." How about it?

"Yes. It's the only feedback you can get. The running stream of attitude is reflected only in these letters. We average about 25 letters a day."

Of the many recognitions and numerous awards he has received, Caniff treasures most the Air Force Exceptional Service Award, its highest civilian award presented to him in January 1957 in recognition of service to military aviation for over 20 years. At Bolling AFB, with Air Force Chief of Staff General Thomas D. White at his side, he took the salute in a parade honoring him. He also received 400 letters extending personal thanks, *one from every general officer in the Air Force.*

Bob Considine once wrote that, "Milton Caniff has done more for the Air Force than any person since Billy Mitchell."

Ours is not to quibble with such a renowned columnist. And, while we won't take sides on the statement, we will say that Steve Canyon is alive, well and has done inestimable good for the United States Air Force.

So has Milton Caniff.

An Interview with Milton Caniff

JAY MAEDER / 1972

From *Rocket's Blast Comic Collector,* Summer 1972, n.p. Reprinted by permission.

A fine storyteller and a highly imaginative craftsman, Milton Caniff, creator of *Terry and the Pirates* and, later, *Steve Canyon,* early brought narrative literacy and graphic sophistication to the burgeoning adventure strip genre of the mid-1930s, and he is considered by many students of American comic art to be the single greatest influential force in the development of the form.

What follows is an edited transcript of an interview with Caniff, done in June 1971, in which he discusses the nature of his own creativity, his relationship with a growing career, and the future of the comics medium.

Caniff is recalling his two-year stint as an Associated Press staff artist in New York City. His work on AP's *Dickie Dare* strip has come to the attention of Captain Joseph Medill Patterson, publisher of the *New York*

Daily News, and one afternoon in September 1934, the young Caniff is summoned before Patterson:

I had this telephone call from Mollie Slott, who was then sort of the executive officer for the Chicago Tribune-New York News syndicate, and she asked if I would like to talk with Captain Patterson about a new strip.

Dickie Dare was actually the same basic proposition of the youngster and an older guy and far-places adventure I didn't know anything about whatever—wishful, Walter Mitty kind of stuff—and clearly, as it developed, Patterson was looking for this same kind of thing for his own syndicate.

So when I was summoned by The Presence, he was very warm, cordial. Not by any means the ogre. And he asked if I would be interested in doing a strip for the Chicago Tribune-New York News syndicate.

And I said I would be very much indeed. By happenchance my contract with the Associated Press was running out, and it was not a problem to break it. AP was not about to have a run-in with their best client in the New York City area.

It was almost a "can you show me something next Thursday" deal. First of all he said, "Let me see some names," and I made a list of about fifty boys' names. He was quite specific that he wanted a youngster as the central figure, and pretty girls, and some humor. And he gave me two books of reference to look at. He said, "The China coast is the last outpost of this kind of adventure," and he had this book on Chinese pirates. And the other book was *Wuthering Heights.*

So I read them both as quickly as I could; the time element was really quite hot here. I was ready and willing to do what he wanted done, you know. I was also equipped to do it—had the general background. But now suddenly I had to go to a real geography hop, and I went from his office to the public library.

And a week after I talked to him, this thing started to run in the *New York News.* My syndication consisted of one paper.

You introduced most of your characters quite early, didn't you?
Yes, Connie was right away, immediately—and Pat Ryan—well, he was the strong character; what I needed was a muscleman. You can't have a kid doing a Jim Hawkins bit of shooting the pirate. At this late date,

when I think of the kid atop the mast shooting someone in the head—I wonder, you know? By devious means, such as hiding in an apple barrel and so forth, fine. But the literal confrontation—not that it was out of order in those days, but . . .

But anyway, I introduced Pat Ryan to handle the muscle. My thought was to bring Terry up to an age when he could then take over, which, by the way, I was able to do in the twelve years that I was incumbent. And Pat Ryan was then phased out, so to speak.

Yes, he became a Navy commander during the war and sort of vanished.
We were able to ease him out of the picture, so that Terry could then be center stage. You've got to have just one leading person at a time. That was the way to do it in those days, or so it seemed to me. By reading and watching movies and so on I knew what was being generally accepted by the buying public. I wasn't trying to plow new furrows, I was trying to grab the handle, you know?

At any rate, Captain Patterson knew pretty specifically what he had in mind.
Yes, he wanted an adventure strip, faraway places, pretty girls, and humor. The Pat Ryan type of back-up character he didn't mention. He wanted a young hero.

So, then he checked the list of fifty names that I'd submitted and picked out "Terry" and wrote it down, and then he added "And the Pirates." Which I always considered to be kind of a drag.

Really?
Well, it could throw you into a mold, in the sense that you couldn't escape from it.

There are only so many stories you can do about Chinese pirates, is that it?
Well, the word "pirates," it's like saying "Johnny and The Gobbledygooks." You know, then you've got to have gobbledygooks.

Personally, I've always felt that "And the Pirates" lent the strip a certain character.
Well, I shouldn't put it down. It was just a drag in my head in terms of trying to do anything other than pirate stories. Which, happily, were very acceptable. Of course they weren't all about pirates, but at the time I felt restricted to some degree.

You hadn't ever spent any time in the Orient, had you?
No, never even been close. California was about as close. Since that time I've been able to make these trips, but not at that time. For a long time, especially because of the war, I never got out of the house.

You developed Terry from a stumbling adolescent into a capable young man during the twelve years you did the strip. What kind of relationship did you have with him, as a character?
To some degree—well, not to some degree—he had to be me. I had to project myself into his head. He was the way I felt I probably would have been if I had found myself in those circumstances.

You identified with Terry rather than with Pat Ryan, then.
Oh yes, Pat Ryan was really Walter Mitty. This was wishful thinking. At that point I was old enough to be Pat Ryan but mentally only capable of being Terry.

Would it be fair to say you grew up with Terry?
Yes, very definitely. Certainly professionally. Because feeling the way all along, in terms of characterization, it was quite intense, much more intense than I realized at the time. Because you say only what you're able to say, you see, out of the Mixmaster of your own background.

Terry went through a lot of changes during his troubled adolescence. I remember especially the sequence (1940) where he asked the Dragon Lady to teach him to dance.
Yes. I'd been waiting for a spot for that. Because this kind of confrontation—this type of situation, where the kid has never even been close to a woman who smelled like that—this can change his life. And this is what I had in mind it would do to him.

Who were your favorite villains?
Kiel and Captain Judas.

You liked your heavyweights, didn't you?
Oh yes, of course: this is the whole key. It's like detective stories: you're only as good as your villain. Sherlock Holmes is the best example of this. Old Conan Doyle was smart in that he never really let you see Moriarty. All this built Holmes up enormously in your imagination. It was a fine device.

So those of us who came along later and couldn't just steal that all outright had to come up with some cuties. The Dragon Lady is the strongest of all because she had the double weapon of beauty and absolute ruthlessness, which everybody, man and woman, dreads and anticipates with shuddering pleasure. Encountering such a person—they don't exist, but it's fun to think about.

Why did you drop Terry?

I didn't own it. The key in these things is to own the package. And when I went over from AP to do *Terry*—the Chicago Tribune, then and now, insists on ownership of the package. And at the time you're so glad to get the job that you don't even question this. You've got no reputation, you've got no bargaining power. You've got one little foot in the door, so you accept the situation.

So, comes the day when your conscience and everything tells you that you've either got to own this thing or get off the pot. Fortunately for me, Marshall Field came along. He'd started the *Chicago Sun* during the war years. He couldn't buy anything, because Hearst wouldn't sell him anything and Colonel McCormick [Robert McCormick, director of the Tribune-News Syndicate's Chicago operation] naturally wouldn't sell him anything either. So he had to start out and build a stable of his own.

He approached me on the subject through intermediaries. I told him I was already contracted and he said, "Of course, we know all that, but will you do a new strip for me?"

I said I'd be glad to. He said, "What do you want?" I said, "Full ownership and editorial control." He said, "Very good." And called the butler for a drink.

That's all there was to the discussion. I'd been thinking about it for all those years, and it took two minutes. We talked about money later; that didn't come up at first.

I'm not sure I completely understand the transitions you were undergoing in your own head at this time. Had you begun at all to grow tired of the idea of *Terry and the Pirates*?

Oh no, not at all. It was purely commercial. It was simply a matter of the difference between working for someone and owning the property.

This being the case, did you approach *Steve Canyon* with great enthusiasm?

Certainly, because of the greater incentive of ownership. It was just as greedy as that. That's what it was, greed.

What is the story behind the search for your replacement that ended with the finding of George Wunder? Had you known him before?
No, I hadn't met him. He used to have the same job at Associated Press that I'd had; it was a retouching-lettering-general assignment staff job, and I hadn't met him just because we hadn't crossed trails. He'd been in the Army, and he got out just at the time they announced they were auditioning people for replacement on *Terry* [fall of 1946]. This was not done publicly; it was mouth-to-mouth.

He was trying to improve his lot and not go back to that spitting-on-pictures job at the AP. So he submitted a couple of Sunday pages which later I got photostats of, and it was a beautiful ghosting job. He got the job. There were about a hundred people, by the way, that tried out. They must have seriously considered several artists, but of course I wasn't consulted, and I never saw any of the finished products except the ones that George did.

By the way, since that time George and I have become good friends.

I was going to ask about that. You continue to follow Terry's adventures?
Oh, very definitely, for a very specific reason—apart from the fact that I'm just interested—because the two strips, naturally, are commercial rivals. If George starts to do something about a dictator in South America being kidnapped, I mustn't come up with something like this two or three months later. It would look as if I'd copied from him. He does the same thing.

Like a cat and mouse game all the time.
It is indeed, and of course we laugh about this when we're sitting around having a beer.

Are you pleased with the character Terry has become in Wunder's hands?
George has done a whale of a job. In the first place, it's a very difficult thing to do. Everybody who's ever taken over from someone else who's still alive has got a horrible job; he knows that the other guy is looking over his shoulder. It's all right if the originator of the strip is dead, because then he's dead; he's not going to haunt you at night.

But when the guy is still around, no matter how good friends you are or anything else, you know he's going to be looking at that thing and saying, hrmpphh if I had done that, I would have done thus and so.

Even though you went on to a new strip you retained some of your old characters.
Yes, I've repeated them. General Phillerie is Flip Corkin, for instance.

Vince Casey became Shanty Town, and the Dragon Lady became Madame Lynx.
Yes, right down the line. This was a deliberate thing. Just running in the faces of copyright facts.

And Terry became Reed Kimberley?
To some extent, except that I had passed beyond the Terry stage and I simply had no further use for him. A closer parallel is the current situation of Oley Olson, Summer Olson Canyon's son; but he is not the aggressive Terry, he's the weak sister. He's had a drug history and that kind of thing.

As far as Canyon himself, would it be reasonable to surmise that he's no one else but Pat Ryan?
He's Pat Ryan, sure. This is Pat Ryan, this is not just the grown-up Terry. It's a Pat Ryan minus a few years. Pat Ryan by this time, of course, would be an elder statesman.

Actually, Canyon is no spring chicken anymore either.
No, he isn't. And this is a problem, because in the Air Force if you don't make it to brigadier general by this time, they'd invite you out. But I've always carefully not pinned it down to dates.

It's hard to avoid, though. Canyon fought in the Korean conflict, and he wasn't a youngster at that time.
Well, he was also a captain and then a major on discharge as the strip opened [January 1947]. He'd had a whole career in the Army Air Corps. We have that all documented, by the way. At the time it happened, the guys in the Pentagon—they didn't have much to do in those days—helped me put together a whole dossier on him. We just made up when he got his wings and when he got his first Purple Heart, and that kind of thing, and it's all on file.

Is it out of the question that he'll make brigadier?
Well, I don't think he will. For one thing, when you have a guy make general, that puts him in a whole different upper-echelon category. People don't think that generals actually go to bed with women at night. It's a whole other thing. As a colonel he can still cat around, in spite of being married. This is a useful device.

The point is that when a guy becomes a general, then you're into Pentagon level things. And that's no good.

In that case, keeping in mind that the cartoonist has the natural problem of the aging process, do you have any plans for Canyon's retirement?
No, not that. I think the simple thing to do would be to ease him into another area. I've been doing this spy-type business, where they need a guy who is able to fly an airplane. It's a counterespionage kind of thing. The transition, I think, will be in that direction.

Would this be essentially a more mature version of the operation that Terry and Chazz got into after the second war, with Air Cathay?
Yes. At that time they were really nothing more than listening posts. Now, we pretty much know what they were listening for. It has come to pass. Not that it ever ceases.

But the use of the female character now, the wife, it's a *Thin Man* kind of relationship. *Mr. and Mrs. North.* Remember Myrna Loy in the *Thin Man* stories? She was not all that smart, and she was not all that happy about it, but she was married to the guy, and she was there and she was lovely, and everybody was happy about the whole thing.

Then you'll keep Summer Canyon in the forefront of the adventures.
Yes. For one thing, she's my counterpoint. For instance, she thinks the whole thing is a bunch of nonsense. "If you both know so much about each other, why don't you call it off?" This is, I think, a woman's logic. "This is stupid. Why spy around on people? Why don't you just go and ask him? Where'd you hide the missiles?"

And, instead of being little boys about it and playing at games, this gives me a chance to pit Canyon against her, and then finally she goes along with it because she loves him.

Canyon went into the military during the Korean conflict and he stayed there. I believe you said once, some years ago, that Canyon would stay in the military because you had come to the realization that American society had become military-industrial in scope. Would you consider yourself a pro-military person?
No, not particularly. This is just simply a matter of facing the situation we're in. The present opposition to armed attitudes is a phase thing, in that we might not want to be caught up in the war situation, the war attitude that occurs when you are a "leading power," but everybody

else on the "leading power" plateau considers us the enemy. We are—reluctantly—in it, you know. World War III is already on.

The key word is "reluctantly."
I think so. The whole Vietnam thing has brought out the attitudes of the younger people. An abhorrence of the whole thing which everybody feels, and the misery of supporting a conflict in an area which they not only don't understand but can't pronounce—the World War II point of view was quite different.

. . . Everyone thinks we should go out and win a war and be a John Wayne movie in the Orient, but when it bogs down they realize somebody guessed wrong here. Guessed wrong in terms of, maybe we should have won it but we didn't. And we're getting our tails burned out there. And everybody hates to be a loser.

You haven't involved Canyon a lot in Southeast Asia.
At the start. First of all I held back to see which way the cat was going to jump, then I did a couple of sequences which involved it. Not so much from a point of view, it was just the fact of involvement. When you're in the flying machine business, you can't very well avoid it.

I'd done one story back during the days of the French surrender. The thing took place in Hanoi when the French were being booted out. But at the time I had no notion what I was getting into. Or what they were getting into. I didn't know what was going to take place.

Essentially what we've been talking about is that this is 1971 and we don't have the G.I. Joe syndrome anymore. We're experiencing the My Lai and the PX scandals and so on; is it possible to be as idealistic about the military institution as it once was?
Not at all. There's no Hitler today, there's no Hirohito, there's none of that. Just a big fat nothing to get killed for, just because you got in the wrong place.

What kind of relationship do you maintain with the Air Force?
Oh, very strong. They understand, for one thing, that I can't use the military in the foreground as I once did simply because of the general attitude toward the military. They dig this better than anybody. They know where they stand.

But you wouldn't, for example, cast the Air Force in an unsympathetic light? Like gross overspending on a defense project or something.
I've found it's better, when these things are happening, to avoid the subject until I get a better perspective on it. I work ten weeks ahead.

And if I say something, and it turns out to go the other direction, either good or bad, then I have no way of regrouping. No way of falling back or restarting. So it's safer not to overcommit.

What are your working habits these days?
They haven't changed over the years—I write the dialogue and rough it out, and send it back to the lettering man first, then he passes it on to my assistant, Dick Rockwell, who puts in backgrounds that I have asked for. For instance, I say "London street," he digs out the file on London streets and puts it in.

Do you ever begin a sequence without knowing full well how it will resolve?
I always have an ending, but I don't always use the same ending I started with. If I sense the thing is becoming obvious—mail will tip you off on that—then you can always give it a twist. That's a break we get in this trade.

You get a lot of mail, do you?
Always have. There was a lag in it at the beginning of television. Television took away a lot of our active audience at the beginning, but the last few years it's been built up again, because we've had a whole new generation of kids who have become bored with television.

For one thing, they've seen the television cartoons at least seventeen times, and that's the one thing we offer, a brand new drawing every day, no matter what. It's always a new drawing, and legitimately so, and they're beginning to sense this.

What other strips do you read regularly, strips you'd call your favorites?
I don't know that "favorite" is the word, because I look at them from a different point of view. But I get a real kick out of *Beetle Bailey.* I love him. And I love *Snuffy Smith.*

Let's put it like this: what strips do you read for fulfillment in the sense of being able to say, well, this man has a good narrative technique, or this man is able to beautifully synthesize his story line with the pictorial representation of what he's trying to get across. . . .
I don't think I read any strips for that reason anymore. Maybe I did once. But I read some of them just to see what the line is, then abandon it if it doesn't overlap me or grab me. Because it's kind of like knowing what the guy's going to do.

What I enjoy reading are those boys who have been coming along recently and knocking down all the barriers. Garry Trudeau [in *Doonesbury*] is doing things I wish I could have done. And Johnny Hart [in *B.C.*] has been one of the real pioneers in doing things that had never been done before. . . .

Doonesbury is the best of the lot right now. It's bright on the part of the syndicate people to grab onto them. As far as the creators are concerned, as long as this "permissive" attitude lasts, I hope that they'll go along with it. . . .

Trudeau is just beginning to feel his oats now. It takes a while. A guy has to find out whether what he's doing is even being looked at. You're an actor in that sense, you have to wait for your applause in this business.

You see, the kind of thing that I got into the business to do—and by the way, I would have done anything, you do whatever will sell; I got into the story strip thing that was taking the place of the old type gag story strip— but the adventure story strip, which is my natural bent, is beside the point. I would have created *Blondie* if I'd known that I could have sold it, you can be damn sure.

That's what makes Picasso tick too. And it happens, the reason Picasso sells is that he does it better than Joe Blow. So it is with any of the rest of us. . . .

Terry (no middle initial) Lee

MILTON CANIFF / 1973

From the *Menomonee Falls Gazette*, Spring 1973, n.d., n.p. Reprinted by permission.

Terry and the Pirates, *which had been shepherded through almost three decades by Caniff's successor, George Wunder, was discontinued with the February 25, 1973, release. Shortly thereafter, Caniff penned the following:*

Terence (no middle initial) Lee, Lt. Col., USAF Born: Oct. 22, 1934 in Rockland County, NY. Killed in the Line of Duty: Feb. 25, 1973.
By Milton Caniff (Past Parent)

In the middle 1940's, when I made the deal to do a new strip for Marshall Field, I had plenty of time to become used to the fact that I would be giving up all of the *Terry* characters. It was not unlike a parent knowing that his children were no longer legally his and that he must relinquish them by court order.

When I heard that *Terry* would be discontinued as of February 1973

I experienced the sensation of a parent learning his long-gone, but alive, children were sentenced to be executed.

It is interesting to note that the Chicago Tribune-New York Daily News Syndicate will make the *Terry* characters available for such charity functions as the U.S. Air Force Salute, sponsored by the Iron Gate Chapter of the Air Force Association each year in New York.

I think George Wunder did a remarkable job of carrying on with *Terry* after I left. It is hard enough to continue a feature when the originator is dead (as John Prentice did so ably after Alex Raymond's tragic demise). Stepping in on a strip when the former artist is still very much alive is a traumatic thing. The old boy is always looking over your shoulder, in effect, and saying in your ear "*I* wouldn't have done it *that* way".

George, of course, had no idea what I had in mind for *Terry* and Company when he got the job. Naturally, I was not asked. I had shaken Wunder's hand once at the Associated Press, but I did not get to know him until after he was well into the new assignment. Then of course, we both avoided mention of future story lines. If you have a good one coming up you don't tell the competition.

I sometimes think back on the plans I had noodled around with and wonder how they would have played out in print. For instance: I had roughed-up a whooping confrontation, between Big Stoop and the

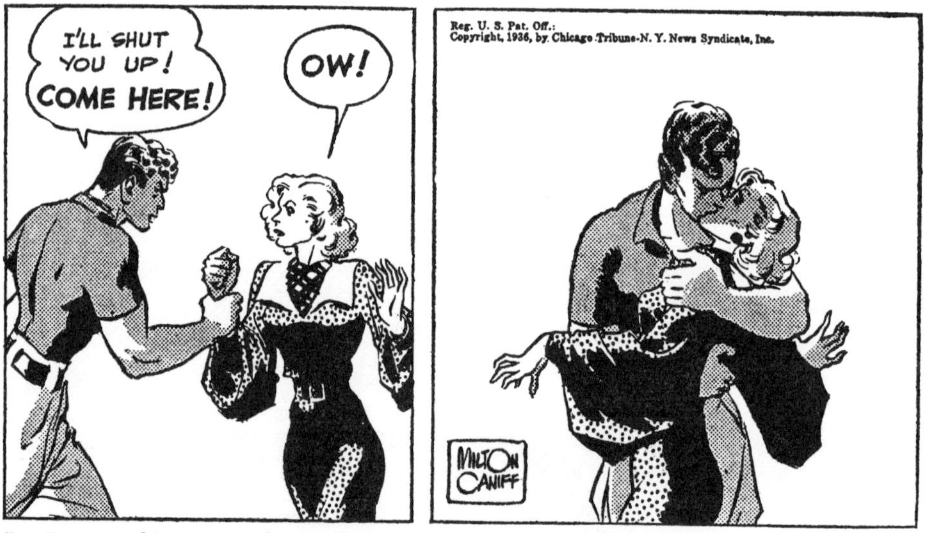

Pat Ryan and Burma strike sparks almost upon first meeting.

Dragon Lady. (I always kept them apart). He was the *only* person she really feared—because he had been her slave when she was a girl and she had ordered his tongue cut out. That could have been a heavy one.

I also planned to have Pat Ryan marry Burma. *That* could have been a Taming of the Shrew at jet speed. I never thought that Terry would take the vows but keeping a hero single these days is a problem. If he is not shown sleeping around, readers begin to ask if he is queer.

There was never a stateside story in my *Terry*. I was going to make a big thing of all these China Hands returning to the U.S. and showing how the picaresque hero from the Far Places does not always fare so well in the conventional surroundings back home.

But is all *damned and over now.*

It was not until I stopped producing *Terry* that I realized just how much of a hold it had on the reading public. With the perspective of 26 years I guess I may feel free to admit that it did accomplish what it was intended to do—which is force the customer to buy tomorrow's paper.

An Interview with Milton Caniff

Shel Dorf / 1978

From *The Buyer's Guide*, Nos. 241 and 243, June 30 and July 14, 1978, n.p. Reprinted by permission.

Dorf was Caniff's letterer on Steve Canyon *for the last twelve years of the strip's run—until Caniff's death.*

Shel: Whenever fans talk about your work, there is always a comparison made between *Canyon* and *Terry,* with the general feeling being that Pat Ryan's adventures were more exciting and, in general, he was a freer spirit. Was there a reason for making Canyon a little more down-to-earth?

Milt: Yes. You had no regard for someone like Pat Ryan. What's this guy doing floating around the world with a young boy, hmmm? You get this feeling that unless he has some mission . . . This is something I thought about quite carefully when I switched over; that I'd better have a full-grown man who has a source of income. I've always said that Ryan was a writer, and this was all right in pre-War days, but today you couldn't get away with this. You never saw him in front of a typewriter. People accepted this before the war, but a lot of people have been a lot of places since those kind of moon-eyed days, and you just simply can't make it stick. It was tough enough then, when sometimes I thought, "Gee, this is not very believable, unless this guy's got a source of income. He's a floater. He's a bum—a gentleman bum, but a bum just the same. So I needed a guy who had a reason for being places, and when you do that, you make a responsible citizen out of him and destroy the whole point. You can't have characters pop up anymore like the "Burma's," who don't ever have to have a passport. Once in a while, I touched on that—casually. Anybody who is not native to the scene today has got to explain his presence, because there's just too much monkey business going on.

Shel: You do have a loophole, however, when Canyon discards his uniform for civilian clothes on a special mission. These stories have the flavor of the pre-war days.

Milt: Yes, but these things just don't happen anymore. You can't get away with a thing. I was in Shanghai earlier . . . or in Hong Kong, for instance . . . you just walk down the street, and if you look like you don't have a job or a place to go or something, the policemen want to see your papers. The British do this with great skill, but they want to know. You just can't float like you used to. Everybody's got to have an excuse for being there. It's the Second World War that caused all this. There was a time when you could live well in Shanghai or Singapore and dribble out a living. But now even the bums who make do are under police surveillance. They just can't move around like I had Pat Ryan move around.

Shel: In one story, after Steve had jumped in to cover for a movie stunt man, he had an offer of a Hollywood contract. Did you at that time seriously consider getting him out of the Air Force?

Milt: Yes. I had gone over this very thing we are talking about now. I'd put him back in service about the time of the Korean War. There was this period between '46 and '51 in which he was a reservist. He was flying an independent airline, etc. And even then he had a job—an angle. When the Korean War came along, it was obvious we were going to have this wartime economy, which would then give him an excuse to be

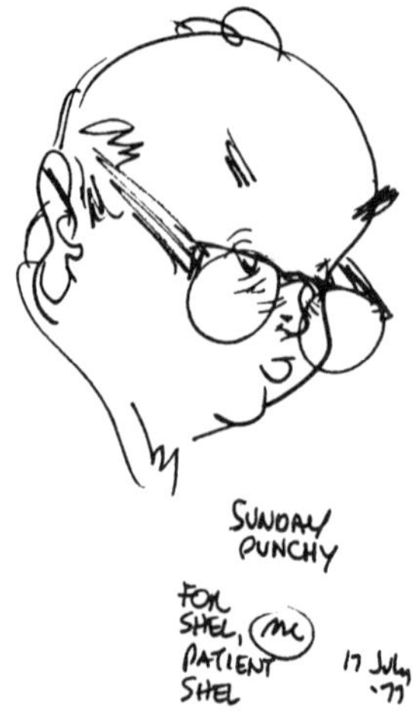

Caniff's self-caricature

a trouble shooter operator, to be sent anywhere. Of course, once you do this, he's got to be loyal. He can't go off somewhere beating the bushes. He's got to make a report, like any cop must do.

Shel: You certainly keep us off-balance in your storytelling. Just when Steve Canyon is headed in one direction, you change locale and we find ourselves in a fresh new situation.
Milt: This is to keep from getting in that awful rut by repeating the same story over and over. This is the break you get by having the whole world for a stage—you can go anywhere.

Shel: You give us an accurate glimpse of parts of the world that are never seen in comics. You make the strip an educational media as well.
Milt: That's a dirty word to editors, by the way. But if you keep the faith and do your homework, and your research is authentic . . .

Shel: If it's Caniff, we know it's pretty authentic!
Milt: Well, that's been not just a trademark, but a way of life for me. When I first started this stuff, nobody was doing this straight kind of illustration and storyline, so you had to find a niche for yourself. And despite the obvious hard work involved, it seemed to be the only place I could turn. The stuff I'd been doing was quite simple. *The Gay Thirties,* a panel, was quite simply drawn. Sort of like *Out Our Way.* So, when I went into the strip thing, I really had to bear down, and I haven't stopped since. I'm stuck with it now. But I must say that of all the jobs of its kind, this is the most interesting you could possibly do because there is never a day that repeats another day. It's not dull. Sometimes you have to repeat a drawing, but this is where an assistant comes in, of course. When you are doing a cockpit shot and you have to draw all those damned instruments—that's where your assistant does the dirty work. Of course, you have all kinds of reference material at hand when you're doing this. The episode of Poteet Canyon at the New York World's Fair of 1964–1965 presented the toughest job, reference-wise. I started gathering data for it since I knew that nobody had any material on hand—the damned fair wasn't even open yet! I had to use archi-

tect's drawings. When the story did appear, the Fair was open, and anybody could go out and check up on it. What I didn't know was what building was next to what other building. So the drawing had to be halfway tentative, yet finished enough so that the average person could recognize it. The colors, too, had to be right. The Fair people printed the episode in booklet form to be given out to the press-aid kids who worked on the fair, as a souvenir. It was also read every day on the closed-circuit television. Great fun!

Shel: Milt, a lot has been written about your leaving *Terry and the Pirates* to do *Canyon,* but I haven't read much from your side of the story.
Milt: I'll tell you the background of the ownership of the *Steve Canyon* strip. I was very happily doing *Terry and the Pirates,* and I got a call one day from a man I had never heard of, and he asked me could I see him at such and such a time in such and such a suite at the Waldorf. And I thought, "If he can afford a suite at the Waldorf, I'd better find out what he wants." So I went to see him, and he said, "I represent Marshall Field. Mr. Field has started this paper in Chicago, and he isn't able to buy features because they are all owned by *Chicago Tribune* or Hearst or etc., and he would be interested in asking you to do a brand new strip. He knows all the technical problems involved—that you couldn't do *Terry,* etc. Would you be interested?" I said I'd like to talk about it, and he said, "Put on your hat!" So we went up the street two blocks to Field's apartment, and he was waiting there—Field and his business manager. We walked in, I was introduced, and Field said, "What would you want?" Now, I'd been thinking about a thing . . . for about a half second! Then I said, "Two things: full ownership of the property and full editorial control." So Mr. Field said (he talked very British, having been educated in England), "Veddy good." I thought, "What was that he said?" And he called the butler and said, "We'll have some drinks now." And that was the end of the conference. He had said yes, just like that! Didn't even argue the point. We didn't talk money until later, and then I discussed details with his business manager, not him. So that's it—full ownership. They can't change a comma unless they call me on the phone.

Shel: I heard that *Steve Canyon* was bought sight unseen by over two hundred newspapers.
Milt: Yes, we were off the nut. We were in the black before the first line was even drawn—before I even had a name for him, as a matter of

fact. Fortunately, Marshall Field and King Features were willing to take this chance, so it worked out fine.

Shel: And now you've been doing *Steve Canyon* more than thirty years. That's twice as long as your work on *Terry.* I don't know why, but *Terry* seemed longer than 12½ years. So much happened. He grew up in the strip. Your style of drawing grew up, too. Some of my [comics] pages from 1935 show the drawing to be very two dimensional, with very heavy shadows not coming in until several months later to give the illustrations more depth.
Milt: I started doing that deliberately. It was very important to do something spectacular. The color and everything in those days was treated so simply. I was looking for some way of just making a noisy bid for attention, and that was the one thing I could think of to do. As I told you before, I wanted to make each panel look like a book illustration. Of course, this took a lot of time. But when you're young and full of beans, you can do it. The whole adventure of it was being young. Once you get the trick and get the hang of the medium, you can work it out.

Shel: Didn't Noel Sickles influence your style of drawing in the early days?
Milt: Noel Sickles (whom I believe to be the best *natural* artist I have ever known) and I shared a studio in Columbus, Ohio after we had both been eased out of our newspaper jobs by the Depression. I lucked into a staff art spot at the Associated Press in New York, and Noel was also hired by AP after I started doing *Gay Thirties* and *Dickie Dare.* Shortly John Terry became ill and Sickles was handed the *Scorchy Smith* strip to ghost until Terry recovered. John died and Noel took on the strip as a full-time chore. And chore it was! Noel was bored stiff after the first few weeks of playing with the technology of the changeover. Since Sickles no longer was required to go to the office every day, he and I again shared a studio, split Frank Engli's salary as a lettering man and later, [Alfred] Andriola's pay as a general assistant. So much for the setting. Sickles was much more concerned with method and technique than with setting up a cartoon character whose name could become a household word and provide a lifetime income (hopefully). It was he who developed the use of the heavy black-and-white, light-and-shade style (which I gratefully followed) using a brush *first* for all shadows, then a quill pen for the light edges. This made the daily strips jump out of the pages composed of more or less straight comic styles, and on Sunday gave the drawings a dramatic sock which was an instant hit.

The important thing here is that the elaborate illustrative style could be applied to six strips and a Sunday page *by one man* during a normal (seven days and nights) working week. The old daily newspaper training paid off now. Sickles and I were fast enough that the staff men at the AP had asked each of us (when we came on from Columbus) to simmer down and not ruin a good thing for the other galley slaves. In sum, Noel Sickles contributed more to the success of the *Terry* drawings than any single person. He was only mildly interested in the story aspects of this field and he finally asked to be relieved of the *Scorchy* headache. Before he left the Associated Press, he turned to editorial cartoons, but found them boring after he had mastered the trick of making a masterful drawing without saying anything that would offend the client newspaper, no matter what its politics. Just before the war, Noel turned to commercial illustration, which gave him a greater scope for his enormous talents. When WWII began, he became a staff civilian illustrator in the Navy Department, then returned to the freelance field in 1945.

Shel: What is Steve Canyon's background?
Milt: Steve was a sophomore in college at the time of Pearl Harbor. He would have had a letter in football—he would have been there long enough for that. He would have been initiated into a fraternity. He would have done all that, yet he would have gone off for basic training in the spring of '42. Therefore, I can date from that, but I don't like to pin it down. People identify with him, "He's old enough to be my father," and stuff like that.

Shel: It's been quite a while since we've seen two of your best femme fatales: Delta and Madame Lynx. Are you ever going to bring them back?
Milt: Each of these puppets you put on the shelf, you know—these marionettes that hang on the string until you need them again. Then you pull them down—happily, because when you've got always enough cast, you've got everything you need. Even if you've left them in a jail somewhere, you could always spring them, as with Delta. It's always useful to have some device like the fact that she's wanted somewhere for something.

Shel: I notice that your famous signature went through a few changes until it looked as it does today.
Milt: Yes. The business about the square around the signature. My father was a printer on a little paper in the midwest, and I used to have

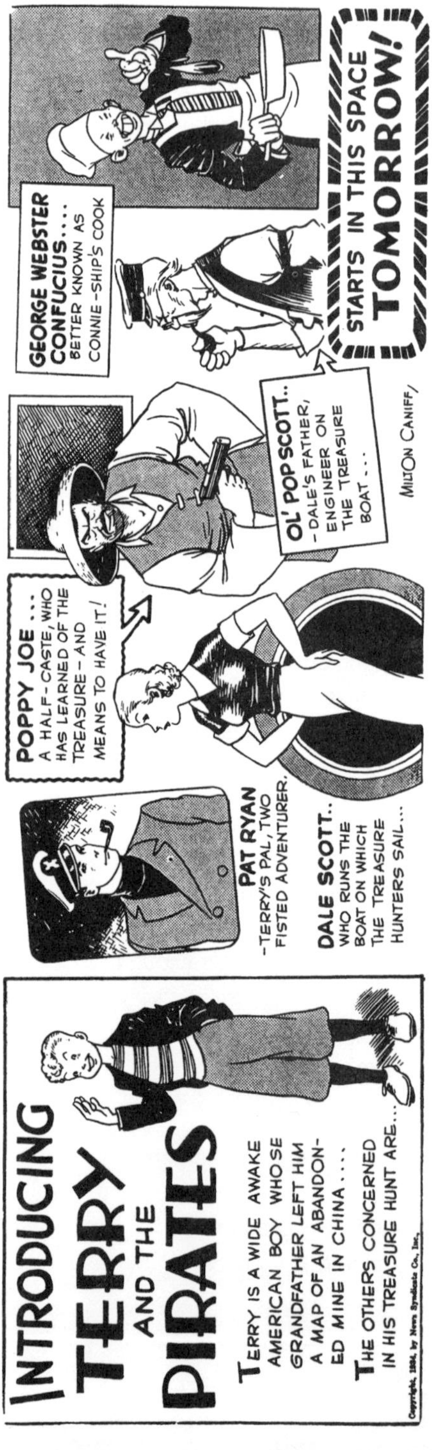
INTRODUCING TERRY AND THE PIRATES
TERRY IS A WIDE AWAKE AMERICAN BOY WHOSE GRANDFATHER LEFT HIM A MAP OF AN ABANDONED MINE IN CHINA . . . .
THE OTHERS CONCERNED IN HIS TREASURE HUNT ARE. . . .
Copyright, 1934, by News Syndicate Co., Inc.
PAT RYAN -TERRY'S PAL, TWO FISTED ADVENTURER.
DALE SCOTT.. WHO RUNS THE BOAT ON WHICH THE TREASURE HUNTERS SAIL...
POPPY JOE . . . A HALF-CASTE, WHO HAS LEARNED OF THE TREASURE - AND MEANS TO HAVE IT!
OL' POP SCOTT.. -DALE'S FATHER, ENGINEER ON THE TREASURE BOAT . . .
MILTON CANIFF
GEORGE WEBSTER CONFUCIUS.... BETTER KNOWN AS CONNIE-SHIP'S COOK
STARTS IN THIS SPACE TOMORROW!

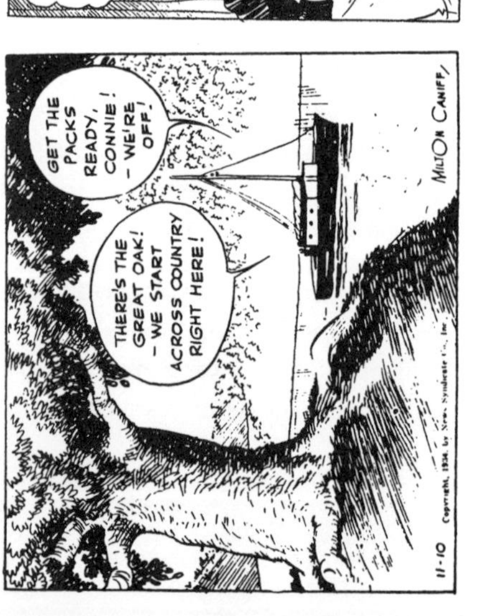
11-10
THERE'S THE GREAT OAK! - WE START ACROSS COUNTRY RIGHT HERE!
GET THE PACKS READY, CONNIE! - WE'RE OFF!
MILTON CANIFF
Copyright, 1934, by News Syndicate Co., Inc.

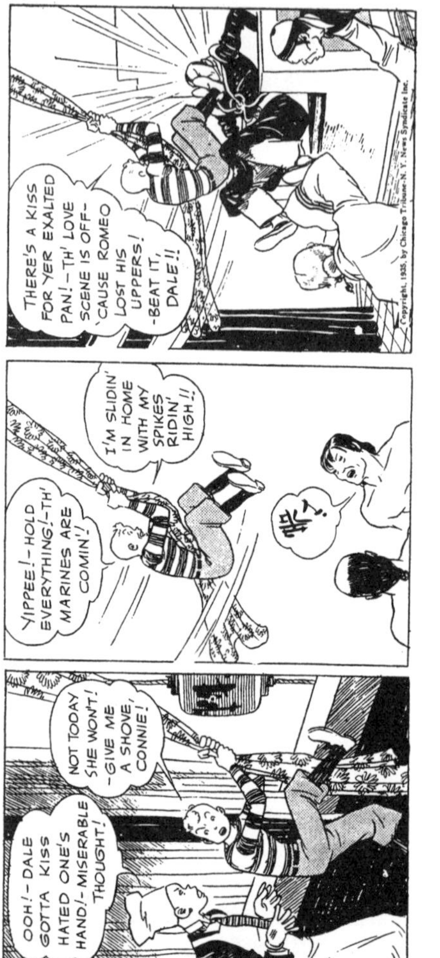
OOH!-DALE GOTTA KISS HATED ONE'S HAND!-MISERABLE THOUGHT!
NOT TODAY SHE WON'T! -GIVE ME A SHOVE, CONNIE!
YIPPEE!-HOLD EVERYTHING!-TH' MARINES ARE COMIN'!
I'M SLIDIN' IN HOME WITH MY SPIKES RIDIN' HIGH!!
THERE'S A KISS FOR YER EXALTED PAN!-TH' LOVE SCENE IS OFF-'CAUSE ROMEO LOST HIS UPPERS! -BEAT IT, DALE!!
Copyright, 1935, by Chicago Tribune-N.Y. News Syndicate Inc.

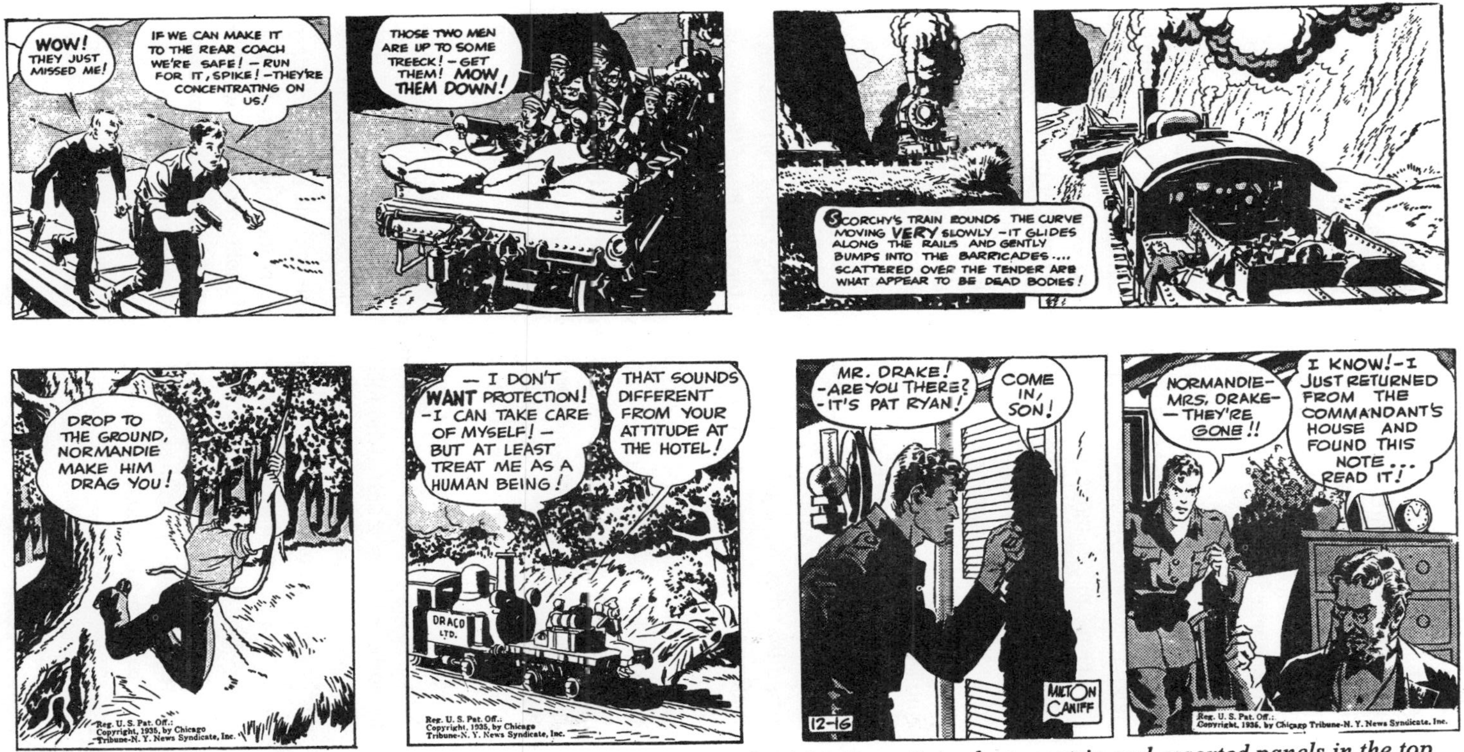

At first, Caniff drew Terry *in the same simple line style he used with* Dickie Dare *(introductory strip and assorted panels in the top two tiers). At about the same time, Noel Sickles was laying in dramatic black solids for shadows in his* Scorchy Smith *strip (third tier); Caniff began doing the same thing (assorted panels from* Terry*, bottom tier).*

trouble finding a place to sign my name. I couldn't sometimes find a place in the sky or the water or the woods, and he said, "Why don't you put the signature in a box like a postage stamp, and you could stick it anywhere!" I've always done that ever since, and I notice that some of the guys now use that same device.

Shel: Where is the best place to begin when one wants to become a cartoonist?
Milt: There are two best places to begin. One is to get a job as an assistant, which is difficult to do, of course. The danger of that is that you learn to draw too much like your boss, and it can get you sidetracked into being an assistant forever. The idea is to work for a guy for a while and then break away for your own things. The other method is to get a job in a publication house or a newspaper so you can learn the mechanics of the trade. Those are the two best ways. There are others, of course, but those are the surest ways in, because you meet the people and learn the trade. If you keep your mouth shut and your ears open, you can really learn the business. You also have guys looking at your work who ordinarily wouldn't see it. For instance, when I started *Dickie Dare* I was doing straight "bullpen" work at the Associated Press. I heard that they were going to drop one of their strips that was not making enough money, or whatever, and the guy (Bruce Russell was doing a strip for them at the time) was withdrawing and I heard this. I wouldn't have known it if I hadn't been working there. So the morning that strip left the service, I was waiting when the man got there. I had two weeks of *Dickie Dare* already drawn! All he had to do was start to run it. No editor can pass up a chance like this. I was already on the staff. We talked about money later. There is never enough money offered, but at least I was in. That was the point.

Shel: How do you view the cartoonist's role in our society?
Milt: We are the minstrel men. We occupy the same position as the banjo boys in this country who followed the wagon trains west and told their tales around the campfire at night, never ending their story so they would continue to eat. As someone has said of the American cartoon strip, two thousand years from today the way the anthropologists will learn how we felt and acted and spoke in our time will be by the daily comic strip—not of the news of the day, but by the way people reacted to things as they happened. We then represent this force. And to protect ourselves we have several devices we use. When you

very carefully develop this story: Boy meets girl, boy has lost girl, boy gets girl again . . . he says, "Darling I love you." She says, "Darling, I love *you.*" And he says we'll live happily ever after, won't we?" And she says, looking over his shoulder out the window, "Yes, sweetheart, but LOOK!" And in the last panel (it's always a French window and it's always raining outside), here is this sinister looking creature with the turned-down hat and the dark moustache. Well, you don't know who this guy is, and you have to buy tomorrow's newspaper to find out! Often, the cartoonist doesn't know who he is either, but he's got twenty-four hours to figure it out.

Shel: Milt, in the early days of your career, you were more of a cartoonist, then you gradually changed over to a realistic style. Why didn't you just stay with a cartoon style?
Milt: Just because the market was there. The market was for illustrations and not for cartooning. Remember, the cycle was going on where the cartoons were being phased out in favor of the semi-illustrated dramatic-story kind of feature. And, I was simply rolling with the punches. I would have stayed with the other thing if that would have sold.

Shel: It comes to mind, though, that you were really the forerunner in that direction. So you're really credited with actually creating the change, or the trend, that made comics more illustrative.
Milt: In terms of noisy acceptance of it, yes. Sickles was doing it in *Scorchy Smith*, but, unfortunately, it didn't run in that many newspapers. We had to search around in exchanges to find them.

Shel: Among your fellow cartoonists you are known as "General" Caniff; they kind of joke about it. You've been playing these war games for years. I know you—you're a very peace-loving man. Why this preoccupation with war?
Milt: Oh, it's the greatest of all dramas. As General Lee said, "It is good that war is so terrible; otherwise, we would come to love it." This is Lee. He was the most peaceful general ever. As skilled as he was, he was a man of peace. The macho comes out in a time of war. A lot of guys love it and they don't admit it. Especially the regular people—the regular army, the regular navy. It's probably what got them into the uniform in the first place. They did have an affinity for this, because it's like courtroom drama. A guy fighting for his life in a courtroom is the ultimate peacetime drama because this is him against the world. And in

wartime it carries that same theme to its ultimate end: a lot of me against a lot of you.

Shel: Do you think we'll ever do away with war?
Milt: No. It's a natural state of life. Everytime you say, "Damn it!" because the traffic's too thick, you're at war!

Shel: The Ohio State School of Journalism now has the Milton Caniff Library. Can you tell me about it?
Milt: It's the Communications Center, really. The library is a part of the Center. In the same building in which they have the library, and an area devoted entirely to my stuff, they have an electronic communications complex, with TV, videotape, and so on.

Shel: The library, then, actually serves a double purpose. It will be the final house, for all time, of your archives?
Milt: Yes. Everything "from the nipple to now" is the way they put it, which is kind of cute itself.

Shel: It comes pretty close, because I remember looking at a scrapbook that your mother kept. It showed a child's drawing you did when you were two years old. It was a crayon scribble, with blue on the top and green on the bottom for grass. So that's got to be the very beginning. I don't know of any cartoonist who has a library in his honor, but of course I don't know any other cartoonist who has pioneered as you have, in the writing as well as drawing. There actually is a Milton Caniff School of Drawing where many of the artists of today have been influenced by your work—clipped it and used it as a guide. This is probably what will happen with future cartoonists. They'll be able to go to the Milton Caniff Library at Ohio State and look up your work and study it.
Milt: What they have to do there is to give the viewer or the student of tomorrow a broad picture of not only what it's like to do these things, but what goes into it, how much it costs for the paper in 1935 and how much it costs today. All of this is catalogued there. The point of all this, of course, is to show how one person does it.

Shel: Your college days at Ohio State were probably the happiest days of your life. You build many of your plots around that college life.
Milt: Yes, it was an enormous experience. No one on either side of my family had ever gone near a college. So the simple experience of going to college was a great adventure to me. Also the simple business of having a library right there. It bugs me when people say there is no

opportunity. It didn't cost you a dime to go down and get a library card and go and read the best book ever written. Nobody is ever going to shove it in your head, you've got to find it yourself.

Shel: Books have always been important to you, haven't they?
Milt: Oh, yes. I've been very fortunate in that my father was a printer, so that introduced me to the simple world of the printed word. But, beyond that, I had great friends who gave me books to read. They were books that kids don't ordinarily find. For instance, I had never dreamed that there was a child's history of England, written by who? Dickens, that's who. And a nice gentleman that I knew was kind enough to let me read his copy in his house. This was simply opening a gate because he was a nice guy and he realized that I was a sponge. Children nowadays would rather watch TV, which is a sad thing. There is a lack of participation. There is nothing wrong with TV except for the fact that you don't do anything except look at it. The important thing about all of this is that you are participating. You have to read the book. You have to see the play.

Shel: You have always been a theater goer, haven't you?
Milt: Yes, I was happily lost in the dark cavern of live theater and films. We had an outdoor summer theater from Chataqua, New York. But then they began to send out road companies. Red Path was the name of one of those. They would set up a tent in town and run for a whole week, and each day a new entertainment feature would come in.

Shel: How old were you when you first saw these?
Milt: The first one I was aware of was when I was about seven or eight.

Shel: Being an impressionable child, when did all this input of seeing plays and movies start to come out in your work? About what time did you stop being an audience and become a performer? Or have you ever stopped becoming an audience?
Milt: No, I don't think you ever do. The point is, at some stage in all of us, I was doing what I am doing right this minute. I had a whole cast of characters in the canyons in Redlands, California, that I was playing with, and I had a hero named Tom Martin. He was the hero image character.

Shel: Was he really you?
Milt: Not me as much as the aspiration of me—the "Walter Mitty."

Shel: Your alter ego?

Milt: Yes. I could never make the athletic teams. At the fifth grade level you might make an intramural team, but you know perfectly well that you were never going to be on the varsity or that kind of stuff. So, almost invariably, the early stages of this was strictly adventures and had nothing to do with girls. That may have come later, if it did come. In the early phases of this, it was a Saturday-afternoon everyman's-heart thing.

Shel: Aren't you lucky that you were able to find a profession that would bring all of these things into a center stage where, through syndication, you would have an audience of millions.
Milt: It's timeless. This is one of the reasons why you can stay alive as long as I have been able to do in this type of work, because the idea of the handsome hero and the damsel in distress is absolutely, utterly endless.

Shel: What caused you to constantly improve your technique? Is there some little bug in the back of your head that says, "Caniff, that's not good enough"?
Milt: I think part of it is running scared, because, as Jack Benny used to say, "I'm always auditioning." In a very real sense, it is that. And Benny also said that one of the biggest problems in his field these days is that there is no place to be lousy anymore. You are always on center stage because of television. In every sense it is true in this field, in that I was able to get away with things as a kid on the *Miami News* or the *Dayton Journal* where there was not much at stake, and I was able to do as if I was doing the big time syndication stuff. We live by the sword, so you've got to keep it sharp.

Shel: What was the first feedback you got from an audience for your nationally syndicated work? When did you realize the effect you were having on the American public?
Milt: It certainly wasn't immediate. You can tell with the syndication list increasing monthly that the people were buying it. The first indication of that, by the way, was the *New York Daily News,* and the *Chicago Tribune* did not start it at the beginning. But two weeks, I think, after it began to run in New York, the *Chicago Tribune* picked it up and ran all of the two weeks that it was missing.

Shel: What was your fan mail like?
Milt: It was good fan mail, right off the bat. People were believing in the characters. They weren't talking about good drawing or any of that

sort of thing. That came later from other cartoonists. From very early on, you realize the one great danger of this thing is that you can't please everybody. You've got to do stuff to please the guy who buys the paper.

Shel: What's the difference?
Milt: The difference is that the guy who buys the paper doesn't see the sweat behind the creation, like another cartoonist does. All the fan sees is the end product.

Shel: If your strip didn't go, would you have made your living in another way?
Milt: Oh, yes, surely. In those days, it was possible to make a pretty good living free-lancing around in New York. You could sell illustrations to magazines and various ad markets. But I was anxious to connect with a steady income, to get the rent paid. The important thing is to pay for the light and the rent and the food. It gives you elbow room. You don't want to be harassed by bill collectors milling around.

Shel: Had you ever thought that you might someday be real competition to Norman Rockwell, for instance, and go after the *Saturday Evening Post* covers?
Milt: Sure, if I could get away with it, I was going to try.

Shel: While you were doing *Terry* did anyone contact you to draw a pretty girl for a magazine cover? For example, the Jon Whitcomb girl became very popular. Were you ever approached to do a Milt Caniff girl?
Milt: No, but I was so immersed in a daily production schedule that I wouldn't have had time in the first place. And mostly, the art directors around town knew that. They knew that I didn't have the time to do 27 illustrations a week and still do covers.

Shel: How did you find the time to put in all that detail?
Milt: I knew these guys were enjoying the wealth of military details. I got letters about that, saying, "Oh, boy, that tank really looks like the one I had."

Shel: And that takes time, to draw all those nuts and bolts and everything.
Milt: Yes, but you're a sucker for your own racket, you know. And all I needed was a little encouragement.

Shel: You really love to draw, don't you?
Milt: Well, actually, the satisfaction of drawing is the one thing that keeps you from going out of your skull from the challenge of every week, having to fill up space, but not having to fill it with a bunch of bookkeeping from last week is the saving thing. Each drawing is a brand-new adventure. If you don't treat it that way, then you really are in trouble. The guy who does the same figures over and over again must have a hard time sleeping at night. With me, it's "Wow, let's shoot that from another angle; let's do it from a low or from the side or from the roof or something." And then it comes out fine.

Shel: After all these years, do you still enjoy seeing your work in the paper?
Milt: Oh, absolutely. It's like eating and drinking. I can't do without it. You are so happy when you see a decent piece of metal or plastic reproduction that you really do your best.

Shel: The business gets pretty hairy at times. You've been the victim of overzealous salesmen from other syndicates who try to push their strip and have your strip dropped. What's your answer to this?
Milt: It's not printable! I know that this is a calculated risk, in that your chances of success are exactly so much and you've got just so many papers that are printed. And you fight for your share of them. But if somebody, without thinking, throws you out, that's not a fair trial. The best example of all this is the incident in Columbia, Missouri, where another strip was being bought by the paper and *Steve Canyon* was to be thrown out. Through some miracle of local loyalty or whatever, they decided to put it up for trial—that is, to show a sampling of the new strip and run a one-on-one poll. Well, *Steve Canyon* won, eleven to one. Now, you don't often get that chance to prove yourself. This is the sad part. They would bring in a new strip without asking anybody about it. They would take a survey, the survey being two guys standing in the men's room, saying, "Well, my cousin Minnie doesn't like this, so out it goes." And, sometimes on that thin level of critical attitude, the editor will throw something out of a paper.

Shel: Well, where does the public come in?
Milt: They don't—they don't get a chance.

Shel: Well, the public buys the paper and adopts comic strip characters as part of their family. This is an American tradition. Now what happens when a strip is dropped? What should the public do?

Milt: Well, the public's got to react immediately, not wait around to see if maybe it was lost in the mail or something. If it's a favorite strip, holler immediately. Call the editor on the phone and give him hell. If you really feel this way about it, he'll listen to you. And this has happened, time and time again. If enough noise is made, the feature will be put back in the paper—it happens all the time. But if no noise is made, they think the public doesn't care. And, unfortunately, sometimes the public does care. There are some people who read *Steve Canyon* who wouldn't dream of writing a letter to the editor. They just aren't letters-to-the-editor writers. And this has cost me a lot of papers—when the chips were down, these people just didn't react. They might have regretted it greatly and said so, but they didn't say it at the right moment and loud enough. This is what must be done.

Shel: If an editor said to you, "Mr. Caniff, you've been doing *Steve Canyon* since 1947 and we feel that we need a newer strip in the paper, what would your answer be?
Milt: I don't think I've ever been asked that question. I'm never consulted about these things.

Shel: Well, how do you feel about keeping up-to-date with the times? Do you think that a new generation of readers is born every few years?
Milt: Yes, about every ten years, roughly. A complete changeover every ten years, and sometimes more rapidly than that. After the war started, I gained a whole new audience because *Stars and Stripes* carried *Terry and the Pirates.* After the war, I was able to make the switch to *Steve Canyon* at the absolute peak of my popularity.

Shel: You once told me that there is a psychology and a way of playing the game in the comic strip business. Some people have it and they survive, and others don't and they fall by the wayside, regardless of the quality of their work. It has to be an understanding of the politics. What are the politics in the comic strip industry?
Milt: The politics are generally supply-and-demand—or, rather, need and fulfillment—[for] something that is obviously grabbing the public, such as *Peanuts.* It is interesting, always, to point out the fact that *Peanuts* took six years to reach the position of being in the enviable circumstances.

Shel: Would an editor these days wait six years for a strip to catch on?
Milt: Six weeks is more like it. Six days is more and more like it. And there is enough material around, with the number of newspapers dimin-

ished as they have in recent times, that you have no recourse. You're on trial for your life. And, boy—thumbs down and out you go. It would be tough to start a new adventure-type strip these days, even though the syndicate editors now are saying, "Continuity, continuity!" *Spider-Man* is the best example that comes to my mind—that this is being bought and accepted. The premise is still there that they don't need us as they once did, simply because we, the continuity people, were used as a come-on for the newspapers to outfox the opposition. "Read my paper because you must find out what happened. Did Andy Gump make it to Congress or not? Did Orphan Annie catch up with Sandy or not?"

All that was a circulation-grabbing device, and a very good one. But now, when all the papers are owned by the same company, it doesn't matter. They don't even want circulation anymore. Most newspapers would like to be able to print ten copies and charge all of their advertisers full national rates.

Shel: To get into the theatrics of a strip, all of your characters have always had a kind of fascinating appeal, and I don't think you have repeated yourself. How do you go about creating a new character for the strip *Steve Canyon*?
Milt: Well, first of all, as you know, there are two ways of bringing the character to life, either taking someone from real life, as I did with Flip Corkin in *Terry and the Pirates,* who was Phil Cochran, an actual colonel in the Air Force and all the rest of it. His speech was so colorful, yet it was soldier talk, a regular Army Air Corpsman.

Shel: Now, Milt, these last few years there have been a lot of *Terry and the Pirates* reprints, and although George Wunder worked on *Terry* for a good 26 years after you left the strip, they just reprint *your* Terry and the Pirates. I don't hear many people really talking about George Wunder's version. You have been doing *Steve Canyon* now, and in *Steve Canyon* you have a much wider range. The plays—the dramas that you present—are much broader and much more exciting than *Terry* was. *Terry,* to me, had a certain naivete as a boy's adventure strip, but *Steve Canyon* really has the whole spectrum of human experience. Does it bother you to see more accent on *Terry* than on *Canyon,* or do you think that someday, maybe twenty years from now, people will be nostalgic about *Steve Canyon*?
Milt: I don't know. I haven't thought about that. But one thing is true, and it has to be accepted as a simple fact: You do a calculated risk here.

Tastes, generally, in cartoons changes. Just about the time that the war ended. Maurice Horn was right about that. Alex Raymond and I didn't realize that at the end of WWII the whole world would be recreated, and we're continuing with those changes. It didn't happen overnight. It took quite a while for it to take place. But the *Terry and the Pirates* way of thinking ended with WWII. The whole approach to cartooning began to change just at that time, and the world that *Terry* represented was no longer going to be. After the war, the cycle of the popular gag strip of today began to assert itself. Suddenly these boys were moving in on us the way we had moved in our predecessors.

Shel: In *Steve Canyon* you've sometimes used the strip as a vehicle to inform the public of a real situation. It was happening and you had your Steve Canyon go in and calm down the townsfolk. Through the strip you were doing more good than all the public relations men in the Service could have done. What compelled you to make your strip more than just a vehicle of entertainment? Because this is the difference between *Canyon* and *Terry*. *Terry* was pure escapist entertainment, but *Canyon* began to get into serious problems.
Milt: Well, go back to one thing. In the *Terry* syndrome the great horrible fact of war hung over everything. This hangs in there and the audience doesn't need to be reminded of it. It's there all the time. When I was doing a drug sequence for *Canyon*, for instance, I had to explain where the danger was. During war time itself, I didn't have to tell them where the danger was or who the enemy was. The enemy very often, in peacetime sequences such as this, was across the street. It may be the kid next door who is pushing.

Shel: I read recently where they caught a teacher who was pushing drugs.
Milt: I'm not surprised. It almost had to come to that. It simply had to. The teacher would need the money and would get trapped into this. I remember a teacher, when I was in college, who was making whiskey downstairs from where I lived. I had an apartment at that time, as I did all through school, because I had to work during holidays. So I had a civilian-type apartment off the campus, and a young professor and his wife lived above me. They made whiskey and they were caught and they were sentenced to stiff terms. We were drinking beer and that kind of thing—just as much a violation of Prohibition as they were doing, except they were making it. Nobody arrested you for drinking it, only for making it. It was a good lesson. It really was. It cost them a

lot, but it certainly taught the rest of us to butt out of that kind of thing. They were nice people, and we hated to see them caught up in this, but they made their own bed. It's kind of like smuggling marijuana in from Mexico. You know what the penalties are. You don't have to be told what happens if you get caught. If you want to take that risk, it's your neck.

Shel: Do you get any feedback from these particular episodes? Do you know when some episode you have written has done some good somewhere?
Milt: A good case in point is something that is current as we are talking. The President's Committee for Employment of the Handicapped is always very pleased when we do something about someone with a handicap. You don't have to give a solution, just show the kind of problems that can occur to a kid in a wheelchair, like having a cop say you are a fake, throw you down on the ground, find out you are not a fake, and be very apologetic about it. You don't encounter this sort of thing in your personal life, but you can imagine how awful it would be, how embarrassing it would be.

Shel: I remember the line where the kid says, after the guy apologizes, "Sorry, but I haven't been ordained." That was great.
Milt: It just ran last week, and people will write in about it. They also write in about such things as my pipeline character [Pipeline Polly, who worked the Alaskan oil pipeline, selling "encyclopedias" to maintenance men], pointing out, to my astonishment, that she's a prostitute!

Shel: I just thought she sold encyclopedias. She *was* friendly!
Milt: The price was high, that's all.

Shel: Has anybody pointed out to you that you are one of the longest-running playwrights since Shakespeare?
Milt: No, I hadn't thought of it in those terms, but it's true.

Shel: You come up with a new play every thirteen weeks, don't you?
Milt: Yes. They are plays, because I am an actor, script girl, camera man, and all the rest. Therefore, it must be treated as theatrical. I'm a director when I have the hat on backwards.

Shel: Milt, for years—ever since you were a young kid yourself—you've done these personal appearances before esteemed groups. Are you still doing this in Palm Springs?

Milt: Yes. One of these is the breakfast held once a month called the Mayor's Breakfast. It's held by the Chamber of Commerce for different groups that are interested in the commercial aspects of Palm Springs. The group of people, men and women, are called ambassadors who meet incoming flights of hotshots, the president or people on that level.

Shel: In your career you've had many honors awarded to you. You and Mrs. Caniff were invited to dinner at the White House as guests of President Ford; the Mayor of New York proclaimed Milton Caniff Day in New York. Why is it that Milton Caniff gets all these honors just through writing and illustrating a comic strip?
Milt: Well, every now and then the thing takes on the tone of extra territoriality, I suppose, in that just supporting the Air Force alone will make a feeling of warmth and gratitude. It's publicity, essentially. Many people are grateful in that sense. And this is just the nature of this product.

Shel: You also feel a responsibility to stress your patriotism, and you are really one of the most prominent patriots of our time. Do you feel a responsibility as an artist who has such a wide audience to give the public a little more than just pure adventure?
Milt: Oh, yes. It's an old adage that you've got to have something to say in order to justify your place. And if you relied entirely on entertainment, then you would be doing an endless tap dance on the street, in effect. You've got to sell your point, whatever your point is.

Shel: But now you have to share your audience with a TV screen. Now, I know that in *Steve Canyon* you would be censored from showing too much sex and violence in your strip. Television doesn't seem to have those restrictions. The public has developed an appetite for this stuff through repetition on TV.
Milt: The appetite was always there, and I'll tell you who is responsible for it. It is U.S. Steel, Proctor & Gamble—it's whoever wants to sell something. They'll buy the shows that the public wants and will go for them, which is violence and sex. The air has opened up commercial exploitation, which doesn't have to be, because the air belongs to everybody. But now you have to pay for it. Television is shoved down your throat. You can't get the set turned off fast enough to avoid the pitch, or some x-rated thing that comes on before you had time to remember it's nine o'clock.

Shel: With *Steve Canyon* you play to a mass audience. How do you get around going into a lot of violence and excess?
Milt: You tell the same tale, but you tell it in a different way. You don't use the explicit sex, or the explicit gore for that matter. And I convey the same feeling. Of course, in very short takes.

Shel: For a playwright, an entertainer, and an illustrator such as you are, to have such a long career—how do you hoped to be remembered? Would you like to be remembered as a great artist, writer, patriot, or would you like to see these *Canyon* stories that you've written for daily newspapers go into another form, say, perhaps a television or radio show in the future? Do you think the future will treat you kindly?
Milt: This is something that I had to examine in my own mind very early on. And I came to one conclusion: There has to be a singleness of purpose. And that is like the alcoholics, one day at a time. The hell with the future. You do the best job, and you do it today. Let the future take care of itself. I simply cannot occupy myself with what I hope will occur, or whatever. I am delighted, for instance, that Ohio State has taken all this memorabilia and so forth, which I cherished and loved deeply. That is one thing I was concerned about. What the hell was going to happen to all this great stuff that I've got piled up which was a tool to me? It's like making a will. You want to leave whatever you have to leave behind you to the right person, but how are you going to know who the right person is? So I've just got to leave this stuff and let posterity take care of itself.

Shel: Would you want your strip to be continued by another artist and writer after you die?
Milt: We're back to the original premise again. If it would make a good income for my heir, in this case my wife, that's the whole thing. If somebody could come along and carry it on and make an income from it, then hurray for him. I hope he's the best in the business, and that he lasts for years and years and years.

Shel: Well, Milton Caniff, you'd be a tough act to follow, and I thank you very much for your time this afternoon.
Milt: Thank you, Shel.

I'm Just a Troubadour Singing for My Supper: An Interview with One of the Masters of Comic Art

ARN SABA / 1978

From *The Comics Journal,* May 1986, pp. 60–102. Reprinted by permission.

Creator of a comic book feature called Neil the Horse, *Saba was a Canadian cartoonist on assignment to interview for radio broadcast some of the masters of the American comic strip arts. Caniff was his first interview, and Saba rented a car in Los Angeles and drove to Caniff's California studio in Palm Springs in September 1978.*

Milton Caniff walked briskly into the room, and the floor seemed to shift under me, throwing me off balance as if there were an earthquake. He smiled warmly, welcomed me, shook my hand, and it was all a dream to me—a dream come true. It was as if I had scaled the heights of Olympus, and was meeting one of the Gods, one the architects of my world and myself. For as long as I have been reading, I have been reading Caniff. His interests, his ideas, his fantasies, and his ways of expression, have had a major influence on the course of my life; and thus I was, in fact, meeting one of my creators.

. . . .

The ostensible aim of all this was for me to create a six-part series of half-hour programs for the CBC Radio Network, about comic strips. My original working title was "Toward a Critical Theory of the Comic Strip," a title which too clearly revealed my tendencies toward academia. My producer re-named the series "The Continuous Art," which was snappier but which said approximately nothing of my aim, which was to examine the very best of the world's comic strips (and comic books), and try to figure out why—why, oh why!?!—this art form is almost universally looked down upon, sneered at, and insulted by the arbiters of taste and culture. This mattered to me, and still does, since comics are among the few species of literature that I really understood. Yet I admitted that with a small number of exceptions, comics have generally failed to hit the heights of sophistication of most literature. So I wanted to know: is there some flaw inherent in the medium? Is there something about the combination of words and pictures that necessarily limits the subject matter? Or were the critics, perhaps, using the wrong standards? Could there be another set of critical standards, a different critical language for considering the merits of this hugely popular medium? As I hurtled down the highway, my intention was to put this kind of question to Milton Caniff, who had, after all, done more to advance the subtlety of comic strips than almost any other single cartoonist—and who was also one of the best-read comic strip artists of all time.

I was given a brief tour of Caniff's comfortable but modest studio. It was explained to me that his home was a few blocks away, and that in fact his "real" home was in New York, where he spent half the year. (He has since given up his Palm Springs residence entirely.) He then suggested that we go for lunch. His friendliness and utter lack of pretension were disarming and immediately endearing. This is a man it would be impossible to dislike. We drove in his big luxurious car to a nearby restaurant, with him all the while chatting and joking as if we had known each other for years. I suspect I must have babbled nervously and foolishly. Caniff regularly hobnobs with Presidents and movie stars. I had come prepared to sit at the master's feet, but I was not quite ready to sit in his car. Over lunch—which he insisted on paying for—he interspersed his answers to my serious questions with a wonderful torrent of reminiscences, jokes and stories about his friends, most of whom also happened to be the greatest cartoonists alive. Need I repeat that I was dazzled?

Back at the studio, he did me the most extraordinary and gracious favor of all, which I failed to really appreciate until a few years later when I became a somewhat professional cartoonist. He submitted without complaint, and with the most perfect gentlemanly generosity, to about five hours of never-ending questions. He must have thought I would never go away, and that he would never get back to his work. Only a cartoonist with perpetual deadlines can truly understand what those five hours meant to him. They probably meant the difference between having a hot dinner and eating a sandwich—and between a good night's sleep and a late night at the studio. Mr. Caniff, eight years later, if you are reading this—thank you. I didn't know what I was doing to you. Those hours are among the most treasured of my life, and the manner in which you gave them makes them all the more precious to me. There is nothing more admirable than generosity.

The result, of course, is the interview which you will read if you manage to get through this introduction (or if you skip this introduction). I think it is a very interesting, enlightening, and complete interview, and gives a very good picture of Milton Caniff's thinking. You will see, however, that despite my repeated rephrasing of the same basic question—are comics Art or aren't they?—that he never truly addressed what I wanted to discuss. And as it turns out, that lack of discussion was his answer. He doesn't think about it. He doesn't care. He probably wouldn't know how to think about that question if he wanted to. At the time, this drove me crazy. I couldn't believe it. How could he *not* think about it, considering his achievements? Didn't he think that his terrific ability to portray character, to convey mood, to evoke emotion, gave him the right to *demand* to be taken seriously? The answer, apparently, was no. His answer was, as he often has said, he just wants to sell newspapers.

It made no difference to me that this was exactly the same attitude held by such historic greats as Bach, Dickens, Hiroshige, and probably even Shakespeare. Dammit, I knew this stuff was serious because it was *my* literature, *my* cultural underpinnings.

. . . .

Today, with *Canyon* nearly 40, and the still incredibly-productive Caniff nearly 80, it is unavoidable to view the strip as being in its twi-

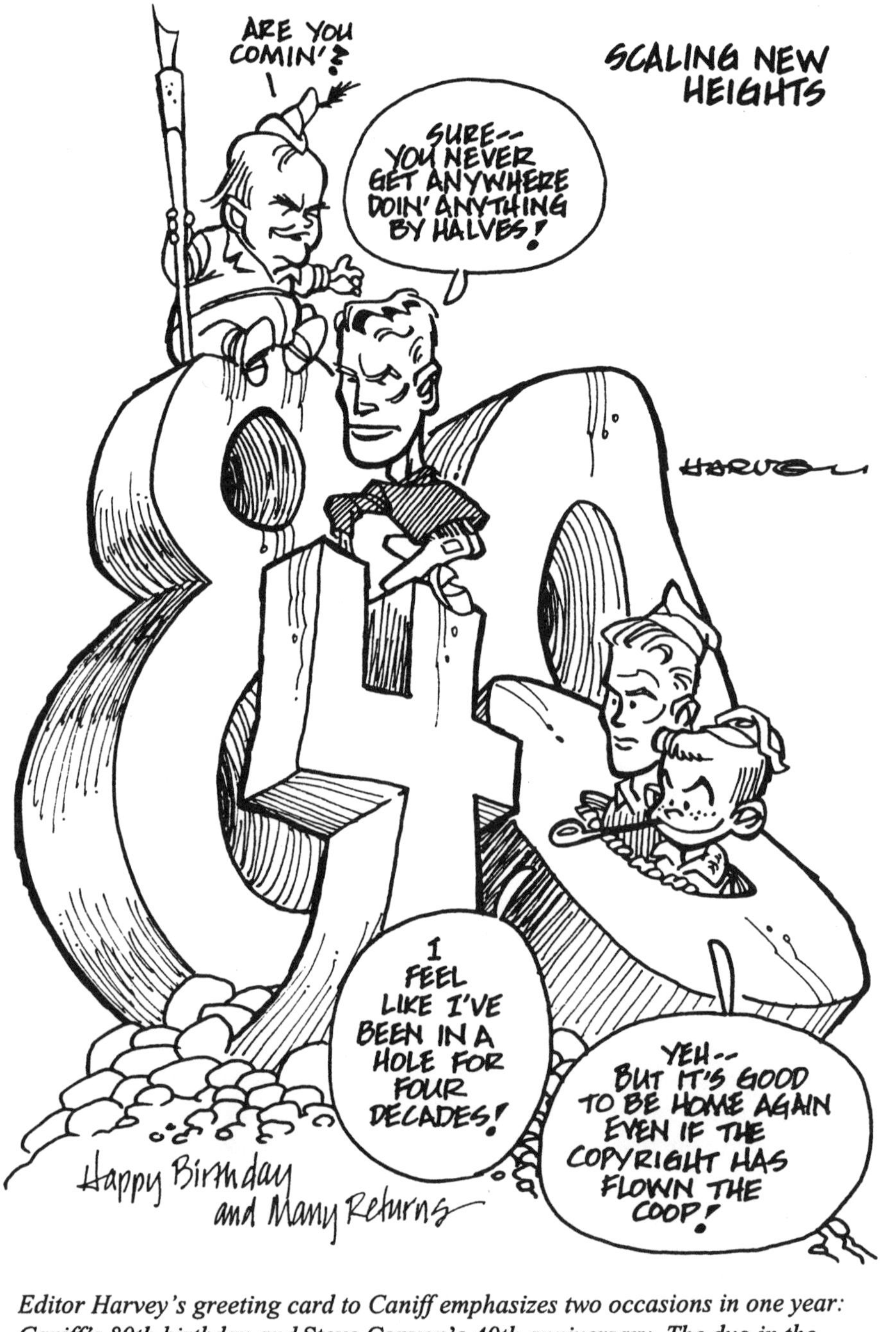

Editor Harvey's greeting card to Caniff emphasizes two occasions in one year: Caniff's 80th birthday and Steve Canyon's *40th anniversary. The duo in the hole are Terry and Hotshot Charlie, who speculates on the status of the vintage strip's copyright.*

light years. Contributing to this feeling are the depradations of Caniff's most difficult challenge of all—the Incredible Shrinking Comic Strip. Daily strips used to be eight or ten inches wide in the newspaper. Now they are about three inches. They cover about one-fifth of the square area that they did when Caniff began his career. The number of words possible in a day's strip is fewer than he used to be able to get into one panel. He has three panels per day, as opposed to four or five much bigger panels that he used to be able to work with. Many papers do not carry the Sunday page, and some carry *only* the Sunday page. Against all these restrictions and diminishments, he is still faced with the requirement of telling a coherent story that is continued from day to day, in which he not only wants to build suspense and invent clever plot twists, but also, if possible, portray character and maybe even draw a few decent pictures once in a while. How could anyone do all that? Ask Caniff. He does it.

With over half a century of experience behind him, he knows how many words to use to keep his readers' attention. He is an expert at pacing, and he knows how to suggest a great deal with very little detail. Caniff's writing has become the narrative equivalent of his famous drawing style—it is impressionistic, telling more than it shows. It is an incredible feat, and yet another innovation in a career that has been notable for innovation. It is Caniff's final triumph, keeping alive the adventure strip in an environment that has become so hostile to it. He not only keeps it alive, but he does so with energy and invention. Fresh new characters and situations continue to appear; plus we have the added resonance which comes with the strip's long tenure. When old friends or enemies return, they bring with them their long histories, and all the sentimentality implicit in ritual exchanges and renewed relationships. There is deep pleasure in seeing the old master storyteller at work.

In the end, any reservations about his politics give way to affection for a man who so obviously loves doing his work, and who is so very good at it. For me, practically weaned on his creations, his artistic and moral influence on me is permanent, and I am very glad. I have the greatest respect for Milton Caniff, as an artist and as a gentleman. Throughout the following interview, you will observe his gentlemanly attitude toward an eager young cartoonist.

Arn Saba: I'll start out with theoretical questions, and we'll see where we go from there. As I showed you with my outline, I'm working on an

attempt to set up some sort of critical standards for comics, because I think they've been greatly misjudged and misunderstood. I'd like to ask, first of all, what you feel about serious criticism of comics.
Milton Caniff: Well, criticism of comics, as such, is a kind of empty phrase. Who cares, really? It's interesting that somebody might decide suddenly that we have a social significance or not. But, we're not in business for that purpose. We're in business to sell newspapers, and the criticism, acceptance, or whatever, lies in the fact that we are in hundreds of newspapers, and that the readership of something like *Peanuts* is in the millions every day. It's in about 1,900 newspapers, as is *Blondie,* which is seldom mentioned any more because everyone takes *Blondie* for granted, but *Blondie*'s in as many papers and as many translations as *Peanuts,* and has been for a lot longer than any of the other strips now extant.

Saba: Now, I understand from what you said that what I call "criticism of comics" doesn't terribly interest you. I would have thought that as an artist you would be interested in people's comments.
Caniff: Oh, I am. I'm speaking generally now. Personally, I'm very much interested in what people think, not just of me, but of the state of the art itself. But I mention this only because of the fact that I've read critical articles that were about to put us all out of business, and the next year some new thing like *Hagar the Horrible* comes along and knocks all of the pins down. People accept it or they don't accept it. If we're suddenly turned out like a government is turned out after an election, then we'd be turned out and that's the end of it. But we have our place simply because we know where the funnybone is. Or the ghoulish attitude, or the storytelling lure of a Scheherazade tale that is endless, because Scheherazade didn't want the old boy to cut the girls' throats.

Saba: And that's exactly what you're doing. [Laughter]
Caniff: Exactly, except it's our throats.

Saba: You said in an interview with Shel Dorf in the *Buyer's Guide* that you feel like you're a troubadour singing for your supper.
Caniff: Of course. And endlessly so. So you become very ingenious just to stay alive. And we must be entertaining. We have no social significance as such, in terms of what we think about it. It may end being socially significant, or accepted, or whatever, but at the time, almost without exceptions, it was a way to make a living. It starts that way, anyway.

Saba: I think I see an interesting dichotomy, because so many people, particularly younger people like myself, who are cartoonists and critics, take comics a lot more seriously, it seems, than the cartoonists themselves. They ascribe a lot of aesthetic motives and a lot of depth to the work of the cartoonists, and I've heard other interviews with cartoonists, such as Carl Barks, who just always say, "Well, we're just making a living, it's not that artistic, it's not that aesthetic," and so on.
Caniff: Let me take it just one step beyond that, in that we are delighted to have somebody think that there is an importance, a significance, or an important significance. [*Laughter*]. The great thing about it is that you start out just making a living. Then, it's rather surprising to learn, as, for instance, a politician will learn, that he can sway people. Suddenly, you feel a surge of power within yourself. The trick is not to take it so seriously that you begin to believe your own press notices, and use it as a tool. I've had kids, for instance, ask me, "Isn't it disconcerting to you to think that these new cartoonists got into this business, and will say so in interviews, because of *you*?" And I say I'm delighted, of course, but essentially all of this is just pleasure, and then I use it as a tool, to make my point. Let them make their own points when the time comes to make it. I'm pleased as punch to think that I've had that much influence, but now suddenly I've created a Frankenstein monster. They're my rivals! Down with this! . . . I'm kidding, of course.

Saba: The longer you go on, the more you're going to see that, of course.
Caniff: Well, the art of survival is what it is. It is with me, it is with them. In the backstage context, that is. You don't tell this to the lay public, of course. You're out there to be entertaining. Am I entertaining or am I not? That's all there is to it. Just like any troubadour.

Saba: From the business point of view, that's exactly what you're up against.
Caniff: Of course. You don't have a choice in this. They'll poke you off the stage without anything you can do. If they don't like you any longer, down you go.

Saba: It's happened to many.
Caniff: Oh, alas. Because the bright new guys are coming along. Which is as it should be. This is a jungle, like any other entertainment, and if you can't cut it, then down you go.

Saba: The theory is, of course, that keeps the best quality being published.
Caniff: Well, when you feel the buckshot on your behind, you run faster.

Saba: You say that you're auditioning every day, and that's obviously what's kept you in the business for so long.
Caniff: Yeah, and I haven't lost my enthusiasm for it, for a couple of reasons. One is the fact that the kind of work I do is no repeats. It's not like a bookkeeping system where you have to do the same thing over and over. That would just drive me nuts. And all the years that I've been at this thing, I've never drawn two panels the same. Ever.

Saba: Not that you know of, anyway.
Caniff: Well, it doesn't occur to you at the time, but when you have two people talking, you still shift the camera around, so to speak, so that it isn't dull for the viewer, and it also isn't dull for you.

Saba: This is one of the things that you're justifiably famous for. You really initiated that technique of being able to have a lot of dialogue go on in a comic strip by shifting the camera angles, as they're called. I don't believe that was done at all before you came along, or at least, not to any extent.
Caniff: No, it wasn't, generally speaking. I was seeking some device, something to make it noisy, and to make a grab for the audience. Part of it was the heavy blacks. It made the thing just look noisy on the page, and draw your attention that way. The other thing was, when you started to read it, you weren't riveted to one point of view across a horizon, you see.

Saba: There's one very famous *Terry and the Pirates* page that I think is reprinted in Ron Goulart's *The Adventurous Decade,* where there's a woman talking to a man behind a desk. First of all, she's getting to the building in a rickshaw, and then she goes into the building, and she's talking to this guy. I think it was Drusilla Crail. But the point is that in that strip, you go up above her, you go behind her, and you go behind him and to one side and the other, and down below, and over the place, and really all that's happened in that page is that these people are talking to each other. And you made this fantastically dramatic. I didn't even notice until it was pointed out to me in this book that nothing physically was going on. And I found that to be a fascinating thing. There's another famous one where Pat Ryan is talking on the telephone

about something. I've forgotten what, and you move literally in a circle around him. He's just sitting, talking on the phone, and you've gone right around in a big circle. And you've made it dramatic. And I think that's an extremely important innovation.
Caniff: It's the kind of thing that the good directors do. Hitchcock, for instance, does this very effectively, and I probably picked it up from him, or from some other director before him that I liked. And I used the movies' technique simply because the movies were accepted, and I was simply trailing along behind them in a different medium. And, I would do this with storylines, too. I would read *Saturday Evening Post* and *Colliers* and things of that day, to see what was being read by people. When I came along in a different medium, I could almost play the same tune on a different horn and grab the same people.

Saba: Aha. So it was quite a conscious attempt to do that.
Caniff: Oh, yes. Indeed. I tried to do that, and it was hard to get established. As I told you earlier, it's always a bad time to start a new comic strip. That's what they told me the first day I ever started in the business. I had six turn-downs before I was able to score with *Dickie Dare.*

Saba: Didn't you do something even before that? You did *Colonel Gilfeather.*
Caniff: Well, that was simultaneously. I was on the staff at the Associated Press when the man who was doing *Gilfeather* became ill, and they put [Al] Capp on the thing, and he was miserable doing this. He wasn't attuned to it at all. It was kind of a road company *Major Hoople* in the story, in the first place. And there was the boarding-house braggart sort of person. So Capp finally just said he wanted no more of it, and went back to Boston. They just dumped it into my lap because I was staff. And, you just do it because you do it. And then, I was able to change that title, with the permission of the AP editors, to *Gay Thirties.*

Saba: Oh, that's where *Gay Thirties* came from.
Caniff: I hated it as much as Capp did, but I could grind it out. But I didn't want to grind it out. I wanted to do something that was fun to do, and *Gay Thirties* was it.

Saba: And when you got to *Terry,* obviously, you really got your teeth into it.
Caniff: Well, *Dickie Dare* was a sort of warm-up for *Terry,* as it turned out. I didn't know that at the time, of course. But I was doing that in

New York, and it appeared in the *New York Sun.* The publisher of the *New York Daily News* saw it, and then asked me if I'd be interested in doing a strip of that sort for the *New York Daily News,* which of course I very much was. So that became *Terry.*

Saba: Well, it's interesting how you say it's always a bad time to start a strip. Your story about *Terry* is encouraging, really.
Caniff: Yes, it should be encouraging. I mean it to be. Don't listen to the howls of ill portent. Just fly in the face of it. Starve a little. A case in point of starving—when I was finishing up on *Dickie Dare,* it was running in the *New York Sun,* and I was paid on acceptance, and that was six weeks lead time. When I started *Terry and the Pirates* I was paid on publication, which was a full six weeks lead time; four weeks dailies. I was caught in between. I had strips running in the *New York Sun,* and the *New York News,* and I couldn't pay my rent.

Saba: [*Laughter*] So you hung in there, as they say.
Caniff: I went to the manager of the building I was living in, and told him this dilemma. He was a layman, who you wouldn't think would understand this. But he did understand it, and he let me hang on the hook for a while, until I got my first paycheck.

Saba: To go back to something that we were talking about before, you said that you studied the films and the stories to learn what techniques might be effective and saleable and so on. Were you conscious, when you were introducing such techniques, that you were expanding the medium?
Caniff: I don't think I was conscious of it from the point of view of what would now be retrospection. At the time I was just trying to forge out ahead of the crowd, like a distance runner, in a marathon, and to get out there and stay out there. I never thought of it in terms of posterity. I didn't even bother to save the originals. It was of the moment.

Saba: That's something that astounds cartoonists now, because we're all hanging on to our originals, and thinking we're all such great artists. You seem to have always had this attitude that you were a craftsman and a businessman, and you did this thing which is now credited as being great innovation, and you're the foremost pioneer of that field, and you didn't think anything of it at the time.
Caniff: Only the newspaper aspect of the thing. The original after it was done, was nothing. There was no intrinsic value. You couldn't have sold

it for a dime. They used to burn them at the *New York Daily News.* They took them out in carts and burned them. Now that the market has occurred for these things, I'm very sorry. But at the time, we didn't bother. We were off on the next week's batch.

Saba: If someone had asked you, in 1934 or 1935 what you thought of yourself as an artist, would you have said that you were an artist at all?
Caniff: I think so. Again, false modesty has no place in these things. You know how good you are. I was not as good an artist as Harold Foster who was appearing on the scene roughly at about the same time. But it didn't bother me that I couldn't draw as well as Harold Foster, I would just do my thing, and he did his thing. I was a great admirer of Harold Foster when he was still doing *Tarzan,* but, and Alex Raymond, when he came along with *Secret Agent,* I remember reading it every day and enjoying it very much, but I never thought of him in terms of a rival. We were rivals because we were shooting for the same audience to some extent. I was doing an adventure thing with faraway places, and he was doing a close-up adventure in this country. It was a different background entirely, a crime story. But I never thought in terms of him being a bitter rival, a mean, old, hate-his-guts rival. I had great admiration for him. And this is nothing about my character at all, it was just that I admired what he did as well as he did. It wasn't my bag at all. As Noel Sickles used to say, "I don't want to draw anybody whose pants are pressed."

Saba: [*Laughter*]
Caniff: It's much more fun to do the wrinkles than a knife edge.

Saba: There was some cartoonist—I don't know if I'm ever going to remember who it was who told me that—during the late '30s and '40s, he used to study the wrinkles in your drawings. And he said that it used to just drive him nuts because nobody could draw wrinkles like you [*both laugh*].
Caniff: Well, I'd been to art school, and I found out where to put the pressure points on the draperies or whatever drape-cloth I drew. Nowadays, we've got 27 separate illustrations to do every week, and if you think of it in those terms, that's an awful lot of work. The trick is to get as much good stuff out of those 27 panels as you can in the time you have available. Sometimes it's easier than others, of course. The ones I was just showing you with all those people: the artist has just got to stop and draw all those people. They can't all just look like

robots, they've got to be people, real people. This is my thing. This is also my bag. To put in a whole audience of people in a football stadium, all listening to something avidly, and with concentration. This is a problem, but if I don't know my trade, I'd better go back to art school.

Saba: Well, it's really a matter of pride in the work you do.
Caniff: Oh, indeed. I've heard a cartoonist say this, and it always saddens me when I hear it—"Oh, good God, I hate to think of sitting at that drawing board today." Well, they ought to get into some other trade if that's the way they feel about it. To just go there under compulsion, as if you've been put in the trireme to pull an oar every day. Of course, it's hard work, but I used to have a managing editor who said to me, "Son, you asked for work when you came here." He's the same editor who said, "Draw this for the old man who buys the paper. Don't worry about the kids." Kids don't read newspaper comics. Everyone thinks they do, but they don't.

Saba: Seems to me you've absorbed a lot of good advice over the years.
Caniff: Oh, yes, heavens. First of all, I've been around a long time. Secondly, if you don't remember these things, then you should. It's just part of the trade. It's like learning to do anything in any field—you don't carry a cigarette in your mouth if you're pumping gas. You learn that the first day, if you live through the initiation.

Saba: You've obviously learned your lessons. I'm going to make one more try at this thing that I find hard to understand, which is how cartoonists of your ilk and of your generation cannot have what seems to me to be the respect for your own work.
Caniff: Oh I'm afraid I'm being unfair to you in that respect. It's pretty hard for the creator of a given thing to tag it himself. Someone else, someone on the outside has got to say it. I'm delighted when somebody says, "This is not just cartoons to be thrown away or to be wrapped around a fish tomorrow, it's *art.*" Well, I'm delighted when people say that, but it's not for me to say.

Saba: One of my questions is, how do you judge yourself aesthetically, and by that I mean in comparison to, say, other literature and other arts. If you were to set yourself up beside the greats of other mediums, how would you judge yourself?
Caniff: Well, I do a good job.

Saba: That's what you'd say?
Caniff: Yeah.

Saba: You won't say more than that?
Caniff: Well, it isn't a matter of not saying more than that. Again, I'm not trying to parade false modesty for you. I'm good at what I do. And, in some respects, I'm the best at what I do. But part of that is because, for one reason or another, I've managed to catch the brass ring enough times to stay alive. But as far as an evaluation is concerned, it's first of all too early to say, and secondly, too fine a line to draw. Where do I stand with John Steinbeck in his field?, or something of that sort. I got fan mail from John Steinbeck. But I also wrote fan mail *to* John Steinbeck. None in exchange, it was just at separate times that it occurred. After *Citizen Kane,* for instance, I got letters from Orson Welles. And so on, and so it goes. Mutual respect is what it amounts to in terms of evaluating it on a scale of 10, say. I'm good at my trade.

Saba: Well, that's an important evaluation right there. Speaking about comics as a medium in the abstract, do you see any reason why the medium could not contain some of the great art that any other medium contains?
Caniff: Anything that's done against a deadline, of course, is always suspect, just because you don't take a year to do it like Picasso did. It doesn't mean that it isn't better than Picasso. Very possibly it is. It takes a lot of time and careful thought to judge that, but people are inclined to think that something that is done against a clock has got to be of lower quality. Well, this is ridiculous, of course. The great moments in history have been done against the clock, in a sense. *The Last Supper* was done against the clock, let me put it that way, but it was a milestone thing in its own context. So you can't use that as a criterion. However, people do, and you've got to face the fact that they do. The French are very good at this kind of evaluation. I had a one-man show in Paris, for instance, and what they did was to just knock out the balloons, because most of the people who were coming to the show wouldn't have been able to read them in English, anyway. They just used the drawings. They would blow up what was a single panel of something that I had done, and they put it on a whole wall.

Saba: Yeah. And how did that turn out?
Caniff: It was marvelous. [*Laughter*] I was surprised myself. I didn't know I had put some of those things in there. You just put them in

because it's built-in to put them in there. Composition is not something that you do consciously. You do it because you're good at drawing, or you're good at composition, or you're not. So some of these things had composition that I had not consciously put there. It was just good composition because I learned composition the second year in art school.

Saba: Well, this makes you a real journeyman, because obviously you've gone beyond having to think about those basic things.
Caniff: Yeah. The tennis player doesn't think, "I must reserve, I must put some topspin on this ball." He just puts the topspin on the ball.

Saba: Have you at any stage been motivated in your work from abstract considerations of the workings as an art form, or have you always been driven by simple necessity? By that I mean to say, do you sometimes sit back and feel that you want to do a certain kind of drawing, put a certain feel in your work? Or are you always thinking more in terms of what has to be done?
Caniff: I think it's a combination of the two. I remember particularly a shot, a Sunday page in which a girl—I think it was Burma, back that far in time—was thinking about something that was happening to her and [that was] reflected in the color scheme of the thing. When she was angry, it was a red drawing, and not just a background of red, but she was red all over. When she simmered down a little bit, she thought, "Well, he was a pretty nice guy," it cooled into a blue, and when she was deeply repentant about something, it was purple. This was in the days when you could ask for and receive that kind of color treatment. That was consciously done. I had to say these things, but the drawing I put together in such a way that I hoped that the colors would make the point. She was alone in this thing, she was not with anybody, no backgrounds at all, just the color. And in black-and-white it would have been pointless. But since it was a color page, it made its point.

Saba: I haven't seen that one.
Caniff: Oh, it goes back so far, I can't even remember exactly when it occurred. But this entire page was devoted to this and nothing more.

Saba: You seem to have always worked, first of all, primarily from an awareness of whatever the audience is going to want or receive. I gather from that that you, in your considerations of what to do, it's usually been from the point of view of what the audience wants. You're not an abstract theorist of the comic strip.

Caniff: No, and I feel very strongly about this. It'd be great to be able to force something down the audience's throat. But that's not the deal, you're out there to give them what they want just as if you were selling oranges. You don't give them rotten oranges because they're rotten people. You give them oranges that they'll buy. If it comes down to that, it's not that mercenary, it's simply realistic. You'll be stuck with a lot of oranges if you don't give them good oranges.

Saba: A lot of younger cartoonists today—and, I must admit, like myself—work primarily from what we want to do. What we think is the best artistic way to do it. Which is what you might call the "art for art's sake" approach.
Caniff: It's dangerous.

Saba: Commercially dangerous.
Caniff: Not just commercially dangerous. It's dangerous in terms of your career. And of course, this comes down to being commercial. If it doesn't sell, you'll finally have to do something else to make a living. But, it's dangerous in the sense that then you're getting into the missionary attitude about what you have to say. Who's to say you're so damn smart, you know? Maybe you're wrong. The trick is to feel your way, like a couple of boxers, feinting around until they find what they hope is the weakness in the other guy, and then letting him have it. And the same way, encountering what he has to offer you. The public can do you in so quickly by ignoring you. We used to have a year. Give a new strip about a year to succeed. Now you've got about two weeks. And I mean *two weeks.* Then, zoom, you're out of there, because the editor has about 200 things to choose from, and he's got 10 slots in his comics page.

Saba: Do you not feel there's a danger of compromising what you would do by feeling what the audience wants?
Caniff: No, I don't regard it as compromise at all. It's a matter of getting your hold. It's like getting on a horse, and the trick is to stay on the horse. And you don't say, "You should obey my bridle." The horse has his own ideas. So the trick is to combine the two. And you must be a good rider. You must have good, strong saddle muscles, or off you go. And he's not going to ask any questions. He's going to throw you, that's all. He's dumb anyway, and you're a big deal about being a hero figure on top of Lochinvar's horse, it's not going to work. You've got to go along with that horse and do it his way, to a certain extent, and your way to a certain extent, and then you end up in a statue.

Saba: I think that could be about the best advice I've heard for a young cartoonist.
Caniff: It's not just practical advice, it's a simple matter-of-survival advice.

Saba: Let's go back to when you were 15 years old. Did you want to be at that time some kind of writer or artist?
Caniff: I was fortunate enough to get a job right out of eighth grade. We had no junior high schools in those days, so this was between eighth grade and freshman year in high school. I got a job as an office boy in a newspaper, so I began to get the town-and-gown thing. I'd go to high school in the daytime. I had a good high school art teacher. And then at night I went to work on the newspaper, where it was really practicality. So the combination of the two is extremely valuable. By the time I finished high school, I was a journeyman newspaper art-department artist. I could do retouching. I went right to work out of high school on the *Miami Daily News* as a full-time journeyman.

Saba: So you've never had the phase that so many of us had time to have in the '50s and '60s, when we were sitting there and dreaming about being a great artist.
Caniff: No, I didn't. Very early on, I think I realized that I was a commercial sort of guy, and if I was going to get into this at all, I had to do it in terms of making it pay. Not just to support me, but making it pay in terms of career. Remember, this is way ahead of the fact that I then studied portrait painting, to find out if I had missed my calling, but at the same time when I was studying portrait painting in the morning, life classes and all this, I was getting a college degree at the same time, and I was working at night on the newspaper downtown. So I had a three-way world going, and from each one I supped. You know, I tried to get as much out of each as I could, and fortunately I was able to put them all together into some kind of approach to the whole thing. And when I got out of college, the Depression was on for real, and the jobs were just nonexistent. I lost my own job, for instance. Fortunately, I was able to connect with the Associated Press in New York, and that saved me from perdition.

Saba: I know the rest of the story from there on.
Caniff: But you see, I'd been learning my trade all this time. By the time I got to the Associated Press, I knew how to do their journeyman stuff.

Saba: So I gather that you would say that you've ended up doing what you wish to do.

Caniff: Not so much what I wish to do, but what I knew I could do, and make it come off, at that moment. Not always exactly wishing to do.

Saba: Looking over your life so far, would you say that you have done what you wanted to do?
Caniff: I think I have taken as great an advantage as I could out of everything that was within my range. I'm not the best artist in the business. I'm not the best whatever, but I know how to put them together in such a way that they will sell.

Saba: As an artist of whatever caliber you want to judge yourself, would you ideally like to look back and say you would have done something differently?
Caniff: Well, I would have if the opportunity had occurred, or if it would have been advantageous to move in that direction. There are a number of things. I've said I would have done *Peanuts* if that would have sold. Obviously, I'm not the *Peanuts* man. Charles Schulz is the *Peanuts* man. That doesn't mean I wouldn't have tried it, if at that moment it would have sold.

Saba: Supposing in 1934, the gag strip had been the most popular, or the coming thing. Can you even begin to see yourself today being the great master of gag strips?
Caniff: I would have given it a hell of a try. [*Laughter*]

Saba: Do you think you'd be satisfied? Could you have done that?
Caniff: I don't know. That's hard to say, of course. But I'm fortunate in that, when I did fall into a slot, it was the kind of thing that I did best. But again, you try to see which way the wind is shifting and go with the wind. If you can.

Saba: I noticed one of the new developments in comics: some people are trying to take an aspect of what you do, but to push it the other way. And I think the primary thing that makes you the top of your field is your ability to tell a story. People are taking that kind of narration that you helped to make possible, through your techniques, and they want to do graphic novels now—start with a beginning, a middle, and an end, as opposed to a strip that goes on and on and on. Would you have ever wanted to do that?
Caniff: Oh, I do it every day. I do six novels a year. The difference is that there's a carefully contrived umbilical between the end of one of my stories and the next, so that the audience doesn't get turned away. When

you say "The End," then lots of people take you at your word, and that's the end of it and you. And, my trick is to hold you from the end of one story to the beginning of another. It's a trick, a technique, that's as old as Scheherazade again, because that's exactly what she did. Just before the end of the story, she would say, "Oh, well, tomorrow . . . ," and so on.

Saba: Are you familiar with the work of the Italian artist Hugo Pratt?
Caniff: Oh, indeed. I finally met Hugo. I admire him greatly, especially the American things that he does, like the American Civil War stuff that he does is great. Wonderful. And I finally caught up with him in Paris. I later saw him here, in this country, and I've corresponded with him. He speaks English, which makes it a lot easier.

Saba: I imagine that Pratt acknowledged his debt to your influence.
Caniff: Oh yes, he did.

Saba: What do you think about the direction he's taken that style?
Caniff: Oh, I love his work. He's done the same sort of thing in his own way, with great skill and great attention to detail, and it's tough because he's not doing something that's his world. He's doing American Civil War stuff. For heaven's sake, I was born in the middle of that stuff, and I still have to look up every button and every rifle, get the bayonet right, and all that. From that distance, he does it.

Saba: Do you see anything vastly different between what he's doing and what you're doing?
Caniff: Well, of course his work is generally published in comic books, and mine is designed for the dailies—two paragraphs of conversation and three drawings, and that's it.

Saba: But in terms of technique?
Caniff: Probably, because he's in a position to demand that. My contention's always been that anyone who can draw, can write. It's just that most of the time, guys have never exercised this extra appendage, and they don't even realize they've got a third arm if they want to use it. So they let editors talk them into giving you a writer.

Saba: What do you think a writer/artist team does to a strip? I gather that you're saying it would make a different kind of story.
Caniff: One great advantage of mine is that I'm the writer, artist, director, the costume designer, the whole works. You can do anything you

want. You can put on any kind of show you want. You can leave it blank if you want to, and I've done that, too.

Saba: You left a strip blank once?
Caniff: Not *blank* exactly, but nothing was happening. In *Terry,* when Raven Sherman died, the last scene was one whole panel of Terry and Dude Hennick looking down at this grave. People had not done this type of thing before, so the impact was such that people realized she was dead. Really dead. She was not going to come up out of that hole and say, "Hello, kids." I set out to make a noise, and I did. I still get letters from people saying, "I remember Raven," and this was 40 years ago, for Pete's sake!

Saba: Do you think you do things in comics that couldn't be done in any other medium?
Caniff: Probably so, although generally speaking, you're not conscious of it at the time. For instance, because of the use of these daily segments of a story, I could use that one panel [with Terry and Dude Hennick], and it needed no explanation, and I didn't have to tell anyone anything else. In a way, you're picking up the attention of the reader that would cause them to read tomorrow's paper to find out what that was all about. Even at that time, I wasn't all that conscious of it, except that you're never *without* consciousness about it. It's like that actor always knows where the camera is.

Saba: And yet, at the same time, he has to forget, too.
Caniff: Exactly. You pretend that there's not a camera there. Yet you always are aware. You don't turn away and mumble something into the scenery. You give it to the microphone so it picks up. This is simple business of the trade.

Saba: It seems like a common thing to say, but comics are, to varying degrees, a combination of words and pictures. I presume that that means that there are ways of telling a story that could not be done in any other way because you can go back and forth between the pictorial and the verbal media.
Caniff: This is something that's often discouraging to young artists who want to draw strips—the story is the most important thing. The drawing is definitely secondary. Therefore, for heaven's sake, learn to tell a story while you're at it. You're two steps up on everybody, because you don't have to split the fees with anyone else, and you also control this thing,

which is more important than splitting the fees. I mentioned the fact that you'll see two names on the strip today, where one is a writer and the other is supposed to be an artist. When I came into the field, one person was supposed to do both. Very often the artist would have a writer under the table, or in the closet, or an assistant artist, or whatever, but it was still credited to one person. And this is the way it manifests itself. The writer comes in, sits down at a typewriter, and types out this paragraph to direct the artist.

Then the artist comes in and has to draw a man and woman on a windswept hill and 10,000 Chinese communists coming up with drawn bayonets. Now, when you're the artist and writer, you do the same scene, but you show a fairly close-up shot of the hero and heroine, show some wind lines and clouds behind with a few leaves going by to show it's a wind-swept hill. The man has his arm around the girl, pointing outside the panel, saying "Look! Here come 10,000 Chinese." This is what you do when you're writing and drawing. And that's to make the point.

Saba: You're making it easier for yourself, is what you're doing [*Laughter*].
Caniff: And that's an exaggeration of the point, that the artist can control it. If he wants to, he can draw the 10,000 Chinese soldiers. But usually, he finds that way out.

Saba: Finds he prefers not to. Although, you are among the people who do, occasionally, do you not?
Caniff: Well, a good example of that is the crowd scene in that Sunday page you looked at before, with all these people. But to make that point, you've really got to show all these people listening to what's being said in that particular instance. Only one shot. If you did it over and over, it would be tiresome old hat. There's just one dirty word in the whole of *The Grapes of Wrath.* It's only one word in *The Grapes of Wrath,* which is such a surprise when you come to it, that it just hits you right between the eyes.

The same thing that used to excite people in, for instance, what we called the Bible Belt, still excites them. Regardless of the fact that all of the permissive things are going on on the front page, they still don't want anything that suggests any deviation on the comics page. For instance, in *Terry,* I used a lesbian character one time, and in those days the word "lesbian" simply wouldn't have been understood by half your audience, and the other half would have resented it.

Saba: You didn't say it, did you?
Caniff: No, not in any way. But there was a sneaky way around it. The character's name was Sanjak, and you first saw her as a woman. You knew she was a woman, but you saw her as a French naval air force officer and her name was Sanjak. Sanjak is the island next to Lesbos, from which comes "lesbian."

Saba: My goodness.
Caniff: Only the insider would know.

Saba: But I remember that character, I guess, first of all, in fact, there's the one that dressed up as the great big fat woman, and then she, yeah, that's one that's in that scrapbook I was telling you about.
Caniff: That was just the way you would do this kind of thing. It wasn't done just to be an inside joke at all, it was just a use of a device. And it was a good word to use. A French naval officer named Sanjak sounded perfectly logical, but the double bounce of it was that Sanjak is the next island to Lesbos.

Saba: Did people get it?
Caniff: Oh, enough people got it that they would say, "Ahhh-hhhaaaaaa." There were enough people who just were aware of the geography.

Saba: Some of them might look it up, because you used geography so often that people might get in the habit of looking things up.
Caniff: Exactly.

Saba: Speaking of *Terry*, Pappa Pyzon intrigued me very much. It was quite early on in the story. He was a rather fat guy who came into the story again later. The Dragon Lady tried to sell Pat Ryan to him as a slave. He hated women, I remember, and he was very effeminate, and had all these weird mannerisms. I remember thinking that you were taking quite a chance with that guy at the time.
Caniff: Not so much a chance as you might think, because that was the kind of thing that Charles Laughton did so effectively, and I probably had Charles Laughton in mind for this guy. But people just thought he was a sissy. The idea of any kind of sexual deviation didn't even enter into people's minds in those days. Of course, I didn't show any sense of that, other than like Nero, who is a fruity sort of character nowadays. Everybody knows about Nero. But in those days, he just was a swish.

Saba: You must have had it in mind.
Caniff: Oh, sure. But you've got to use the tools that are at hand, and people such as that—the Neros and whatnots—have caused history to change, and for the very reason that they were deviants. They did the things they did because they were deviants. Witness Nero.

Saba: How closely does an artist have to identify with his audience?
Caniff: Essentially, you're a pretty good cross-section of an audience in the first place, or you wouldn't be doing it. So you can trust your own judgment, generally speaking. This isn't always true, and of course, you can go off in all kinds of tangents, like Percy Crosby did. Poor guy, he lost his marbles. But in the beginning, he was his own best audience.

Saba: What is the story behind him? I've heard various references to his demise, but I don't know what happened to him.
Caniff: Well, he ended up in an insane asylum. He finally just flipped his lid, and when that happened he became paranoid and schizophrenic, too, but paranoid, particularly. Yet, a brilliant guy in many respects, as so often happens with paranoid people.

Saba: You knew him, I gather?
Caniff: I never knew him personally. I never met him.

Saba: So you don't know why this happened or anything like that.
Caniff: No, no. I suppose there's a background to it, but I don't know what it is.

Saba: I've often heard he was drinking.
Caniff: Oh, there's that too, of course. He went through the same stages. There was a lot of F. Scott Fitzgerald in him. For one thing, they were more or less contemporaries, and they were caught up in the euphoria of public acceptance and they were both from middle-income level families. Fitzgerald from Minnesota, and Crosby was from Staten Island or someplace like that. A city boy, essentially.

Saba: He was quite dashing and handsome, I believe.
Caniff: They both were. This was World War I time, when there was still a romantic overtone to all of that. *The Great Gatsby* came along, and then their careers were or less parallel in that respect. He was drawing for *Life* [humor] magazine when Fitzgerald was being published as widely as he was.

Saba: I love Crosby's work, too.
Caniff: Yes. Oh, Jesus.

Saba: We'd better get back onto the track. When you are writing your strips, do you think of your characters as real? Do they live within you as real characters?
Caniff: Yes. You must sell yourself first on this thing. You must convince yourself, because if you feel a shakiness about it, then it's shaky. My art teacher in high school said that there's only one way to judge your own work, and that's if it looks right, it's right. If it looks wrong, change it. That's all you need to know.

Saba: And it's the same with writing. It's the way you feel.
Caniff: Yeah, exactly. It doesn't mean that you're going to change it for the better, but if it feels wrong to you, then it's wrong. I've had this happen many times. I don't want to go back and erase all that, but, that little voice says it's wrong. It's wrong.

Saba: I know. I've done the same. I've walked away from something thinking, "Oh, that'll do." Five or 10 minutes later, I'll come back and think it won't do.
Caniff: Yeah, it isn't just conscience, it's simple integrity. You try to do your best shot every day, every line.

Saba: This is what I do when I'm writing a story—rather than saying, "Okay, then I think I'll have them do this, then I think I'll have them do that," I think, "What would he do?" Or I look and I see what he's doing.
Caniff: Put yourself in his skull. That's why it's hard for men to write about women and women to write about men. Some people do it with great skill. But that doesn't mean they're always that good at it. For instance, I've always felt that Agatha Christie was a great plot-person, but she didn't ever write realistic people. At least that's my reaction. On the other hand, the Sherlock Holmes characters are utterly believable to me. They do what it seems they should do, or would do.

Saba: Now, your characters have always had a great individuality, perhaps more than any other cartoonist's.
Caniff: You try for this, of course, because you must. The guy must look different. You put a guy with a headful of curls in a scene with a lot of

other people, like a college campus, and then you put a couple of other guys in there to show he's the only person with a headful of curls. You make the point. He's always the one person with that style, or the girl with this hairdo. In spite of the fact that you've got all kinds of other people milling around. That keeps the focus on him. It's what they call in films "key lighting." They'll keep one spotlight on that central character, no matter what else is going on. It might be West Point, where everybody looks alike, but still that key light's on the hero. They can do it so subtly that you're not even aware that your attention is being riveted always on that character, no matter where he is, that the key light is always on him. It's just part of his being the hero, or the heroine.

Saba: In your case, it's more than such things as a hairdo. It seems to be also very much the entire conception of the personality.
Caniff: When I do it it has to be tight, because you're only doing eight weeks. In the old days it used to be 13 weeks in *Terry.* Now eight weeks. Not that that's the attention span of the reader, but it's better not to just linger with the thing. Get on with it—boy meets girl, boy loses girl, boy gets girl, and then go on to the next thing.

Saba: Do you wish you could have a longer story at times?
Caniff: Oh, it might be fun to do, but I find it punches it up to not wander off, stay with your point. The situation of Poteet, for instance, comes about because she thinks that Steve needs her. She goes out to American Samoa, is almost raped—wind it up and get her out of there. You've made the point that she's come out to chase down her endlessly unrequited romantic situation.

Saba: It's the world's most unrequited love affair. It's been going on ever since I can remember.
Caniff: You have to keep on thinking of ways of Charlie Brown to kick that football and for Lucy to pull it out and make him fall on his face.

Saba: You have an interesting way of repeating elements often enough that people look for them and recognize them, and at the same time you have constantly new twists.
Caniff: Remember, when I first started in this whole thing, the *New York Daily News* people suggested that I write to Harold Gray and to Chet Gould, who at that point had just ascended. They had become widely read. I was supposed to ask if they could offer me any advice. I wouldn't have done this on my own, by the way. Not that I didn't high-

ly respect them, but I didn't want them to feel obligated, and I didn't want to feel obligated to them. But I did because the editor suggested it. Harold Gray said something that was so pertinent: he said that each day you tell a little of what happened yesterday, and tell something of what's going on now, and then tease them into reading tomorrow's strip. But always a little new, a little old, and a little maybe. Very good advice. And he used this, because nothing in his drawing ever gave him the chance that I have of shooting all around the character with the telephone and so on. It was always the same drawing, more or less. But his storytelling was so skilled that he was able to hold you to *Orphan Annie.* If you became an addict, you were hooked.

Saba: It's often been pointed out that the dialogue really carried his stories, because his drawings were symbolic. They were not real drawings.
Caniff: Yeah, and every villain looked like the last villain, unlike in Chet Gould's work. Of course, the villains were his great thing, like Scarface, the Mole, and all those wonderful guys. Vitamin [Flintheart], the one who was always popping pills. Long before people were popping pills, he was popping pills.

Saba: At least these were vitamin pills he was popping, anyway.
Caniff: That's what it said.

Saba: Another theoretical question that I have—what would you say would be the limitations of the medium? Suppose someone wanted to go about writing a long, psychological novel or something like that in comics form, leaving aside the question of daily readership. Through all your years of working in the medium, do you feel that there's a certain limit to what can be done? That there are certain things that just could not be pulled off, physically?
Caniff: No, I don't think so. I don't think there's any limit at all. It's in the way you do it. You can make the point with the people who would get the point that Sanjak was a lesbian character by the use of the word "Lesbos." Never at any point did she ever do anything overt. You had to read into the character. Nowadays you could do it more overtly, for instance. But you do what you can do or must do at the moment, to make your point. And the skill, the trick is to be able to pull it off. Garry Trudeau is the best example of this. Nobody before him ever used the word "gay," until one character announced to the gal who was the law student [Joanie] that he was gay. And she said, "Oh, I'm good-

natured, too." [*Both laugh*] Then it hit her what he meant. Now, nobody had ever attempted that before. And she took a lover, and they went to bed together, and all this was in a strip. Lots of papers stupidly left it out, and people really let them have it, saying, "Who do you think we are? Who's the boob in this case? You're the boob for not printing the thing!" Because anybody who cared immediately called up their friends in the next town and said, "Send me prints of this."

Saba: It ended up being reprinted all over the place because of that.
Caniff: Endlessly! *Time* magazine, television stations and so on. It made fools out of the editors. In most cases they printed pages of the protest letters, none of them approving of having left it out. Because having left it out, the people who would have disapproved just didn't see it. But the ones who were following the story avidly, which is the whole point of having it in there in the first place, were *enraged* at this. In Columbus, Ohio friends of mine sent me copies of the *Columbus Citizen-Journal* where the editor had printed a couple of full pages of the letters of protest.

Saba: Bill Blackbeard has an interesting opinion, which is that once a comic has too many words, particularly outside of balloons, it is dangerously weakening the medium, and in fact he ceases to consider them to be comic strips beyond a certain point. He says, for instance, *Prince Valiant* is not a comic strip. I can see his point there, but what he's saying is that the strength of the medium lies in the pictorial element, in the action that can be shown. It is my feeling that an educated comic-strip reader could read a whole novel-length story that had a lot of talking and a lot of narration, and you could have a story of equal depth and importance to *Moby Dick* or something like that in the comic strip form.
Caniff: The one refutation that I can think of off-hand to Bill— whose opinions I respect enormously—is the fact that Andy Gump, which at its peak was about as popular as any comic strip has ever been, had one of his balloons so long that he had to show Andy Gump lying flat on his back on the bottom line to accommodate all the words. This was at its peak, at the time when Andy Gump was running for Congress, and so on. It was the most popular strip in the *Chicago Tribune*, and for that matter, all over the Syndicate. So that's the other side of the coin. If you're interested enough in what the guy has to say, then you'll read it.

Saba: I noticed something when I was doing *Neil the Horse* as a continuity before I did it in the gag format: I could only go on for so long—a certain number of panels or a certain number of pages—without some kind of action. I couldn't have people forever talking, reading, or sitting. There had to be some fight or some running. Something had to happen.
Caniff: Well, that's another string to your bow, of course. In Sidney Smith's case, he had his audience. He didn't do anything but just show up. But that had its limitations, too. There was an end to that, and the scene changed. Part of this was the fact that in those days the things reproduced about seven columns wide, or certainly six, and the people could read it. If that same panel that I described, where he's lying flat on his back in the last panel, were reduced down as we are today, you couldn't have read it, and he would have lost his audience.

Saba: Do you feel confined in your writing of stories to the necessity of that kind of pacing—that relatively often you have to have some kind of physical movement within the story?
Caniff: Well, of course, it's part and parcel of this thing. Yes, I do. After so many talking heads in an adventure story, it seems a little ridiculous. I'm not doing Andy Gump. I'm doing what used to be called an adventure story, or a suspense strip. You don't even hear these terms any longer. I don't know exactly why, except that the term just has drifted out of the vocabulary, out of the lexicon.

Saba: One of my very favorite writers is Robert Louis Stevenson. I love that kind of adventure story. But even so, I would like to believe that the comics medium can be a medium for any kind of comics writer—even a serious, philosophical writer.
Caniff: In fact, you have a leg up on them, because you grab them with the pictures. Trudeau's a good example of that—one of the attractions of his drawing is that it's so non-drawing (he says so himself) that people go, "What's this thing?" They can't even see it, let alone read it. Then they get hooked, and they're *gone.* He suffers from the reduced size as much as we do. More so, in a way, because his lettering is not his strongest suit. If you shrink it down to postage-stamp size, it becomes harder to read.

When we went from six to five to four columns, we had to do larger lettering. This was before Frank Engli died, who was my original lettering-man, and before Shel Dorf took over. I had another man in the middle who didn't work out. He didn't like doing this kind of thing. He was

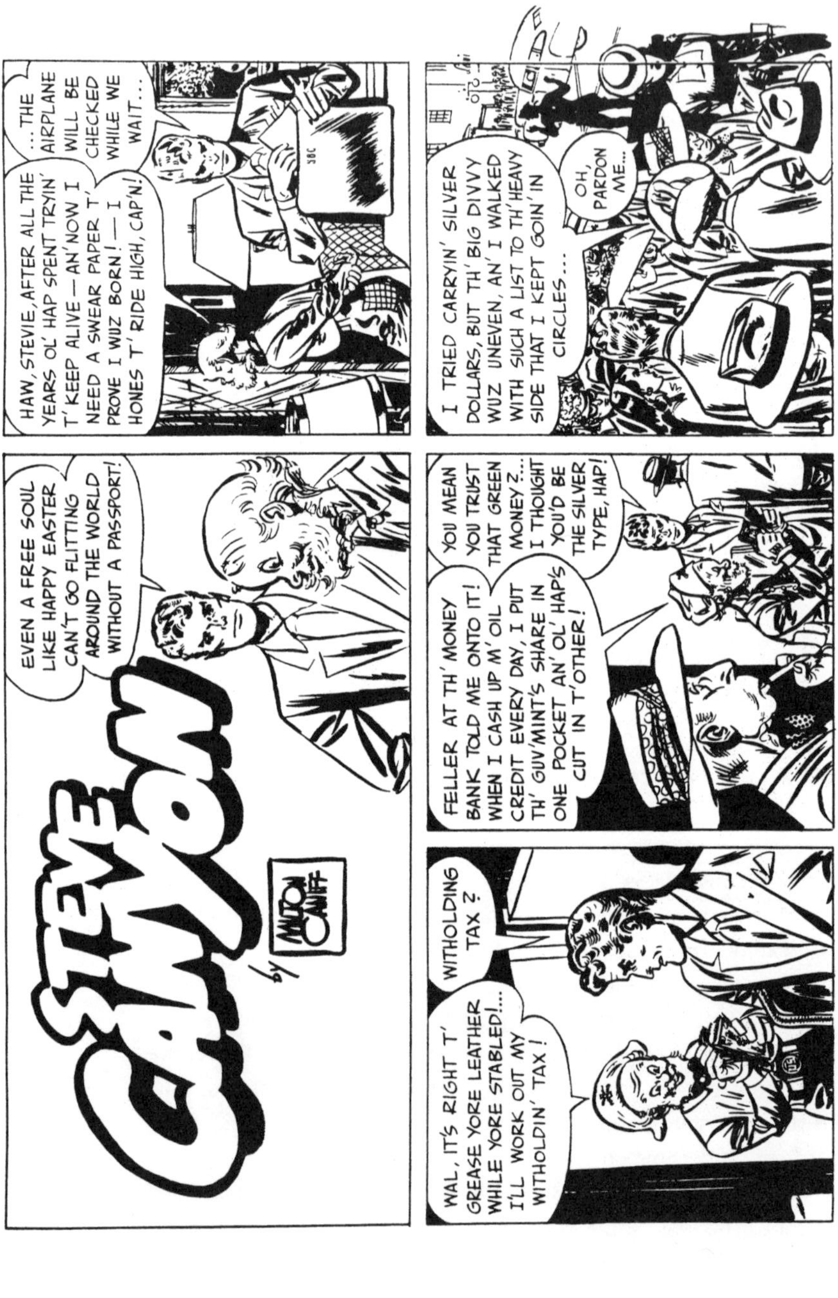
STEVE CANYON
by MILTON CANIFF
EVEN A FREE SOUL LIKE HAPPY EASTER CAN'T GO FLITTING AROUND THE WORLD WITHOUT A PASSPORT!
HAW, STEVIE, AFTER ALL THE YEARS OL' HAP SPENT TRYIN' T' KEEP ALIVE — AN' NOW I NEED A SWEAR PAPER T' PROVE I WUZ BORN! — I HONES T' RIDE HIGH, CAP'N!
...THE AIRPLANE WILL BE CHECKED WHILE WE WAIT...
WAL, IT'S RIGHT T' GREASE YORE LEATHER WHILE YORE STABLED!... I'LL WORK OUT MY WITHOLDIN' TAX!
WITHOLDING TAX?
FELLER AT TH' MONEY BANK TOLD ME ONTO IT! WHEN I CASH UP M' OIL CREDIT EVERY DAY, I PUT TH' GUV'MINT'S SHARE IN ONE POCKET AN' OL' HAP'S CUT IN T'OTHER!
YOU MEAN YOU TRUST THAT GREEN MONEY?... I THOUGHT YOU'D BE THE SILVER TYPE, HAP!
I TRIED CARRYIN' SILVER DOLLARS, BUT TH' BIG DIVVY WUZ UNEVEN, AN' I WALKED WITH SUCH A LIST TO TH' HEAVY SIDE THAT I KEPT GOIN' IN CIRCLES...
OH, PARDON ME...

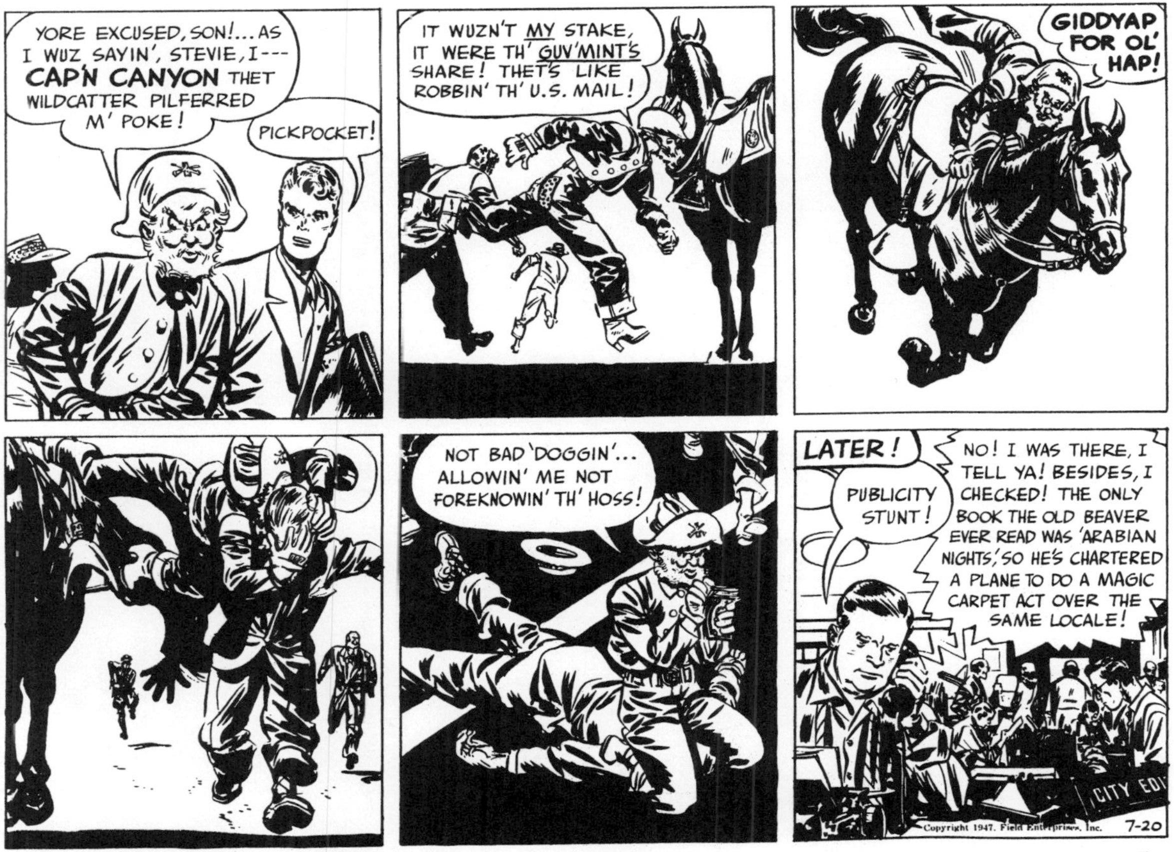

While Caniff's characters do a lot of talking (their verbiage establishing personality and advancing the plot), Caniff could slip into an action sequence effortlessly, and he knew when to turn off the persiflage in favor of fast-moving visuals.

a deeply religious person, and he felt that some of the things I was doing were not according to his way of thinking.

Saba: It's hard to imagine that he'd find something in your work to object to.
Caniff: He read things into it very often that I hadn't intended at all. One time, for instance, he brought a Sunday page back, and he had not lettered one whole balloon, because he had read into it something that I didn't mean at all. I was furious, because I was right on the deadline. He wanted to talk ethics, and me with five hours to get this thing on the plane.

Saba: Did you letter it yourself, finally?
Caniff: I didn't have time for him to letter, so I said, "This is the deal—if the syndicate objects to what I have to say, then you're right." Because they read it with a fine-toothed comb, up, down, and backwards to see if there's any hidden meaning. I said, "I'm going to letter it now. If they don't change it, then you are wrong." So shortly after that, he quit. He had a missionary attitude—he was going to save me from myself. He was a good lettering-man, though. That's when I called Shel, with whom I'd had a long-term acquaintance, and I knew he's studied lettering. I said, "Shel, I'm gonna shove you in the pool. I've got to have this stuff done. Just do it, and don't ask any questions." And he said, "I'll try," but he plunged right in, and as you can see now, it's very strong and readable.

Saba: It took me years to learn to letter. I do my own lettering, and I don't mind it now.
Caniff: Well, I used to do it all the time. When I started out, I couldn't afford to have a lettering-man. Finally, when I was able to hire somebody, I was delighted, because it was a chore. It wasn't something I enjoyed doing. It took a day's time to do a week's worth of strips, and it took you away from the drawing.

Saba: Blackbeard feels as you and I seem not to feel, that the comic strip has a certain limitation on it, and that it can only be used for humor or certain situations, like an adventure strip. He feels that a philosophical novel-length effort would be a total failure, that the medium could not support it.
Caniff: Again, it always comes back to personalities. I wouldn't have thought, in my wildest dreams, that a thing like *Doonesbury* could succeed, and yet he did it. He did it because he's who he is. Nobody else

could have done it. As he says himself, he is a non-drawer, but he non-draws very well [*Laughter*].

Saba: I understand he doesn't do his own inking at all.
Caniff: Not at all. He does it in pencil. But he must have inked it himself years ago, when he was a student at Yale.

Saba: I guess it goes without saying that you're an admirer of what he's doing.
Caniff: Oh yes, indeed. I'm always apprehensive about the new guy coming along, because he's going to threaten my position. But that doesn't mean that I don't admire him. I don't consider Garry Trudeau a rival, because we're not dealing with the same thing. But an editor has to dump something to buy something new, and therefore he's a rival. But I admire his work very much.

Garry gave me an original that's very amusing, and on this theme. A kid is talking to his father, and the father says, "We have nothing in common, and we don't agree on anything—I don't know what to do about it." And the kid says, "Have you considered voluntary euthanasia?," which is exactly Garry's and my situation [*laughter*]. He picked that one out to give to me.

Saba: I wouldn't be surprised to hear you say that you didn't like what he was doing because it's so different from what you're doing in the sense that his strips are static and verbal. It doesn't use any of the camera angles and personalities.
Caniff: Well, it's his thing. Just as *Li'l Abner* is *Li'l Abner,* and although Capp and I were rivals, we were old friends. I even took over *Colonel Gilfeather* from him. Capp once wrote a story about that. He said, "My work was once given to a guy named Milton Caniff—what ever happened to him?" [*laughter*]

Part of the reason Capp lost interest in *Li'l Abner* was the reduction in size. He felt an awful, pounding limitation. You may recall that, as a counterpoint, he started doing lettering billboard-sized.

Saba: I could never understand why he did that.
Caniff: He was just mad at the syndicate for demanding that it be done larger. So he said, "They want it larger, I'll make it larger." So he made it billboard-sized. This was Al. He overreacted.*

**This interview was conducted prior to Capp's death in 1979.*

Saba: It was all part of his personality, wasn't it.
Caniff: Exactly. I won't say there is nothing subtle about him, because there is plenty subtle about him, but when he reacts, he reacts big. Then, he had some personal problems, as you know. His daughter committed suicide, and his granddaughter was killed in an automobile accident. One was almost right on top of the other.

Saba: I understand that he's still in bad health.
Caniff: Yes, he is.

Saba: Are you still in touch with him?
Caniff: Yes, we talked on the phone a little while ago. I called him on a Sunday morning, which is the low point of anybody's week. We had a long talk about . . . oh, everything.

Saba: It's good that you keep in touch with each other.
Caniff: Yes, we're old friends. People used to think we were bitter rivals, which we never were, because *Li'l Abner* and my stuff had no rival points. We always got along well together. He was always very generous to me. In the times that he was doing a lot of radio and television appearances, he had nice things to say about me. In fact, he would turn the conversation around to that end. He always liked Alex Raymond, and while Alex was alive, he used to do the same thing for Alex.

Saba: You've said how you keep on auditioning, and you have a healthy attitude towards your work, because you don't allow yourself to get inflated. But at the same time, you must realize that an awful large body of fans and professionals regard you as a great artist and a pioneer. I was just wondering how that feels?
Caniff: There's danger in becoming a "cartoonist's cartoonist," because you can begin to believe your own press notices. It's the same with the theatre, or any other publicly offered medium. You've got to use all of this as a tool. "Tool" is the only word I can think of. It's a tool to bolster your ego, to make you feel good, but it's a tool. For heaven's sake, don't believe it, but do use it.

Saba: So you still wake up in the morning and feel like a regular guy?
Caniff: Very much so. In fact, more so, because as you get older you've got less energy, so you've got to make maximum use of every hour of energy. I can't do as I used to do when I was a kid—as all kids do—have a big night, wake up with a hangover, then say, "Gee, I'll knock

off today, and make it up tomorrow." I can't do that any more. First of all, I can't do it physically, and second, I'm not as fast as I once was. I don't draw as fast as I used to.

I have nothing to collect. Nobody owes me a living. It's either get out there and prove it, or get off the pot.

Saba: You're obviously going to keep working as long as you can.
Caniff: Well, it's a simple business of nothing better to do—it keeps me off the streets at night [*laughter*]. But more importantly, there's a great satisfaction in doing it. As long as you can produce, it'd be ridiculous to sit back and cry in your beer.

Saba: You're the owner, or at least part-owner of *Steve Canyon,* I understand.
Caniff: I own the title completely. I lease it, in effect, to Marshall Field. Marshall Field, in turn, has a distribution arrangement with King Features Syndicate.

Saba: I've never quite been able to figure out how all that works [*laughter*].
Caniff: I put it in cinema terms. You can go out and do an independent film, like Stallone did. You have to raise the money to get backing, but in my case, I don't have to do that. Field leases it by paying me a fee, just as you would lease a house, or anything else. It's yours to use during the time of that lease. At the end of that lease, it reverts back to me. During that time, he copyrights it. You'll notice that it says "copyright Field Enterprises."

Saba: Does that mean, for example, that if I wanted to reproduce some old *Steve Canyons* that I would have to approach them, not you?
Caniff: No, the way the contract reads, you would approach me. But that's really a fairly minor aspect of the thing. Let's use the film metaphor again. You create the film, and you go to MGM to produce the film, although it still belongs to you in terms of production. MGM, in turn, goes to United Artists to distribute the thing. The deal is not between you and United Artists, but it's between them and United Artists. So it is with Field Enterprises and King Features.

Saba: Is this only for *Steve Canyon*? I've noticed that in *Cartoonist Profiles* that Field advertises separately from King Features. But your name is in both. So a newspaper could order *Steve Canyon* from either address?

Caniff: As it is now. But in the beginning, there was a reason why it was like this. They wanted it to come out with the widest possible coverage, as quickly as possible. To get off the nut, for one thing, that they were guaranteed to give me, as well as to get the strip out as fast as they could. So their sales directors sat down with a map. They circled the cities in red and blue, and said, "The red cities are my cities, and the blue cities are your cities." For whatever reasons—"I've got a great friend in St. Louis, so I'll take St. Louis, and you take Montreal," and so on down the line. And as a result, they had 200 papers lined up before the first line was drawn. It was a big, noisy boost, and it didn't cost them a nickel. They were off the nut, as they say in the movie business. Happily, it's remained that way, so the guarantee has held.

Arn Saba: I wanted to ask your opinion of such cartoons as the simple gag strips. As much as I admire their skill, I bitterly resent them. I don't like what the Mort Walkers and the Charles Schulzes are doing to the medium, and I wonder what you think.

Caniff: First, you have to realize that the guys who are making it big in that area are good at it. The ones who are not so good make your point for you much more forcefully. If a guy can grab the audience with a minimum of physical effort, great. It's sad to see a good narrative strip knocked out by a second-rate gag strip, where the guy's using ancient gags, once-over lightly, and there's nothing coming through at all. In the case of Walker and Schultz, they're coming through, and that's why they hold the audience.

Saba: Well, they're not good examples to use, because they obviously are originators.

Caniff: But again, they started the trend, and when they were successful, a whole train of less skilled people came along to try to imitate this, and picked up a second-string audience. But it doesn't work that way. The audience is much more discriminating than you think. They'll stay with the goodies, and the others fall to the wayside.

I don't feel a competition with these people at all, in terms of content. But to get back to the space again, that's the same space that could be occupied by *Spider-Man,* or whatever. By the way, the *Spider-Man* people have had an enormous impact and they did a very highly skilled sales job on the strip. The Des Moines Register-Tribune Syndicate is responsible for a good part of that, and they've knocked out a lot of things in papers all over the country, just because they did a good sales job.

Saba: Well, *Spider-Man* has all the television coverage, and toys in the stores, and all that stuff.
Caniff: And the comic-book exposure. A lot of editors thought they were going to grab the youthful audience again by doing this, and it is simply not so. The same kids go out with their hot little quarter and buy a comic book, but they won't buy a newspaper.

Saba: I was really sorry to see it happen. People were talking about the resurgence of the continuity strip, but it's happening the wrong way, I think.
Caniff: A good example of an unfortunate manifestation is the condensation of novels [in comic strip form] that was done by Universal Press Syndicate. They were good novels, obviously, but boiling them down in that manner . . . I couldn't even find out who the hero was before it was already over.

Saba: I thought Elliot Caplin was involved with that.
Caniff: Elliot Caplin was condensing them, which is a hard job in itself.

Saba: I thought he'd do better than that.
Caniff: Well, he was stuck with a novel, which might have been a great novel about the recovery of the *Titanic,* but it tipped 900 pages, and all he could do was say, "We went down there, and brought it up." That's about all the time he had to do this thing. It was an enormous research job for the guy who had to do the drawing. It's hard work to draw all that stuff. There was no sense of continuity about the thing, when it was only going to last eight weeks.

I don't know what the disposition of the thing is. I haven't checked out *Editor & Publisher* to see. I know the *Los Angeles Times* carried it for six months or so, and then it just disappeared.

Saba: What do you think of *Star Hawks*?
Caniff: I don't see it as often as I should to make a comment on it. I like the art. I haven't been able to follow it, because I haven't seen it often enough, which is because it doesn't appear locally, and it isn't in any of the papers I subscribe to. But I like what I've seen.

Saba: What are your favorite strips these days?
Caniff: I think I'd have to rephrase the question slightly. I read strips that are not at all my favorites, but I read them because I feel as if I should. For instance, I don't warm to the *Spider-Man* premise, but I

read it, because this is the opposition, for one thing. I want to see it. It's beautifully drawn, and Stan Lee and his people do a great job of it. But it's not my bag. I don't warm to any science fiction. It doesn't grab me. Not only doesn't it grab me to try some, but it doesn't grab me to read. Never has. This goes all the way back to the great Martian stories, and even Ray Bradbury, whom I admire greatly. His work in that area would not be the kind of thing I seek out, although I think he does it with the greatest skill. So did H. G. Wells. It's just not my thing, that's all.

Saba: It's so much less realistic, I think. I don't care for super-heroes at all, and the thing that makes a great difference between your work and their work is that you're dealing with people who you could conceivably believe exist.
Caniff: Exactly. And in a curious way, and I'm sure you understand, it's too easy. In other words, I could say, "They fly off to the moon," and I don't have to explain how. When one of my characters says, "I'm going to fly this thing across the country in an hour and a half," this is within the realm of possibility these days. This is the sort of thing that can be done. But flying off to Mars is for the future, for somebody else to do. Not me.

Saba: You had an interesting story where they find Poteet in the hold of this ship. A superhero would just come in and rip the ship apart, and it wouldn't be as interesting as them looking around.
Caniff: As we've always said, it's like painting a sunset in Albuquerque. If you can't paint a sunset in Albuquerque, you ain't trying, boy. [*Laughter*] There it is, every night for you to try. The great thing is to paint a sunset over the North Pole. That would be tough to do with the same skill.

Saba: I think it gives an artist a greater sense of satisfaction to do something with greater challenge, and it gives the reader the same feeling, ultimately.
Caniff: I think so. As far as my own work is concerned, this has always been my theory. But it's also true with what I enjoy reading. I'm a sucker for my own racket. I can sit there and watch somebody on television, as if I were a first-year art student. "Wow, how does he do that?" [*laughter*]

Saba: That's terrific, because if you'd lost your enthusiasm, you wouldn't be in business.
Caniff: It's awful to see somebody who says, "Oh, I'm bored." Anybody who's bored is a boob. If you're bored, it's because you haven't

got the mother wit to be unbored. If you're bored, then just stay bored and shut up.

Saba: I hate to bring up names to use as examples, because a lot of these people are good people. What is happening with Alfred Andriola's Kerry Drake? He doesn't seem to be doing it.*

Caniff: Well, Sururi Gumen is his assistant, and Al was able to ease off on the greasy grind of daily production by giving him a byline, and everybody needs the ego-boast of having a byline. So Al is able to take more time now for research and all the other things he's able to do. That doesn't mean that he doesn't participate in the production of the strip, just as Chet Gould participates in the production of *Dick Tracy.* And you notice that his name is still on it. The young men do the hard, physical labor, but Chet can still move in and say, "I think you're wrong." and the Chicago Tribune-New York Daily News Syndicate will back him up, if he needs to be backed up. I'm sure he doesn't overuse this privilege, but he's still there, and his name is still on it.

It's a happy arrangement, and I hear he's pleased by it. He hasn't lost his equity in it. Everybody still regards it as his baby, but he doesn't have to sit down every morning and take a fresh sheet of paper out. He can go out and tend to his real-estate interests [*laughter*].

Saba: Well, his age is quite advanced.

Caniff: Yes, that's part of it, of course. It's an awful job to do even the kind of drawing Chet was doing in the beginning. It looks simple, but it's never simple. Nothing like that is ever simple. And he worked hard at it. A real conscientious guy.

Saba: What plans are you making for *Steve Canyon* to outlive you?

Caniff: None at all. There's nothing in the world you can do about it in the first place, because if it carries on the same tradition, it has to be topical. It has to be current. The minute I can't continue it, the best person to do it will continue it. And I hope to God they get the best person, even if I'm disabled, much less dead and gone.

I own *Steve Canyon.* It's a vested interest I can leave to my wife or to my heirs and assigns, as they say. But as far as trying to make any plans for it, that's ridiculous, because I don't know what I'll be drawing next week. It'll turn as the world turns. With that in mind, I just hope

**Since this interview was conducted, Andriola has died.*

they get the best possible people to carry it on. If it can't be carried on, then it just goes into the stable.

Saba: I thought you might be training an assistant or something.
Caniff: I wish I could. I would love to be able to train an assistant. But I would never say to Dick Rockwell, for example, "You must do thus-and-so for me, because you work for me." I want him to be his own man. I told him when I hired him, "Either you get so good you take over this strip, or you get so good you spin off your own strip." He's not going to take it over because I won't let him, and he knows this.

Saba: How long have you had him?
Caniff: Twenty-five years.

Saba: When did you first start using an assistant?
Caniff: Twenty-five years ago. All during those war years, during what I consider to be the peak years of *Terry,* I had no assistant at all.

Saba: So you never used anyone for airplanes, or anything like that?
Caniff: No. I had done the research, and during the war years, people were not available. Every guy who would want to do the thing was in the Army. I was stuck out in the country with too few gasoline stamps to go to the Post Office. I just had to do it myself. I didn't do anything else, because I couldn't anyway, so I just stayed home and did it as well as I could.

When Rockwell came back from the war, he was just getting started doing comic books. He lived nearby, and he said, "If you've got any extra work to be done, I need the work." I gave him a couple of things to do that were really nothing but samples, just some pictures of pinup girls, and a shot of Canyon in his uniform of the day. He was versatile enough that he could do almost any kind of thing, so gradually, I gave him a little more to do, and a little more, until he now does what I showed you.

Saba: That's good, because he takes the backbreaking load off you.
Caniff: But he never does the finished inking of figures, because this is where ghosting shows. You can do all kinds of ghosting in the background, but he doesn't draw the figures the same way I draw them. He draws them his way. It's all right in the pencilling, but in the inking, I ink them my way. The end product of that is that it still looks like my stuff, even though he might have inked the background. Still, figures are what you remember.

Saba: I was interested to see what loose pencils you use. You don't go for very tight pencilling.
Caniff: No, because sometimes I compose in mid-air, so to speak. I change it in mid-air.

Saba: That's one of the reasons I'm so slow—I go for very tight pencils.
Caniff: I sometimes will put down two lines and then white one out, rather than decide which one to use. I'll just put them both down. I used to use a razorblade, but the retouch white is so much better. I do some pasting over, too. I have these little stickertype things that I can just slap down to change a whole face, if I need to, or a mouth, or eyes. In the old days, I used to have to paste down, but it was likely to come loose, but now these things really stay put. It's a nice little tool that turned up—happy day.

Saba: Since we're talking about ghosts, I'll just add a couple of more questions. I recently got those two books that reprinted *Steve Canyon.* They weren't very good printing jobs.
Caniff: No. Unfortunately, they didn't realize that you can't just take them out of old newspapers and slap them down. They have to be retouched with tender loving care.

Saba: I found a very interesting thing when I was reading them. I was extremely aware of something you must have been going through. When you started *Terry,* there was a vast difference between starting that and starting *Steve Canyon.* You had an unknown strip with *Terry,* and you had a chance to build it up

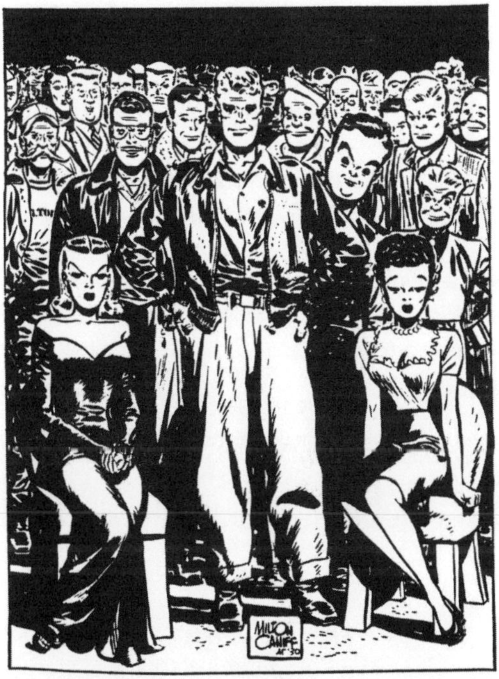

For the cover of the January 1947 issue of The Magazine of Sigma Chi, *Caniff produced this drawing of the cast of his new strip—and inserted himself into the picture just over Steve's left shoulder. That's the Sigma Chi pin on Steve's shirt over his heart. Pat Ryan was also a brother.*

slowly. You had the chance to figure out your characters, keep some of them and drop some of them, and all that. But you had to start in full-flight in *Steve Canyon.* It must have been a very rough time—you had a lot of papers signed on, and you had to have what would pass for a fully developed strip right from the very start. You had no chance to get your legs. It was very interesting to see you come in with a very professional strip. Over the first four or five years of the strip, you did improve in many ways, from your first conception of it. But your first conception was masterful enough that it held together. But it was interesting for me to try to guess what you were trying for.
Caniff: It was rough. Not the least thing was that I didn't dare do anything that was the least bit reminiscent of *Terry,* because the legal eagles were just waiting for me to copy myself, and shove it down my throat. But the thing I feared most, and it happened in many instances, was when people said, "I don't like this as well as *Terry.*" Because they were devoted to the characters, and in *Terry* at that time, an emotional peak had been reached that was higher than at wartime. I had a character called Big Jane, and she saw a picture of Snake Tomlin, who was her lover, and she was going back to see him in Australia, because she thought he was in a hospital in Australia.

Saba: I've seen that page. That's how you ended it. Terry kisses her goodbye, and off she goes. You must have felt an emotional wrench.
Caniff: Oh yes, indeed. We talked earlier about how you have to believe this stuff before you can sell it to anyone else, and the deeper I got into that, the more poignant it was for me. Especially knowing that I was going to have to hang my children by the neck. It was almost as bad when, 26 years later, *Terry* was chopped off. I felt again that my distant children were being executed in far-off Hindustan, and I couldn't do anything about it.

Saba: They ended it very unceremoniously, too.
Caniff: Unfortunately, it had reached the point where it was paying its way, but just barely, so the editors were anxious just to get it out of there. I'll give the syndicate credit—they tried to get someone who could carry it on, but they couldn't get anyone to do it for the price they wanted to pay for both writing and drawing it. So there was nothing else to do but just cut it off.

Saba: I guess it was the Vietnam War that killed it, really.
Caniff: To a great extent, yes. It was identified too closely with the baby bombings and all that stuff.

Saba: I must say that 10 years ago, you and I would have probably been on very different sides of the war.
Caniff: Not necessarily, and this is a funny thing. It's come up quite frequently. Let me put it this way: the people who were fighting the war in Vietnam were not there of their own choosing. They were there because they were drafted. They didn't enlist for "Down with Hitler," and "Down with Hirohito," which would cause a lot of guys to enlist. Almost without exception, they were there because they were drafted. Once a guy is drafted and he's stuck in a place, that's where my relationship with him begins. I never got into the reasons for him being there. It's just the fact that *he was there,* that's all. Then he became my way of mirroring what was going on, what a miserable job it was being there. But not *why* he was there.

I didn't like that war any more than you liked that war. But because I was showing these GIs doing their thing, it sounded as if I were a hawk. I didn't feel that way about it at all.

Saba: I have to say that during those years it wasn't printed in Canada, so I didn't see it then.
Caniff: I think that the perceived pro-war stance was why it was dropped in Canada, largely, accentuated by the use of Canadian territory as the base for an American bomber experiment.

Saba: It insulted the sensitive Canadians [*laughter*].
Caniff: Well, why should they be made the target for a Russian missile?

Saba: My interpretation of why it was dropped is, more than anything, you deal so much with American politics and military situations, and the Canadians have this hypersensitivity about nationalism. It's a funny thing, because they're running all these other American strips, but they didn't deal with the subject matter you were concerned with.
Caniff: Just as *Blondie* and *Beetle Bailey* are translated into all those languages, they're just as Yankee Doodle as they can be. Especially *Beetle Bailey.* But with *Blondie,* as well as *Bringing Up Father,* it's considered enormously funny that a woman could dominate her husband. *That's* what's funny.

Saba: To get back to my readings of the early *Steve Canyon*s in that book, I felt something that I can now perhaps interpret more easily. All of the characters in *Steve Canyon* had a tremendous nostalgia for the War. I feel it must have been you feeling how much easier it was to write this strip during those years. You kept looking backward as well.

Caniff: That's what war could do—you could always have an explosion upstairs, and *boom!* you're into another story.

Saba: But I think that you must have unconsciously, or consciously, been looking back and feeling a sort of nostalgia.

Caniff: I was, I'm sure. But everybody around me was. Every guy who came back from the war was so glad to get home, but after a while it was, "Gee whiz, we had a pretty good time out there." You forget the pain. You forget the stench. You only remember the time you went into London and did the town.

Saba: I only read the first year, because that's what was in the book, but I found that the crew of [Canyon's] plane didn't come off as individuals. There was too many of them all at once.

Caniff: Yes. I had them come out too strong in too many directions. What I had in mind in the beginning was to have each one have a segment as the strip progressed. You needed that many people to crew that type of aircraft. It was a four-engine aircraft.

Saba: Well, it did give you characters.

Caniff: And it gave me something to talk about. Each of these guys had his own world to come back to. In the wartime, they would have been just GIs, but once the war was over, the jockey had a big, beautiful dame at home, one guy was the familyman, somebody else was the radio nut, and so forth down the line.

Saba: They all seemed to me to be like caricatures. They didn't last. As you developed better characters, they dropped out.

Caniff: I had to have some tools to work with, and they were it. They were the most useful device I could think of to get this thing off. What happened was, a lot of real people did exactly that same thing. They'd buy one airplane, and a bunch of guys would start a one-man airline. Then they blew out one tire and they were out of business. Usually, that happened in Afghanistan [*laughter*]. That was the end of it. They never got the airplane out of Afghanistan. The only group who succeeded in this was the Flying Tigers.

Saba: I have a lot of *Steve Canyon* Sunday pages from the '40s and '50s. I looked through them, and I failed to find the moment at which he re-enlists.

Caniff: I don't think it was shown. He was off-stage. It was in the early stages of the Korean War, and somebody else was center-stage. When he reentered the strip, he was in uniform. There was no single scene where he reenlisted.

Saba: I didn't realize, until I looked through my Sunday pages, how early Happy Easter came along. It struck me that he was very much like the Connie figure in *Terry.*
Caniff: He was someone to talk to. You need a Mutt and a Jeff to do almost anything. It gives you a chance to explain: "How are you going to make it, Steve?" and then Steve explains how. You need that in a narrative strip.

Saba: And he's comedy relief, also.
Caniff: It starts with comedy relief, of course.

Saba: Did you plan Happy Easter from the time you started the strip?
Caniff: I don't think so. I don't think it was part of my original concept. But I needed somebody who wasn't really connected with anything.

Saba: It struck me that it was such a vital element to have the comedy relief in the strip. I'm surprised to hear that you didn't realize that before you started the strip.
Caniff: Let's go back a bit, using *Terry* as a test-ground for the thing. The Connie character was introduced deliberately for the comedy relief. Connie was right out of a Somerset Maugham story—he had a character who was the Chinese servant. Maugham knew what he was talking about, and I was flying blind, with this phony pidgin English that was never before heard by man nor beast. The Big Stoop character was out of real life. I had a picture of a guy, a big Mongolian character, and he looked as if he didn't speak. I got around to revealing that he had his tongue cut out a long time later. But he just looked like a guy who wouldn't speak anybody's language, and was therefore catatonic. But he was the perfect counterpoint. Mutt and Jeff, again.

I used them a lot, and then, when the war came along, they were sort of incongruous, except that nobody in China in those days was incongruous. It was perfectly logical that each of them would be in the Chinese Army. It wasn't hard to bring them in on that level, and it gave me an excuse for the comedy relief.

It wasn't so easy to come by in *Canyon,* because I couldn't fall back on these outback people. I had to come up with some that *could be.*

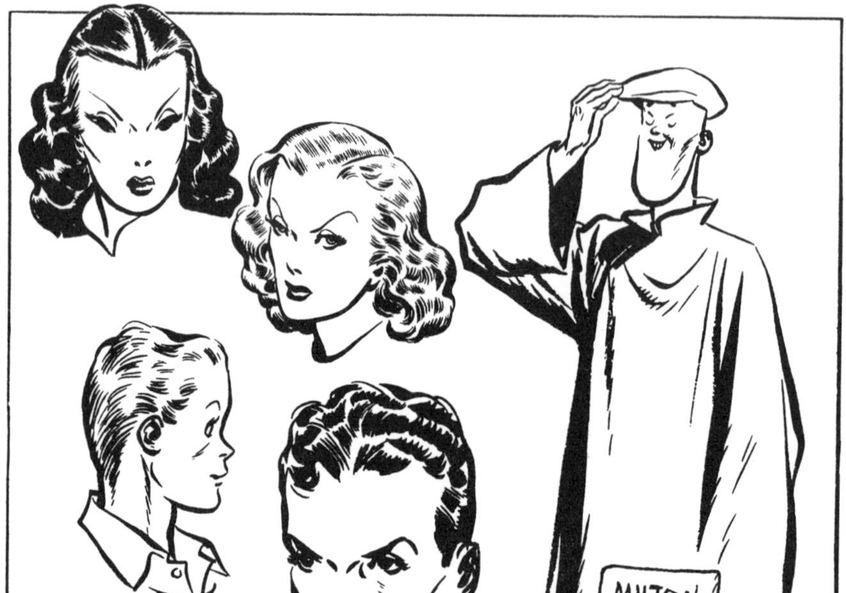

Model sheet for Terry characters—the Dragon Lady, Burma, Big Stoop, Terry, Pat Ryan, and Connie—shows the relative size of the four principals.

The Happy Easter cavalry had been obsolete for so long that it's unlikely that he would have outlived the Spanish Civil War, or whatever he was involved in.

Saba: [*Laughter*] I thought of that myself. "How old is this guy, anyway?"
Caniff: The cavalry characters, whether they ever rode anything but a tank in World War II, they were still members of the cavalry.

Saba: In Jim Steranko's *History of Comics*, he mentions that Noel Sickles actually ghosted a sequence of *Terry and the Pirates*.
Caniff: When he was doing *Scorchy Smith* and I was just starting *Terry*, we used to have a studio together. We often would help each other out. Noel hated to write. It was not his bag. So I would write a whole storyline for him sometimes, or just pick up in the middle of one he was bored by, just so he could make his deadline. He would help me sometimes under the same conditions. We were sitting there, and I'm left handed and he's right-handed, so we were always facing each other. Just to make the deadline, sometimes we would bat these things back and forth. But he never ghosted a whole sequence. I never wrote all of his stories. I never did any of his drawing. He was only interested in the drawing problem, he got bored with that too. He just gave it up.

Saba: That's what he said. He licked it and he wanted to go on.
Caniff: Then he did editorial cartoons for the Associated Press after he'd given up the strip thing. But he found that the Associated Press editorial cartoons were so vapid, and so blah, that that was nothing but an exercise in drawing. The ideas were nothing. He got tired of it, and he just quit.

Saba: I read this about four or five years ago, and it was really exciting. It was the Nostalgia Press volume of your first 14 months of *Terry*. I really got excited about how your style changed over such a short period of time. You could see it week by week. If you turned one page, you couldn't see it, but if you turned back six pages, my God, there's a real difference.
Caniff: That was Sickles' doing, by the way. It was Sickles who said there wasn't enough drama in it. He was doing all that in *Scorchy*, and we were doing the strips facing each other. He said, "Why don't you use more black, and jazz it up?" So I started rather gingerly at first, coming down heavily on the blacks. There was more drama in the night

scenes, and that's when you notice it. I was just not quite sure of my ground up until then.

Saba: I can see you tentatively going one step forward and two steps back, but it became your own style.
Caniff: In a very real sense, it was Sickles' style, because he was the one experimenting with it in *Scorchy,* which he didn't give a damn about really. But it was a great canvas to noodle and doodle around with. He was developing this stuff day-by-day. He had no Sunday page, and he was playing around with it on the dailies, and I was doing it daily *and* Sunday. As a result, I had an even broader canvas to play with. Except that I wasn't all that certain of myself.

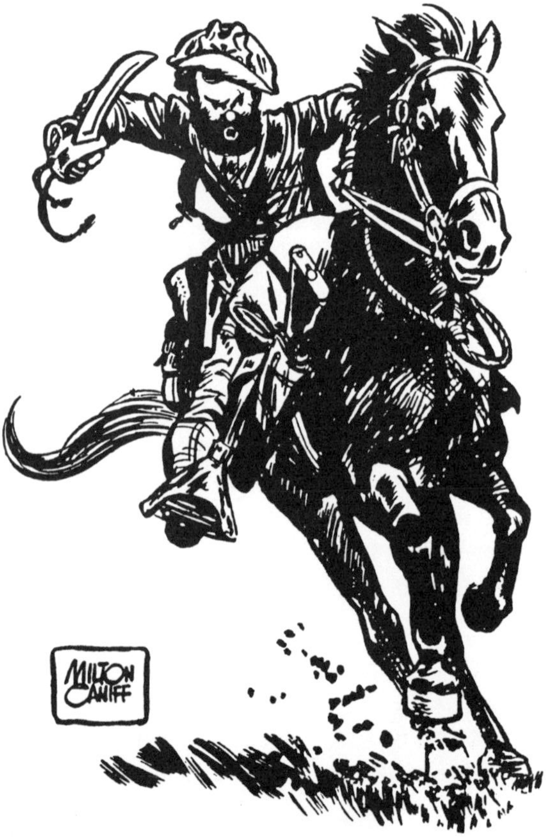

In a fanciful mood once, Caniff drew Happy Easter as a young trooper in the Seventh Cavalry—an impossibility since Hap was too young to have kept company with General Armstrong Custer.

Saba: I could see you in that book trying things, and I could see the development of an artist, who becomes a really supreme artist. It's very rare for the public to see, over the span of time in a reprint edition a great artist develop right before your eyes. It's like stop-motion photography of a flower opening.
Caniff: We would throw anything out there, just to see what the reaction would be. If it was good, we'd use it again, or continue on that theme. Fortunately, in those days, we were dealing with a background that was so little known—China—

that you could do anything. You could show up with a battleship in the middle of the desert. Why not?

Saba: You know, I'm envious that you could do that.
Caniff: It was an absolute blank check. You could do anything at all. Of course, once we got the bit in our teeth, it was great to play with this. Except Sickles got bored. But I didn't get bored, because I had to go on with it.

Saba: Are you aware of the similarity between your work on *Terry* and Oriental brushwork?
Caniff: Yes. Actually, I set out to learn to do it the way they do. I'm not that skilled at it, but I know how to hold the brush to get those snappy lines that they do. I don't say that I do it well, but I try. When it comes down to when I can't make it the way they do, I simply go back to an actual character and copy it. But you've got to practice it more often than I have the chance to do.

Saba: It seems to me that the art of cartooning is very similar to the Chinese brushwork technique of painting and drawing. The speed and spontaneity that's important in the Chinese work is also an important part of cartoons.
Caniff: Percy Crosby is the best example of all. You could tell that when he made a speed line, he made a speed line, the way the Chinese and Japanese do.

Saba: You could feel the action in the line when you look at it.
Caniff: Definitely. That's where the skill comes in, in making the point.

Saba: I think a great argument for the worthwhileness of comic art is in comparing it to the Chinese and Japanese art.
Caniff: Especially if that is the point you want to make, and if you do it successfully, as Crosby did. Boy, there's nothing faster than watching Skippy run the way Crosby drew him. That was real speed. You felt it.

Saba: You must feel some of the same things when you're drawing. When you're drawing a running figure, I'll bet you ink it faster.
Caniff: Probably. I haven't thought about it before, but I'm sure I do. I have that sense of impatience. Once I've got what I want in terms of general position, I'll just whip it in, even if it's wrong, and I have to do it over. Or do two lines, and have to knock out one of them, so just that one line will give the impression of the boxing stance, or whatever it is.

Saba: It's interesting that you were setting the story in China, and you were using that style.
Caniff: Of course, I was milking the Chinese thing for everything I could, because I knew nothing of China before.

Saba: Do you think your style is still progressing?
Caniff: I hope so. It must. It *has* to. If it doesn't, I'm turning to stone. I'm not about to atrophy. I'm not about to preside at the dissolution of the British Empire, as Churchill said.

Dragon Lady, We Still Love You!

Austin Stevens / 1979

From *Yankee*, December 1979, pp. 68–69, 71–73, 150–58. Reprinted by permission.

James Reston once described Milton Caniff as "a very odd character . . . with a very few special loves: one wife, one craft, and one country to whose conflicts and troubles he devoted his skills and patriotic instincts." He also had an eerie ability to get to history before the world made it. . . .

Sundays were always the same at our house. After church and before dinner, the *Boston Herald* and the *New York Times* were divided, five ways.

Being the youngest in the family, I had the first shot at the comic section and I always saved *Terry and the Pirates* until last, because it was the best of the bunch. I'd read it three or four times and then I'd get out some paper and a pencil and try to copy the drawings. Lying on the floor, my head not more than five inches from the paper, I'd work for an hour or more—always just time enough to worry the drawing into a smudgy mess.

What I didn't know at the time, however, was that children all across the country were doing the same thing and, like me, a large number of them were learning how to draw.

Milton Caniff, creator of *Terry and the Pirates* and *Steve Canyon,* is the most imitated cartoonist in the country. He's led the pack for 40 years: four drawings a day each weekday, plus the Sunday panels; 35 a week; 1,820 a year; a total of more than 72,000 pen and ink illustrations so far, and some so fine that the originals hang in museums.

As a master of black and white he has been ranked with Toulouse-Lautrec, Gluyas Williams, and Charles Dana Gibson. With the exception of Hal Foster, creator of *Prince Valiant,* there was, in the late thirties and early forties, simply no one in his league.

But as important as his draftsmanship is to his strips, equally compelling is his ability to tell a lively story, full of surprises and mood, with characters so convincing that when one died in 1941 the whole country mourned the loss. *Newsweek,* April 1950, reported: "When the heiress Raven Sherman was pushed off a truck by villains and died at the base of a Chinese cliff, millions of Americans mourned her. College students, heads bared, reverently faced east. Flowers and condolences by the thousands streamed in, one from a Florida man who wistfully wrote: 'Most of us would like to die in such a manner.' " Yet Raven had never lived except in the inkwell of Milton Caniff. When Terry received his wings on October 17, 1943, the message of the lecture given by his mentor, Colonel Flip Corkin, seemed so important to the spirit and direction of America at that time that it was actually inserted in the *Congressional Record.*

Currently, *Steve Canyon* is followed by more than 30 million readers. Its appeal is broad—from the housewife to the intellectual, from the man on the street to the leaders of our country. According to Bob Considine, "Milton Caniff has done more for the Air Force than any person since Billy Mitchell." He goes on to explain that since "so many of the jams in which Steve Canyon finds himself show up later in real life, to pester real airmen and bedevil U.S. relations with the enemy, that the comic strip has become required reading in Washington. Air Force files actually list 'Colonel Canyon . . .' " (His file number is AO #041044.)

In the history of mankind there have been only a handful of spokesmen who have ever managed to talk to 30 million people at one time, on a daily basis, for a period of over four decades. Perhaps one of his secrets is that he does not talk *down* to his audience. He assumes them to be as intelligent and sophisticated as he is himself.

In the beginning, the Caniff family came to Boston from Ireland. "We weren't lace-curtain Irish," he hastens to point out. "They had fruit on the table. We did, too, but only when somebody was sick in the family." When Milton Caniff does return to New England these days, it's usually to lecture. "I feel as if I've come home," he continues. "Whether I'm talking to a group at Symphony Hall or on the campus at Harvard or in a backwater town in Maine, the audience is always right there with me. Heavens, yes," he laughs, "sometimes way out ahead of me."

When Milton Caniff started *Terry and the Pirates* in 1934, it was as conventional a strip as was ever launched. The drawing was adequate, the story line dogged: a straight-on adventure that was an irregular mix of *Treasure Island* and *The Rover Boys.* But within four years he had transformed it into a stylish, amusing, American fantasy, treating adventure with a tongue-in-cheek nonchalance Hollywood wouldn't achieve for years.

In one two-day sequence, the Dragon Lady would recognize that she was in love with Pat Ryan—only to take him up the river on the following day to sell him to another pirate. This was the kind of light-hearted skullduggery that only Truman Capote would dare handle, in a movie like *Beat the Devil,* 20 years later. And Pat Ryan's offhand manner with the Dragon Lady wouldn't be put into a movie until Rhett Butler finally said to Scarlett O'Hara, "Frankly, my dear, I don't give a damn."

By 1939 Milton Caniff's panels were so subtly planned that they looked like a story board for a movie to be produced ten years in the future. His use of extreme "camera angles," dramatic contrasts, the push and pull of a pictorial sequence, was paralleled only once during that period, and then in the very advanced movie *Citizen Kane,* which may or may not be a coincidence. Along with fan mail from John Steinbeck, the Duke of Windsor, and Hap Arnold, Milton Caniff actually *did* have correspondence with Orson Welles in those days. . . . .

Most of his characters were taken from Hollywood: Pat Ryan from Fred MacMurray, the Dragon Lady from Joan Crawford, the villainous Sandhurst from Charles Laughton.

"Burgess Meredith brought Charles Laughton around to my studio," said Milton Caniff. "Mr. Laughton didn't read comic strips and was absolutely delighted to discover himself in the part of Sandhurst."

To the newspaper reader, a comic-strip artist is somebody who draws four drawings a day with either a gag line or a cliff-hanger in the fourth picture box. But for a strip with the dimensions of *Terry and the Pirates* and *Steve Canyon*, the "artist" should be, as well, director, producer, writer, set and costume designer, and all of the actors: hero, villain, heroine, and the cast of thousands. Of course, he must also be able to draw everything he can dream up—and with precision and strength—for every picture will be reduced to 2" × 2", photostated, embossed on a mat, and finally printed on a cheap piece of absorbent newsprint.

By some fluke of nature's eternal unfairness, Caniff was given enough talent in all these areas to put together a comic strip of immeasurable impact—a strip that would enter World War II as innocently as the nation, and reflect through its duration the country's growing burden.

Considering his place at the outset of the war and Terry's age and location in the Orient at the time the Japanese bombed Pearl Harbor, the coincidence now seems destined. There was no TV in those days and most war movies seemed to be directed by Hopalong Cassidy. So it would fall to Mr. Caniff, working alone in the quiet of his studio, with only the scratching of his pen and the ticking of his clock to keep him company, to speak to the American public responsibly about war: telling them, gently, how to face the enemy and death and how to live through a war without losing their courage, or style, or ability to love, or their sense of purpose. He did more to this end, reaching more of us graphically, than any other individual, including President Roosevelt himself. It was "his hour upon the stage," and he had arrived at it by a combination of hard work, some luck, and a considerable talent.

"When I was in the eighth grade I took the Landon course. It was an art student's correspondence course—a forerunner of the Famous Artists' School in Connecticut [he later was head of the cartoon division of this school], but it was better insofar as it cost only $25 to sign up. The Famous Artists' School's enrollment was $400, which was simply too much money for most young people. And what I learned from the Landon School, that one simple and direct course, is of value to me even today."

But from the beginning, drawing just wasn't Milton Caniff's problem. Deadlines were. In the early years of *Terry and the Pirates,* he was always in trouble. He shared a studio with Noel Sickles. It was located about a block away from the *Daily News.* ". . . At five minutes to five on deadline days, we'd go out the window and gallop over there, the top panel still wet when we arrived. It was always that close."

Had it not been for the pressure of time and Sickles' help, Milton Caniff might never have developed as a draftsman. In the beginning the strip's drawings were indecisive both in the craft of the work itself and in the intent. Many of the characters seemed transposed from Sagendorf's panels of "Popeye," and while "Popeye" is a classic in its own right, it was an idea headed in quite another direction. The story line, too, fluctuated from an adventure strip to a "funny strip." Milton Caniff hadn't made up his mind, or soul, or something.

From panel to panel the drawings varied in quality, but even the best boxes lacked the sure knowledge, the telling line, the stark contrasts that set patterns dancing on a four-panel strip, patterns designed to catch the eye—all qualities that would later distinguish a Caniff strip and put him far in front of the pack.

"Sickles was doing *Scorchy Smith* in those days," Caniff explains. "That man could draw anything, and all from memory. He could even draw things he *hadn't* seen; that is, if they were described to him. And he was forever experimenting."

Milton Caniff stood up and walked over to the wall. He took down two framed reproductions of full-color illustrations and handed them to me. They were western themes, beautifully executed. Bright, smart color, strongly designed, their sharp detail suggested even more than it stated. They were pictures by Noel Sickles—but in the tradition of Frederic Remington, they were more than illustrations. These were paintings.

"Well, Sickles was trying to find a way to help both of us draw faster, and as I've told you, he was a great experimenter. He started fooling around with the chiaroscuro technique . . . you know, developing an image with just lights and darks." It was a technique introduced by woodcutters of the 16th century. Using different values (or tones) of one color they managed to create their image through a contrast of patterns.

"Well, it worked. He figured out how to translate the approach to our strips. We used brushes on the shadow side of our drawing, grouping our blacks and then coming in with pen and ink on the light side. It was fast and that's what we needed, but it was also very effective."

Mr. Caniff sat back in his chair and looked out the window on East 45th Street. "In those days, all we were trying to do was earn a living. We had started out in the Depression. I suppose that's when I got my $50-a-week mind."

Beyond speed, the chiaroscuro approach offered a greater opportunity for saying more and suggesting more. The drawings, however frisky in the subject matter, were taking on an illustrative quality that was far more appropriate to the telling of an adventure story.

Terry looked less like Blondie's son, and developed, instead, the clean good looks of a young William Holden. Pat Ryan looked less like Smiling Jack and more like Fred MacMurray, and he grew stronger and braver panel by panel.

The Dragon Lady lost two pounds around her waist and somehow regained them at her bust line. She had, moreover, developed into a rather willful female person. Compared to her, Gloria Steinem, Jane Fonda, and Vanessa Redgrave come over as a gaggle of teenagers at their first prom. The Dragon Lady was by now the nation's leading anima figure. And every American male reader from age 13 to 103 had fallen quite in love with her. John Steinbeck wrote, "When my grandchildren speak of their sugarplum eroticisms, I can say, 'You see? This is how it was in my day. This Dragon Lady, with the figure of a debutante . . . was one of your old man's girlfriends.' "

From 1938 to 1940 she developed from a river pirate to a guerrilla leader in China. Milton Caniff was beginning to display an eerie ability to get to history before the world made it. As early as 1937 and 1938, the war in China became more and more a part of the strip. America was neutral in this matter but Terry Lee and Pat Ryan could ill afford to be. Though the syndicate required that the Japanese be referred to as the "invaders," by 1939 everybody who read the strip knew exactly whom Mr. Caniff was talking about.

When, on December 7, 1941, the Japanese bombed Pearl Harbor, all Caniff's people were in the thick of it. Young America had grown up with Terry and identified with him and now every mother and father could identify realistically with his danger. Terry Lee, like Pinocchio, had somehow mysteriously become a "real" live boy in the very real target center of world action.

In those days, there were no arguments about whether we should be in the war. It had not been our choice. So we simply went to work to win it. Overnight, factories converted from paperclip production to producing tanks, jeeps, rifles, and airplanes. As in the Revolutionary War, when Yankee farmers adapted their building skills to producing the finest sailing ships in the sea, so it was at the outset of World War II.

Instantly America became the innovative leader in the development of a war machine that would astound the world.

Milton Caniff tried to join a service, but he was 4F. If you, who are reading this, are under the age of 45, it will be hard for you to imagine the fervor of the time, the personal disappointment (almost shame) of being turned down by a service. The fever ran so high that one young man, knowing he was eight pounds underweight, actually consumed 10 pounds of bananas in a single sitting so that he might tip the scales properly at his physical.

Women kissed their sons and husbands good-bye and went to work nights turning out bullets and boots, bayonets and bombs. Children collected scrap metal and housewives rolled bandages and saved frying fat for the war effort. On the home front all of this was done in the spirit of a community preparing exhibits for a county fair. Only the soldiers on the front lines knew what war was all about. And only men like Caniff guessed what the soldiers knew and the mothers suffered and the world needed.

"Not being in the service put me in an awkward position," he confesses. "I couldn't speak with the same authority as, say, Bill Mauldin. I couldn't form the same kinds of personal statements *he* was free to make. It could too easily be said, 'What does *he* know.' "

But speak to us he did, from the general taproot of our collective spirit. And he did so with another and very serious authority. He knew by now a great deal about China. Through his research he had become something of an expert on Far Eastern warfare. He had been drawing planes, tanks, and uniforms for over four years and he had become a master draftsman. He spoke with sentiment, never with sentimentality. He was intelligent and dedicated. Even today, his studio time runs 12 to 14 hours every day of a seven-day week. And in those days he would often work into the lonely hours of the morning, his wife Bunny helping him stay awake by reading aloud to him. (He also did a strip for the *Stars and Stripes* called *Male Call.*)

By 1943 his strip had become so important that its content was twice discussed in Congress, and the F.B.I. made it required reading because of Caniff's innocent habit of disclosing top secrets.

And now a strange new game developed among the nation's war-watchers. They were called armchair generals and they simply couldn't get enough information too quickly. A cartoon appeared in *The New Yorker* on this subject by George Price: one of his hopeless male types is sitting at a table. Before him blares his radio. The chair and table, even his head, are perches for pigeons. He's examining a message and his harried wife is complaining to a friend, "It's the *Times* bulletins every hour on the hour, the *Daily News* bulletins every hour on the half-hour, and those damned carrier pigeons in between."

But for Caniff the role of armchair general was an important part of his career. "I used to sit at the drawing table and try to figure what I would do if I were MacArthur or Chennault. After a while, if you do something long enough, you begin to be right. Well, one day the F.B.I. came around, and I never had to talk so fast in my life."

Months before he had seen a small news item about a whole group of soldiers, in fatigues, who had been picked up by the M.P.'s, because, to a man, they were out of uniform. They were *all* wearing black shoes. "That's all there was to the news item. They had to be Navy personnel. But what would the Navy be doing out there? If you're planning an invasion of the Chinese mainland you ought to have checkpoints. So you send in the Navy observers to do the triangulation, I reasoned.

"So I repeated the black-shoe bit in *Terry and the Pirates* and set up my checkpoint back in the hills—but here's the startling part. For no special reason that I could remember I called the checkpoint 'Happy Valley.' I had to give it a code name. I hit it right on the mark that time. It turns out there *was* such a strategy afoot and the checkpoint *was* called 'Happy Valley.' My dialogue with the F.B.I. was fairly intense when I told them I just made the name up. They quite simply didn't believe me.

"And then I remembered where I'd borrowed the name. I piled the F.B.I. in *their* car (we didn't have any gas then, either) and we drove down the road to a summer camp I pass every day on my way to the studio. There was a sign there, tucked under the trees. It read, 'Happy Valley Boys' Camp.' And I was off the hook."

His soothsaying at times was appallingly accurate. When Flip Corkin in *Terry and the Pirates* blueprinted a 1943 paratroop invasion of Burma, it actually happened *and* only two days after it appeared in his strip. And of course Caniff developed his strips weeks in advance.

"Once," he said, "I had prefabricated submarines being carried by the Russians overland to the warm-water ports of the Persian Gulf. The F.B.I. came back to see me. Again I learned through a very suspicious interrogation that, indeed, the Russians *were* doing just that.

"Make no mistake, I had a rule of thumb on this kind of thing: if an authority *ever* told me something he shouldn't have, I would *never* use it. Beyond the interest of national security, I wouldn't want to get my friend in trouble. And anyway the F.B.I. visits were always a strain."

When the war ended, Milton Caniff was still making only $70,000 a year. *Terry and the Pirates* had always been owned by a syndicate. In 1944, Marshall Field offered him a five-year contract, a guarantee of $2,000 a week, to create a new strip for the *Chicago Sun* syndicate. The new strip, *Steve Canyon,* would be owned by Mr. Caniff and "rented" to the *Sun.* That was more than 22 years ago.

According to King Features Syndicate, Inc., it is *still* the most widely read adventure strip in the world today. But more surprising than Caniff's continued success with *Steve Canyon* is the widespread interest in a strip he gave up some 30 years ago. *Terry and the Pirates* has now become an antique. A comic book reprinting Terry's newspaper adventures that you could purchase off the newsstands in the forties for ten cents will now cost you $45. Young students working for their master's degree study his correspondence with people all over the country. A library at Ohio State University has been given his name; and photostats of *Terry and the Pirates* (*not* original art) are kept under lock and key. It's far easier to examine original Rembrandt etchings at the Boston Museum of Fine Arts than Caniff photostats in Columbus, Ohio.

"I'm not sure why *Terry* is so durable," says Mr. Caniff today. "I'm *still* getting a great deal of mail on that strip. Perhaps it has something to do with the idea of the American hero. He lives within all of us. In our tradition any native-born child may grow up to be President. We're not heroes ourselves, but we *are* all hero-ridden."

When we were through talking, Mr. Caniff invited me to have lunch with him at the Palm Restaurant on Second Avenue in New York.

"It's an old speakeasy," he said. "We all lunched there in the old days. After prohibition, the owner threatened to redecorate the place, but such a hue and cry was set up that he didn't dare. And he hasn't dared since. It still has sawdust on the floor. Not the same sawdust, of course."

Along the walls hang a parade of all the famous cartoonists of the mid-thirties.* The drawings are yellowed and stained by time, but they hold their own against a changing world.

*The walls of the Palm, a hang-out for cartoonists, are decorated with an array of merry murals—drawings on the plaster of famous comic strip characters painted there by their creators when they were, presumably, in their cups. The walls have been repainted occasionally but usually by a fine arts student or portrait painter, who steers carefully around the priceless original works of art. In various places, as Stevens notes, framed original artwork hangs among the murals.—RCH

Mr. Caniff picked one of his own off the wall: a Christmas card, he told me, circa 1939. It was a night scene. Through the window of the building to the right, Terry Lee, Pat Ryan, Connie and Big Stoop could be seen celebrating their Christmas dinner. The mood was warm, tucked-in and joyous. But outside their door, in the snow, stood a guard, an "invader"—an Oriental dressed in exotic winter garb, head-gear, cuffed and collared in fur, holding a rifle. Behind him rose an awesome landscape of mountains, cold and brooding. As a pen and ink drawing, it was a humdinger.

I looked at it, smiled and shook my head. But the best thing about the business of the day was that I could tell that Milton Caniff was just as tickled as I was with the drawing.

I mean, you might have thought he'd done it the day before.

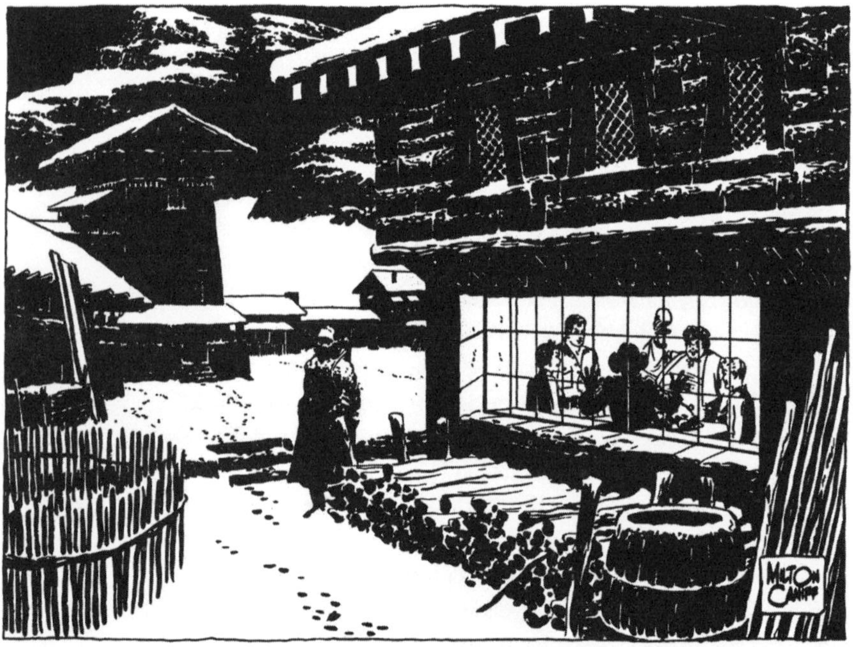

Homefront Commando

MASTER SERGEANT ALAN PROCHOROFF / 1982

From *Airman*, October 1982,
pp. 37–41.

They used to call Milton Caniff a "home-front commando." It wasn't meant to be a compliment.

It was, instead, a label of shame during World War II, used sneeringly to imply that a male civilian in the United States couldn't measure up to the standards of those in uniform.

Caniff was 4-F. But even though a bad leg kept him out of the fighting, he measured up in other ways, graphically proving you don't have to use a sword to make a point. An artist's pen can be every bit as mighty.

He is, of course, famous as the creator of comic strips like *Terry and the Pirates; Male Call,* which appeared during World War II; and later *Steve Canyon.*

He has drawn *Steve Canyon* for 35 years, and the popular strip—equivalent in scope to six adventure novels each year—continues to reflect Caniff's respect for the military, something that was readily evident in his earliest work.

It comes as no surprise to anyone who knows him. The military tradition has deep roots in the Caniff family. His great-grandfather, who came to the United States to escape the potato famine in Ireland, joined the 1st Ohio Cavalry and served with Gen. William T. Sherman during the Civil War.

His father, too, had military ties. He was a first sergeant in the Ohio National Guard. Even the elder Caniff's civilian jobs gave a hint of what was to come for his son—he was a printer for a Hillsboro, Ohio newspaper and later repaired and sold automobiles in Dayton, including that of Lt. Gen. Jimmy Doolittle. None of this was lost on an impressionable Milton Caniff.

"We were always near the edge of greatness in Dayton," he recalled. "We lived close to Wright and Patterson air bases where new airplanes were constantly being tested. There was a feeling in the town of a special closeness with the military, especially the aviation part of it. 'Hap' Arnold and Jimmy Doolittle were just second lieutenants then, but they were often in the news because they were always trying to do things with an airplane that were thought to be impossible.

"It was quite an amazing time," he told *Airman,* propping his foot under the drawing board in his New York City apartment, which is located near United Nations headquarters.

Living close to the place where people from all nations come together seems somehow ironic. Caniff, wielding his pen to create adventurous alter egos, habitually places his characters in exotic, faraway places. He never left New York to visit China, but that's where it all began for him and *Terry.*

"The publisher of the *New York Daily News* thought the strip should have an adventure theme, and that it should take place in the Orient. At the time, China was still filled with romance, and I saw it as a place where anything could happen."

On October 22, 1934, Caniff became the nation's youngest major cartoonist with the birth of *Terry and the Pirates.* From the beginning, *Terry* was no ordinary comic strip; Caniff's unique art style saw to that.

Instead of drawing in the two-dimensional manner of the day, Caniff made "Terry" look like a real person. The strip was also vibrant and gutsy. Additionally, "I caught readers' interest by using vivid color and illustration in the artwork."

Terry and the Pirates became the first of the "every-wrinkle-must-show" school of illustration. Caniff was also the first to incorporate movie-making techniques into his strips, experimenting with "camera" angles, sudden switches from long shots to close-ups, and with light sources and their relation to moods.

"I wanted to have the strip look as true-to-life as possible," he said.

Equally important were the stories that accompanied the [pictures in the] strip. Caniff pioneered the use of current events in the news as a backdrop for his stories.

His reason was simple. "While your art technique may attract readers initially, it's the story that keeps them coming back. I try to keep the subject matter as topical as I can because using subjects in the news keeps readers that much more interested."

It's also a natural device to use for an adventure series. "The military in war is always a big news story," said Caniff. "There's hardly been a day go by in history when there wasn't some fighting somewhere in the world.

"If you have that as a backdrop, the rest is easy. You look at a situation and try to work in the 'what if?' factor."

His formula has been a huge success, but it hasn't been without its problems. The realistic illustrations and intricate story lines created a vexation from the outset for Caniff—accuracy. But accuracy would become Caniff's hallmark, and he has gone to great lengths to ensure everything in his strips is "just so."

His philosophy is simple. "When it comes to being accurate, there is no gray—you're either right or you're wrong. I'd rather be right.

"I've made a fetish of it. One reason is that during the early years of World War II, nobody else was drawing a war/adventure strip, and that gave me a leg up on everyone else." The adherence to absolute accuracy began almost from the beginning of *Terry and the Pirates.*

He decided Terry needed to have mobility to be able to travel easily for his adventures. Being a military pilot seemed a logical occupation, since that would give him mobility and a reason for getting into unusual situations.

That created a problem right away, though, because Terry was in China, and he didn't know how to fly when the strip began. "I couldn't just have him jump in an airplane and fly it without learning how first," explained Caniff. "That wouldn't have been realistic or fair to the readers.

And I didn't want to bring him all the way back to the United States just to learn how to fly.

"Then I remembered seeing something in the news about Chinese pilots being taught to fly in the United States. I asked the War Department if it would be practical for something similar to be worked in reverse—for Terry to be taught to fly in China. My contacts thought it highly unusual, but agreed that it might occur."

That presented yet another challenge for Caniff. He didn't know how to fly, either. "I needed to have at least a rough idea of what it was you did before you got your wings. Once again, the Air Corps came through and gave me some pointers."

Caniff earned his wings, so to speak, and eventually Terry did, too. Caniff used that occasion to ink a still-famous strip in which Flip Corkin gives fatherly advice to a youthful Terry about what it means to be a military pilot.

Going to extremes was one way Caniff made sure he was accurate. There were other lessons, too, some more painful to learn.

"One strip in particular convinced me to go over the edge and use straight reality rather than pseudo-realism. I had been putting Terry through his paces in the Yellow Sea when I began getting letters saying my characters were floating east on rivers that coursed west. And I was told they were holding up Chinese pants with buttons that were sold exclusively by an Ohio dime-store chain."

Such a hue and cry forced realism into the comics as it had never been emphasized before, according to the cartoonist-writer. "I didn't sell comic strip realism to my readers," Caniff said. "They sold it to me."

The combination of realism and current events has made for some interesting reading, but has also gotten Caniff into trouble occasionally. There was the time, for instance, when he predicted the invasion of Burma during World War II. His strip showed Terry working on plans for a move his unit was going to make, saying, "Gee, it sounds like we're going to invade Burma." And Flip Corkin lifted an eyebrow and said, "Wellll. . . ."

The strip was carried two days before the actual invasion and raised more than eyebrows in some circles. On the day of the invasion, one London newspaper reproduced the strip on its front page with a story demanding to know how he found out.

"The British thought I was a spy," Caniff said, "but actually all I did was put two and two together and sit back and play general. You only had to look at the situation as it existed then.

"The Japanese were in strength in the east, and we were massed in the west. Somebody obviously was going to move in and fill the vacuum, and Burma seemed the logical place to do it. The timing of publication was purely a coincidence."

In another strip, he toyed with submarine tactics. "My idea was to disguise the snorkle as a flagstick for a life raft," Caniff explained. "When a freighter came in for the rescue, the submarine would launch its torpedos."

It was a great idea—one, it turned out, German U-boats had secretly used in the early days of the war.

He was also questioned by the Federal Bureau of Investigation about other information he included in *Terry and the Pirates.*

Caniff had fabricated a story about a military group that was operating a secret radio transmitter behind enemy lines. "I hypothesized that if you were going to invade a coastline—something I was contemplating for an upcoming story—you'd need a land-based radio station to send out homing signals."

He "established" such a radio station, giving it the code name Happy Valley. That was all there was to it until the FBI agent showed up, demanding to know how he'd found out about Happy Valley.

"It was another of those wild coincidences," Caniff explained. "There actually was a secret Allied radio station whose code name was Happy Valley that was being used to prepare for an invasion. The planners had gotten the name from a race track in Hong Kong: I had chosen mine from a boys' summer camp near my home."

Another strip Caniff produced was, in his own words, by far his most popular, *Male Call* was drawn exclusively for camp newspapers.

"Right after the war started it occurred to Al Capp [the author-illustrator of *Li'l Abner*] and me that camp newspapers were going to need some material. Capp was an amputee and I had been disqualified from serving because of my leg, so we had a common desire to contribute to the war effort."

A survey showed their efforts succeeded tremendously. *Male Call* was said to be the most popular single feature distributed to military papers, topping even news from home.

Anyone who was in uniform in those days remembers *Male Call* and, in particular, Miss Lace. It was about the gorgeously seductive

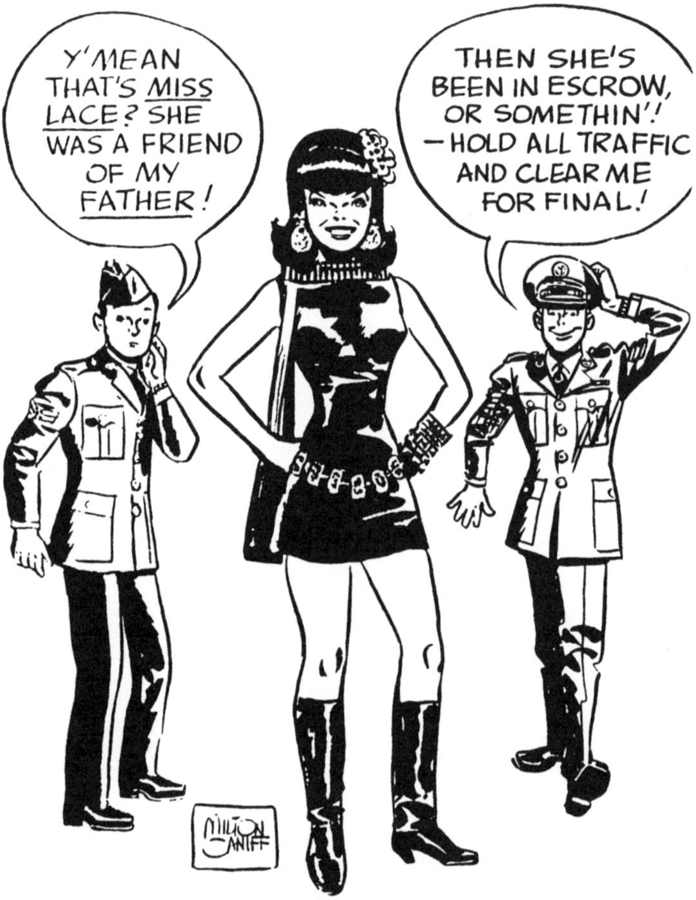

Here's the first Miss Lace drawing since she retired after WWII, done for Airman *magazine in 1970.*

character that Gen. Nathan F. Twining, while chief of staff of the Air Force, said, "I don't know of anyone who didn't fall in love with Miss Lace. She was everything we'd left behind—a pal, a pinup, and a laugh when we needed one. She was Milt's gift to service morale."

. . . .

The realism made famous in *Terry and the Pirates* didn't end in 1947 when Caniff discontinued drawing the strip to start a new adventure series called *"Steve Canyon."*

The new strip's hero began as a civilian setting up his own business—just like countless numbers of men at the time who were returning to civilian life after mustering out of uniform.

Back then, Steve Canyon's connection with the military was his Reserve officer status. He was a major then, with his own serial number: A0041044.

When the strip first appeared in 234 newspapers on Jan. 13, 1947, Canyon's business was flying and his business, Horizons Unlimited, was a charter service that would fly anything or anybody to anyplace in the world, providing the price was right.

As in the case of *Terry and the Pirates,* Canyon was made a pilot to give him the mobility he needed to travel in search of adventure. But unlike other heroes of the day, Steve Canyon was not a "James Bond" kind of guy. In keeping with the basic tenent of Caniff's art ("Characters in the strips live, exist, enjoy, or simply bear life as all other mortals enjoy or bear it."), Canyon had his weaknesses.

"I wanted him to be able to defeat his foes but, as with other mortals, there are things Canyon can do well, and there are other things at which he can be beaten." This element injected realism into the strip—vulnerability. It was a trait with which the average reader could identify.

His business was one area in which he was particularly vulnerable. It was shaky—just like many other postwar businesses that were started on a wing and a prayer.

"Like most guys, Canyon had good intentions, but he forgot you needed money, not just an airplane, to start a business," said Caniff. "He was operating on a shoestring and running into the same problems as everyone in real life: He'd get a lucrative charter, but then would blow a tire in the middle of Timbuktu and be out of business."

The strip continued to mirror the times as Canyon found himself more and more vulnerable to bill collectors. Eventually he found he had to expand, go out of business, or go to work for someone else. That was around the time the Korean War broke out and like so many real-world reservists, Maj. Canyon was recalled to active duty.

"I could easily have left Canyon a civilian, but the renewed military fervor was the temper of the times, just as returning to civilian life had been at the end of World War II. Getting him back in uniform was logical."

Steve Canyon has been on active duty—although not necessarily in uniform—ever since. Although *Steve Canyon* was originally designed to be a civilian adventure series, Caniff stuck with a military theme for many of the same reasons he started with it in *Terry and the Pirates.*

"From a scripting viewpoint, the military is one of the few groups with whom Canyon could be affiliated that made it reasonable for him to be in these exotic situations," Caniff said.

"One of the toughest things I had to reconcile with *Terry* was having a reason for him and the others to be in China. In reality, there was no reason—I put them there to begin with, but there was no compelling reason why they should stay. That used to bother me, and I wanted to avoid it with the *Canyon* strip."

Caniff admits to another, less obvious reason for the military theme. "Let's face it," he admitted. "I'm just an out-and-out unabashed patriot."

Today, Stevenson B. Canyon is a full colonel, but his date of rank is one of the few elements in Caniff's make-believe world that isn't accurate.

"I've deliberately kept him from becoming a general," said Caniff. "Generals can't go out and raise hell with the boys. They have to stay off by themselves or with other generals. That just doesn't work in an adventure story."

He still gets queries from his readers about that, so to make the situation less obvious, Canyon has been quietly eased out of uniform. That doesn't mean his connection with the military has been severed, though.

These days, Col. Canyon is assigned to the Air Force Intelligence Service, a true-life organization whose headquarters is in Washington, D.C. That move came at the same time Canyon was eased out of the cockpit. Both moves, Caniff explained, were a concession to the hero's advancing age.

"Flying fighters is a young man's occupation; it's a tough job keeping current in the airplane you fly. I have Canyon fly light aircraft from time to time, but nobody Canyon's age flies military jets regularly anymore, so I don't have him do it in the strip.

"I'm reminded of Sir Edmund Hillary's comment about conquering Mount Everest. All the pictures showed his Sherpa guide on the summit. When people asked Hillary why his photo wasn't taken, he'd say, 'The top of Mount Everest is no place to teach someone how to work a camera.'

"That lesson holds true for modern jet aircraft—you can't just go out to the airplane, jump into it, and fly off. That just isn't realistic."

On the other hand, Canyon's current assignment with the intelligence group does ring true.

"I liken his position to that of cavalry scouts of the Old West like Buffalo Bill Cody," Caniff explained. "They were on the government payroll because they knew all there was to know about one certain area. The government needed that kind of expertise. And the civilian clothes gave them the freedom to do all kinds of things a uniform would restrict them from getting involved with."

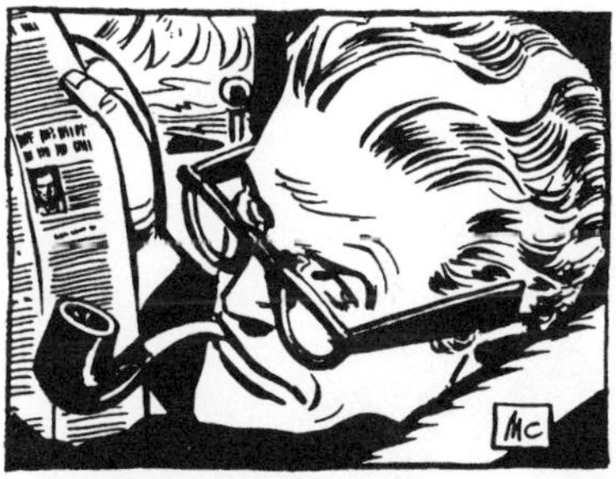

In 1948, Caniff drew this picture of an aging Steve Canyon, saying: "This represents the pipe and slippers routine all adventure strip heroes are purported to seek. Note that the black streak in Canyon's wig is burned gray from the rigors of the life he has led. Of course, this retirement implication is so much guff since S.C. has a family to support —the Caniff family."

As with *Terry and the Pirates,* the use of current events has continued in *Steve Canyon.* Some have involved voodoo in the Caribbean as well as adventure in the oil fields of the Middle East. The strips are usually pure adventure, but occasionally there is a message Caniff is trying to get across.

About four years ago, for instance, one Canyon segment involved the Soviet navy in the Persian Gulf.

"I thought it was important to show the Russians were in that area for a reason. At the time they desperately needed warm-water ports for their navy. They still do."

Using current events isn't the only touch of realism in Caniff's strips.

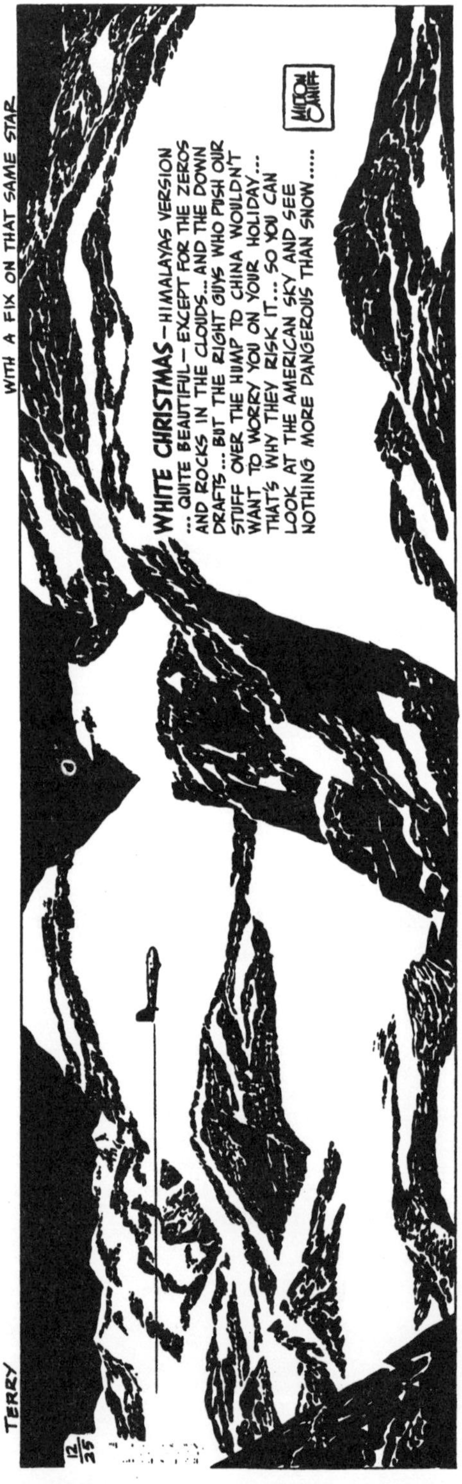

TERRY
WITH A FIX ON THAT SAME STAR
12/25
WHITE CHRISTMAS—HIMALAYAS VERSION ...QUITE BEAUTIFUL—EXCEPT FOR THE ZEROS AND ROCKS IN THE CLOUDS... AND THE DOWN DRAFTS... BUT THE RIGHT GUYS WHO PUSH OUR STUFF OVER THE HUMP TO CHINA WOULDN'T WANT TO WORRY YOU ON YOUR HOLIDAY... THAT'S WHY THEY RISK IT... SO YOU CAN LOOK AT THE AMERICAN SKY AND SEE NOTHING MORE DANGEROUS THAN SNOW......
MILTON CANIFF

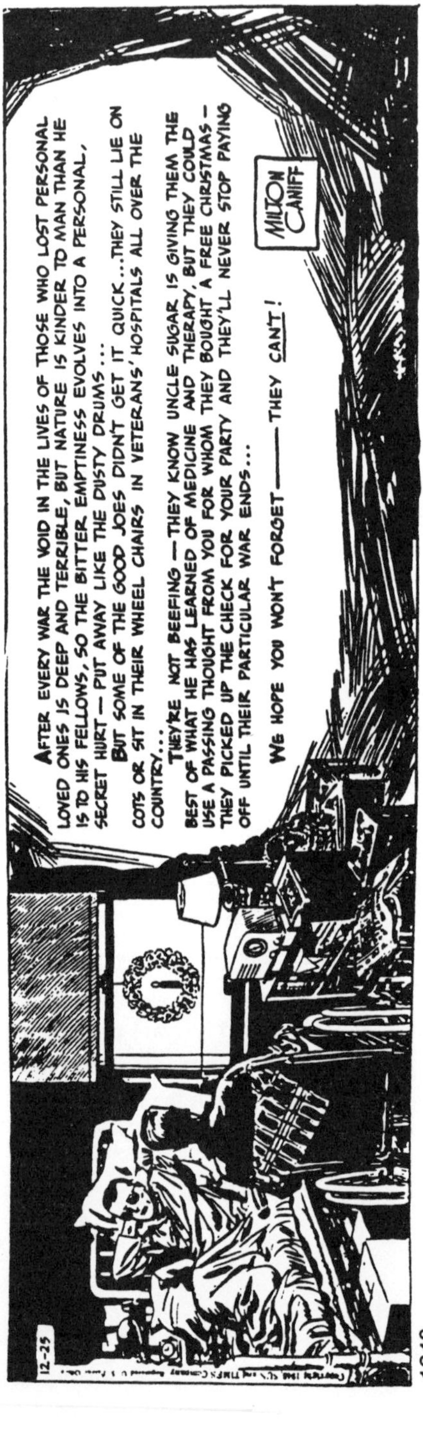

12-25
AFTER EVERY WAR THE VOID IN THE LIVES OF THOSE WHO LOST PERSONAL LOVED ONES IS DEEP AND TERRIBLE, BUT NATURE IS KINDER TO MAN THAN HE IS TO HIS FELLOWS, SO THE BITTER EMPTINESS EVOLVES INTO A PERSONAL, SECRET HURT—PUT AWAY LIKE THE DUSTY DRUMS...
BUT SOME OF THE GOOD JOES DIDN'T GET IT QUICK... THEY STILL LIE ON COTS OR SIT IN THEIR WHEEL CHAIRS IN VETERANS' HOSPITALS ALL OVER THE COUNTRY...
THEY'RE NOT BEEFING—THEY KNOW UNCLE SUGAR IS GIVING THEM THE BEST OF WHAT HE HAS LEARNED OF MEDICINE AND THERAPY, BUT THEY COULD USE A PASSING THOUGHT FROM YOU FOR WHOM THEY BOUGHT A FREE CHRISTMAS—THEY PICKED UP THE CHECK FOR YOUR PARTY AND THEY'LL NEVER STOP PAYING OFF UNTIL THEIR PARTICULAR WAR ENDS...
WE HOPE YOU WON'T FORGET———THEY CAN'T!
MILTON CANIFF

1948

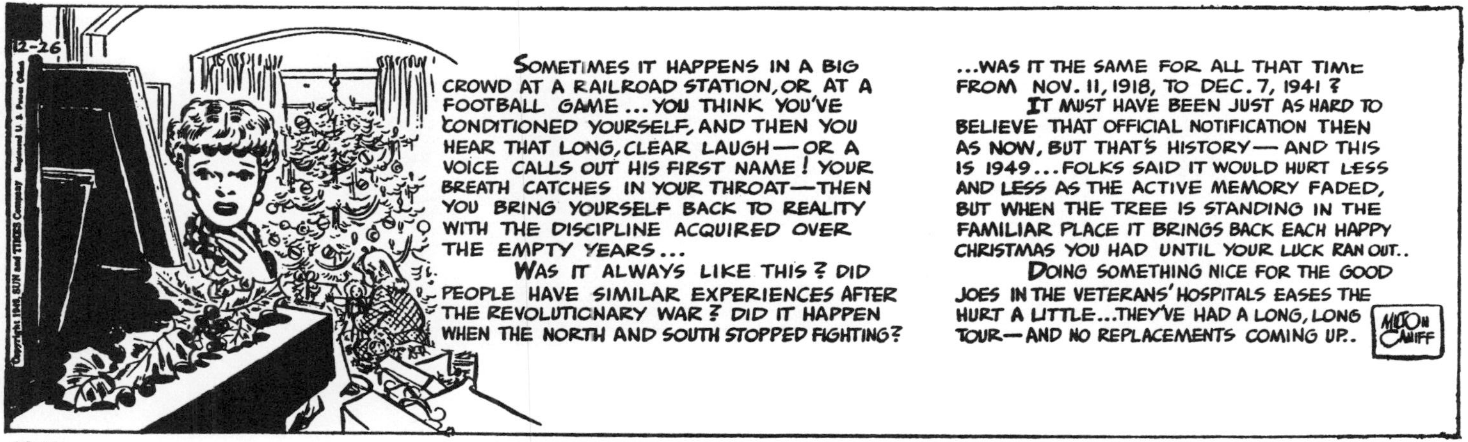

1949

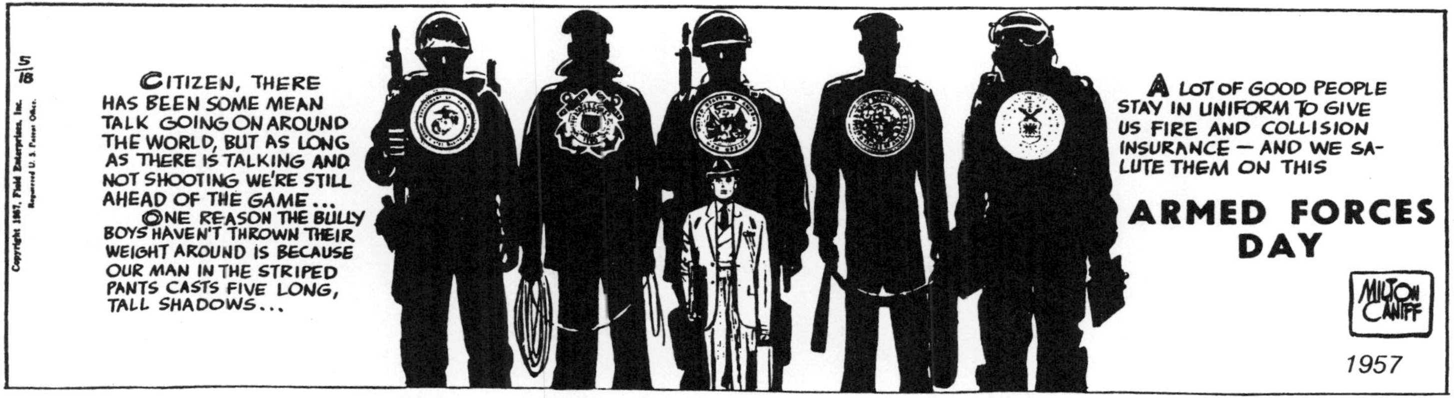

Caniff's first Christmas Day strip was in 1943 (top) during Terry. *It invoked Irving Berlin's 1942 hit song while picturing "the hump" in northern Burma over which supplies were flown to troops in western China. Caniff also recognized Armed Forces Day.*

He also uses real people as models for some of his characters; it's another innovation that's made him one of the comics' most imitated cartoonists.

"I've never asked permission, but I have yet to run across anyone who objected to being a character; in fact, most of them enjoy it."

Among his most famous characters were Flip Corkin, who first appeared in *Terry* in 1942, and Gen. Philerie, who dropped in from time to time to give assignments to Steve Canyon. Both characters were based on real-life Philip G. Cochran, a former Ohio State University classmate and a famed military pilot.

Corkin pulled some pretty wild stunts in print but, as Caniff himself will admit, "Everyone I used for characters did something in life more spectacular by far than anything I ever did with them in fiction."

Cochran was no exception. Much has been said of his bravery and innovative combat methods. His feats were not restricted to the CBI theater.

"The Germans had hung their communications lines in North Africa in the open, with no attempt to conceal them," Caniff said. "When Cochran got there, he attached an old engine block to the tail of his P-40 with cable. Then he flew up and down in between each length of the wires, cutting the sections as he went along. It was weeks before the Germans could restring their telephone lines."

As entertaining as they are, Caniff's strips of today and yesterday are often more than illustrated adventure stories. Many are editorials in disguise.

He is particularly noted for his Christmas Day strips that carry a holiday theme. They began as a practical arrangement so that newspapers that were printed on the holiday could have something to run and those that didn't print wouldn't miss a day's episode in a continuing story. They've become more than that to many followers.

"I've built quite an audience of people who look forward to the Christmas Day strips," Caniff said.

Through the years, he has boldly made a statement about America when, for example, he illustrated the readjustments of veterans to civilian life and the Russian threat in the Mediterranean. However, editorializing in the comics hasn't been without some personal cost.

During Vietnam, for instance, many newspapers canceled *Steve Canyon* because of the way the war was being presented in the Sunday funnies. The impression was that Caniff was trying to glorify the Vietnam conflict. Caniff disagrees with that point of view.

"I was simply showing a military person in a military situation doing a military job," he countered. "The reasons why we were there had nothing to do with it. The fact was we were there and I didn't think we should turn our backs on the situation."

Unfortunately, a lot of people, including editors who bought the strip, disagreed with him and dropped *Steve Canyon* from their papers.

During those difficult times he continued to portray the Air Force in a favorable light to the general public. He has no regrets. Nothing that's happened has ever altered his warm affection for the military. "They're the ones who keep the guns warm until the civilian population rises up to defend the country," he said.

But if you press him, he'll tell you there's more to it than that, *Terry and the Pirates*, *Male Call*, and, later, *Steve Canyon* have served as a small penance for the "home-front neurosis" he suffered for not serving in uniform.

"There was a slight tinge of guilt because being in the military was something I had always wanted to do. It's just like a small boy who dreams of catching the game-winning touchdown pass or rescuing the heroine from the villain. Fortunately, the strips have allowed me to have this close association with the military."

And that 50-year association has been one of mutual admiration. The Air Force has awarded Caniff the Air Force Exceptional Service Award, the highest award it can give to a civilian, in recognition of his service to military aviation.

Earlier this year many of his friends both in and out of uniform gathered in Columbus, Ohio, or sent letters of congratulations applauding Caniff's 75th birthday and the 35th anniversary of the publishing of *Steve Canyon.*

His career has been long and distinguished, characterized best, perhaps, by the name he chose for Steve Canyon's civilian enterprise—Horizons Unlimited. The words say much about Milton Caniff, capturing both his character and the theme upon which he has based his life. Truly, he has expanded the horizons of thousands of readers who now better understand the mission of real-life commandos in uniform.

And he did it all from the home front.

Shop Talk with Milton Caniff

Will Eisner / 1982

From *Will Eisner's Spirit Magazine*, Nos. 34 and 35, April and June, 1982, pp. 30–39 and pp. 32–43. Reprinted by permission.

Creator of the comic book crime-fighter the Spirit, Will Eisner has made a life's work of pioneering in the medium. His late 1930s work before inventing the Spirit helped shape the infant comic book medium, and during World War II, he devised instructional uses of comics, an endeavor he continued for about twenty years. And then in the 1970s, he came back to the comic book format to explore its literary capacities with a series of graphic novels. The following interview, conducted in February 1982 at the Princeton Club in New York, is one of a series that Eisner arranged with masters of the medium. All of the series is reprinted in Will Eisner's Shop Talk *published by Dark Horse Comics, Inc., 10956 SW Main Street, Milwaukie, OR 97222.*

Will Eisner: So, we're in the studio . . . with our feet up and we've just washed the brushes . . . and we're talking [laughter]. I wonder, Milt, how much "shop talk" goes on now? People seem too widely separated now. I learned a lot by talking, comparing . . .
Milton Caniff: Of course you do. You find out things about the business that way.

Eisner: I remember in my studio back in 1941 . . . there were five of us then. We did a lot of that. I was still working with Japanese brushes—they were 3 or 4 cents then. Cheap!—and Lou Fine also used 'em. He was by far the best draftsman in the shop. Well, anyhow, Lou and I would start talking about line and inking and how the Japanese print art related to comics. Pretty soon the others would join in and soon, like two local bullies hand-wrestling, one of us would draw a long line and the idea was for the other to go over it without appreciably thickening it until one or the other would waver his line. I usually lost and bought the beers [laughter] but it was a great learning process.

Let's start with a very basic concept. We are dealing with a medium that is irrevocably and interactively composed of words and pictures. Are you in agreement with me on that?
Caniff: Yes, and you've got to have something to say.

Eisner: Okay. Now, what is your method, your style of working? Mostly your work is daily strips, is that right?
Caniff: Well, it works a little differently for me because I have to tie up a daily strip and a Sunday page.

Eisner: Are they connected? The daily and the Sunday?
Caniff: They're connected. They read straight through seven days a week, or they must be readable from Monday to Saturday, or they must be readable from Sunday to Sunday. So the bookkeeping is pretty heavy.

Eisner: All right.
Caniff: And a Sunday page because it's done so much further ahead in time, sets the tone, and sets the plot, not just the tone. And I try to define the end of the story first because that way you've got a goal to work toward. My approach is that you have a goal to work toward, but also you have set yourself a time box. You've got to get things said that lead up to that Sunday page when you come back later—a Sunday page [is produced] ten weeks ahead, for instance, and daily strips, five

or six, whichever you can manage. But they still have to match between the last week's Sunday page and next week's Sunday page.

Eisner: How many weeks does your story usually run?
Caniff: Fortunately, I finally decided to stop worrying about that. I used to go for two months—say ten weeks—and then I realized that sometimes I was chopping it off. If I had a good thing going it seemed a shame to chop it off just because it was ten weeks, so I started letting it run its course. I still haven't gone beyond thirteen or fourteen weeks, or very rarely have, but I don't feel constrained.

Eisner: When I was doing a daily strip six to ten weeks seemed to be almost a requirement of the syndicate salesman.
Caniff: Yes.

Eisner: I suspected later as I became a little bit more sophisticated that they felt that they were going to get a cancellation [laughter]. They could avoid hard feelings with a paper if they could break it off at a point where the editor would feel that they could cancel, so . . .
Caniff: By the way, in that respect—and this is something that has annoyed me over the years—a newspaper will ask a syndicate to tell them when a story ends so they can cancel. They don't always say they're going to cancel, but you don't want them to ask those questions.

Eisner: Yes, that's right, that's right [groan].
Caniff: Now it always seemed to me only fair play for them to stop the strip right in the middle of a sequence so if there are going to be any protests, you'll get the protests. Who's going to protest after a sequence ends? Why should they? But in the middle of it, if the reader is held and entertained they'll say, "Where's whoever?" or "What ever happened to so-and-so?"

Eisner: Yeah, yeah . . . but it rarely happened.
Caniff: It's only fair to the cartoonist to give him that kind of break, but they seldom do.

Eisner: Well, I found from my own syndicate experience that this business is very corrosive in many ways to a cartoonist. I don't know if you've had this experience, but one initially enters the syndicate strip business with a new idea and a fresh approach and a fresh personality. And your strip becomes widely bought. A year or two later, being the inventive person you are, you want to add new things and do new

things and then your hand is stayed because they say, "Now wait a minute. We bought you for this particular strip. We want you to be what you were when we bought you. We don't want you to be anybody else." And suddenly you find yourself just turning knobs [laughter] and the machine is just turning, turning. Did you experience this? Have you gotten that?
Caniff: Well, yes. Fortunately for me, when I stopped doing *Terry and the Pirates* and started *Steve Canyon* I was able to get the kind of contract which gives me the final cut, as they say in the movie business. I haven't had that problem as much recently as I used to have with *Terry,* especially when the war was going on because the overtone of propaganda was there and had to be there and should have been there. But propaganda can be handled in so many ways. It can be cheap and shoddy and offhand and Jerry-come-lately, or it can be most persuasive in times of emergency. It's not the kind of yelling "fire" in a crowded theater that you . . .

Eisner: No. no. I know what you mean. You were working on presenting a point of view. More intellectual than . . .
Caniff: Yes, exactly.

Eisner: "Point of view," depending on who it comes from and why, is different than propaganda.
Caniff: Oh yes, yes it is.

Eisner: By the way, do you know that Mao Tse-tung used comics widely in his early days?
Caniff: I've seen some drawings that were very heavy-handed and although the Chinese generally are very good with graphics they were just falling for their own line; his line. Of course, nobody was going to talk back to the big man. But they had very often the overtone that the boss did it. The publisher wrote the book.

Eisner: Yeah. That of course was "the word." So . . . you start with the end of the story, so to speak. You know how it is going to end, where you want to go . . .
Caniff: Let me interupt here a moment.

Eisner: Sure.
Caniff: You set it up and let it be as fragile as needs to be because, for instance, in the case of right in the middle of the story [incoming fan]

letters indicate they know how it's going to come out. They've out-guessed me! So then I can still switch the ending and cross them up.

Eisner: I see. So, by being loose as you go, you can alter your course when you sense you're becoming too obvious.
Caniff: And it works that way as long as I'm not too deeply into the Sunday series; I can still do a switch on the end. It makes me look smart as hell [laughter].

Eisner: Arthur Miller, in an interview some time ago, said that he likes to set up characters and let them go . . . and follow them where they go, as they develop themselves so to speak.
Caniff: Yes, exactly.

Eisner: In *Life On Another Planet,* I found that it worked that way for me. Create a situation where they're going to go ultimately, but set them up and follow them rather than direct them. Let them react to events you impose.
Caniff: Yes, throw up all of the red herrings and the things that are necessary.

Eisner: Well now, since we're talking about a continuing set of characters like Steve Canyon, your plots do take on a kind of similarity, do they not? Or are they violently different?
Caniff: No, the plot structure is similar enough, but you change the pace as much or as little as you choose. For instance, essentially my kind of thing is: hang him on the cliff and get him off the cliff.

Eisner: You mean a basic line.
Caniff: Or boy meets girl, boy loses girl, boy gets girl.

Eisner: Uh huh . . . Fundamental?
Caniff: The *most* fundamental. Not only the soundest but the most endlessly used, of course. And this can be employed whether it's a love story or not; it's still true.

Eisner: Do I understand that to mean you superimpose a problem over a boy-meets-girl frame?
Caniff: Yes, well, to give you a for instance . . . I had a character named Raven Sherman when I was doing *Terry and the Pirates* who began as a very austere teacher—a missionary-type teacher—but a teacher. She had her hair pulled back starched, proper—oh, Katharine Hepburn in *The African Queen.* In the beginning she was one person and then in

the ending she was another. And the total result of this is that the basic script was that she was like this: she was doubtful, then she capitulated to the guy, and then she went back to being herself again, you assumed. Now, this gives you the opportunity to switch that ending and make her not what you assume. So, time gives you that privilege.

Eisner: Uh huh. I see what you mean here.
Caniff: But sometimes when you start you don't. You think you know the payoff and you've established an ending, but it's very comfortable and it can be made to switch and fool the reader, because I think it is true that readers like to be fooled.

Eisner: Oh, readers love surprises. Also, they don't like to be disappointed, but they do want to be surprised.
Caniff: It isn't just the whodunit kind of murder mystery.

Eisner: Well, in that frame, let me ask you about something that has troubled me all these years, but you have always seemed to have had really no trouble with it—"claustrophobia." A daily strip to me is like trying to conduct an orchestra in a telephone booth. On *The Spirit* dailies I always seemed to wind up choked up because I have so much to say in any one strip.
Caniff: Yes . . .

Eisner: And I'll either go tight and say nothing, which is disastrous and stupid, or say too much, which is equally as stupid. Have you ever felt the daily strip closing in on you as a form? And how do you deal with it?
Caniff: Well, when I first started, I'd been doing a daily strip for the Associated Press called *Dickie Dare,* which had no Sunday page so I didn't have to worry about that. It just jumped from Saturday to Monday and that was that. But once into the Sunday page thing, which had to mesh, I was facing a problem [and I took it to] Mollie Slott, who at that time was the editor of the Chicago Tribune-New York News Syndicate. She said, "Why don't you ask some of the old boys who've been at it awhile and see what they do." So, I wouldn't have dreamed of asking Harold Gray or even Chester Gould, who was not all that old—he'd been around for [only] a couple of years at this point—but, anyhow, I wrote a letter to Harold Gray, and waited for the blow to fall of no answer or a negative answer or a nasty something. Instead I got a four-page single-spaced typewritten letter from Harold saying various things, but this in particular: On Monday morning, any given Monday, I

have to use at least one panel to recapitulate the weekend thing which has all been in the Sunday page. And then another panel to conjecture on what I might have been able to do with whatever the dilemna is. And in the last panel you advance the strip; in other words, you use something you had not used in the Sunday page. Maybe the first two incidents which you view from a different point of view. There's a fight in the Sunday page, for instance. You see that fight. On Monday two guys will say, "Hey, did you see those two guys fighting over there?" Well, you've told exactly the same story over again from another point of view. And a perfectly legitimate thing is that gimmick-wise, in the last panel you have the door open and in comes the man with the gun. Then you're off into Tuesday, you're off and running.

Eisner: Well, how much story did he say that leaves you? He leaves you one panel to develope your plot?
Caniff: Again, it's more a matter of what your plot is *going* to be. In other words, in the Raymond Chandler thing—the door opens and there's the man with the gun. That's all you need to start a mystery story.

Eisner: That's true, but . . .
Caniff: Well, in effect, that's what he was doing here. That one panel is enough to suck you into tomorrow. Then tomorrow is all going to be new gravy. Now, you may have needed the second panel just because [the reader] missed yesterday's Sunday paper. But surely you need that last panel because he doesn't know what's going on out there in the hall or what's going to happen when the door opens and admits the man with the gun. That panel is usually enough to hold the audience and to advance the story. Then on Tuesday you can jump around any way you want to, assuming the reader is with you.

Eisner: Well, do you work in that frame . . . today?
Caniff: Essentially, I still do it.

Eisner: Do I understand, Milt, that you start with a total view of a story? Okay, so let's just fabricate a plot from the man with the gun who enters the room and deal with it, okay?
Caniff: Yes.

Eisner: In that plot you know that for the next two weeks you're going to have a running account of a man who is behind the door with a gun. He's a hit man from Chicago, let's say, and he's here to get, to kill this guy who turns out to be a sleuth himself. And through some sort of

mistaken identity they think—and the guy from Chicago thinks—he's another hood. Okay, that's the essential theme of that plot. How many weeks or days to you deal with something as explanatory as that?
Caniff: The exposition is not really very necessary when you're showing this very graphic thing of a man with a gun. That's enough. He doesn't have to *say* he's got a gun; he's *got* a gun. It may be a phony, but he's got a gun or you think he has. And you can make it turn any way you want. This is where I jump to the end of the story and make everything that happens after that incident, whatever path it takes, lead to that culmination.

Eisner: Lead to that killing culmination?
Caniff: It's awful to kill off bad guys because you hate to get rid of anybody if you've got a really good one.

Eisner: [laughter]
Caniff: You know Chet Gould never does that, or if he does, the death is so questionable that it's harder . . .

Eisner: [laughter] Bring him back . . .
Caniff: So you can bring him back: "Poof!"

Eisner: I have problems with villains myself. I've never been able to see a villain as absolute! Always in the back of my mind I say, "I bet he's good to his mother." [laughter]
Caniff: Well, I think your self-criticism is sound and I don't know exactly how to categorize it because when something is unfinished it's unfinished; you have to pick up the story line and so forth.

Eisner: True.
Caniff: But the reader gets very clever. Some of these readers will do anything to keep from being made fools of themselves.

Eisner: Uh huh.
Caniff: It's not their favorite thing.

Eisner: So now we have a fair concept of what you do for a story. By the way, do you, when you have a story idea for your next ten or fifteen weeks, do you first rough it out? What are the mechanics?
Caniff: As I go along in the beginning of the story, I'm cranking up sometime before the story begins, stockpiling places and events or cross reference events, referrals, something that actually happened. Naturally I'm going to be dealing in fictitious characters, but I want to have done

a little homework between—sometimes—just me and the ceiling. I think this girl would be vulnerable to soft music, or I think she'd go out of her mind if she were invaluable. She wants to be free . . .

Eisner: Let's go back and talk about your actual technique. What about pen and ink and style? Just to make it fast and easy, why don't you go through the current procedure. You know, you write the story and . . .

Caniff: Yes. The way I'm working now, unlike the old days when I used to letter in pencil right on the drawing paper, is to take ordinary foolscap and lay it out as if it were strips. Two to a page of foolscap. I divide that into panels of three each and start writing it then exactly the same way except roughly this time because I'm going to dictate this over the telephone to Shel Dorf in San Diego. In doing so I've got to be able to change pace in the middle of it. If I realized that I've said something I didn't want to say or I want to add a word I can just make a note to myself as I go along. Then he only gets what I want him to hear. He takes it down in a kind of comic strip shorthand.

Eisner: What's that? [laughter]

Caniff: And he's a very fast lettering man. In other words, I can dictate this to him—as I did just yesterday—six strips and a Sunday page, and he will have it lettered and in the mail that same afternoon by air express so it will be back here the following morning.

Eisner: Well, then . . . you get it back with balloons already on the board, on the Strathmore, or whatever board you use.

Caniff: He just rules it up so he can anticipate what I want. Sometimes I want a single panel with no smaller panels at all, just one great big panel as on New Year's Day, Christmas Day, something of that sort.

Eisner: Oh, yeah.

Caniff: And when he letters—left-handed, by the way, which I don't see how he does . . .

Eisner: Well, *you* draw left-handed, don't you?

Caniff: Uh huh. And my lettering is terrible, as most left-handed people's lettering is. Yet there are many left-handed people in this business. George Wunder is left-handed, as is Bill Mauldin.

Eisner: Oh, I didn't know that.

Caniff: Irv Moore was left-handed.

Eisner: Really?
Caniff: Uh huh. Good lettering men too.

Eisner: Leonardo da Vinci was left-handed. [laughter]
Caniff: Of course, of course. But having to *push* the pen in lettering has always been a problem. Even back in high school, in mechanical drawing class, it was a real handicap to me. And as a result, I've always been a little gun-shy of lettering. I can do it, but I just don't want to do it. I hate to do it. Did it for a long time before I could afford a lettering man.

Eisner: Well, join the club. I think most of us hate lettering. Currently I do most of my own lettering because of the kind of story . . . and treatment. It means the lettering and art must be handled by the same person.
Caniff: Yeah, I guess so. In any case, I *can* do it. I can always fake it if I have to. And sometimes I do, for instance, when it comes back from Shel. I send it right on to Dick Rockwell because I've written whatever notes I'm going to make. Sometimes it's just a stage direction word background, "storm at sea," for instance. That's all I have to tell Dick, who then really lays out the strip in tight pencil.
Then it comes back to me and I finish it, and I'm the last one to see it. The final cut, so to speak. And in the interim time I can change it around if I don't like what Dick has pencilled or I want to change it. I seldom dislike what he pencils because he's very good. It's just that I change my mind sometimes.

Eisner: Is he related to Norman?
Caniff: Yes, he's Norman's nephew.

Eisner: Oh, all right.
Caniff: His father was Norman's brother, Jarvis Rockwell.

Eisner: Oh, I see.
Caniff: Who was also an artist, by the way. Designer, I should say. He designed childrens' toys.

Eisner: Really? I didn't know that.
Caniff: So Dick grew up almost in the shadow of Norman, which is unfortunate in that people always equate him with Norman. He's very good on his own, but he doesn't paint the way Rockwell—Norman Rockwell—did, or anything else. He's his own man.

Eisner: How long has Dick Rockwell been working on your stuff?
Caniff: Twenty years now.

Eisner: On your work? Oh, I didn't know it was as long as that.
Caniff: Just after the war. He was a pilot in the European Theatre and when he came back he was freelancing, doing comic books and that kind of thing. And he lived down the road from me in Rockland County.

Eisner: Uh huh.
Caniff: One day he brought some samples to my studio and said he was too busy one week and not busy at all the next, and if I had anything that I needed done that he would be available probably. So I asked him to do a couple of sample things cold turkey. He did and they were very good. He'd never drawn a strip.

Eisner: Uh huh. There's a considerable difference in panel treatment . . . composition.
Caniff: Dick had always worked in a page form. I need that too, of course . . .

Eisner: So, he pencils tightly then, right? Reasonably tightly?
Caniff: Right.* When I do a pencil of a situation, for instance, which I can't describe in one sentence [laughter]—hand written or lettered is too loose. What I need is what he supplies. I've always been a very sloppy penciller and only in very tight facial situations and so on have I pencilled this tightly. I actually almost pencil with a brush, you know?

Eisner: Well, I understand. There's an advantage to it because you know what you're doing and you get a freedom of flow of movement. When it's very tight you're tracing rather than drawing.
Caniff: That's exactly it. And sometimes I intensify a situation—where I have the guy running down the road, for instance, to escape the bad guys. Dick will draw it correctly and very well, but I want to intensify it; I want to make him look more scared. So I'll bend him over a little more and put him in a position of intense effort instead of just a jogging kind of scene.

---

*I think Caniff is answering too quickly here—or perhaps without listening carefully to Eisner's question. Caniff penciled very loosely, as he subsequently says, and his remarks here make better sense if we assume that Rockwell pencils loosely, too, giving Caniff, as he says, what he "needs"—sketchy blocking of scenes, which Caniff then tightens up a little either while he inks or with a few pencil strokes beforehand. The penciled strips that I've seen of Rockwell's are loosely penciled. In the last years, Rockwell also outlined backgrounds and props in ink; Caniff then added solid black shadows to Rockwell's drawings.—RCH

Eisner: Well, then, actually Dick Rockwell will compose the panels too.
Caniff: Yeah.

Eisner: And you'll get back something that you can alter if you wish. Isn't that what you're saying?
Caniff: Yeah, that's what it all comes down to. But I don't have to do it very often because he's so good, especially after this many years.

Eisner: Sure, yeah.
Caniff: But every now and then there will be something that I had in mind to be more "something else" than what he does and it's just a simple matter of changing it.

Eisner: Yeah.
Caniff: And, by the way, every once in a while, quite deliberately, not just to pick up time—although it helps the schedule—I'll just block out a Sunday page or a whole set of strips and do them all myself. It's like a hostess, you know, will sleep in her guest room once in a while.

Eisner: Yeah. Yeah, right. In other words you can't keep your hand out of the soup, so to speak. [laughter]
Caniff: Well, I'll say you don't want to lose your touch either.

Eisner: I think that's very important; I agree with you.
Caniff: And doing it from cold scratch is the only way to find out . . .

Eisner: Yes, yes, yes.
Caniff: It isn't a matter of picking an easy one! [laughter]

Eisner: Well, let me interrupt because this brings up something I've been wanting to ask you. I've spent a lot of time in recent years—now I use myself here because I'm the only comparison I have—I find myself more and more concerned about composing a panel, that is, staging. I know you and I have talked about our theatrical background. I was hardly theatrical but I'm interested in the theatre and I mentioned to you about my early life with my father doing back sets and stage sets, and you were of course involved in college and amateur theater. I think professional too, weren't you?
Caniff: Well, just as I could grab a job as a super in downtown professional companies while I was in college and high school.

Eisner: Well, anyway, what I'm trying to get at is that I regard the panel as a stage.

Caniff: Uh huh. So do I.

Eisner: And I move the furniture, the elements, around . . . until I get the story told. I spend a lot of time arranging my characters. I literally compose a panel. Now, do you feel the same way? Do you do the same thing?

Caniff: Oh definitely. And, also, we're saddled with one problem—I don't know if you have to do this or not—I draw for third color page size because that's the greatest number of clients I have. Sunday, that is. But about three inches from the bottom, I always have to keep expendable—about two and a half inches, actually—which means this is where they're going to cut it off for tabloid size and that one half of standard page, one quarter size. Real postage stamp stuff, which is annoying as hell.

Eisner: I know. It's terrible. I had to deal with this in *The Spirit* sections . . . drew for both tabloid and small comic book page. I don't have that problem now . . .

Caniff: However, for composition I will often add a whole thing down there that I know is going to be cut out and thrown away in a lot of papers. But, still, I can't stand seeing it just sloughed off.

Eisner: Well, Milt, does that mean you are laying out or composing each of these panels as much for the purpose of the newspaper as for clarity and the fact that it's coming down to a postage stamp, as it is for story telling?

Caniff: Yes, that's the function every day, every minute of every day.

Eisner: Well, let's get into pen and ink. As students always ask, "What pen do you use?" As a matter of fact, I recall going down to the *New York American* looking for a job and I went into the bullpen there and the first question I asked the old timers was, "What pen do you use?" somehow thinking mystically that if I get the right pen I'll draw like him. [laughter]

Caniff: There's one thing about it on the negative side. If you want to draw a given way, if you like the line work that James Montgomery Flagg did, it's a good idea to use his pen. [laughter] And maybe that's not for you. I found this out and I'm sure you did too. I was using a 290 or something like that and I found the crow quill 659 was a better pen for me because it was stronger. It was not quite as resilient or soft.

Eisner: I started out with a 290 and it was a very soft pen.

Caniff: I still don't know what James Montgomery Flagg used.

Eisner: I think he used that.
Caniff: He probably did because you couldn't get lines like that unless you did.

Eisner: I think he did and I think [Charles Dana] Gibson before him.
Caniff: Yes.

Eisner: He used a soft . . .
Caniff: He was always saddled with that Gibson thing.

Eisner: Well, they literally painted with those lines. You know it seemed to me like they were just prongs on a brush, so to speak.
Caniff: What amazed me, and still does, is how they could hold that much ink that long.

Eisner: Yes. Incredible.
Caniff: Some of those lines were halfway down the page. A girl's hair which Gibson would draw curling down below her face seemed like one continuous line.

Eisner: There's just no going over those lines. I've seen those originals and you just didn't go over those lines, you just snapped them in.
Caniff: And no white [ink] as I remember. I don't remember seeing any.

Eisner: That's right. That's right. They used razor blades for white-out. I remember, talking about my first job at the *New York American* newspaper, there was this old guy with a green visor sitting next to me. You know, an old grizzled old newspaper artist. I asked him about "tools" and he just picked up this razor blade—which he would also use to sharpen his pencil—and an art gum erasor and the crusted pen and he said, "Kid, these are the only tools you'll ever need!" [laughter] He'd work on a hard surface, you know, on a plate-finish paper and razor blade errors off . . . Well, you use a pen to outline the figures, do you?
Caniff: Not entirely. It depends on the time element, for one thing. If I'm lush with time, which is rare, I'll draw out a whole scene. But usually I have to take a brush full of ink and throw in the blacks, shadow side of the picture, whatever the incident pictured.

Eisner: Yeah.
Caniff: Whether it's a person—daylight's a little tougher—at night you can use those wonderful things that *you* do with streetlamps over feet and hands. [laughter]

Eisner: Yeah.
Caniff: Show their feet by the shadows of the legs against the light of the streetlamp on the cobblestones. [laughter]

Eisner: Uh huh. Well I guess that's my way of dealing with city drama. You handle shadows beautifully as story-telling devices.
Caniff: They are really part of the thing. I've got, for instance—to give you a "for instance"—which takes place at night on the beach on a Caribbean island and you see silhouettes of people, including the hero, who is tailgating this woman, thinking that she's going to be mugged. And the muggers come out of the bushes. All this is in silhouette. She's the one with the awful face.

Eisner: [laughter] The one you're currently doing?
Caniff: And the two muggers approach her from the rear and then, just at the moment they're about to pounce on her, she hears them coming. Of course, *we* know that she has a flashlight in her hand and she flashes the light on her face. You don't see her face but the muggers do and they run in horror.

Eisner: Oh, that's great!
Caniff: It's all shadows except you see the edges of the light around her head. You're looking right into the flashlight; the bare bulb.

Eisner: Yeah, and then you see the faces of these characters, right?
Caniff: No, they just run.

Eisner: Are these recent *Steve Canyon* sequences?
Caniff: This is one I just did.

Eisner: A current *Steve Canyon.* Great. Real good.
Caniff: Anyhow, to play up the fact that she has this horrible face which nobody ever sees except the characters, they all say, "That horrible face!" But you don't know why it's horrible.

Eisner: Well, there you use blacks for story-telling, right?
Caniff: Yeah.

Eisner: I recall the old *Terry* series . . . and your way of handling black, which really influenced me you know. I must tell you that when you were doing *Terry*—there's a little difference in our ages—I was in high school while you were out there in the major leagues.
Caniff: Oh yes, yes. [laughter]

Eisner: And I was carefully watching what you did on *Terry* . . . My God, you know, I'm beginning to sound like a young fan that comes on saying, "When I was three years old you were a great cartoonist!" Oy!! [laughter] No, please don't accept this as adulation. [laughter]
Caniff: I understand very well. I . . . [laughter]

Eisner: What I wanted to say is that you've used blacks in snow scenes where you drop the blacks on the paper with almost no outline.
Caniff: I really stole that from Roy Crane [in *Wash Tubbs*].

Eisner: Oh, did you?
Caniff: Oh, he was the best. When he was kind of young he had a sequence once in the Alps and the foreground people were all cartoony as the dickens, the way he could draw cartoons . . .

Eisner: Uh huh.
Caniff: . . . [in] the *Wash Tubbs* era. But the backgrounds, those mountains and the Alps were just magnificent. I don't think anybody has ever done them as well.

Eisner: I didn't remember. I thought you originated it. Well, okay . . .
Caniff: What happens is you take it on from there.

Eisner: Well, of course. We all pick up where others leave off and make our own contribution.
Caniff: When he did it, it was really almost decorative. When I do it, very often it's a practical application.

Eisner: Well, that's why I said you do it for the story. Just as I see a great difference between your work and [Noel] Sickles and yet you will constantly say, "Well, Sickles did it first." But actually I see different values in it, just as I recognize different styles in anybody else. Well, at any rate, in a round-about way we're getting back to the finished board. So, you use a pen and ink to outline the faces or the heads?
Caniff: Well, to outline the light side of the thing.

Eisner: I see. You can go all the way down the figure with that pen then?
Caniff: Well, you can if the circumstances call for it. For close-up drawing, of course, I use a pen, then come back in with a brush and do hairs especially. Blond hair is hard to do, simply because if you get too fine lines it will fade out in some papers. With a brunette, of course, it's much simpler to make the point with highlights. I

have a tousled-haired girl, for instance, who's in a sequence I just finished, and it was fairly easy to slop in there with a brush and still just highlight on her bouncy hair. Then the next woman character is blonde with very fixed beauty salon type set hair where everything is exactly so.

Eisner: Uh huh.
Caniff: The danger there is using a brush and getting it too thin, so I often use a pen.

Eisner: To hold the line?
Caniff: Just to hold the line strong enough to reproduce it in Sheboygan.

Eisner: Well, I've been using, I've gone back to pen for the backgrounds now. I use a hard, that is, an unresilient quill for backgrounds. I've suddenly rediscovered it again and I'm really enjoying it. I still prefer a brush for figures and I will use a brush for figures wherever I can.
Caniff: Well, nobody does it better than you, by the way, because I was following you from the very first. That Philadelphia book, whatever it was, was the first time I saw your stuff and it was really . . .

Eisner: Well, it's nice to hear your memory's so good! [laughter]
Caniff: Well, my young friend in Bryn Mawr, the one I told you about, the girl who made the book on the outcome of your stories . . .

Eisner: Well, it was a novelty when you think about it. It was the first newspaper comic strip that was doing complete stories every week. No one had ever done that before.
Caniff: Those kids ate it up, by the way. We've talked about this before; about how amused I've always been—and you have too—about ruining these kids' lives and here are these college kids drinking with a spoon and going down and stealing proofs at the *Bulletin* . . .

Eisner: Well, I never knew that. I wish I had known that then; I'd have demanded more attention from the syndicate! Actually, the complete-each-week story was *their* requirement, but no one had done it before. So that gave me, I guess, the historical advantage just by accident.
Caniff: I think that's one of the things the kids liked, especially because I remember following my kind of strips and I'd lose a day or two during the week and I'd lose the thread.

Eisner: Well, that's the reason I questioned you so closely about how you conduct a story because I still can't conceive in my mind that if you have

panel one for recap and panel three or four is the cliffhanger—I mean, you've got two panels left, it seems . . . My God, how can I tell a story in ten weeks or even twelve weeks in two panels a day? It just really almost seems impossible to get much of a story in ten or whatever number of weeks. Well, it's a totally different medium from comic books, isn't it?
Caniff: Yeah, uh huh.

Eisner: I mean, a complete seven page story versus a story told in daily segments, you know . . .
Caniff: I did it. In the early days when they didn't really go for the reprint comic books—we'd sort of run the course there—I wrote some original comic book pages, stories, complete . . .

Eisner: Did you really? When was this?
Caniff: '50s I suppose.

Eisner: Oh, yeah, approximately . . .
Caniff: It had to be that far back because we'd run through the reprints of the early *Canyons* and the kids weren't buying them as avidly as we thought they should. So we tried the original story thing thing and it worked. All of a sudden they didn't know how the story came out. They hadn't read it in the newspaper. And this was the reason for switching, but someone had to write this . . .

Eisner: So you had your teeth into some complete stories all at one . . .
Caniff: In the beginning I did it all myself, but then it got to be just too much work and I had to delegate it then. But at least I learned how to do it. I learned the technique.

Eisner: Did you find it very different from the daily strips?
Caniff: Oh yes, quite different. You stalled in different places for one thing. When you're doing it day by day you've got to . . . Capp described it best. He would take the beginning and the ending of a story and then put a string between them and hang baubles of incidents on the string.

Eisner: Oh, that was very well put. That was Al. He could say things like that. It's very, very, very apt.
Caniff: I think that one of the things he failed to do, though, was to build his climaxes as effectively as he should have. He would get bored with a story after the first few weeks, then let it peter out. Not always, of course. He was a master of the other thing that we talked about, having this girl with the Veronica Lake hair-do and beautiful body and an awful face.

Eisner: Well, I think Al had a devilish streak in that he loved to shock. I think even more than you and I do or anybody else I know.
Caniff: Yes, he did.

Eisner: In your work I don't see a desire for sense of shock more than I sense a desire for romance and atmosphere.
Caniff: Yes.

Eisner: It has to do with personality, I guess. Capp—I can still hear him roaring with laughter. That leonine head would go back and he'd laugh out loud at his own stuff!
Caniff: Yes, yes.

Eisner: Every time he talked with me, if he told me something funny, he was the first guy to laugh.
Caniff: He'd start to laugh before he told it! [laughter]

Eisner: Yeah! [laughter]
Caniff: He'd start when he thought of it.

Eisner: Yeah, yeah, yeah.
Caniff: And in his broadcasting too.

Eisner: We've strayed from our discussion. So now, back to your strip. Rockwell has pencilled it, you have inked it and now what does it look like when it's finished? Do you . . . is it a very clean page or is it. . . ?
Caniff: I use a lot of detail, of course, so that it's a busy—almost without exception—a busy page. But it looks good to me if the drawing feels good.

Eisner: Uh huh.
Caniff: I had a high school art teacher who said this is a very simple business. She said, "If it looks good, let it lie. And if it looks wrong, change it. And that's all you have to know."

Eisner: I had an anatomy teacher once say, "Don't worry about where the bones are. If it looks good, it's right." [laughter]
Caniff: Exactly so. She [was] the same teacher I told you about who would look at a drawing of mine, long after I was out of school, to see how much I had erased. If I hadn't erased enough, in other words, tried and failed and tried and failed, she didn't think I'd worked enough.

Eisner: That's an interesting point.
Caniff: If I'd been someone who traced and then did my erasing on the tracing paper then . . . but she *knew* how I worked. She knew that I was . . .

Eisner: That brings up an interesting question. There are artists who start drawing the top of the head, down the side of the nose and down right around. You know what I mean . . .
Caniff: Sure, sure, sure.

Eisner: And other artists are busy running all over the page. I'm talking about pencilling. For example, I do a lot of constructing. My pencil is like a dancer. It just keeps moving around. I do a lot of probing in construction. How about you?
Caniff: Well, first of all I use the same old armature, the thing that they had in the stick figure body to get action before the clay is applied in sculpturing. A guy is putting his arm around a girl, for instance. Have his hand come out where it should and not have too long an arm or too short an arm or whatever.

Eisner: Uh huh.
Caniff: But especially on action type of stuff, and then just flesh it out. But I work all over the composition. I had a painting instructor in art school who said, "Work all over the canvas. Don't pick an eye or an ear or something. Get laid out first before you go back."

Eisner: You work with a hard pencil or a soft pencil?
Caniff: 2H or 3H.

Eisner: Uh huh. I'll use a 2H to lay down a drawing if it's a toothy surface.
Caniff: Sometimes if I'm in a big hurry to get some effect or I'm playing, I'll use a soft pencil and then it's a mess and it's hard to erase.

Eisner: You work on a plate finish paper or kid finish?
Caniff: No. Kid finish. 3-ply kid finish Strathmore.

Eisner: A toothy surface.
Caniff: I've used the same paper since I was in high school. I've tried everything else, of course, to find out whether it would work, and that was my bag.

Eisner: Well, the only originals I've seen of yours looked awfully clean. But somebody the other day told me they saw some of your work and it had a lot of white paint on it.
Caniff: Yes, I've used more white paint recently.

Eisner: Yeah?
Caniff: I never used to use white paint. In the first place, not because I didn't need it, but because the touch-up white they had in those days was not good enough.

Eisner: Yeah, it would chip. I use Rich Art poster white now.
Caniff: You couldn't mark over it. It would chip, mush up and if anybody dropped a tear on it you'd have a mess. But in more recent times, I've found two reasons. One for speed and, secondly, certain effects that I want to get I can only get with white. And speed is the main reason. I'll go through a whole set of strips, for instance, and just make a check mark above the head of a character that I want to change in some way. And if I've forgotten what it was I wanted to change I go back and I only have to think a minute or two to recall that the face is too long or too short or too wide.

Eisner: We are, after all, working for reproduction, not for a gallery exhibition.
Caniff: Just one stroke of white along the edges of it and it'll be more of what I want. And I'm always fighting the clock. Always have been, but more so now, in recent times.

Eisner: Uh huh.
Caniff: I've slowed up. That's what it comes down to.

Eisner: Well, I don't know whether we slow up. I think what we do is become more selective. I find myself being dissatisfied with the first effort.
Caniff: Well, that too.

Eisner: Whereas before I was willing to go with the first shot. [laughter]
Caniff: I used to work, for instance, consecutively through, just straight through. Stay with it, stay with it, stay with it. And my doctor finally told me two things: that my circulation is lousy, that you've got to get up and move around and take a break every ten minutes, a break at least every hour. The old army way. And, also, if you begin to feel eye weary, don't push it. Go lie down, take a nap or do something else. Go

look out the window. I welcome it because it does make a difference. I can go through a whole night like that by knocking out a half hour some where along the line, take a nap, drink some coffee. I drink coffee all the time.

Eisner: Uh huh.
Caniff: But do something else.

Eisner: Sounds like you were a disciplined worker. Talking about being a disciplined worker—what about your studio life? You worked alone for the most part or with an assistant?
Caniff: The chronology of it was simply this: I worked in a newspaper art department until I was fired at the *Columbus Dispatch* back in Ohio in the Depression and was lucky enough to get a job at the AP Feature Service in New York. A month later—I had to borrow money to get to New York—I was in what used to be called the Fraternity Club, now called the Hotel something-or-other at 38th and Madison, in a one room cell Allenton-House-kind-of-hotel room. Meanwhile I checked in at the art department at the Associated Press, which was a bullpen. They brought in guys from outside New York like Al Capp and me.

Eisner: How did they discover you?
Caniff: The bureau managers at the AP forward to the main office in New York any outstanding work by a writer or artist.

Eisner: I see . . .
Caniff: A guy named Brophy was head of the [Columbus] AP bureau, which was in the same building as the *Columbus Dispatch* and he had been sending back clippings of my work to the feature service editor here [New York]. A guy named Brooks. They had an opening coming up in the bullpen. Then I got a query from Wilson Hicks, who was his assistant.

Eisner: Mmmm Hmmm. Well, anyway, that got you to New York.
Caniff: Very often it's somebody who is following your work whom you don't even know exists who gives you this break or who refers you to someone and they ask to see your work. Samples are *so* important. I had a good batch that had been turned down by everybody else [laughter]. The only place I hadn't applied for a job was the AP. I didn't even know they *had* an art department. I had tried the United Features

and King Features and all the others but got a polite turn-down from all of them.

Eisner: There you are in New York from Ohio . . .
Caniff: So I'm sitting in New York and you were asking about whether I worked alone. During the day then, I worked at the AP in the bullpen on straightaway general assignments. The first job was crossword puzzles. The new guy always had to fill in the blanks of the crossword puzzles. [laughter] You make one mistake and you've got every crossword puzzle nut calling!

Eisner: Yeah, that's right!
Caniff: And the editors hated to edit these and find those mistakes that the artists made. I didn't last too long at that, fortunately. Anyway, I learned lettering. The election was coming up and I'd done a lot of portrait stuff—you know, the pebbleboard portraits.

Eisner: Oh yes. The Coquille board they called it.
Caniff: I did all the candidates of both parties. I did thirty-two portraits of these clowns. [laughter] And, fortunately, with the AP photo lab department I could get small heads blown up large enough to trace them on the Coquille board—pantograph them up, which is a big convenience of course.

Eisner: Mmmm Hmmm.
Caniff: Surprisingly, the two final nominees were the hardest to draw. The two worst portraits I did out of the whole bunch were Hoover and Roosevelt, and, of course, they're the ones . . .

Eisner: [laughter] They're the ones you had to use all over the place! Yes . . .
Caniff: Working on a daily newspaper you learn to get fast with this kind of stuff. I think I told you that the other guys at the AP said, "Lay off—cool it, kid. We've got a good thing going here! Don't spoil it." [laughter] Most of them had come from individual newspapers too, so they knew exactly . . . You catch on very quickly. Now, about the studio: when I reached New York I called Bil Dwyer who had also worked on the *Columbus Dispatch.*

Eisner: Oh—he did *Dumb Dora,* that was it.
Caniff: Well, it's pertinent here. I called him just socially and told him I was in town to say hello. I didn't know where he lived, on Christopher

Street. I didn't even know where Christopher Street *was.* So he said, "My God, I'm glad you called! I've got a problem here. Come on down!" This was like the first night I was in town and he had been submitting things to King Features and selling gags, by the way, to the magazines, *Collier's* and the *New Yorker.* Anyway, he had submitted a gag-type strip to King Features and he got a call back saying that Paul Fung was being pulled off *Dumb Dora* and Dwyer had the assignment. Here he was suddenly with six strips and a Sunday page to do and he'd never done anything except single panels.

Eisner: Oh boy!
Caniff: And he was in trouble. Frank Engli was helping him.

Eisner: Frank Engli . . . He was a sports cartoonist, right?
Caniff: No, he did lettering. He later on did a strip called *Looking Back,* about stoneage characters—

Eisner: Oh, I see.
Caniff: —very well done cartooning. But his lettering was especially good. So I went down to see them and they were laboring away at the first release. Bil was a good gag writer, but he'd never had this kind of assignment before. So he said to me, "Will you sit in on this thing and especially draw the girls?" So I laid out the first batch of stuff and, again, it was not hard for me to do because I had those eleven o'clock deadlines every morning. And so then I inked the girls and he inked the other characters; very simple drawing.

Eisner: Who wrote the stuff?
Caniff: Dwyer. He was a very good gag man. Chic Young had originated the character and then Paul finally took over from Chic when Chic started *Blondie.* Paul was drawing it before Dwyer. I never did find out, by the way, why he withdrew.

Eisner: *Dumb Dora* was a very successful strip in its day.
Caniff: Maybe Fung had a fight with King Features. I don't know and I never did ask. So we made the deadline, which was the thing that was bothering Dwyer, but in the meantime I had to go to work the next morning at eight o'clock. So, for the first weeks of this thing, I was moonlighting at night for him and doing my regular job during the day. I had a hell of a time staying awake.

Eisner: Oh boy, that *is* a hell of a schedule . . .
Caniff: But, again, when you're 25 years old you can stand that.

Eisner: Yeah, yeah . . .
Caniff: And at that time my wife had not come out yet so I had nothing else to do at night. Bunny was still in Columbus closing up our things out there, trying to find a way to pay the rent we still owed [laughter]—so right off the bat I was into this moonlighting thing. It was necessary financially because I was only getting sixty dollars a week from the AP. And you couldn't make it even then on sixty dollars a week living in Tudor City. Well, about a year after this time Wilson Hicks had taken over at the AP as head of the feature service. He came around and said, "Do you know somebody who could do this general assignment illustration?" And I said, "I sure do!" There was [Noel] Sickles back there doing movie ads for RKO in Cincinnati and hating every minute of it. I didn't even have to send for his work. I already had it. They looked at it and, sure enough, they thought, "Sheesh, this'll cost us!" But he didn't know any more about New York than I did and they got *him* for peanuts too. He was glad to make it though.

Eisner: What year was this now?
Caniff: This was in the spring of 1933.

Eisner: Well, this was at the tail end of the big Depression.
Caniff: Oh, it wasn't over.

Eisner: It wasn't over yet, no. In fact, it really hit in '31, '32. I know.
Caniff: Well, we caught it late in Columbus and the Midwest. We knew all about what had happened to friends of ours who had eastern interests and stocks and so forth. But at that age you don't move in those circles. My mother and dad lost everything they had in Dayton a year later.

Eisner: I know, because I was selling papers downtown in '31.
Caniff: Exactly. My dad and I lost our jobs on the same day. I got fired at the *Dispatch* the same day he was fired. He worked at that time for an automobile company, although he was a printer by trade.

Eisner: Oh yes. So you already had a little of that ink in your blood.
Caniff: Oh, very definitely.

Eisner: What about Sickles now?
Caniff: Well, Sickles was better in *high school* than any newspaper staff artist in Columbus or Cleveland or Cincinnati, which was our world at

that time. He could do the sort of work we were doing in New York because he had practiced at home making "comps," layouts, retouching; he'd taken the Landon course. Landon used to touch on this sort of thing. He really trained you to be a newspaper artist.

Eisner: Landon? I don't remember that now.
Caniff: C. N. Landon was his name . . . Charles.

Eisner: Yeah, yeah . . . That's right. Now I remember: "Draw me."
Caniff: "Draw me" was Minneapolis. "Copy me" was Landon—in Cleveland. It was Uncle Sam. That's what I used when I applied for the course and, of course, was accepted immediately. [laughter] No one was ever turned down, unless you were under 15. That was one rule he had—you had to be 15. I think the reason for that was that below 15 you couldn't get financial responsibility. Usually it was your father or—

Eisner: Well, also it was signing an agreement. Minors can't.
Caniff: Yes, that too. Under 15 a kid is not responsible, with rare exception. I took it when I was 16 or so. I never finished it—nobody ever did—because I got a job. Then, who needed the damn thing? [laughter] I got a job as an office boy in the Dayton, Ohio *Herald-Journal* art department. I got to know Landon later, because by the time I got to New York he had come to Manhattan as the art editor of *Cosmopolitan.* So I went around to see him with my hat in hand. I had never met him before, only corresponded. I showed him things I had been doing for the AP here and he said, "Well," and he took out his pencil and wrote corrections on my drawings!

Eisner: And started criticizing. [chuckle] And marking up your art. [groan]
Caniff: And in *red!* But, he was always right. Oh, he was absolutely great at this stuff. He could teach you to draw for the worst reproduction in the world. If he were doing chalk plates, they'd come out good.

Eisner: Oh, that's just marvelous.
Caniff: He taught you not to put crosshatch too tightly together and all that. It was very valuable. He used single lines with his crayon stuff on that Coquille board for his portraits and he said, "You should always remember that a single stroke of a crayon is better than mushing around with it, because it leaves some error room in there for the reduction."

Eisner: Very good, yeah. Most of the younger artists I see from this generation are really very casual about reproduction. They don't worry about it. The technology is so sophisticated today.
Caniff: An old engraver from the *Dayton Journal* said, "I'll teach you engraving and you'll make a better living than in that dumb art department." [chuckle] And I thought about it quite seriously because I could have done this at night and those guys were making a lot more money than we were. They were on union scale, even back then. This is back in '21, '22. I told him I was very grateful but I had to go to school and I just didn't have time to do both these things. But along the way he let me listen in and he would talk. He loved to talk, and he'd tell me, "This is something you shouldn't do here." He would give me an assignment to do down there on a piece of paper and he taught me to *not* do more things than *how* to. He taught me not to let my brush ink gray out and to always use strong black so the engraver can pick it up, and to not isolate something in the middle of white space. Don't just put a blob of something without connections so when we rout the thing out it would hold up. And he showed me the actual routing machine. It gave me something to hang on to.

Eisner: Isn't that valuable? Right after high school I spent some time in a print shop cleaning presses for three dollars a week and I consider that one of the most valuable experiences I had. I could sit there with a typesetter, a compositor, a big fat guy who would pick type out of the rack and set it in a stick—you know. I learned about engraving and printing there. I know it's been as useful to me as it has been to you.
Caniff: It has. My dad gave me some of the stuff, but at the time my dad was actively carrying a stick around in that little bag that they had—

Eisner: Yes.
Caniff: —and I still have all that, by the way.

Eisner: You still have all that: the old apron?
Caniff: My dad's old apron and also his stick. But by the time I got old enough to really assimilate this stuff, my dad had become ill with lead poisoning, because of the miserable conditions they worked under.

Eisner: Oh sure. All that type was lead. It wasn't really zinc.
Caniff: It was a very bad thing; leads to tuberculosis. He had to get a job outside, so he did, and that was the end of my contact with the print shop, per se. But my contact with the people still remains. I was named after the editor of my dad's paper.

Eisner: Is that right!
Caniff: Milton Wedding was his name.

Eisner: What town in Ohio was that?
Caniff: Hillsboro. It's between Cincinnati and Columbus.

Eisner: I see.
Caniff: It was then a little weekly newspaper, now a daily. A little population that hasn't altered that much. The advertising has. They have supermarket advertising and that makes it possible.

Eisner: But let me get back on the Sickles thing because you've left me hanging. Now Sickles came along, and he came from Ohio too, didn't he?
Caniff: Yes. Chillicothe. He was working in Cincinnati. He and I had tried to start up a studio. Both of us were fired. He from the *Ohio State Journal* and I was dropped by the *Columbus Dispatch.* So we set up a business in which I would go out and sell in the morning and he would stay inside and then when I would get back in the afternoon we would both work on what I had sold in the morning. And our big thing was to deliver you a finished rough the next morning. We were trying to beat the existing ad agencies. We had friends enough among the art directors from Frigidaire and General Motors and big companies like that. We had entre like that and right off the bat we had good assignments. But it nearly killed us trying to do what we set out to do: to turn in a finished rough the next morning. We'd put it on a bus to go to Cincinnati or Cleveland from Columbus and it would get there by noon. It was great except that we couldn't have kept it up. Well, anyway, we were doing very well. We made a good impression; a good initial impact. And then I got this wire from the Associated Press in New York and I had to decide whether to stay with the advertising or take the AP job. We talked it over, of course, and Sickles said the chance to go to New York was worth everything so he encouraged me to go ahead and not worry about our little thing back there. We had some free space in an advertising agency, so we didn't owe anybody. Our billings were still coming in so we had a little money, thank goodness, or we wouldn't have been able to do anything. Sickles then went freelance on his own. He stayed with the same agency. Again, he wasn't paying any rent and they weren't paying him, but it looked good when a client came in if they had an artist working. It was really an exchange of space for a body. He'd take jobs from them if they had jobs. The trouble was they

didn't have that many jobs. [laughter] Anyway, we stayed warm friends until the man died—the owner of the agency. Meanwhile I was stockpiling Sickles' past and present work and he went on to RKO in Cincinnati to do their daily ads, which was a fulltime job. They had several theatres and he hated it. Sickles was a good lettering man among other things, and so these were beautiful ads, more than RKO deserved really. But nobody ever really pays you enough.

Eisner: That's so true!
Caniff: Anyway, he was ready to come to New York, and he was single, so he didn't have to ask anybody anything. He just got on the train and came. I called him and told him that this was in the works and to be on the alert for it because he had to negotiate his own deal. I wasn't about to act as his agent. It was none of my business anyway; it was up to him. He didn't know how much I was getting and it was up to him to make his own mark. So I imagine he settled for about the same amount. I don't even remember now. He earned much more later, when he started doing features. He could live on $60 a week in New York. I couldn't, so I *had* to moonlight. Anyway, he came out and the AP was so delighted to get him because he could do anything. He could take over making maps of the European War or whatever was going on at the time. He was also an expert lettering man. John Terry was doing a strip on [Charles] Lindbergh. It didn't look very much like Lindbergh because poor Terry couldn't draw, but the impact was there so it sold like crazy. But the AP's method of selling was that they offered the whole service, not an individual strip. They handed the assignment to Sickles but said, "You have to draw it lousy, as John Terry does." [laughter] So, he drew it lousy. He could imitate anybody. So he got to take over . . .

Eisner: *Scorchy Smith.*
Caniff: *Scorchy Smith,* then, at the AP. He just walked out of the building as far as working in the office was concerned. They didn't bother him with the general assignments. Nominally, he was still in the bullpen, still a working stiff.

Eisner: Sickles then, is he still working?
Caniff: Oh yes, he's doing western paintings out in Tucson.

Eisner: Oh, I see.
Caniff: He was still on this assignment thing in the office but he was doing this full six strips a week in that miserable style. But he didn't

want to hang around the office anymore, because every once in a while they'd say, "Hey Noel, there's a crisis in Bolivia,"—or something—"Draw a map!" And he said, "Oh to hell with that! You can't do both. If I'm going to do *Scorchy Smith,* I better do it at home." He had to do the research on the thing and he was writing it too. So they said, "All right, all right." They wanted him under their thumb but they didn't want to lose him. He was living and working in the Tudor Hotel.

Eisner: Oh yeah? Well, I had a studio in Tudor City in 1940.
Caniff: He got tired of imitating this thing, but he agreed to do it and it wasn't fair to poor old John Terry not to continue drawing it the way he did. Then Terry died. Immediately Sickles said, "Now can I go, coach?" So they said, "All right, but gradually." So he gradually shifted to his own style and, of course, he drew like the blazes.

Eisner: Oh yes. His work was brilliant; a brilliant draftsman. Well, he exercised an influence on your own style . . .
Caniff: Oh, definitely. Now, right about this time I had started to do *Dickie Dare.* I was still doing *The Gay Thirties.* I had been able to get away from the office just about the time Sickles came on there. I took a room at the YMCA on 47th Street so I could get away from the apartment and still have a place to work. He was living at the Tudor Hotel in Tudor City so we said, "Why the hell don't we join forces again and get a decent place in Woodstock Tower?" It was right next door to the hotel. So we rented an apartment there and it was much better all around. You had your own bathroom and everything else. Sickles continued to live in the Tudor Hotel and I lived in the Windsor Tower.

Eisner: I lived at No. 5.
Caniff: Mmmm Hmmm. That's the one. And I lived there right up until 1937 when I moved out to the country. By that time the strip had begun to sell. By that time I had switched over to *Terry and the Pirates* of course. The whole business took place during that time from 1930 . . .

Eisner: You went to *Terry* from *Dickie Dare?*
Caniff: Yes, Joseph Patterson saw *Dickie* in *The Sun,* the old *New York Sun,* and then I got a call asking if I'd like to do a strip for them and we discussed that. He had *The Teenie Weenies* running as a daily and Sunday strip. I think they felt that they were not quite *New York Daily*

News level stuff. He wanted an adventure strip, real blood and thunder adventure. That's why I got the nod, because that's what I was doing in *Dickie Dare* in *The Sun.* This is what he wanted: a kid, an older guy with muscles, pretty girls.

Eisner: Well, it was in the tradition of *Tim Tyler's Luck.*
Caniff: Yeah, exactly. *Tim Tyler,* I remember, was into the flying stuff right from the beginning, wasn't he?

Eisner: *Tim Tyler* was pretty much like *Tin Tin,* Herge's strip. Tim Tyler would go off on African adventures and so forth. He was a little like—do you remember the books?—I grew up on them; I'm sure you did too, the Boy Allies, the Tom Swifts . . .
Caniff: Oh sure. Read 'em all twice.

Eisner: Of course. [chuckle] But those are the books that influenced the early adventure strips.
Caniff: Well, that's when I began to pick Sickles' brain. It was important that he was doing *Scorchy Smith* "his" way and he could knock out those six strips in time to make the deadline, and that is what influenced my drawing style more than anything else, being able to do that on a Sunday page *in time.* Oh, they were a headache! At that time we were doing all our own work—no lettering man. It was at that time also that we decided that between the two of us we'd hire a lettering man. We went back to Engli—with whom I had worked on *Dumb Dora*—and called him and asked. He was working for an animation studio in midtown New York, still living in the same apartment down on Christopher Street. All this had taken place in a fairly short period of time. I was no longer, of course, associated with Dwyer. He had fired me because I was making too much money [laughter]—$20 a week, and he thought he could get it done cheaper elsewhere. Things began to break better for me around that time. I could make it without the $20. These things all overlap, overmesh. I can't remember which came first. Oh, back to Engli again. Between Sickles and me we were able to afford to have him quit his job and come to work for us. He was glad to be able to leave the animation place. It was a backbreaker—hell on the eyes.

Eisner: So you took him on as a letterer and that made a studio. I'm interested in something you said a minute ago, that you were picking Sickles' brain. What exactly did you get from Sickles?

Caniff: Well, first of all, the use of the blacks, the specific shadows and things. I first learned from him that I could do the heavy black shadows with a brush first and then come back with a pen and do the faces. This was something he was so skilled at.

Eisner: That takes a hell of a lot of confidence to do a thing like that.
Caniff: He pencils tighter than I do, so his compositions and everything were all set. He didn't work on the faces as much as I did. I went more for character and he went more for general effect. He hated *Scorchy Smith* anyway. It didn't have a strong enough leading man. The Lindbergh association was fine, but he was not as assertive as he should have been.
So Sickles then was drawing him unassertively. The secondary character was better than his main character. He had a couple of bad guys who were marvelous. This so often happens, you know. He had an ex-World War I German fighter pilot who had come to this country. His name was Himmelstoss, as I recall. Right out of *All Quiet on the Western Front.*

Eisner: Oh gees . . .
Caniff: And by this time the German had a monocle and was paired off with Scorchy—flying stuff. With that and the Lindbergh thing, Sickles had a ball. Whenever it came to that, he was happy. He used every technique imaginable: chemical Benday paper, crayon . . . He used everything in the book and it was all great. But as soon as he'd licked it, he lost interest. So he was so bored with the feature—and by that time they had suspected that might happen at the AP—so they had Bert Christman warming up in the bullpen. So he took over. Sickles started doing editorial cartoons for the AP. You could never say anything about anybody.

Eisner: No, that's right, because they had so many newspapers and they didn't want to offend anybody.
Caniff: You couldn't even say Hitler was a bad guy! [chuckle] You could show what Hitler was doing and let the reader make up his mind about it. But you could never say *any*thing. Sickles had fun with this for a while, but after a time it was just this milquetoast business. So he quit.

Eisner: Yeah. Well, he was a courageous man. Getting back to the technology, what you picked up from Sickles was being able to lay the black on the figure and then outline.

Caniff: And in *time.* That was always the biggest thing: time. He could do it fast *and* good. With me, it took me a while to get the hang of it, and when I finally did it was right in the nick of time because this is right when I was tapering off on *Dickie Dare* and starting *Terry.*

Eisner: I see. So you really needed this.
Caniff: Starting *Terry* was more or less the old style because I was afraid to jump into the pool.

Eisner: You were using a pen then pretty much the way you are today.
Caniff: And afterward, when I began to get more adept at the brush, I finally started. Fortunately, the background of things in China at that time—the war was imminent—allowed you to do a lot of military stuff, explosions and things being blown up in the water.

Eisner: Yeah, that kind of thing. You also had more space to work in.
Caniff: Oh God, yes. I was working in tabloid size then; in the tabloid configuration. Now I work in the eight columns wide, 1/3 page deep configuration, simply because so do the greatest number of clients. Let the rescale come as it will.

Eisner: I want to talk a little bit about the business we're in. I really grew up in comic books. My newspaper experience was really as a comic book artist. As a matter of fact, you first met me during the National Cartoonist Society's first meeting, when it was being formed, and I was kind of the token comic book artist. [laughter] I think the Society felt they ought to have a comic book artist just for appearances. You were the hierarchy. [laughter] Yes, you were the aristocracy and we were the—[laughter] I felt somehow I was different than you fellows. I remember standing around as an awed youth listening to you pros—you guys seemed old to me then—talking about circulation. You had a relationship with circulation far greater than we did in comic books. We never really knew how many copies actually sold because our salary and our fees were not predicated on how well it sold, but simply on how much the publisher liked us or how well he thought we did.
Caniff: And he wouldn't tell you anyway.

Eisner: No, of course not.
Caniff: He didn't want you to ask for a raise.

Eisner: What I'm getting at, Milt, with this long opening, is to point out that I have always regarded comic books as having a position of their

own in popular literature. Did you and your contemporaries see yourselves as working in a valid art form, or just as comical artists doing an extension of features in a newspaper?
Caniff: Well, the art form, yes, but not in so many words. I think, first of all, we were a circulation device. I had an editor once who said, "Remember always that the old man pays for the paper. So draw for the person who pays for it." This was in the 20's. Because if the old man doesn't bring the paper home it won't be read in the house. At the same time you have to remember that sometimes there's home delivery circulation and the lady of the house will decide which newspaper—and in those days there was a choice, very often a multiple choice, of which paper to subscribe to or to have delivered to your house. Very often the old man would read the paper on the way to the office if he went on the bus or subway—depending on the transportation, if it was a big city where there was time to be read—and the wife of the house would be having her second cup of coffee or be in the bathroom or wherever there was a moment in which you had your little tete-a-tete. Now that hardly exists even today. Home delivery still exists, but reading it on the bus is almost gone because most men drive to work anyway, no matter where they go, or they go to car pools in the big industrial cities. So, generally speaking, it's read at home now. Now the same editor said, "You've got to remember you're not selling today's newspaper. They already *have* today's newspaper. You're selling *tomorrow's* paper." He was talking generally about anything in the newspaper, but he said, "You cliffhanger boys"—already my bent was toward that sort of thing—"have a better chance to do this than gag-a-day people." If somebody likes to read *Blondie,* they'll just read it tomorrow because they want to see if the postman gets knocked down again by Dagwood. But with the cliffhangers, you're selling tomorrow's paper. That is why at that time we were on the ascendency—the *Dick Tracys* and the *Little Orphan Annies.*

Eisner: Well, did you regard yourselves as newsboys, that is, newspaper salesmen, or did you regard yourselves as people involved in some kind of art form or entertainers? Did you think of yourself as an entertainer?
Caniff: Entertainer, first of all.

Eisner: Rube Goldberg used to refer to himself, whenever I heard him chat in private conversations, as an entertainer.
Caniff: Well, this editor's contention—and I think I learned more from him than from any other single editor—his point was that with entertain-

ing you must be entertaining no matter what you do or say—whether you have a message or whether you're just showing off your skill. If you are not entertaining and the pleasure dies in your reader, then you're failing in your mission. The newspaper itself is an entertainment medium. You read the news headlines, but almost from there on, you're reading for entertainment. You're enjoying reading about Babe Ruth scoring another home run or whatever. "You should always remember, no matter who reads the paper it's primarily the man who pays for the paper,"—back to the editor—"So always show a little skin above the stockings as a bonus." [laughter] And he was right. Of course you had to be judicious as hell as to how you showed that skin above the stockings. I found, just as movies have been finding, that it's much more provocative to allude to the premise rather than the realization.

Eisner: Exactly! At any rate, what I'm probing is how you people saw yourselves, because across the street or down in the valley where us comic book artists were working, most of them saw themselves really as drones, drudges working in a galley with everybody pulling oars. [laugh]
Caniff: Right. Sometimes it's like that too.

Eisner: Occasionally some cocky guy like me would come along and think, rather presumptuously, that he is in some kind of an art form and what he's doing is literature. But when I got to talking to the strip artists on the newspaper side of this business, the newspaper artists, writers like yourself, thought of themselves as entertainers and in show business, if you will. Didn't Rube Goldberg do a lot of vaudeville acts for a time?
Caniff: Oh he had one. I forget what you call it but he drew pictures and talked . . . a chalk talk.

Eisner: Yes, chalk talk.
Caniff: Just a spotlight and a drawing board. And he did it big time.

Eisner: Yeah, and very funny too. I remember seeing him in the RKO Palace.
Caniff: Successful. He probably would have traveled more except that he still had to grind out a strip. Yes, he used to be very good. One of the incentive things in the strip field is that you're being paid on a percentage basis, based on circulation. You had this big chance to make as much money as you could make on the same simple syndication level.

So that always, like a performer in the movies, the one more successful would make more money than the other one. Very seldom did anyone ever better their percentage base, but some people did. You'd go from 50-50 to 70-30 or 60-40 or whatever.

Eisner: Do you know, Milt, any of your contemporaries who would admit that what they were doing was art?
Caniff: I don't think it was ever quite put on that basis, but it was certainly put on the basis that it was a "form." It was a communication form rather than an art form. I don't think I ever heard anybody ever use the phrase "art form" as such. It started out being a job which could be improved—a rent payer to begin with, and then as it improved it became a better and better rent payer, but still you were married to the simple business of making a living.

Eisner: You didn't think of yourselves as being on the same level as, say, a novelist, a fiction writer, let's say?
Caniff: Yes, I think so, without ever having expressed it so.

Eisner: Did you all think that way?
Caniff: We were shooting in a sense for the mass audience, a provable mass audience. One break that the syndicate people always got was the syndication list. When it was up that always meant more readership as well as more income, so you began to feel more important because of this, and with good reason, because you could *prove* it. When a syndicate hires a guy on an employment contract, it's quite different than when an artist signs or renews a contract because he has built up 600 newspaper. He doesn't have to argue the point! There it is. It's there because he did it. Of course, it works the other way too. This is the greatest break we ever had. The president of General Motors can't prove anything if many cars are sold! Neither is it entirely his fault if GM has a bad year.

Eisner: That's right.
Caniff: So he's on a contract. If the guy in the interior of General Motors works out a new gear, it belongs to GM.

Eisner: So, in the main, your satisfaction or self-measurement came from the amount of papers you sold or the build-up in circulation. I was really trying to get at how we see ourselves, because things have changed. Candidly, I have been devoting myself to the theory that what we have here is a medium which is capable of far more than what has been done so far.

Caniff: I agree with that. I think it hasn't been plumbed. We've been doing the best we can, but timorously. Once in a while I will do something I was told not to do and bend the rules. I'll give you a for-instance: When I went to the *News* to do *Terry and the Pirates,* I had not been doing a Sunday page, so they had no track record of me doing anything in color. Joe Patterson himself said, "This is a mass printing of course, so you have to keep it simple." He said, "Jiggs always wears a red vest. So-and-so always wears a plain flat blue, and you've only got three colors to work with." He prided himself on his real knowledge of the mechanics of the business, as well as the less easily identified skills. And he said, "Keep the colors simple." And I said to myself, "I'm not going to do this. They've got the best newspaper engravers on this paper and the *Chicago Tribune.*" They always made two sets of plates on *Terry* and all the others. The one-half page size standard was made in Chicago while the tabloid was being made in New York. That was all they offered at the beginning. An editor couldn't buy 3⁄4 pages or other odd sizes. They were very arbitrary about it. If the papers out on the circuit didn't like it, they'd tell 'em to lump it. Patterson didn't give a damn about anything except the *New York News* and *Chicago Tribune.* And they had all those great old German engravers! I thought, "God, I never had a chance like this in my life to do real newspaper color; to really paint a picture with a color scheme indicator or color chart or whatever they called it. I'm just going to do it!" So, right from the start, I started using the most elaborate color schemes I could get. And these engravers were challenged for the first time for some of them in a long time, and they really came through. Gradually, Patterson himself began to like this. He didn't say he did, but he did. I heard it through the grapevine. Finally, they took one of those veteran engravers at the *News* and put him on *Terry,* on that tabloid page. All week he did nothing else but that. I learned all this through whispers. Patterson ordered this himself. All the backgrounds. Boy, you could do a sunrise and they'd make it glow!

Eisner: Oh, that had dot etching in those days, you know! Let's get back to the question of the art form and where comics are going, because I think this is really the most important thing. What we're living through now is what Dickens referred to as "the best of times and the worst of times." The syndicate business seems to be drying up under the face of most of us who are in the adventure continuity. How do you see it?

Caniff: The adventure story as such and whatever form it takes before it gets to production as films or newspaper, hard paper or soft paper, or any other thing, is going to remain. Everyone is going to want to know what's going to happen next, tomorrow, or the next page or whatever, and I've always gone on that pretext. Well, it's not a pretext at all, but a simple thesis that anything can make the reader, viewer, whatever want to turn the page or see tomorrow or next week's episode of M-A-S-H or whatever. These guys are all doing the same, making the same propositions for the same reasons, to hold you one way or another. The gag men have a harder time. But that's not the point now. As to where it's going, it's a matter of how it's going to be produced. The cable television, for example, is going to change the whole aspect of syndicates, syndicate contracts, everything else, because of its ability to be put in your house or before your eyes or ears or whatever, in another form than the way we've been doing it. Getting down now to the point where the postage stamp size of a comic strip is too much for the older reader. Older readers can't even read the damn thing. Well, it's going to topple, but it will topple into another form. It will take a form where it will communicate itself to the listener, viewer, consumer. Unfortunately, not one of us knows what that form will be. Along the way it has not lost its steam. For instance, there are more clients now for *Prince Valiant* than ever before—

Eisner: Is that a fact? I'm surprised.
Caniff: —because it isn't in New York, it isn't in Chicago, but the other papers around the country and overseas as well have raised that list to higher than when Hal Foster was doing it.

Eisner: Now, that's a Sunday paper only. That's only a Sunday feature . . .
Caniff: Yes, but the point is that this is with all the Sunday papers folding and the cries of horror that you hear.

Eisner: Yes, that's astonishing.
Caniff: I heard this from Ben at King Features. That's right from the horse's mouth.

Eisner: Incredible!
Caniff: That's at the same time they're crying havoc about every other feature. Charlie Schulz is making more money than anybody has ever made. He's the highest paid person in the United States.

Eisner: Incredible!
Caniff: And Mort Walker has three strips and is going to start another one. You don't do this in a dying entertainment form. This is no Titanic we are working with.

Eisner: But the daily humor strips, they're not the—
Caniff: Well, in these instances, yes, but it still is "What happens to *Beetle Bailey* tomorrow?" This is what causes you to continue. You laughed today but still—

Eisner: You want to see what he's going to do tomorrow.
Caniff: You want to see more of him.

Eisner: Is it that the other newspapers are proliferating or—
Caniff: No, they're shrinking.

Eisner: Shrinking. So how is it possible that these strips are—
Caniff: Well, here's how it is going, and this is the simplest kind of economics: The *Chicago Tribune* used to "protect" the territory, as they said, around Chicago. You couldn't buy *Terry and the Pirates* in Illinois, Indiana, Iowa or Wisconsin. When I started *Steve Canyon,* every paper in the daily size cities all around there—a very tight little skein around Chicago—were available as customers and suddenly, *boom!* Oh, I had papers in Indianapolis, and Iowa City and Milwaukee which I didn't have before with *Terry.* So, that kind of thing has happened. Now the neighborhood papers are the ones who have done it. I was living in Rockland County, New York and the Nyack, New York *Journal News* was a good little country paper; a daily, but still a country paper. Now it's a big metropolitan-size thing, and that's where the business is. Across the river in Westchester there are metropolitan-size newspapers in every city. You open those up and here's *Hagar the Horrible* in all these papers that are now up to 2,000. I think *Hagar* is now into 1,900 papers.

Eisner: Nineteen hundred papers. That's incredible.
Caniff: Which is really saturation. You can't get any tighter than that. *Peanuts* might be in a few more than that because he's been around longer and has more foreign papers.

Eisner: *Blondie* is supposed to have had the largest circulation.
Caniff: *Blondie* still has the largest circulation because it's widely read and has been for a long time, for all the wrong reasons. That is, in South America they think it's funny. They think it's ridiculous, ludicrous

that a woman can dominate her husband like that. And that's why they read it in the Latin countries. *Hagar* is funny because Hagar is funny. Schulz is so universal that translating it is easy; little kids are little kids in every country. There's a third one . . . *Hagar, Peanuts* . . .

Eisner: Oh, *Beetle Bailey?*
Caniff: *Beetle Bailey* is the third. There are four. King Features has three and United Press has one.

Eisner: *Incredible!*
Caniff: And they're the saturation. They can't go anywhere. They can't sell anybody because there isn't anybody left to sell.

Eisner: Incredible. [chuckle] Isn't that wonderful!
Caniff: This is not a falling-down-depression. This is very big stuff and Mort's coming up with another strip.

Eisner: Yeah, well he's an industry. I think he's a one-man conglomerate.
Caniff: He calls his studio "King Features East" out there in Connecticut.

Eisner: He's got four strips and all of them are successful.
Caniff: Oh, some of the things he does are more appealing. *Hi and Lois* is appealing for the obvious reasons: the suburban life, which does well. He's a hell of a gag man. He's also a very disciplined person and he doesn't even appear to sweat. And here he is coming out with a new one. He does one called *Boner's Ark* which we don't see around here, and one called *Sam and Silo,* which is a—

Eisner: Yeah, I've seen that . . .
Caniff: —comedy thing. All of them are gag. Don't know what the new one is.

Eisner: Well, talking about the future, where is all this going? You think the newspaper business is going to be around for some time and daily strips are going to be around for some time in whatever form they take. Is that what you're saying?
Caniff: Well, let me play something and you'll see what I mean about the changing device of the medium, or the idiom, not the medium. Back before the war, I think it was NBC that was playing around with a device like a ticker tape from which you could get your whole newspaper in the morning, but it came on the floor like loops from a ticker tape. So they used the *Columbus Dispatch* as a testing ground for this, and they reduced the whole thing down so that when you received it

on your machine it was like coming out of a typewriter or a copying machine about that wide, legal size. It was the whole page, a completely legible thing on a facsimile basis. And the comic strips were right there, reduced slightly. As of that day in 1939 we were being reproduced at least five or six columns. That's when all this happened. The reason I got it was that a friend of mine was on the *Dispatch* and sent it to me. They did this experimenting out in Ohio. Then the war came and they had to stop. Now we'll probably be going back to something like that. This was 40 years ago; something similar to having a newspaper in your house and perfectly legible, and you tore off— [chuckle] if Mama wanted a food section, she'd just—

Eisner: Tear it off—
Caniff: Tear it off the machine, except that the paper would be there on the floor like a—

Eisner: —a UP ticker—
Caniff: Except that it was silent and it could come in during the night, or some form of it would. As of 1939, reproduction was good, but not the quality you'd have today.

Eisner: When I was running the Bell-McClure North American Newspaper Alliance, you remember we syndicated all those old-timey features. Well, we were approached at the time on the possibility of a facsimile thing which would go out as a total service with art and so forth. Since I was cartoon-art oriented I was trying to make it carry strips, but there were a lot of impracticalities.
Caniff: Oh, sure.

Eisner: That was in the early 60's.
Caniff: The most legible thing about this 1939 effort was that it was small enough that the type was pretty tight and the reproduction wasn't that good, but the strips were perfect. *Moon Mullins* or *Winnie Winkle* or whatever . . .

Eisner: So, in other words, you see the strip potential as being still very much there.
Caniff: Very much there, and if anything, more explosive than before because people find their niche. In other words, television took the immediate audience away because they could do in a half hour what I

took ten weeks to do. So there was no comparison. I had editors saying, "Why don't you speed up your continuity and just make it eight weeks instead of ten?" [laughter] But that just wouldn't make any difference, you know. Jesus, that this guy could be editing a metropolitan newspaper and his reasoning could be so short-sighted as that! He knows I can't do it. If I'm going to try to compete with television, I'm not going to make it because you can't. You've got to find a whole other audience.

Eisner: Exactly!
Caniff: For one thing, it's a person-to-person medium. Television is usually a shared thing. You're almost never by yourself; you're almost always watching with someone either in your home or at the club or bar or wherever you are. If you're reading the newspaper, you're alone. In fact, you *want* to be alone when you read it. You don't want somebody yakking in your ear. In time this personalization will be the one salvation of our kind of viewed image. It'll be simply a continuation of it, a new format of the old thesis. Again, selling tomorrow's ticker tape or whatever the device is, which will again change by the next year. Just as it has changed since last year.

Eisner: Well, tell me, as an adventure cartoonist, which is after all the category you are in, do you find in the feedback from the syndicate that there is any feeling about where adventure strips are going? What have you heard?
Caniff: Of course, nobody has an absolutely locked-in view. They're all living day-to-day, like an alcoholic. They don't do anything to live tomorrow. At the same time, they're prospering. This is the thing that King Features pointed out at the Comics Council the other day. The advertising has fallen off on the newspaper comic sections, which is a secret rejoicing among the cartoonists because that's what stole all the space away. Patterson rationed advertising as one page either in a full page or half-page form, and gradually he had to increase that to a page and a half, due to the pressure that was on advertisers, especially during wartime. They were desperate to advertise. Comics sections had an audience and the people had money, but they couldn't get their ads in the news sections of the paper because the newsprint was so short. So they turned to the comics sections and that's how *Metro* and *Puck* were born.

Here we are with these people crying havoc because their ads are going to television. But the comics, going back to *Prince Valiant* again, are on the rise. King Features has never done better in terms of their income. They've raised their rates, of course, but the strips that are doing well are doing better than last year at this time. And these suburban papers are the reason for that. They have more clients because they don't have the restrictions now. There's no place in the country now where a paper is holding a territory as the *Chicago Tribune* once did. Even around Los Angeles, for instance, it used to be fifty miles to the next nearest paper. It has shrunk gradually now so that, just last year, Palm Springs was able to print my strip because it was no longer in no-no territory.

Eisner: Oh, I see; it was their given territory. Back then, our salesmen used to come back off the road and complain about the fact that they had a lot of peripheral papers they couldn't sell to. We even tried organizing a regional alliance around Cleveland—the whole ring of papers around Cleveland—trying to pull them out from the big *plain Dealer* who had a lock on the whole area. But we couldn't because they also bought our blanket service which contained news features.
Caniff: Still does, to the extent that it is the paper of record—where you advertise that you are leaving your wife's bed and board.

Eisner: That's the place to do it. They have the sheriff's notices. [laughter]
Caniff: All the legal notices.

Eisner: That's an interesting point, because to the beginning cartoonists, the syndicate business seems a bastion into which they cannot get. What's more, as the comic pages get smaller and smaller, opportunities diminish. It seems advertising gets to take up more and more of the paper. Most of the kids see only big city papers. They're not impressed by being in the Rockland County or the *Woodstock Dispatch* or whatever.
Caniff: Any continuity strip is in hot water now because when it does get printed they reproduce it so small that the older readers can't read it and the younger readers will slough it off. But now I'm beginning to get letters from kids again. For a long time the older readers—who are still my readers—were still there. The young kids that I lost for a whole generation or so are the middle group, the young marrieds or new marrieds; but now I get mail from young kids saying they'd like to be cartoonists.

Eisner: You're getting more mail now. That's interesting.
Caniff: Just in the last three or four years it has begun to expand in volume and intensity. There's hope in that they realize that new strips come along, such as *Hagar. Hagar* is a good example. Of course Dik Browne is an old pro. He was not a kid who had to break in. But still, *Hagar* was never there before. There's no red-hot success except *Doonesbury,* which is in a whole class by itself.

Eisner: That's a political, an editorial strip, unique in that he is commenting on the contemporary political scene.
Caniff: But it's also entertainment. This is what editors have to decide, whether while [Garry] Trudeau was winning the Pulitzer prize—which he did for the political aspects of it—it was still a comic strip. Just because it was not done in a single panel, it was political but at the same time it was entertaining; a damn sight more entertaining than many of the strips on the comics page. I think editors who pulled it out of the comics page and put it by itself on the editorial page were just ducking the issue. Their decision was a hedge rather than a decision. The *Los Angeles Times,* for instance, which, of course, is a bullwark newspaper and can do what it pleases, didn't budge. They let it stay right where it was.

Eisner: On the comics page?
Caniff: Yes. Other editors felt that Garry was being too specific by having an unmarried man and woman living together, and in another place he . . .

Eisner: Editors really didn't feel it belonged on the comics page because that was a family page?
Caniff: Mmmm Hmmm. Exactly! And they felt it should go with the political stuff. The *L.A. Times* didn't do any of this. In one strip a girl was being courted by a man who said, "I'm gay," and she said, "Well, I'm good-natured too." [laughter] Other papers threw that out. Where I lived the Riverside paper immediately threw that out, but I read it that same day in the *L.A. Times.*

Eisner: Well, there is still that mystique that the comics page is the "family" page or is regarded that way by editors and—
Caniff: Many editors hate the comics.

Eisner: Yes! I noticed that even from the days I used to go out with the syndicate salesmen. The editor would hold up the comic page gingerly and say, "Well, we *have to have* these!"

Caniff: Yes, that's the attitude they took, and very often their method of choosing strips would be the gent's room poll, asking the guy in the next urinal, "Did you read this?" Or they would pass proofs around the city room. This, of course, is no place to take a poll of anything, because the guy has to go for what he thinks the boss *wants* him to go for.

Eisner: Of course. As a matter of fact, I always felt that syndicate cartoonists suffered from the kind of "surveys" they take. They'd say, "Well, we made a survey!" Actually, they'd run a small box in the newspaper and ask, "Which comic do you like the most?" Those people who wrote in at all usually put in *Little Orphan Annie,* in the days when nobody read *Orphan Annie* except little old ladies. Norman Isaacs once told me—this was years ago—that he was trying to drop *Little Orphan Annie* and he said he couldn't because the bulk of his subscription circulation were nice little old ladies in the suburbs who had nothing else to do but write long nostalgic letters about *Annie* and threaten to cancel if he dropped it. He said he *couldn't* drop the damn feature.
Caniff: Norman was a very conscientious editor. He had his own favorites but he acted as an editor should act. He'd raise hell with you over a single word.

Eisner: Yeah, yeah. You could hear from him. Well, that was a welcome thing, really. Better than sullen silence and then-*bang!*—a cancellation.
Caniff: For me too. I loved it.

Eisner: Because we always seem to be working in a vacuum.
Caniff: I'd rather have the guy mad at me than ignore me.

Eisner: That's right. I always thought, yeah, say something: do you like it or don't you? In the world of comic books the reaction is much more immediate. A newspaper never really knows how popular a given strip is.
Caniff: No, they don't.

Eisner: I never really heard of a proper scientific way of testing.
Caniff: No—no newspaper really has. The closest thing I've really ever seen to a decent survey, at least a fair survey, was taken by the *Philadelphia Inquirer.* On the ballot they broke up the comics page. It was one of those which asks which strip you want to keep in the paper, and if features are to be dropped, which ones would you prefer. Then the next thing the *Inquirer* did, which was a big break for us, they put

the adventure cartoons in one category so you'd be voting only for those . . .

Eisner: Ah, yes.
Caniff: More noise or more attention does not necessarily mean more readership of a feature. I'm sure you found this to be true. Charlie Schulz said that there are a lot of people who don't even know that he does a comic strip. All they know is the animated television specials and greeting cards; Snoopy and stuff. He said he gets letters from people saying that they just found out he draws a strip in the newspaper [laughter] and it makes him mad. Then he looks at the paycheck and—

Eisner: —and he feels a *lot* better! [chuckle]
Caniff: This is so often true, that people learn about a thing from the noise it makes elsewhere. An actor, for instance, whom you have never seen on stage or in a movie, you suddenly know all about the fact that he just divorced his wife.

Eisner: Well, our media is so parochial.
Caniff: Jack Benny used to talk about that; that it makes you mad but you can't show it when somebody comes up to you and says, "Oh, I enjoy your work. You do great imitations," and you know he's talking about Red Skelton. [laughter] Actually, not so many were familiar with his work, but they heard about Jack Benny; he's a famous guy. We get that too. Of course, as it's happened with you, we're obscure in personal terms I'd get called Al Capp; I was even *introduced* once as Al Capp! Al and I did not look anything alike, yet in the mind of the person I was he.

Eisner: I've been introduced as the artist who creates "The Saint." What do you say?
Caniff: Yes, you don't say anything; you just say, "Thank you."

Eisner: Well, it's getting on in time. One of the disappointments of this interview is that we haven't really had an argument. I've been throwing out things hoping you would say, "I disagree with you. You're all wet." But you haven't. [laughter] And I thank you for it. [laughter]
Caniff: One thing about this business—and I'm sure you've found it true—and I quote John Wayne on this: "M'am, we've got enough trouble in this business without fighting each other." Yup! [laughter] So you won't find me talking about—

Eisner: No, there aren't too many people in this business that I'm mad at. Maybe there's something wrong with me, but—[laughter]
Caniff: Well, there's something Burgess Meredith said. Burgess used to drink too much and I'd have to take him home sometimes, that kind of thing. This is when we used to live in the east all year 'round, but we still see Burgess here and there. Anyway, he said, "Milt, we get along fine." And then there was a pause and he said, "We don't see each other very often, do we?" [laughter]

Shel Dorf Interviews Milton Caniff

Shel Dorf / 1985

From *Terry and the Pirates: Volume 3, 1936–1937,* Flying Buttress Classics Library of Nantier, Beall, Minoustchine Publishing Company, New York, 1985, n.p. Reprinted by permission.

The New York World's Fair of 1964–65 was a highlight in my life. It brought me to Manhattan and led to my first meeting with Milton Caniff. In the two hours we talked, I asked him as much as I could about *Terry and the Pirates.* By this time (July of 1964) he'd been writing and drawing his third strip, *Steve Canyon,* for seventeen years. Milton Caniff is constantly looking ahead and I had the feeling that he preferred talking about his current work. I'm as big a fan of *Canyon,* having saved and read each strip since 1947, so we did talk about the current story which used the World's Fair as a background. He'd done it using blueprints of the fair buildings since it was drawn months before the buildings were finished. He'd timed it to start when the fair opened. There was an actual "Steve Canyon Day" at the fair as well. His current career was indeed exciting, but I had to get those *Terry* questions answered. I persisted.

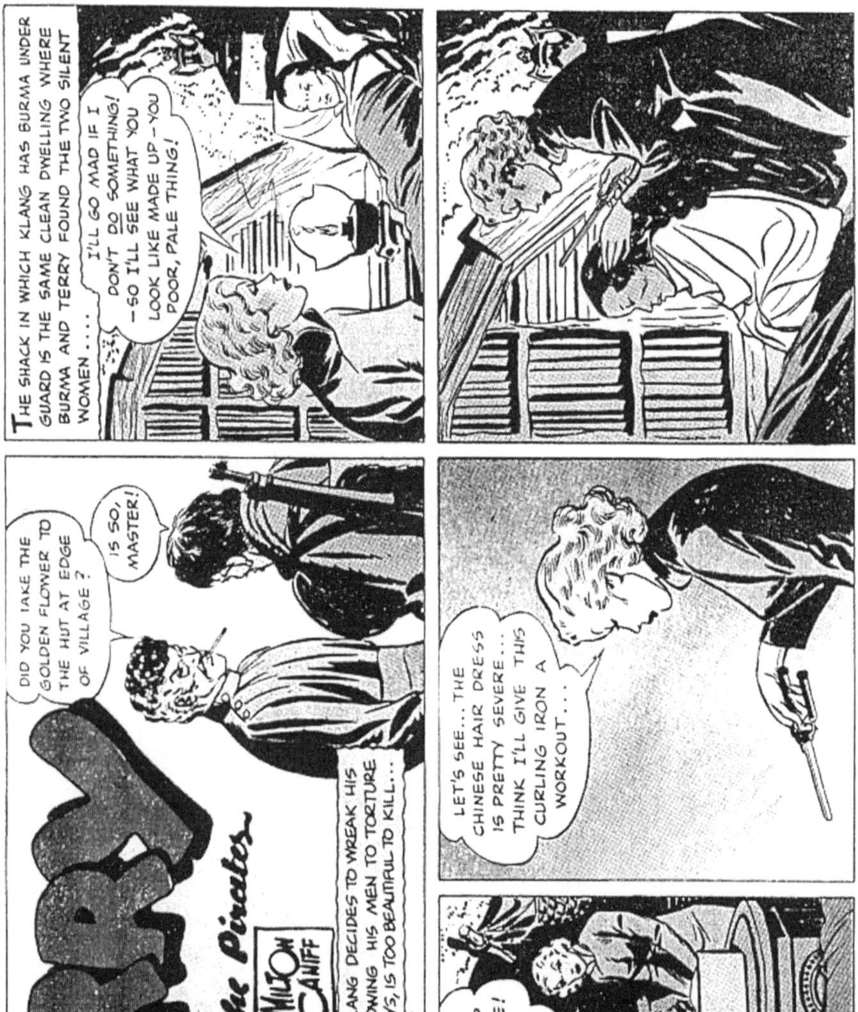
TERRY and the Pirates
by MILTON CANIFF
AFTER TERRY'S ESCAPE, KLANG DECIDES TO WREAK HIS WRATH ON CONNIE BY ALLOWING HIS MEN TO TORTURE THE LAD... BURMA, HE SAYS, IS TOO BEAUTIFUL TO KILL...
DID YOU TAKE THE GOLDEN FLOWER TO THE HUT AT EDGE OF VILLAGE?
IS SO, MASTER!
THE SHACK IN WHICH KLANG HAS BURMA UNDER GUARD IS THE SAME CLEAN DWELLING WHERE BURMA AND TERRY FOUND THE TWO SILENT WOMEN....
I'LL GO MAD IF I DON'T DO SOMETHING! —SO I'LL SEE WHAT YOU LOOK LIKE MADE UP—YOU POOR, PALE THING!
THIS WOMAN'S TRUNK JUDAS TOOK FROM THE SUNKEN SHIP HAS COME IN HANDY FOR ME! YOU MIGHT AS WELL HAVE SOME FUN FROM THE STUFF IN IT, TOO...
LET'S SEE... THE CHINESE HAIR DRESS IS PRETTY SEVERE... THINK I'LL GIVE THIS CURLING IRON A WORKOUT...

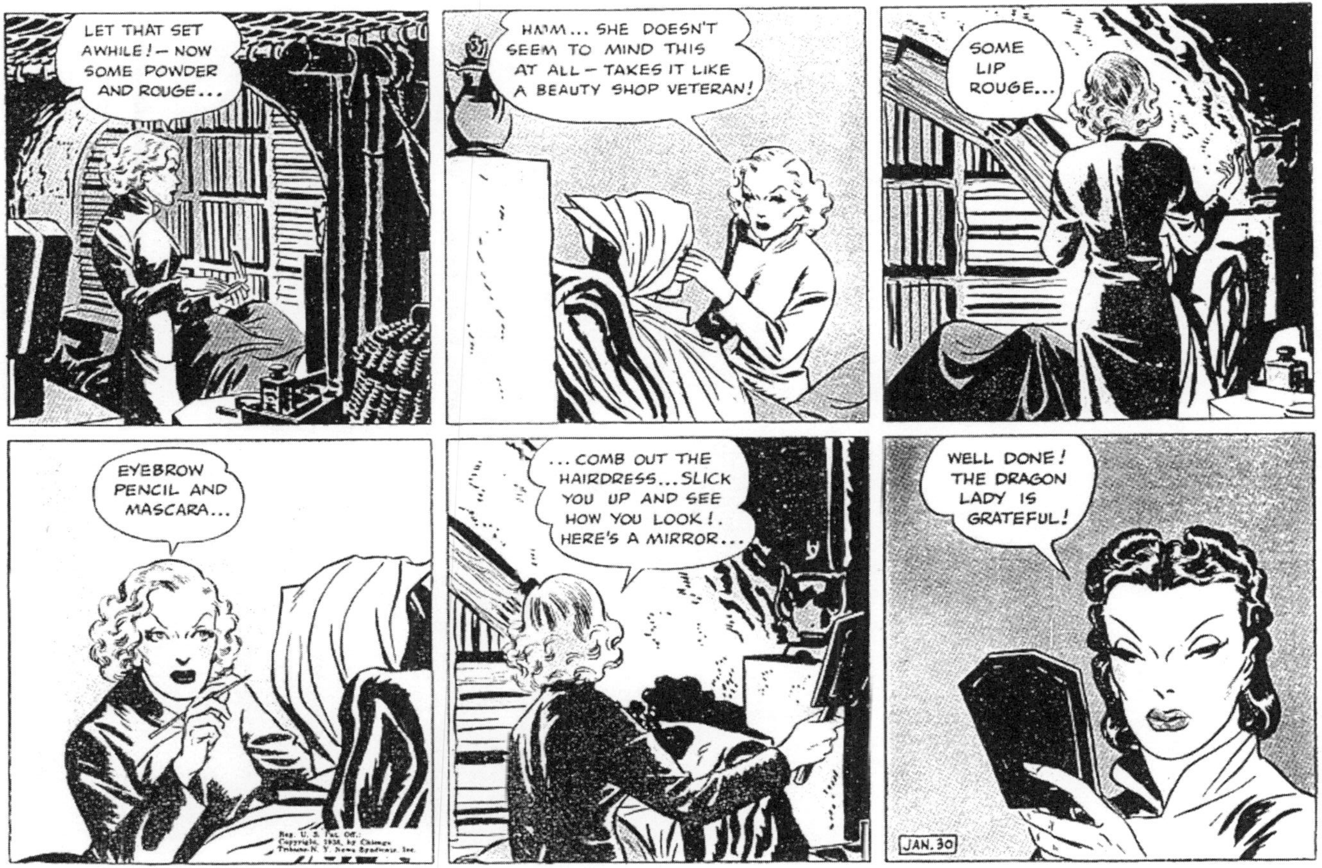

Caniff's two celebrated femmes fatales appeared together in only one adventure, and their initial encounter (above) was unusual.

"Mr. Caniff, remember Captain Judas' mini-submarine which crawled along the ocean bottom? You were years ahead on that one!" His eyes lit up and he smiled. "Oh, yes, I haven't thought of that in a long time. It's getting common place now. Jon Lindbergh is experimenting with something like that, living under water. It was easier for me to do it. All I had to worry about was a bottle of ink and a pen!"

I continued, "Remember when Burma, Terry and Connie find this invalid Chinese woman in a hut on the edge of a village and she turns out to be . . ." [the Dragon Lady].

"Oh, sure", he replied, "That's something you can only do once. I guess it did have impact. Burma, of course, was the 'Sadie-Thompson'-like character. The slightly shady but good-hearted dame."

I kept going. "That 'Pappy Pyzon! What a character he was! Oh, and remember when Burma talked jive-talk to fool the Nazis? Uh, and what was the dirty joke that inspired the 'Hotshot Charlie' character? And tell me—was little Gloria Vanderbilt the inspiration for 'Nastalthia Smythe-Heatherstone?"

To the last question, Caniff replied, "She probably was, I suspect. The poor-little-rich-girl thing. I always feel sorry for those kids. They never have any fun and they're blamed for everything."

This was my once-in-a-lifetime chance and I had to get all those questions answered by the man himself! I was on a roll. Mr. Caniff was enjoying it too. He became like a kid remembering exciting events from his childhood. Each question triggered little recollections associated with the *Terry* stories I'd mentioned.

He said that all his China research came from the New York Public Library. He had no time to travel for many years. As you look at all the detail work in these strips, you can see why. It takes hours to pencil and ink the settings which establish reality for *Terry* people, even if you're not supposed to notice those things.

His storyline and dialogue often get overlooked because of the brilliant art. If he had only done the writing or only done the drawing it would have been enough. But doing both so well makes him indeed a giant in American Art and Literature.

When I asked him why he eased Pat Ryan out of the strip as Terry grew up, his answer surprised me. It had something to do with people thinking there may be a gay element involved with Pat going around the world with this young boy! I disagreed. Ryan was too macho for that. But there was a definite lesbian angle to a story he did in 1939.

"Oh yes," he replied. "The 'Sanjak' character with April Kane. Nobody ever caught on that 'Sanjak' is the name of the island next to the isle of Lesbos."

We spoke fondly of the Dragon Lady. I mentioned that each time he brought her back, her chest became more awesome! This amused him as if he hadn't realized it before. He said it was always the second or third time around that he really (no pun intended) developed a character.

That first visit I had with him in 1964 lasted two hours and could have been savored all my life. I never dreamed that eleven years later I would begin working for him, but fate had some surprises in store.

Frank Engli, the skilled artist who had done all the Caniff lettering on *Terry and the Pirates, Male Call* and *Steve Canyon* became ill with a nerve disease which eventually caused his death. He notified Mr. Caniff he could no longer do his lettering. Willie (Mrs. Otis) Tuck, studio manager, suggested to Milton that, since I was an artist so dedicated to the study of his career, I should be tested for the job. I was. I passed the test, and since October of 1975, have been doing the lettering (following the established "Engli look") on *Steve Canyon.*

Milton Caniff is a unique individual, a remarkable genius. His *Terry and the Pirates* is the classic work of his youth in the same way the film *Citizen Kane* was to Orson Welles.

Being on the inside, there have been many opportunities for casual chats or formal Interviews. I've done several. Here's a transcription of one of them.

Shel: Milt, let's just toss out a few words: *Ethics.* What's your thinking on the subject?
Milt: Ethics are at the absolute heart of the matter in comic strips, in your writing, your drawing, your attitude, your sales ability, and every other aspect of the business.

Shel: Where does *Pride* fit in?
Milt: Oh, pride—not false pride, which is just put-on, but inner-satisfaction pride—is necessary. Without it, you're kicking yourself so that you jar the ink bottle loose!

Shel: How do you feel about *Service?*

Milt: It's a very important part of the comic strip business, as relates to public relations, etc. But beyond that I think it's something that everybody owes as part of their dues to "the club"—the human race.

Shel: What is *Fun* for you?
Milt: Actually, the hardest, most grinding labor is fun if you are doing what you enjoy doing. And, of course, in my case I would be doing what I'm doing, or some version of it, if I got paid for it or not. That's fun!

Shel: What is your feeling about people who are *Parasites?*
Milt: Well, parasites are a natural phenomenon and have to be accepted as part of the scene. But, unfortunately, they can disconcert you and make you angry, unhappy, mean-tempered beyond their value. The parasite is a natural part of the life of the large animal. The lion has his parasites, the monkey has his, and even the parasite has parasites! The drug business is a splendid example of it. The addict becomes a pusher so that he can feed his habit. He's eating his own tail, in effect. His habit is his own parasite.

Shel: How important is *Organization?*
Milt: Oh, you've got to have that! The minute you forget that this is a business, and the minute you think of this as "holy public service," you can go down the drain!

Shel: Let's look at two kinds of *Evil:* other people's and one's own.
Milt: The jungle in which we exist—and always have—makes you wary of other people, and you are able to anticipate it in many cases. Without it, I wouldn't be in business. If we were not evil, I wouldn't have good guys to be heroic. I once got a letter from a church in Boston that said, "You paint evil so black that it's disconcerting to the members of my parrish." I wrote back saying, "I have the same job you have, Dr. Rogers, because I must paint evil black so that heaven will appear more desirable. You do the same thing on Sunday." He wrote back saying, "The ladies from the committee were in my office when I dictated that letter. Personally, I read your stuff every day, and enjoy it very much."

Shel: What are your own evils?
Milt: I have a horrible temper. It's a dangerous and expensive luxury to be able to tell off somebody. It's much better to keep your control.

Shel: Must everyone have a *Duty* in life?

Milt: It's a matter of justifying your existence. It's getting back to the dues-to-the-club thing. I think anybody who fails to pull his oar deserves to splash out. There are lots of goodies to be had just by getting along with people. And if you're not willing to contribute your share of the "getting along with," then you get short rations at the other end of the stick.

Shel: What is *Fame* to you?
Milt: Fame is a tool. You use fame to get better contracts. It's very satisfying, of course, and I have no false modesty, as I've told you before. I have a certain amount of modesty and a great deal of conceit, but the trick is to channel the conceit into a desirable product that someone else will want to spend money for.

Shel: When you first signed your contract with Marshall Field to create *Steve Canyon,* you asked for two things: ownership of the property and complete editorial control. Has this been a liberating thing for you, or has it created its own problems?
Milt: It's created its own problems in that you've got to earn your own liberty, so to speak, but it hasn't created a difficulty. It's been liberating, to use your phrase, in that I don't have to sit here and think that I can't do that because if I do something and want to barrel it through, then the wrath comes back on my head.

Shel: How do you feel about the demise of *Terry and the Pirates?*
Milt: In some ways it's a monkey off my back, and all these years I've had nothing to do with it. But now, at least, I can discuss it. I couldn't even discuss it before. I couldn't make a comment on it because it would sound critical of George Wunder. I would not necessarily have done it that way myself, but it doesn't mean that I think it was wrong for him to do it that way. It's too bad that the thing's out of business, because once it's dead, it's dead! You can't revive one of these things. That part I regret.

Shel: Are you having as much fun doing *Steve Canyon* as you did with *Terry?*
Milt: Well, I'm having more fun in the sense that I have more time to myself. When I was doing *Terry,* I was doing it all. I didn't have any time to myself. I couldn't even go to a movie. It was an awful, greedy grind. Of course, I was much younger, so I could take it, but I couldn't get out of the house! It was just too damned much work! I'd been

doing just six daily strips of *Dickie Dare,* but to do a Sunday page *and* six daily strips of *Terry* was a sudden and all-absorbing task. It was just murder to get that stuff out.

Shel: Yet you were your own task master, because you determined that you wanted to produce an illustrative-type strip, and each panel was like a book illustration! Couldn't you cut corners or something?
Milt: Sure you could cut corners, but the way to survive was to give them something that the other people were not doing. The extra care on the drawing, plus the kind of writing I thought I was producing, was the kicker to push ahead of the other strips of that day.

Shel: Do you think *Terry* will be looked upon as folklore one hundred years from today?
Milt: I doubt it. It'll be something to look back on, as we look at "The Yellow Kid" now. It's a part of the generic genre of the day. It was a pretty good chronicle, and sometimes pretty naive, but that's because we were naive at that time during the World War II years.

Shel: Does it annoy you when people go on and on about your *Terry?*
Milt: Oh, no. I'm pleased. I'm very pleased. What's hard to handle is the fact that you can't explain to them the situation with *Terry.* "Why did you sell *Terry*?" they'll ask.

Shel: I actually had someone ask, "Why didn't he do them both?"
Milt: Jesus Christ Superstar! Ha! Well you can't explain this to a lay questioner unless he has been around a studio. It's hard to explain to them why it sometimes took me longer to do one *Male Call* strip than to do six strips and a Sunday page of *Terry*—trying to get the gag, or some piece of research, exactly right.

Shel: You have been an influence on at least two generations of artists, and I'd like to ask, who have been *your* influences? Who are the people who shaped *your* life and style?
Milt: People like Billy Ireland, editorial cartoonist of the *Columbus Dispatch,* who said, "Actors don't eat regularly, kid, so stick to your inkpots." In terms of work, production, and quality, Noel Sickles had the greatest influence on my personal life. Going way back beyond that, the art director of the first job I ever had with the *Dayton Journal,* a gentleman by the name of Ferd Appel, put my foot into many right stirrups. He pointed out, for instance, when I'd admire certain illustrators in *The Saturday Evening Post,* he'd say, "Now this is good, of course, but so-

and-so is best, because . . ." And he'd tell me why one drawing was better than the other. And it was this guy whose practical instruction was so valuable.

Shel: What motivates you to keep going?
Milt: Greed! I told you that before. Once you're into this, it's like John Wayne, you continue to make pictures. And you're just paying last year's taxman, til they finally come and take you away.

Shel: What keeps your interest?
Milt: That isn't so difficult. Anybody who has half a wit can never be bored, so I'm never bored.

Shel: Is there an area you don't know about and want to learn?
Milt: Sure! I don't know how they make thread, do you? This is the kind of thing I mean. There's so much that goes on around you that you should know about, or that it would be nice to know about.

Shel: What kind of a diet do you have to keep your energy up for those long sessions at the drawing board?
Milt: Well, it must be the high-protein diet. Steak, certain green vegetables, etc. It's sometimes hard to stick to, but it works pretty well, thanks to Bunny and Willie. They look after me. If I were left alone, I'd eat chocolate cake all the time. I have a sweet tooth a mile wide!

Shel: Do you have any unfulfilled desires?
Milt: Yes. The one big thing that bugs everybody who's stuck with this sort of thing—the travel I would like to do and can't. I have to do this sort of production, and if I stop the production, I can't travel either. I'd like to have another month in the Orient, but it took a month of work-ahead to get the month in the Orient.* That was the longest I've ever been able to get away. That was 1960. It took me so long to get that month ahead that I came down with the flu in San Francisco, from exhaustion. We had to cancel flights and so on, but we made it, finally, and had a marvelous time. It was wonderful to be away that long.

Shel: What's your approach when you travel in a foreign country?

*Syndicated comic strips must be delivered to the distributing syndicate 4–6 weeks before publication date—without fail, every week of every year, year after year after year. The only way Caniff or any other syndicated cartoonist can get a vacation is to work ahead, producing as many weeks in advance of the deadline as he or she wishes to take on vacation.

Milt: It depends on the job. If I have no work to do at all, then I just do the standard sightseeing trip—rent a car and go around and look. But if I have to do work that I have to send back, then the trip can go any way.

Shel: How do you keep abreast of the times and know so much about everything?
Milt: Actually, between the radio, television, and the newspapers I get a pretty good cross section of what's up.

Shel: Doing such a realistic strip, how much fantasy do you put in to keep it interesting? Isn't it yourself you must please first?
Milt: Sure. You've got to use your own reaction and instincts for outguessing the other people's reactions. You try to be far enough ahead of the public that you'll know what they want before they know they want it. A certain amount of fantasy is always desirable. It's really the heart of the adventure story. Much more so than identification or relevancy.

Shel: You lived for many years in an ultra-modern home on top of High Tor Mountain in Rockland County. Who were your friends and neighbors in the thirties and forties?
Milt: The people we were closest to were the musicians and playwrights of those days. For instance, there was Maxwell Anderson, Lenya and Kurt Weill, Henry Poor, the painter, and John Houseman, the stage director. Then as the war shifted gears, Marion Hargrove ("See Here, Private Hargrove") and Bill Maudlin moved in, and the whole place began to take on the tone that goes with fresh blood—fresh blood with big, fat credits. It was fascinating to watch these two currents try to mix, which couldn't, quite.

Shel: Milt, in the early days from dusk to dawn, your Terry studio was a kind of meeting place for these very celebrated people, wasn't it?
Milt: Yes, in many respects. I listened to some pretty famous people talk about their personal affairs as if I were the neighborhood psychiatrist. One time I asked one guy, whose name you'd know instantly if I told you, "Why do you ask my advice?" He got angry and said, "Well, I ask your advice, but I don't have to take it!" He just wanted to talk to somebody. I didn't try to offer advice. He'd been around a lot longer than I had.

Shel: Were you much affected by TV?
Milt: Oh, yes. One result of television was that some editors thought that, in order to compete, we story-strip people should shorten continu-

ities—as if we could compete with a tube tale that was complete in one half-hour or an hour. The really grim harvest of television is the shrinkage of the list of daily newspapers. This has leveled off. Each medium has its own niche. Those of us who had followings have survived, but it would not be easy to sell a story strip to the syndicates today.

Strip-time: The Comics Observed

MILTON CANIFF AND JULES FEIFFER / 1986

Excerpted from *The Festival of Cartoon Art* (catalogue), Ohio State University Libraries, Columbus, Ohio, 1986, pp. 7–29. Reprinted by permission.

The following is in the character of a meditation on comics in which Caniff's remarks serve to inspire Feiffer's musing on the medium. Feiffer (whose cartooning career includes an apprenticeship with Will Eisner as well as a long run with a celebrated weekly cartoon of political and social comment that originated in the Village Voice*) interviewed Caniff on three occasions for a total of about four-and-a-half hours, and then he edited the transcription "down to a monologue," as he put it. "I have eliminated my own questions, interjections and comments," he continues, "so that the gist of what Milton has to say will flow with more fluency than it did in our confused back-and-forth-devouring-our-own-entrails conversations. My own reflections were put on tape later, have been revised, edited and appended to the text. They are italicized."*

My father was a printer. He wasn't near the editorial side; he was a mechanical guy. This was in Hillsboro, Ohio, at a weekly newspaper, which then went to twice weekly and years later switched to daily. He never moved into linotype. My father was a hand set guy. I have a book here which he set by hand. And seeing a book set by hand by anybody nowadays is something to behold. All of this must have eased into my system, whether I wanted it to or not, the presence of the newspaper world around me. I didn't know that I wanted it. It was just a bunch of fun, that world, rather than the universe of my one uncle who was a carpenter, another uncle who was a plumber, another who was a barber. None of these things appealed to me like the smelly world of ink.

There were many more newspapers in those days. For instance, in Dayton there was a morning paper and two afternoon papers, each of which carried ten or fifteen strips by different syndicates. Full size papers, five or six columns. My aunt picked up the Cincinnati papers, and that was a different world entirely. And she would save the comics pages out of the *Cincinnati Post.* So like it or not, know it or not I was already into it.

The Dayton papers, with rare exceptions, did not carry the Scripps-Howard comic sections, the various family strips of that day. In Dayton we had the *Chicago Tribune* crowd and the Hearst strips of the day, Billy DeBeck and others. And in three newspapers you got quite a number of strips. Only two were Sunday papers, but they carried a lot of comics. They printed their own in those days. They weren't printed in a central place such as the Greater Buffalo Press, so you had great variations on the quality of printing depending on how papers like the *Dayton News* printed them.

The syndicate would send out mattes, the curved kind, mattes which were cast and done with great care. You see old reprints now and it's amazing how good they were considering the fact that it was local level stuff and they didn't change a thing after it was on that curved plate, rolling. They would roll comics on the off-times of the week, Saturday morning for instance. Not tomorrow's comics but maybe next week's. They'd stockpile them.

[James] "Scotty" Reston used to stack comics at the *Dayton News,* that's how he got into the business. He was a caddy for then-Governor Cox, who ran with Roosevelt in 1920 against Harding. The old man said "Would you like a job on the newspaper?" and the kid went to work in the mailing room, stacking comics, stuffing them. Each paper was stuffed by hand.

The Sunday supplements would run about eight pages, which is more than they do now. And the things were printed larger, of course. They didn't split up the pages as much in those days. Even when I started doing *Terry,* for instance, we did no splits. We did a half-page and a tabloid and that was it. Already it had dropped from the full page, which was merciful, really. Some of those things didn't deserve a full page; they didn't need a full page to make their point.

The four panels of the daily strip were not four panels to me. They extended into infinity. They were a world, a time, a place. I'm still amazed at how much time could be compressed in the short space of four panels where, after all, the first panel had to reprise the scene from yesterday. And yet, as a young reader on my knees in the living room, those four panels could last hours, could last days. Depending on the action, time was lengthened or compressed. A Popeye *fight of five or six panels could last fifteen rounds, but fifteen rounds of extraordinarily violent, fast and funny action while a* Flash Gordon *fight by the more realistic Alex Raymond seemed to be shot in slow motion, demanded study, close examination: How the figures filled space in action. How the fists connected to the jaw. How the victim gracefully fell back under the elegant impact of the blow, a dancerly right cross, an art school life drawing topple. Not a fight really, not crunch, wham, powey, biff, wacko, but choreography.*

If you wanted crunch, wham, powey, you went to Roy Crane. Also choreography, but of a more vulgar sort. Characters whacking away at each other with abandon. Fists swinging in ragtime. Villians falling in high-spirited jitterbug motions. Alex Raymond's characters operated out of a world of silence, a narrative seriousness that rendered his universe mute. Roy Crane's Wash Tubbs, *on the other hand, played out to the sound of a brass band, not nearly as slick or sophisticated as Raymond's world, representing a less urban America. Small town rowdyness versus big city slickness.*

I read both versions of Hans and Fritz, *The Katzenjammer Kids* and *The Captain and the Kids*. I wasn't aware of any of the backstage goings-on, who owned what and so on.

And I read *Little Jimmy.* Jimmy Swinnerton was one of the giants, very unusual guy. He was a big shot, a bigger shot than we realize now. Hearst had sent him down to Palm Springs to die in 1903 and he outlived all the doctors. He had tuberculosis and acute alcoholism and he managed to out-live them all.

He was a President of the Bohemian Club, up in San Francisco. Being President of that club is like being President of the Skull and Bones at Yale. He was Hearst's favorite favorite, down the line. Hearst paid his bills in his nursing home to the day he died to the utter confusion of King Features. The younger auditors had never heard of Jimmy Swinnerton and here was this check that went out every week. Joe D'Angelo told me that when he came in as an auditor, he wondered, "Who the hell is this guy?" He was taking care of some of the old man's favorite things, and Swinnerton was certainly one of them. He was loyal about old employees. It sounds like *Citizen Kane.*

Swinnerton was a painter, too. Desert stuff, almost entirely. While we were still in California, in Palm Springs, I went around and asked the price on those things and they wanted ten thousand bucks.

I also read Harry Hershfield's *Abie the Agent.* He was in one of those litigation fights with Hearst over the ownership.* Swinnerton, Dirks and Bud Fisher—they set the tone. Fisher set the tone that everybody tried to achieve ever since: right at the start he owned *Mutt and Jeff* and never let it go.

Gasoline Alley has always been one of my favorites. Frank King used to do magnificent color things on Sunday. In the fall we would look forward to seeing his use of color. A full standard page. Beautiful. We enjoyed the *Little Nemo* also for color. Much more for that than content, although we liked *Gasoline Alley* for content. The [Sunday] story was self-contained; you didn't have to remember anything.

Polly and her Pals was another one, although it didn't grab me in quite the way *Gasoline Alley* did. I didn't identify with it, but it was beautiful to look at. Often I'd look at it and not even read it because to some extent it was one-joke. But even today, when you see how he distributed those blacks and on Sunday, the color. . . . He did the same thing that McCay had done except that McCay was almost ethereal. Cliff Sterrett was heavily influenced by all kinds of people, such as the German poster artists of that day. The greatest period of German posters was around that time.

*Hershfield's fight with Hearst over the rights to his comic strip took a couple of years to resolve, and Hearst won. As soon as he had secured his ownership, Hearst arranged to pay all of Hershfield's legal costs in the case!—RCH

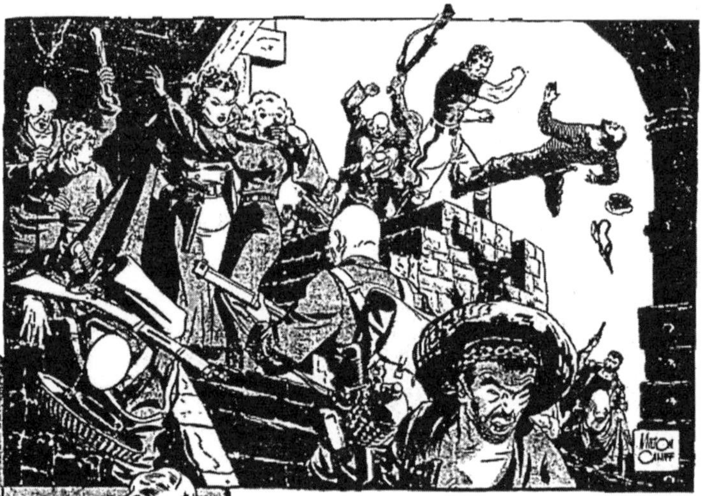

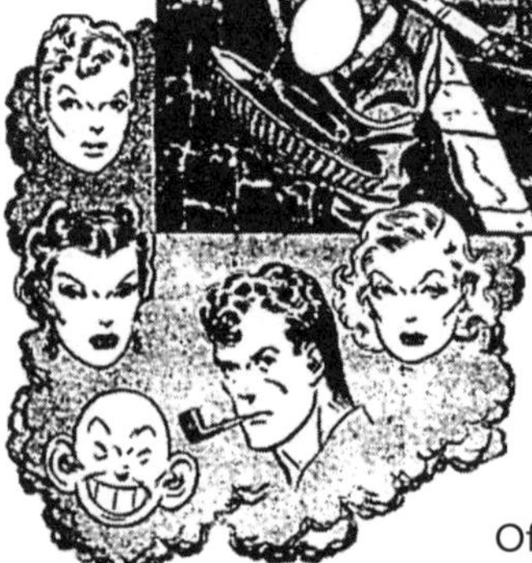

An action-packed promotional drawing for Terry.

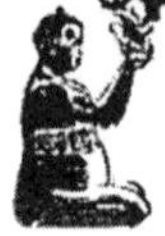

Of course, Sidney Smith's *The Gumps* was a grabber if ever there was. Andy Gump running for Congress was a big deal. There was a man who was writing for Smith at the time, feeding him the fuel with which he ran the engine. This guy was a jeweler in Chicago, Sol Hess, who later did *The Nebbs.* He worked for Smith in the beginning.

Smith was very proud of his physical fitness. There's a story connected with that: he came into New York once a year, he liked New York but he wasn't known here. In Chicago he was king of the mountain. He apparently was a pretty difficult man. Everybody in the syndicate, of course, cowtowed to him because he was the head duck in the parade. And he was describing his physical condition and the admiring syndicate employees were standing around. He said "I'm hard, I'm hard." He said to this one office boy, "Hit me. Hit me." He said, "Come on now, come on, hit me." "You sure sir?" He said, "Yes." Well the kid was a golden gloves champion and he let him have it right in the middle. And boy, he went back against the wall and sank to the floor. He got up and left and went back to Chicago and never came back. The kid said, "Well, there goes the job," but everybody cheered.

Caniff I saw as a halfway house between Crane and Raymond. The violence in Terry *was cinematic, not cartoony as in* Wash Tubbs, not illustrative as in Flash Gordon. *But no question there was a touch of Crane's jazziness when Caniff drew Pat Ryan slugging a bad guy. The scene was less breezy, less* Hardy Boys *than Crane. Caniff's world was far more realistic. Not gritty-realistic as in Eisner. Not* Collier's *realism as in Raymond. But RKO—M-G-M movie realism. Heavy shadows, heavy folds, great light and dark contrasts. Light and dark leaped at you, actually danced as in no other comic strip. And when Caniff's characters were in action, that light and dark gave them an authenticity, a reality—wherein one actually felt the scene, felt the crunch, felt speed, the speed of the car, the boat, the plane. Felt it not as in a dream or as in life but in the idealized version of both, the movie version.*

Caniff used action infrequently, he saved it up. Most of the time his characters were talking and talking and talking. As a little boy reader, the talk in Terry *passed over me, frequently made me impatient. Only as I hit eleven or twelve did I realize how truly good that talk was, so that after a while it became as riveting as the action. The talk became one with the action. Caniff, in fact, is one of those cartoonists where one doesn't distinguish between the words and the pictures, where one can't imagine one person doing the writing and another the drawing.*

One could say the same for Crane. He was the master boy's story teller of comics. No one dealt better with the boy's world. No one made it more fun or more adventurous or, in its own terms, more real. Not Caniff real: Caniff gave us a post-pubescent reality; Crane's reality never ventured past the age of nine. But what a glorious nine! No one was seriously injured in a Crane fist fight, although it could go on for days. As in Segar's Popeye, *getting your lumps was half the fun. Getting your lumps in* Terry *was a more serious business. Caniff would lead us slowly up to it. By the time he was ready to explode, we the readers imputed to the outcome a profundity that went beyond pure comic strip mayhem. Caniff's battles implied consequences. One was surely not going to live to fight another day. Crane took us to exotic places, as did Caniff, but where Crane took us never hinted at a world of harsh darks and lights. It was a boy's world, eternally lighthearted.*

The continuity strip really didn't come into its own—although there were mild attempts, short bursts—until the *Orphan Annie/Dick Tracy* period in the twenties [and thirties] that really exploded the continuity.

You wouldn't accept *Dick Tracy* from another artist. Alex Raymond, for instance, could never have done this stuff. You had to be from an Oklahoma farm and go to the University of Oklahoma and grow up and beat your brains out in Chicago trying to get a job. . . . When Gould said something, he meant it—that kind of Oklahoma farm boy sincerity which sometimes bordered on the absurd except it never was absurd. It was what he had to say. Just as you'd see Henry Fonda doing *Grapes of Wrath.* Completely believable. You knew he was going to be there.

And another thing you've got to remember about those people is that they could have been on either side. Dillinger was a folk hero. He was a Robin Hood to these farm boys who had no hope of ever getting away from the plow out in Illinois or Indiana or Oklahoma. . . . Dillinger went out and did something about it. He just went out and held up a bank. John Dillinger was a farm boy who said to hell with it and he went out and consorted with ladies in red—and boy that's the way to really live! Tracy could just as easily have been John Dillinger. The same amount of energy, the same effort, the same purpose: getting away from this awful plow and this furrough and the mess—the seeking of the farm boy trying to break the bonds holding him. Many people didn't want to accept the violence in *Tracy.* Chet's answer was that there it is on the front pages. "I'm just mirroring the front pages." There was a time when the violence was enough to have committee hearings in the Senate.

Orphan Annie problems went deeper than that. It was so reactionary that it was considered to be endangering the future of the country. Gray was a better artist than he knew. His politics were a great part of his armor. I'm sure he felt beaten and bruised from the reactions, but he stayed with his guns. And he had the newspaper editors behind him. Most of them felt pretty much the way he did. Editors in those days were in no sense a liberal lot. They were conservative as hell. Sometimes they had to be closet conservatives in big cities. But in smaller towns, the *Columbus Dispatch,* for instance, there isn't any question that *Orphan Annie* spoke for them. I think Gray sensed that. Long balloons or no long balloons, they were reading it. You were perfectly willing to stay there and hear him out day after day.

I got to know him a little bit. His letters were warm and very friendly. But I think he was caught up in this awful prison of his shyness. He must have been an essentially shy person. When Harold was working for Sidney Smith on *The Gumps*—Smith was such an outgoing sort of guy—Harold was the character in the closet with a ten watt bulb. He was the drawing assistant, not the writing assistant. If any of his writing got into *The Gumps* it would surprise me. Smith apparently was such a loud mouth, he wasn't even listening. He should have, although he did damned well for himself. The night Smith was killed he had just signed the first million dollar contract. The first one.* He was coming home from Lake Geneva, Wisconsin, to celebrate it and *crash!*

I've got the yearbook that George Bellows did when he was the art editor at Ohio State. He was a good cartoonist too, a damn good cartoonist. He imitated the hot shots of the day: Charles Dana Gibson was ascending in those days. A lot of influences everywhere, but no hint of Bellow's later abilities. It probably was there, but you had to look hard for it. He did some paintings on campus which were used in the yearbook. The reproduction was so sketchy in those days. You couldn't get a decent reproduction of a painting, but you could get pretty good black and white pencil. That in itself had no influence on me. That was my natural bent. I got a degree in fine arts.

The theater, and all of the arts, were a kind of island: us against the world. In the midwest you got this much more than you did in New York, for instance, because in New York it was around for the choosing. But there, there would be one little group, all the people who were interested in all of these things. They all went to the same places and ate in the same restaurants. They were railed against by the better folk in the town, the better element. It was true in Dayton, when I was in the theater. It was true in Columbus. In Dayton, for instance, we had one young friend who was darn good as an advertising artist. But his father was a toolmaker and he just simply couldn't accept the idea of his son working in a place where he couldn't get a guaranteed union contract. The artist's world was much too loose-ended and hapless from a toolmaker's point of view.

*Actually, the first million-dollar contract with a cartoonist was signed in 1922—$100,000 per year for ten years. And it was with Sidney Smith for *The Gumps.* The occasion to which Caniff refers here was the second renewal of Smith's contract (this time, for $150,000 per year for five years) in October 1935.—RCH

An observation seldom made about comic strips seems to be in order: Readers expect, no, they take for granted, the unfailing steadiness, the unflagging quality of their favorite comic strips. Readers and editors find nothing surprising in the notion that a cartoonist should be expected to turn out peak work six days a week plus a Sunday page, year after year, decade after decade. Even the best cartoonists slip after a while. They run out of steam, energy, inspiration and/or patience with the job. They may love it—but want to leave it. But they can't leave it, they've got to eat. And besides it's what they do; it's all that they do.

For me the strip thing was so unassailable, was so far away, I thought I could sneak into the business through the editorial side. There was no syndication of editorial cartoons in those days. It was always local. There were very few people who were syndicated—Ding Darling maybe, and Donahey out of Cleveland. But even the big shots in New York and Chicago were not syndicated. They were almost all local. And I wasn't thinking big in those days about that. I was hoping to get a job as an editorial cartoonist. And just in the normal course of events we'd get a chance to substitute for the boss, who took vacations or sick leave. So I was beginning to build a little wad of samples. This is now about high school. Later at the college level I began to do even more of this sort of thing in the *Columbus Dispatch* which carried a lot more clout than the *Dayton Journal*. It was seen by more people. And as it turned out that's how I got out of Columbus. The head of the AP bureau there sent my samples into the New York office, unbeknownst to me. It was part of the job of an AP bureau manager, just like a baseball talent scout. They did it well. They did it with careful thought. Sickles, for instance, was brought on under the same circumstances. They didn't approach him or anyone else. It wasn't a matter of presenting a portfolio. The portfolio was already on the guy's desk before he sent you the telegram, the previous year or two of the man's work. And they knew that he could be reproduced in the newspaper level of quality. I hadn't thought about comic strips. I was just decorating the paper.

As Milton says, Frank King's Sunday pages were a joy to behold and lessons to learn from. His use of composition and color to give us not just pretty pictures, but a mood and story which was subtle and moving. He had in abundance all the gifts a cartoonist should have—except the gift of making me care about his characters.

I didn't give a damn that Skeezix grew from boyhood to manhood. Skeezix as a grown man always seemed to me to be that little boy's head pasted on to someone else's body. He didn't so much age as grow freakish.

And who cares about cartoon characters aging anyway? Blondie and Dagwood didn't age, but Baby Dumpling—an adorable little character—grew into this boring teenager, Alexander. And Terry Lee was more interesting as a wise guy adolescent than he was as a serious, manly flight officer.

Growing up is enough of a drag in real life. Why impose it on our favorite characters? The whole idea of cartoon characters is, or should be, to represent us in place, a better place than the place we now occupy; certainly a funnier, a more entertaining place. When we let them grow, we let them jar the form, displace the place.

After Pat Ryan left Terry, *I was happiest when Dude Hennick or Flip Corkin took over. They came in as men and I could accept them as men. Full bodied heroes. But Terry as a grown man always left me uneasy and Skeezix as a young man was a wimp. Only King's extraordinary artistry on Sundays overcame that fact. But what, after all, did Skeezix and Uncle Walt do on their Sunday afternoon treks through the changing autumn leaves? They looked, the observed, they commented. They didn't argue. They weren't set upon by pirates or marrauders. And to my knowledge they never got into a single fist fight. King was good enough to get away with this—barely—but I would argue that there are some burdens comic art should not be asked to carry: unsatirized nature is one of them. I say it's Thoreau, and I say the hell with it.*

Each paper in the town had its own person who was highly regarded. We thought more of him, for instance, than we did of the syndicated guy who would come visit, like Bud Fisher or someone like that. I remember Billy DeBeck did a cross country race with Spark Plug and some other dog. He hit every town where he was syndicated—good local stuff. It was a big noise—the local printed it on the front page of the paper.

I suppose I had some aspirations in that direction, but the other thing was here at hand, the bread in the basket. I was watching for a chance to break into the editorial side, not political; the cartoons were simply an echo of the editor's view. Very few of the guys had their own head. Maybe Ding, maybe John McCutcheon.

Billy Ireland was the man at the *Columbus Dispatch* when I was there: top dog of the paper, top dog of the town—top dog of the territory. He was a big shot. His power was very real. He earned it, he could point to it. He was a member of the firm. No cartoonist I ever knew was a member of any firm, but he was. He was offered a post on the board of directors. It was awe inspiring to the rest of us.

"Don't ever rule a line with a pen," Billy Ireland used to say. You look at his drawings to this day and they have that free-flowing feeling. Never once in them do you have a sense that he got a t-square out.

He was this funny little guy behind the drawing board. He used to do this full page of Strathmore for a Sunday release and that's a lot of paper. He would pencil the thing at night at home and ink it at the office. He could talk, for instance, and still be inking. He held the bottle of ink in his hand because he began to get fatter and fatter and couldn't get close to the board. Here was this huge page, looming up there, and he sat back like this and drew with a pen. It was amazing, the kind of detail he got.

It was a comfortable kind of existence. Damn little hard cash, but we had lots of chances to show our things: illustrations one day and a silly cartoon the next and a sports drawing the next. Many times you would volunteer your services. The sports editor, the amusements editor were glad to get these things. It made their pages look rich, although they didn't spend a dime. I'd get tickets to the movies. That was the payoff. However, it was very nice. You would go to a local beer garden or somewhere that I couldn't mention in the cartoon. You got used to this after a while.

In those days there was a lot of glamour in the magazines. The Jon Whitcombs and people like that. All those guys, whenever they appeared anywhere were introduced from the stage of the Casino de Paris and places like that. They certainly were celebrities, much more so than many of the theater people who were in the same category. Friends of friends, Rube Goldberg and Billy Gaxton, people like that were a sort of Broadway group. Not having it, you desire it, seek it. So there was envy involved. To be all of those things, getting recognized. I was lusting to make some kind of a place in the newspaper sun.

Roy Crane was working in Cleveland at the time that I was on the *Columbus Dispatch*. He was doing *Wash Tubbs* out of Cleveland. He worked right in the central office. NEA was syndicating it. And he was unhappy. NEA was chintzy as hell. They didn't treat their people as well as King Features treated them. He was almost on a staff job, in effect.

I wasn't thinking about doing adventure at that time, I just liked the way Crane did it. He had the kind of wild approach. Great cartooning. He could draw—the sets that he drew, the little trains in the background and things. I didn't really get grabbed and hog tied by Crane until he introduced Captain Easy. Right up to the very end of his tenure I wondered about the background of Captain Easy. He was such a good character. What happened to that little southern town—it was always southern—what happened to that little southern town? I still am wondering.

Crane's women were exotic. His villainesses—or rather bad girls, because they were not always villainesses—all blowzy, all wonderfully drawn, wonderfully built, existing as equals in this world of rough men. They could run, jump and fight with the best of them and look a hell of a lot better doing it. Crane's bad girls had a kind of masculine sexiness. They liked to stand legs spread wide apart in jodhpurs, feet planted firmly on the ground, hands balled into fists on the hips. If a Crane woman didn't like what you said, she'd just as likely put the slug on you as one of the male characters. In fact Crane's women were better fighters than they were lovers, better big sisters than sex objects.

There were no true sex objects in Crane's world, certainly not in the sense that one found them in Caniff's. Crane's women denied puberty. Caniff's women were its paradigms. Caniff introduced serious sexual inference into the comic strip—the Dragon Lady for certain, but even more markedly with the character of Burma: the one an out-and-out villainess, the other an archetypal bad girl. Burma, more so than the Dragon Lady, let us know in drawing and wisecrack that she had a sex life and that she wasn't going to quit having it just because she was in the funny papers.

Caniff brought sex to the comic strip. Not sexiness, that was there before: all the pretty girl cartoons from Boots and Her Buddies *and Tillie the Toiler to the flapper panels of Russell Patterson. But one never slept with those girls. One ogled, yes. One whistled at them, fantasized about them, dreamed about dating them—but going to bed with any of them? Spending the night? Unimaginable!*

Not so with Burma. No so with the Dragon Lady. One knew—even the eleven year old suspected—that a man—say, a very young man—

could spend the night and that Burma would please him beyond his wildest dreams and that the Dragon Lady would please herself.

Alex Raymond's women had no life off the paper. They existed in a series of fashion poses, slick, thick-and-thin brush lines, pure white bread women in decorative still poses. The lack of dimension in Raymond's characters was more than made up for by the extraordinary draftmanship. But Raymond's best work was saved for men in action—surprisingly he wasn't much for backgrounds and his women were cookie cutter visions from the pages of Collier's *and* Vogue.

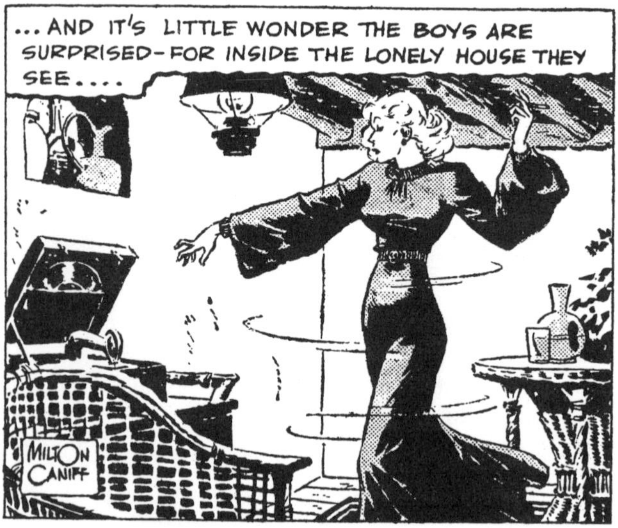

Burma's first appearance in *Terry*—dancing by herself to a recording of *St. Louis Blues*; W.C. Handy's tune became her theme song, and whenever the gang heard it, they knew Burma was not far away.

In fairness, I have to say that this is an afterthought. As a boy, no woman in comics was more beautiful to me than Dale Arden. She seemed the comic strip equivalent of Oliva DeHavilland. There was no disaster so imminent that Dale Arden couldn't pose prettily within it; no peril so risky that she couldn't show a little leg. If Flash were ever to be thrown into a pit of horned lions, Dale would dress right for the occasion.

Captain Easy was certainly an influence on Pat Ryan. But I always carried on that mildly Heathcliff attitude: you don't know the background of this guy and he has an unrequited love, Cathy or somebody down the street, partly the Clark Gable thing of *Gone with the Wind.* I wanted Pat Ryan to be a picaresque, scarred character who had a temper that was too strong. I wanted Terry to be afraid in a situation, "My

God he's going to lose his temper, and blow the whole thing up!"—and then have him *not* lose it.

Easy never did have a romance that was touching, physically touching. I suspect Crane thought about it and realized that he couldn't hack it. Local editors were scared of anything that resembled a normal erection—in the head or elsewhere. Somehow I was determined to pull this off if I could. I was walking the razor's edge. I knew what people liked to see, but getting away with it was something else. Then I got bold and even went into the Sanjak sequence with a lesbian angle. But nobody recognized it except a cult few. I never had one complaint about it.

Alex Raymond drew models, Caniff drew women, Crane drew gals and Will Eisner drew dames. In Eisner's The Spirit *the female was always on the prowl. Good or bad, heroine, spy princess or gangster's moll, if there was any love-making to be done, she would have to be the aggressor.* The Spirit *was as reticent about sex as Capp's* Li'l Abner*—or for that matter, Gary Cooper and John Wayne in their early films. Eisner's dames were from the city. They looked tough and they posed tough. They reeked of a combination of street smarts and vulnerability. So much vulnerability in fact that the toughness never lasted long. It turned out in every case to be a facade. Eisner's dames were easily hurt, had hearts easily broken, had to frequently swallow pride.*

Eisner's world had less libido than Caniff's, but more than Crane's. Raymond's, of course, had no libido at all. Crane's world was pre-pubescent, Eisner's world was post-pubescent, just barely, and Caniff's characters knew. *Eisner's characters understood sex to be fooling around, necking parties, wrestling in the moonlight. Gal meets boy, gal chases boy, gal catches boy who squirms and goes "yich." When gal walks off in triumph, boy is left shame-faced, with big red lipstick blotches all over his face.*

Most of the things that I do, whether I do them well or not, had to be learned. I had a hell of a time learning to draw women, for which I've been given great credit, like the Dragon Lady. But it was a hell of a hard road for me to learn to draw them. Finally, somewhere along the line I learned the trick, but it was a slow process.

Sickles, on the other hand, was a natural artist. He could do anything. He wasn't that interested in women, so he didn't draw them as well as he should have. But he drew everything else well, especially long-shots of things rather than close-ups.

I went just the other way, the personality first. So even if it wasn't drawn the way I wanted, somehow it was able to make it. I haven't had success with anything where I haven't had to gestate. Nothing ever came naturally.

There were no two better story tellers than Eisner and Caniff in the business. Eisner's stories came out of the Ben Hecht–Baghdad-on-the-Hudson tradition. Small characters caught up in big events triggering great and violent actions. And within these stories inspired not only by Ben Hecht, but O'Henry, Ring Lardner, Clifford Odets and all Warner Brothers big-city movies, Eisner fashioned surprisingly complex personal relations and entanglements. Characters with needs beyond the winning of a fist fight or the robbing of a bank. Characters who cared, who were obsessed. *Characters with whom a reader could identify, not on fantasy terms, not on idealized terms, but in terms of one's own wishes, aspirations and experiences.*

Will is the master. The opening scenes in that book about God, *The Contract with God,* that Eisner drew were beautiful. Right from the first panel I'm with it, I know exactly what the old boy's thinking, how cold it is out there. Will's always been a master of despair. Nobody else could do despair. . . . I didn't even know what it was like. We didn't think we were poor or disadvantaged. We never experienced it. We had disappointments, but they were disappointments that kids in the Midwest see due to circumstance. But when you see something the way Will did it—Jesus, this guy was a loser. This is despair incarnate. Down these mean streets, but how beautifully handled. I wouldn't want to live there. I'd rather live on Maple Street or Walnut Street. I'd rather draw about things I know best. So I end up doing this Chinese stuff—and I've never been there either.

Only Caniff's world was as serious and complex as Eisner's. Only Caniff's stories interwove action and character so intricately that one could not tell where one began and how it led inexorably to the other. Only Caniff conveyed that sense of grown-up characters with grown-up feelings and grown-up sexiness, operating in a universe of boy's adventure and girl's romance.

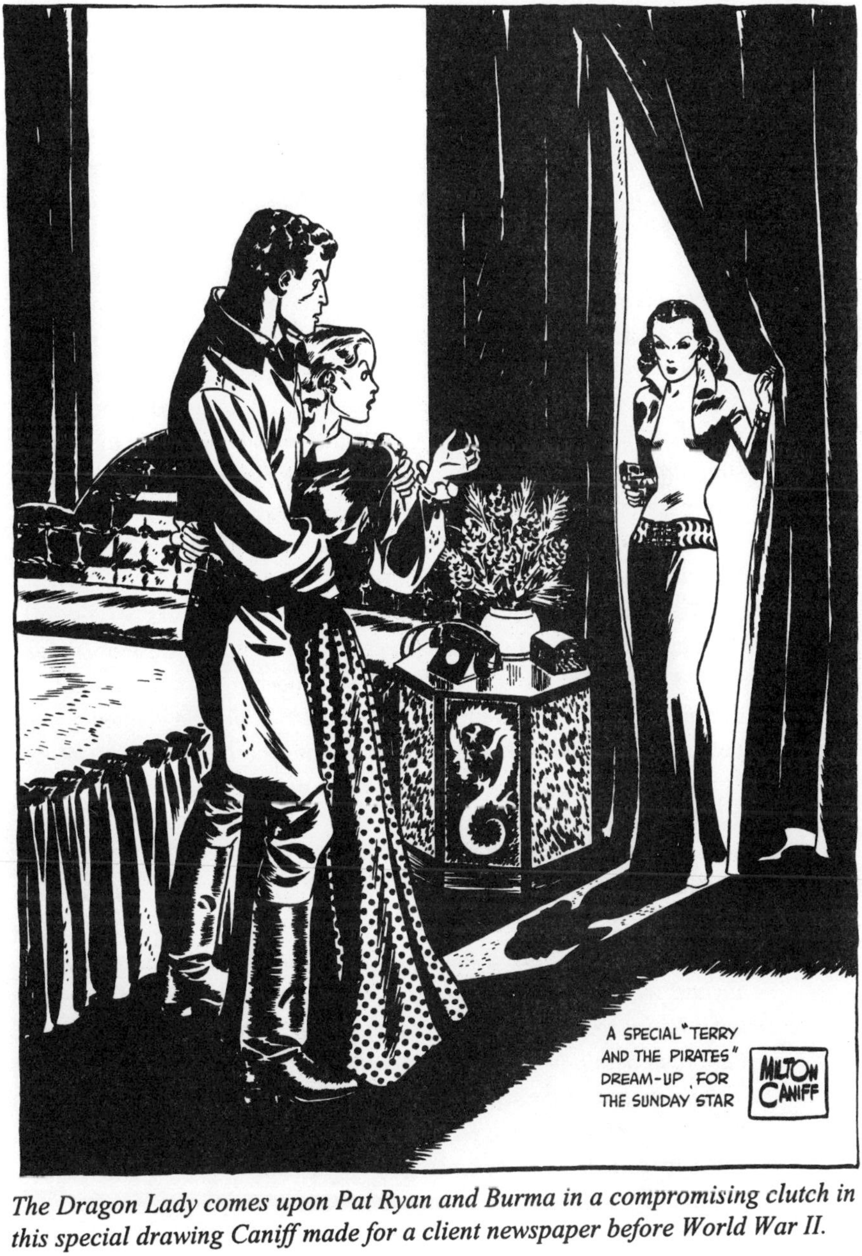

The Dragon Lady comes upon Pat Ryan and Burma in a compromising clutch in this special drawing Caniff made for a client newspaper before World War II.

And both artists, more than any others, were masters of silence in the adventure strip. No one came close to Caniff at writing dialogue and only Eisner was his equal at writing silences. Two, three or more panels where not a word was spoken, not a balloon appeared, nothing but pure, unvarnished story telling, whether action or not, in its purest form. A kind of poetry of silence where time stretches out dreamlike and one reruns the drama of the drawings as if in instant replay, over and over, letting the action sink in with a depth not possible were the drawings with dialogue.

We were all desperate to get syndicated, to get bought. I jumped in on the AP, for instance, because they had a solid page of comics which the local editor could buy as it was or chop up, whatever he wanted. Bruce Russell was a good editorial cartoonist. He preceded Conrad on the *Los Angeles Times.* I guess Russell just got tired of doing the daily strip. I heard about this. The great advantage of being on the staff anywhere is that you hear about these things ahead of time. So come Monday, I was there. *Dickie Dare* was a school for me, getting ready for the *Terry* blast that was to come.

Walter Berndt, who did *Smitty,* told me later that it was because of the *Gay Thirties* that Joe Patterson called me in, not because of *Dickie Dare.* The content of the *Gay Thirties* was much more to his way of thinking. Yet he didn't want a panel, which that was, he wanted a strip. I was putting more stuff into the *Gay Thirties* than into *Dickie Dare.* So he just let me find my own way down the path. It took me years to find this out.

Caniff is generous in his praise of Noel Sickles, as he should be. Sickles' contribution to the look of the modern comic strip, to the look of Caniff's comic strips, is fundamental. Sickles, possibly more than anyone else, gave the modern adventure strip its style. But he cared not a fig for story or character or atmosphere. His interest was in illustration: in detail, in airplanes, tanks, weapons of war. He was a brilliant technician, but of the two, Caniff was the artist. Caniff was able to take all the elements that Sickles introduced, add story to them, add character to them, add cinematography, and out of the blend create a genuine full-bodied vision. It was remarkable friendship, Caniff's and Sickles', an awesome collaboration.

Patterson ran the syndicate. This was sort of his agreement with McCormick after the war. When they came back from France, they talked about founding a new tabloid paper which became the *News*. They had to go out and buy it. But they never got along, editorially. This is why Patterson moved to New York. Whatever else about McCormick, he knew how to delegate authority to the guy who could do it better, and Patterson could do it better.

Patterson always said he didn't care what a strip looked like in the *Chicago Tribune*. If he thought it sold the *New York* [*Daily*] *News*, then it was OK and to hell with the rest of it.

Let's take a moment for *Dick Tracy*. I don't think Hearst would have touched *Dick Tracy*. Hearst lived in another world. Patterson dug the gangster thing. He was a Chicago boy and knew about the bootleggers and all that stuff much more than Hearst.

Hearst liked certain things and King Features ran what Hearst liked. It didn't matter what anybody else thought. This is why *Little Jimmy* lived on beyond his natural life. It had run its course, but he was Hearst's boy.

And Herriman was just enough of an oddball to intrigue Hearst, I imagine. *Krazy Kat* ended with 40 papers or so but it was still in there. And beautiful! God Almighty, those Sunday pages in the old *Journal!* Those posters, they were beautiful posters, each one, right down the line.

When Alex Raymond came along, this is the kind of thing that Hearst personally liked. I don't think that Alex could have sold *Flash Gordon* to Joe Patterson. I don't think so.

. . . .

Now somebody began to mention to Patterson that these so-called invaders in *Terry* were Japanese troops. I'm sure he was aware of it from the beginning. He was a very discerning guy. But other people began to mention it; it began to be a little more than casual, because they were too well done in terms of the recognizable Japanese uniform. The newsreels were already carrying that stuff. Everything. The meatball flag and the fact that I called them the invaders. And so he called me in and said that he didn't think this was exactly the thing to do at this point. He said it might be just a little too much politics. Not that we were going to lose any Japanese circulation—that's a quote—and then he laughed, ha-ha, that's a joke; but maybe we'd tone it down. Now this is November of 1941.

He never got in your hair, by the way. Very rarely ever called you in for a personal interview. He always relayed it through Molly Slott or Arthur Crawford, who was the general manager.

He was sitting in his office. Crawford and Molly were across the desk—a long desk, completely barren, but at the end was a cage-like wastebasket exactly flush with the top so he could slide papers and things, like a beer down the bar. He would sail whatever he didn't want down into that trash can. So his desk was clear when he started to talk to me. He put his feet up on the desk, all the way up. He was a tall, rangey person. He'd been an athlete at Yale, a Lincolnesque-looking guy. Lincoln keeps coming to mind because of the rumpled clothes. He always dressed like a well-turned-out bum, wrinkled pants and all that. So that's when I said, "Sir, I disagree with you."

There was this silence you couldn't imagine. Molly was sitting there. And Crawford too. Nobody ever said that to the man. A stage situation. You could see it coming. He said, "Son, by an accident of birth, we're going to do it my way." And then he took his feet down and this was it, the party was over. We all stood up and said thank you. About one more week and Pearl Harbor happened.

Now, when the war began, all this criticism stopped; anything I did was all right. I decided right from the start to play the Japanese, if not sensitively, at least, by thinking it through in the case of any one character. I got some good mail on that, too, from people who recognized this. They were soldiers: they were there because they were sent there. And they were good soldiers and they got their heads blown off, too.

It seemed to me that we were going to be in this thing for at least four years because such wars usually last four years, until they run out of young men. Then they have to wait another generation. I thought: four years, Terry's got to be in this thing. He can't be on the sidelines. I've got to spend four years on this greatest story that ever happened to anybody: this guy's gotta be in it! At the end of it, he'll step back and then it's behind him. It's happened with so many guys, they walked away from it.

In this case when it was over, Terry would go back to whatever opportunity, flying for a private airline—or a public airline. That was what happened to most of those guys. It was the only thing they knew how to do. It was the only thing they had a skill at. Couldn't even get a drivers license when they first got their airplane license.

Among all the cartoonists I've loved, the hardest to assess is Al Capp. As a boy he was up there with my favorites, was my favorite for a period of time, preferred to Caniff, to Eisner, to Raymond, to anybody. The humor, vulgarity and sentimentality of Li'l Abner, *mixed with its outlandishly satirical vision of the world, was to my taste entirely.*

And Capp was no less the story teller than he was the satirist. No one was better than he at making building blocks of panels. Turning the four panel form into a model structure of picture and event. If in Caniff's world plot evolved largely out of character conflict, if in Segar's plot was accident, and in Crane's plot was the excuse for action, adventure and derring-do, in Capp's best work plot became an extraordinary mechanism, a master craftsman's overview.

Capp was more godlike in his plot conniptions than any other cartoonist. He was the great script carpenter in the sky. Nothing escaped his notice. No action went unobserved, unplanned, unprovoked. In the vision of every other cartoonist one can expect the intrusion of surprise and accident. But with Capp, softness of structure was to be sneered at. Like Dickens, he was a know-it-all, and knowing it all he somehow made it pay off. Capp could plant weird credibility in his unlikely stories. Whatever the premise, it didn't matter how off-beat, he knew how to set it up. He knew how to build it. He knew how to bring in outside observers to comment on it. He knew how to drag it out day by day. He knew how to keep the reader in suspense. He knew, as many cartoonists did not, the importance, the sexiness, of off-screen actions; radio-like events happening outside of the panel. He was not only the great humorist of his time, he was an equally adept manipulator. Who was that character in silhouette in the last panel, making plans about characters as yet unheard of? Who belongs to that shiny new car driving up to the Yokum shack? What is the meaning of this dialogue coming from unseen persons in an unseen office in a Manhattan highrise?

Capp, as good as anyone, perhaps better than anyone else, could seduce the reader, keep us on edge. OK, so why doesn't he hold up?

Al [Capp] and I met under such personally destroying circumstances. We were both hard up. Al was at the AP. He was doing *Gilfeather* which had just been dumped in his lap. It wasn't his cartoon at all. Tad Dorgan had originated the thing. And Tad's brother took it over, a very poor Tad. So Al had to take over. He did the best he could, but he wasn't ready for it. He hadn't done his servitude. Then it was dumped in my lap. It was a nuisance; it wasn't a fun thing in any respect. And Al was so far behind, it made things difficult. But it gave us a curious kind of bond. We worked at night. Al used to come up there at night. He hated to come up during the day because he didn't know the routine things to do in an art department.

He was not assertive in any way. In fact, just the opposite. Catherine, his wife, used to come with him and he would erase down to the other side of the paper, you could see the drawing through the paper, just fighting every inch. I worked the nights, too, and this is probably where we hit a thread.

God knows we couldn't be more unalike. Al used to write about me later on—these wonderful exaggerations—that he used to advise me how to draw faces of the presidential candidates of that year, stuff like that. Invariably the opposite of what happened. That I introduced him, later on, to movie actresses—none of which was true. But somewhere along the line it made a good paragraph. He just forgot about facts whenever he was writing. He considered it promotion.

Capp's caricature of this whole *Tracy* business, *Fearless Fosdick,* was an absolute dream. You could see the daylight through the bullet holes, the whole landscape. I think Gould was ambivalent about it. He was flattered by the fact that Capp singled him out to roast; at the same time he was annoyed.

Charlie Schulz has the same reaction to criticism. You may recall when Capp took off on Charlie at some point back along the line. You could almost write the script in your mind: he caricatured Charlie Brown just as he caricatured Fearless Fosdick. It was good fun, except Charlie Schulz didn't think so. It made him very angry; and long after the fact, angry. He just didn't think it was nice. We argued the point, by the way, I've argued it with Charlie. Jesus, when Capp took off on me a couple of times, I was so flattered that he did it. Al was riding high at that time and just to be mentioned in *Li'l Abner* . . .

Why don't I go back to Capp the way I go back to Caniff, the way I go back to Crane and Eisner? Is it politics? Is it partly politics? Is it only politics? Is it that Capp alone among my boyhood idols had feet of clay? And I mean more than right wing clay here. I'm not crazy about Caniff's politics either. The militarism in Terry *and* Steve Canyon *has always disturbed me. But Caniff's hawkishness is by no means the heart and soul of his output. Regrettably Capp's meanness became the heart and soul of his. Capp didn't just turn right, he turned ugly.*

From the beginning he had a tendency to make boobs of his characters. He used to boast about it in interviews; i.e., that readers loved Abner because he was even dumber than they were. But as he got older the ante on boobism, stupidity, cupidity, and unsatiric nastiness escalated alarmingly. Capp started out in stripland as a professed liberal during the New Deal days but when the going got tough, when Joe McCarthy appeared on the scene, when liberals began running for the hills, the hill that Capp ran for was Dogpatch. At the very time that Walt Kelly was taking on Joe McCarthy, Capp was announcing in the pages of Look *or* Life*, I forget which, that a satirist couldn't do politics anymore and that's why he was getting L'il Abner married.*

In the early years of Capp's work it contained a fancifulness, even a whimsey, that took the curse off its harshness. Capp's bleak vision, not very different whether left or right, lost its subtlety not so much because of politics, I suspect, as because of age. As he got older, Capp was less interested in seduction than assault. Less interested in charm than abuse. Less interested in story telling than in people-smashing. For all sorts of public reasons, and he was our most public of cartoonists, he had turned bitter.

Cynics can be funny; bitter cynics cannot be. Fred Allen, always a cynic and always a funny man, turned bitter in the days of TV—and in the days that followed, most of us stopped laughing. Walt Kelly was never a cynic, but his wrath was righteous. And as forceful as he got, as objectionable to some editors as he got, he never veered off into bitterness. But Capp spent his latter years truly pissed off and unforgiving. I never accepted his public reasons and I have no insight into his private ones.

The day after the incident in Wisconsin, when they did the badger game job on [Capp] out there, framed him with a coed in a motel room, I sent him a telegram saying "Who do we slug?" It was just down Al's alley, exactly what he needed. I'm sure he got lots of communications from people, but what he needed was somebody to say, "All right, let's shoot it out with these bastards." He wrote me a long letter about that little telegram.

He lost a lot of papers after that. It finished him. He was tottering, more so than any of us realized. He said of himself he hadn't done any good work for two years.

I think part of it with Al was just a manifestation of his anger about the leg happening to him, losing it at age nine or whatever. He still had some grudges to settle with the Fates. So he would throw up these wild balloons that were not himself at all, just to see who shot at them. Meanwhile, taking good care of his family; he never lost tract of that. He was in good financial shape.

And then his peccadillos with women—he was a womanizer. And a womanizer womanizes, he doesn't have to have a reason for it.

We used to do things together, personal appearances. He never failed to mention me warmly. On a TV show, somebody would ask him the state of the art as of now and he would mention Alex Raymond and me. A lot of crazy guys around, but Alex and Milt were all right. Never ever heard him say anything other than that.

. . . .

In the case of Canyon, of course, you didn't know anything about his military time; coming out and being demobed and trying to start an airline with one airplane which is ridiculous, that phase of it. But that was the only thing he knew how to do. So it was my stepping off place, my kickoff.

In the early days, with the freelance flying, all I had to do was use the World War II references for the aircraft. Then it gradually became obsolete so that then I had to either go to the new equipment or get off the pot. About that time I figured Canyon would have lost his business. He would have to turn freelance, hiring out as a muscleman or whatever. Pilot yes, perhaps; he would hire out to whoever and that was the next phase. Which also happened to actual guys who tried to do that. And few succeeded, the Flying Tigers and two or three other spinoffs of the war. But pretty soon afterward they were glad to get back to the insurance business.

Guys in my age bracket were foundering just as I was foundering; they couldn't find a place to put their burden down. They were skilled, but the flyboy glamour was absolutely nothing. If they tried to do it on their own they failed. If they went into commercial aviation, just flying TWA to the coast, it didn't pay enough to justify the risks. So it was a time of flux.

Flux on my part, too. I couldn't quite get the act together. It was the coming of the Korean War which gave me the chance to call Canyon back. I knew he was going to stay around the edges of aviation

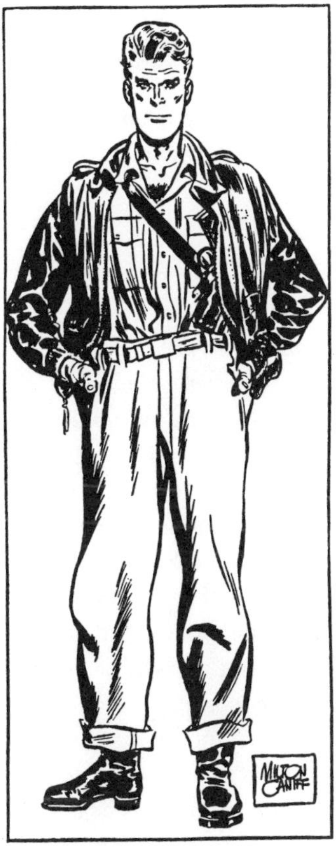

Steve Canyon

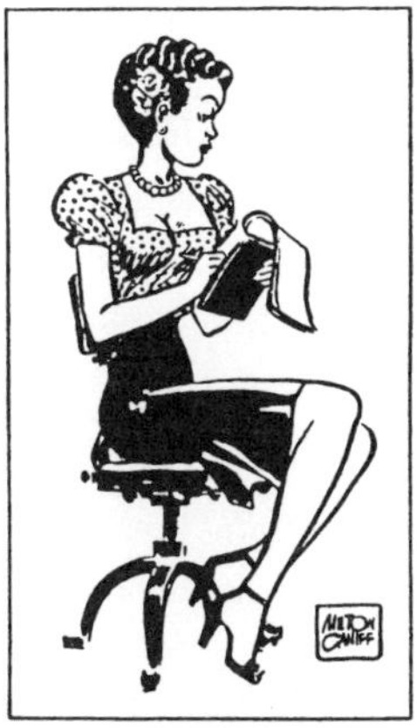

Feeta Feeta
An E & P preview of the characters in Milt Caniff's new strip. Sketches and "Steve Canyon" copyright (1946) by Field Enterprises, Inc.

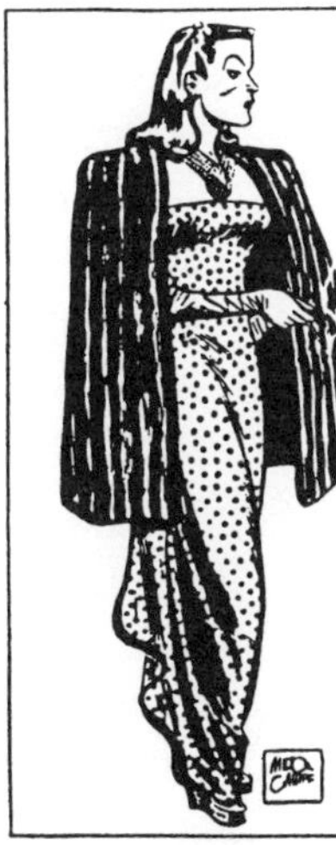

Copper Calhoon

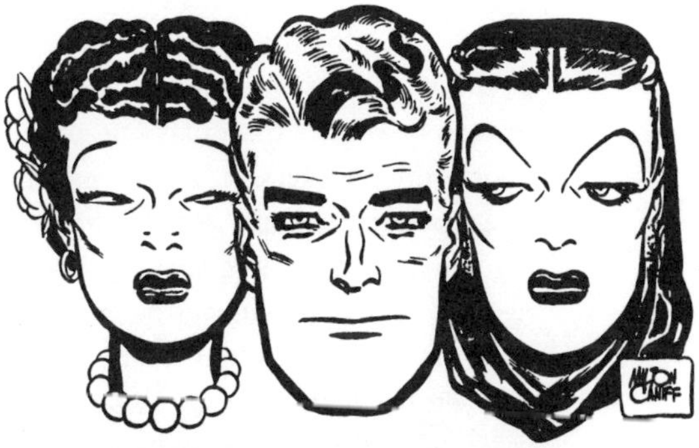

Here are the first published promotional drawings for Steve Canyon. *The full-length drawings appeared in* Editor & Publisher, *November 23, 1946; the trio mug shot came along a little later.*

whether military or not, if for no other reason than in an adventure story your hero has got to be able to fly an airplane. He can't go aboard and say sorry, I don't know how to fly this. It's the only way he can move on to the next scene. Or save Pearl White. He can't do it in a handcar. He's got to be able to fly. It's almost as if these things are required by law.

Then I had to decide whether to keep him out of uniform or not. I kept thinking of James Bond; when he was sent out on an assignment he was a lieutenant in the British Navy. He was sent out by British Intelligence, but he was a guy in uniform. I started thinking of this when I sent Canyon out on assignment. He was in that service. He didn't go by choice. If he went wherever under questionable circumstances, I could fall back on the fact that he was sent there. There's more freedom to operate, because he had no freedom. He's in the military and he's sent there which takes me off the hook.

. . . .

I did sequences involving both Korea and Vietnam. They were not the main issue. I never talked about the reasons. It was just the fact that there were guys there being shot at. Americans, especially, but not entirely so. I had two or three allied characters: Canadians, Australians, Frenchmen. The French were getting their tails kicked out of Vietnam. I came in just on the end of that.

I just talked about what happened to people, a guy who knew nothing more about that rifle than that he could lie on his back with his bare toes and pull the trigger and he would hit the pilot and he would come down. It was the simplest kind of ground fire sharp shooter. That's all he needed to know. I used that kind of thing. And didn't say why or hooray or damn him. It just was a fact. This was happening.

Surprisingly, I didn't get flack from anybody on it. I never once had to argue this out with an editor—or a reader for that matter. It was simply a news story, we knew it was happening: these black pajama kids who knew nothing at all about weapons except which end was the trigger; and yet they were winning a war against us. I would try just to show it as it was in dispatches or in the newspaper. Not talk about the reasons.

I remember reading about the horrors of British rule in India. I would read Kipling, and Tommy Atkins was a pretty nice guy. Tommy Atkins might wish he were elsewhere, too, but he's in the British army and he goes where he's told. He glorified the British Colonial military. In the beginning I never gave it a thought as to why they were there. All I thought of was Gunga Din. This Kipling did with great skill. He had us pro-British in World War I before we even gave it a thought.

. . . .

The last page I did of Terry, he says his goodbye to Big Jane. Both their lives were in that last strip, but there's very little dialogue, almost none. She's going to try to find this guy, her number one main guy, in an Australian hospital. But along the way she's crossed paths with this nice young kid, Terry Lee. And neither of them want to break it off and yet both of them have to go and do what they have to do. I liked that page. I liked being able to kiss it off with style. There was a poster on the wall that said, "Off with the old and on with the new," because it was New Year's Eve, the last Sunday.

Remembering Caniff

RICHARD WARING ROCKWELL / 1989

From *Cartoonist PROfiles*, No. 83, September 1989, pp. 32–37. Reprinted by permission.

Of all my memories of my long association with Milton Caniff the one I drew here is the most vivid. I never sat down, not because I wasn't asked, I just always stood while we talked. It was always late. Day or night it was a hurried trip to pick-up new work and deliver the work I had just done. But we talked about a lot of things and often about the strip, about what was going to happen next.

I always assumed he had a story plan but he seemed to develop the story as he wrote it. Occasionally when it seemed appropriate I'd make a suggestion, but he wouldn't allow me to get away with just an idea, I had to show how my idea would work. It was a good practice. The exploding oil reservoir mountain that caused "Steve" to be separated from "Happy Easter" and "Pipeline Polly" was one of my suggestions.

There were others but only a few. Mostly I read each new set of strips or Sunday Page as avidly as any reader.

The *Steve Canyon* operation was a well oiled machine long before I joined the ranks. Adelaide Gilchrest, secretary, Frank Engli, letterer, and Wilhelmina (Willie) Tuck, general purpose aide, whose frantic last minute runs to the city to deliver the strips to the Syndicate were legendary, accepted my arrival on the job with kindness and patience.

When the Caniffs moved to the city and then to Palm Springs, California I joined Willie in making those drives to the Post Office and the airport.

The decade in California reduced our conversations considerably. Adelaide had gone, no one ever quite filled that post after that. Frank Engli who had preceded Milt in the westward trip also left the job after suffering a terrible attack of desert fever. Shel Dorf ably took up Frank's pen and Willie broadened her shoulders a bit to manage the whole operation.

When they returned to New York and 45th Street the talking ses-

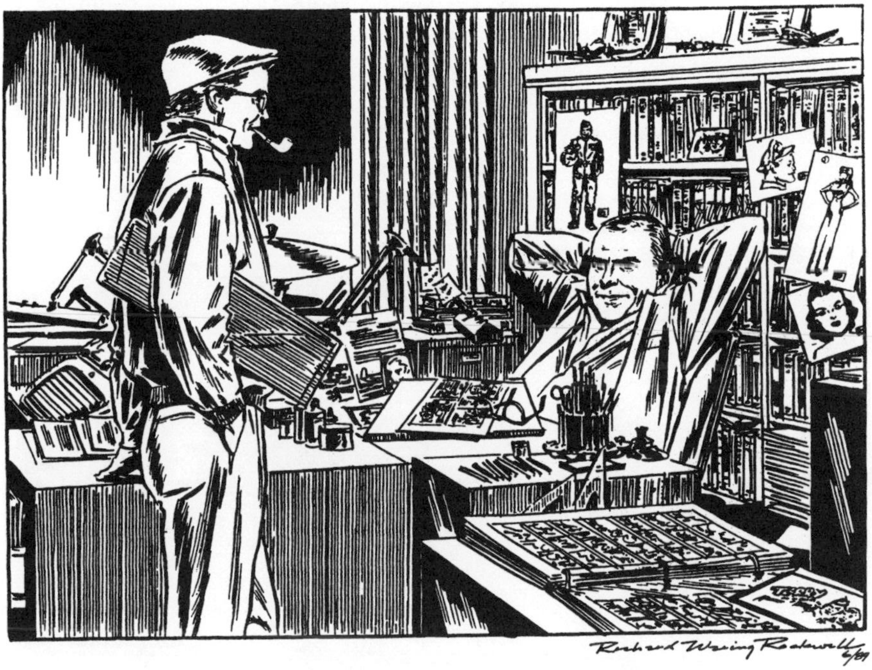

Rockwell pictures himself and Caniff in the latter's 45th Street studio.

sions began again just as before. Sometimes if Bunny was there I would sit down but the habit of standing was hard to break. It probably comes from sitting at the board so much. Milt always had trouble standing because of his bad leg.

I brought with me some special qualities as an assistant on *Steve Canyon.* I was a pilot trained by the Army Air Corps. A WWII throttle jock, and I would draw most of what I knew from memory. It helped because Milton drew flight action better than most pilots could fly it.

I was not so qualified when it came to drawing women. Caniff's women are world class. He had that mystique of style known only to a few. But my anatomy was sound and that helped.

Our last talks dealt a few times on the fate of the story strips. Diminishing size left little room to draw anything but heads. It was like performing the opera in a subway car at rush hour. And Steve too suffered from obsolescence. The resourceful defender of the good guys became suspect in a culture of conflicting ideologies and social contradictions. Milt knew this and wrote his stories with a distinct note of irony.

When it was over and beyond the emotional separation in the loss of a friend we were stunned by the sudden silence of our lives. Milton, the characters he created, Bunny, Willie, Adelaide, Frank, Shel and many others had served with dedication a man and his art of humor and ideas. Maybe that's why I was always standing.

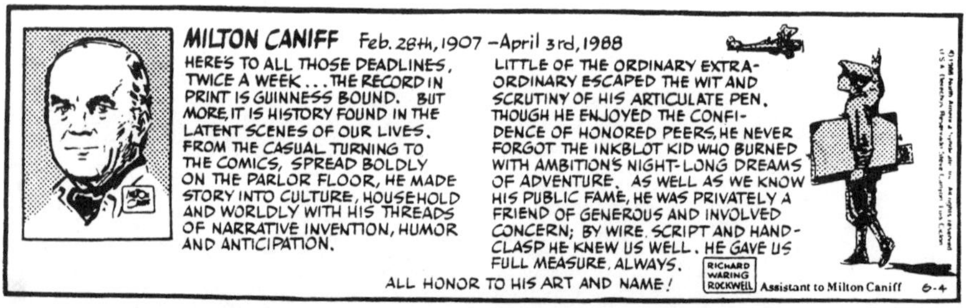

The last Steve Canyon *daily strip, June 4, 1988, by Rockwell and Dorf.*

Index

References to illustrations appear in **boldface.**